Psychological Aspects of Inflammatory Bowel Disease

In the Western world, around 360 in every 100,000 individuals have inflammatory bowel disease (IBD), a relapsing-remitting immune disease that affects the gastrointestinal tract. Its impact on individual functioning across physical and psychosocial domains is significant, and psychological distress is a common feature, with research suggesting that active IBD is associated with one of the highest rates of depression and anxiety of all chronic illnesses.

Despite the high prevalence of mental health co-morbidities in IBD, psychological illness remains largely undertreated, with studies showing that 60 per cent of IBD patients experiencing mental health problems do not receive adequate help. In this book, Knowles and Mikocka-Walus bring together world experts who practice an integrated and holistic approach in their care for IBD patients, to provide an overview of research across a range of topics associated with the biopsychosocial treatment of IBD. Each chapter provides an up-to-date comprehensive consolidation and evaluation of the current literature alongside recommendations for practice.

Key themes include:

- current understanding of the interrelationship of the neurological and biological aspects of IBD;
- common concerns and issues individuals with IBD face;
- exploring challenges across individual life-stages;
- current evidence for psychosocial interventions;
- recommendations for future directions of biopsychosocial work.

Psychological Aspects of Inflammatory Bowel Disease: A biopsychosocial approach is a key resource for researchers, practitioners and academics considering psychosocial aspects of the disease and psychological interventions. It will also appeal to health psychologists and mental health practitioners working with clients with IBD, as well as gastroenterologists interested in a comprehensive and holistic approach to IBD management.

Simon R. Knowles is Senior Lecturer of Psychology at Swinburne University of Technology, Australia. His research and clinical interests include biopsychosocial aspects of gastroenterology. Simon runs an active private clinical psychology practice that specialises in working with individuals with chronic illnesses of the gastrointestinal system. He has several honorary positions including at Melbourne University, Royal Melbourne Hospital, and St Vincent's Hospital (Melbourne).

Antonina A. Mikocka-Walus is Senior Lecturer and Lead of Psychology in Relation to Health at the University of York, UK, and Visiting Associate Professor in Psychology at the University of Adelaide, Australia. She specialises in psycho-gastroenterology and conducts studies on psychotherapies and antidepressant treatment in chronic gastrointestinal conditions.

Psychological Aspects of Inflammatory Bowel Disease

A biopsychosocial approach

Edited by Simon R. Knowles
and Antonina A. Mikocka-Walus

LONDON AND NEW YORK

First published 2015
by Routledge
27 Church Road, Hove, East Sussex, BN3 2FA

and by Routledge
711 Third Avenue, New York, NY 10017

Routledge is an imprint of the Taylor & Francis Group, an informa business

© 2015 S. R. Knowles and A. A. Mikocka-Walus

The right of the editor to be identified as the author of the
editorial material, and of the authors for their individual chapters,
has been asserted in accordance with sections 77 and 78 of the
Copyright, Designs and Patents Act 1988.

All rights reserved. No part of this book may be reprinted
or reproduced or utilised in any form or by any electronic,
mechanical, or other means, now known or hereafter invented,
including photocopying and recording, or in any information
storage or retrieval system, without permission in writing from
the publishers.

Trademark notice: Product or corporate names may be trademarks
or registered trademarks, and are used only for identification and
explanation without intent to infringe.

British Library Cataloguing in Publication Data
A catalogue record for this book is available from the British
Library

Library of Congress Cataloging in Publication Data
   Psychological aspects of inflammatory bowel disease:
   a biopsychosocial approach/edited by Simon R. Knowles and
   Antonina A. Mikocka-Walus.
      p. cm.
   Includes bibliographical references.
   I. Knowles, Simon R., editor. II. Mikocka-Walus, Antonina A.,
   editor.
   [DNLM: I. Inflammatory Bowel Diseases–psychology.
   2. Anxiety. 3. Comorbidity. 4. Depression. 5. Inflammatory
   Bowel Diseases–complications. 6. Inflammatory Bowel
   Diseases–therapy. WI 420]
   RC862.I53
   616.3'440651–dc23   2014015476

ISBN: 978-0-415-74125-5 (hbk)
ISBN: 978-1-315-81537-4 (ebk)

Typeset in Galliard and Gill Sans
by Sunrise Setting Ltd, Paignton, UK

Simon R. Knowles: I dedicate this book to my amazing and ever tolerant wife, Shani.

Antonina A. Mikocka-Walus: I dedicate this book to my beloved husband, Bart. Thank you for being my soulmate these fourteen years.

Contents

List of illustrations	x
List of contributors	xii
Acknowledgements	xvii
Preface	xviii
Foreword	xxv

1 IBD: what is it and does psyche have anything to do with it?   1
JANE M. ANDREWS

2 Stress, distress and IBD   10
KATHRYN A. SEXTON AND CHARLES N. BERNSTEIN

3 The brain-gut axis and psychological processes in IBD   20
EMERAN A. MAYER, SYLVIE BRADESI, ARPANA GUPTA
AND DAVID J. KATIBIAN

4 Microbiota and psychological processes and IBD   30
PETER DE CRUZ

5 Diagnostic procedures in IBD: addressing common
client concerns   40
GREGORY T. C. MOORE

6 Psychosocial aspects of IBD in paediatric and
adolescent patients: the impact of transition   47
JAMES LINDSAY

7 IBD in the elderly   56
MARCI REISS AND SUNANDA KANE

viii Contents

8 Sexual function, contraception and IBD 65
REME MOUNTIFIELD

9 Fertility and pregnancy in patients with IBD 74
C. JANNEKE VAN DER WOUDE

10 IBS in IBD and psychological implications 84
ANIL K. ASTHANA AND PETER R. GIBSON

11 IBD, cancer, and its psychosocial impact 93
SIMON R. KNOWLES AND FINLAY A. MACRAE

12 Patients and IBD surgery: rightful fears and
preconceptions 102
ANTONINO SPINELLI AND FRANCESCO PAGNINI

13 Standard medical care, side effects and compliance 109
PHILIP HENDY, YORAM INSPECTOR AND AILSA HART

14 Diet, nutrition and mental health in IBD 118
SUE SHEPHERD

15 Fatigue and IBD 130
DANIEL VAN LANGENBERG

16 Cross-cultural aspects of IBD 140
RAY BOYAPATI AND CHRISTOPHER LEUNG

17 Psychological assessment and the use of questionnaires
in IBD cohorts 150
SIMON R. KNOWLES

18 IBD, psychosocial functioning and the role of nurses 164
JULIE DUNCAN

19 Psychological treatment outcomes in IBD, methodological
issues, and future directions 172
LESLEY A. GRAFF

20 Cognitive behaviour therapy and hypnotherapy for IBD 183
LAURIE KEEFER

Contents ix

21 **Antidepressants and IBD** 191
ANTONINA A. MIKOCKA-WALUS

22 **Complementary and alternative medicine in IBD** 199
RANDI OPHEIM AND BJØRN MOUM

23 **Future directions in IBD: eHealth** 207
SIMON R. KNOWLES

24 **Future directions in IBD: the biopsychosocial care, the integrated care** 216
ANTONINA A. MIKOCKA-WALUS

Index 223

Illustrations

Figures

7.1	Formula for best outcomes in inflammatory bowel disease	57
7.2	Psychosocial world of a patient	58
9.1	Rotterdam preconceptional pregnancy IBD care, pale arrow head indicates 'proceed', dark arrow head indicates 'adjust current strategy'. IBD: inflammatory bowel disease. OBGYN: obstetrician, gynaecology	78
13.1	The cycle of deteriorating psychological wellbeing, disease activity and medication adherence	110
15.1	Proposed management algorithm for the fatigued patient with inflammatory bowel disease (IBD) using a dimension-based (physical or cognitive fatigue) approach	135

Tables

10.1	Pathophysiological changes described in the function and structure of the enteric nervous system in patients with inflammatory bowel disease (IBD) in remission with or without irritable bowel syndrome (IBS)-like symptoms	86
10.2	Studies comparing levels of faecal calprotectin (FC) in inflammatory bowel disease (IBD) patients with and without irritable bowel syndrome (IBS)-like symptoms	87
13.1	A review of both the important and the common adverse effects of inflammatory bowel disease (IBD) medications	112
14.1	Contributions to malnutrition in inflammatory bowel disease (IBD)	119
14.2	Examples of high FODMAP foods	125
15.1	Potentially important contributors to fatigue in Crohn's disease	134
17.1	Key components of a psychological assessment	152
17.2	Standard formulation matrix	153

17.3	Summary of questionnaires that can be utilised in inflammatory bowel disease (IBD) cohorts to assess multiple psychosocial domains (e.g. anxiety, depression, stress, disease activity, illness perceptions, and quality of life)	156
19.1	Recommendations to improve psychological treatment trials in IBD	177

Contributors

Jane M. Andrews is currently Head of the IBD Service and Education in the Department of Gastroenterology and Hepatology and Clinical Professor in the School of Medicine at the Royal Adelaide Hospital, and University of Adelaide, Australia. She is also the current chair of the Australian IBD Association. Her research interests include all aspects of IBD, health access, models of care and equity issues in addition to optimising standard clinical management.

Anil K. Asthana graduated with honours from Kings College Medical School in London, UK. He trained in Gastroenterology at Box Hill and the Alfred Hospital, Melbourne. He trained in intestinal ultrasound in Italy and Germany after receiving a fellowship from the Victorian Government. He is currently the IBD fellow at The Alfred Hospital and his current PhD is focused on the mechanisms of IBS symptoms in quiescent/mild IBD.

Charles N. Bernstein is a Distinguished Professor of Medicine at the University of Manitoba. He is also Director of the University of Manitoba IBD Clinical and Research Centre, and in 2009, he was named the University of Manitoba Bingham Chair in Gastroenterology. He was elected a fellow of the Canadian Academy of Health Sciences (2008) and to the Royal Society of Canada-Life Sciences Division of the Academy (2012).

Ray Boyapati is currently an IBD Fellow at the Western General Hospital in Edinburgh. He completed his gastroenterology training through Monash University having received the University Scholarship for Excellence. He was awarded the Royal Australasian College of Physicians medal for the highest achieving candidate in clinical medicine.

Sylvie Bradesi is an assistant Adjunct Professor at the Center for Neurobiology of Stress at the School of Medicine, University of California, Los Angeles. Her research interests include the development of animal models to study the neurobiology of stress and stress-associated gastrointestinal disorders including visceral pain.

Contributors   xiii

Peter De Cruz is a Gastroenterologist and Head of the IBD Service at the Austin Hospital in Melbourne and a Senior Lecturer at the University of Melbourne. His research has focussed on the prevention of the postoperative recurrence of Crohn's disease and the role of the microbiota in IBD.

Julie Duncan is the Lead IBD Clinical Nurse Specialist at Guy's and St Thomas' Hospitals, London UK. In addition to an extensive clinical role, Julie has an active teaching and research portfolio and, strategically, is National Chair of the RCN IBD Network and UK N-ECCO rep. She is co-editor of *Inflammatory bowel disease nursing*, the first nursing textbook on IBD.

Peter R. Gibson is Professor and Director of Gastroenterology at The Alfred Hospital and Monash University. From a background of research in epithelial cell biology, he now directs a program of translational research in inflammatory bowel disease, coeliac disease and irritable bowel syndrome, a major focus being in the use of diet to control gut symptoms and influence outcomes.

Lesley A. Graff is a Professor in the Department of Clinical Health Psychology, University of Manitoba. Her work as a clinician, scientist, and teacher is in the area of health psychology, and includes psychological consultation for a range of gastrointestinal conditions. Research and clinical interests specifically focus on inflammatory bowel disease, and broadly encompass stress and health, and evidence-based psychological interventions for medical conditions.

Arpana Gupta is a Postdoctoral Fellow in David Geffen School of Medicine at the UCLA. Dr Gupta's research examines the influence of brain in the underlying pathophysiology of disorders with altered interoceptive processing. Dr Gupta is dedicated to developing and testing biopsychosocial models that address the interactions between psychosocial, environmental, and biological factors in shaping brain structure and function.

Ailsa Hart leads the IBD Unit at St Mark's Hospital in London. Her clinical work covers the spectrum of gastrointestinal diseases, with a particular interest in inflammatory bowel diseases. Her research interests focus on intestinal immunology and bacteriology aiming to further our understanding of the pathogenesis of inflammatory intestinal disorders.

Philip Hendy is a gastroenterology and general medical registrar in training within the North-west London Deanery. He is currently working toward a PhD, and his clinical and academic interests include inflammatory bowel disease, mucosal immunology and the microbiome and metabolome.

Yoram Inspector is a Consultant Psychiatrist, Psychotherapist, Jungian Analyst (member of the International Association of Analytical Psychology) and a specialist in Eating Disorders psychiatry. He is Head, Psychological Medicine Unit of St Mark's Hospital, which provides psychiatric and psychological treatments and support for people who suffer from various gastrointestinal diseases and disorders.

xiv Contributors

Sunanda Kane is Professor of Medicine at Mayo Clinic in Rochester, Minnesota. Her areas of research include medication-taking behaviour and adherence, as well as gender specific issues. She has written extensively on issues dealing with inflammatory bowel disease, is one of the Medical Advisors to the IBD Support Foundation and is the former Chair of Patient Education for the Crohn's and Colitis Foundation of America.

David J. Katibian received his Bachelor of Science in Physiology and Neuroscience from UC San Diego. As an undergraduate, he was involved in clinical research pertaining to Alzheimer's disease and neuroimaging. He is currently working at the UCLA Center for Neurobiology of Stress, focusing on IBD's role in structural/functional brain alterations. He will be attending medical school starting this Fall 2014.

Laurie Keefer is a clinical health psychologist specializing in digestive diseases. An Associate Professor in the Division of Gastroenterology and Hepatology at Northwestern University, Feinberg School of Medicine, Dr. Keefer's Center for Psychosocial Research in GI is nationally recognized for its state-of-the art behavioural medicine program and NIH-funded research.

Simon R. Knowles is Senior Lecturer of Psychology at Swinburne University of Technology, Australia. His research and clinical interests include biopsychosocial aspects of gastroenterology. Simon runs an active private clinical psychology practice that specialises in working with individuals with chronic illnesses of the gastrointestinal system. He has several honorary positions including at Melbourne University, Royal Melbourne Hospital and St Vincent's Hospital (Melbourne).

Christopher Leung is the Vice-President of the Australian Chinese Medical Association of Victoria and a gastroenterologist working in IBD, luminal dysmotility disorders and hepatology at Austin hospital and Royal Melbourne hospital in Melbourne, Australia. His other roles include being an Educational Supervisor and Professional Development Advisor for the Royal Australasian College of Physicians, and a Clinical Supervisor at the University of Melbourne.

James Lindsay is a Senior Lecturer and Consultant in Gastroenterology at Barts and the London School of Medicine. Along with a full multidisciplinary team, he runs the adolescent IBD service at The Royal London Hospital and the Adult IBD service at Barts Hospital. He is Chair of the ECCO education committee and has chaired working groups for the ECCO consensus on the management of Crohn's disease and ulcerative colitis.

Finlay A. Macrae is the Head of the Inflammatory Bowel Disease Service, The Royal Melbourne Hospital. He has lead the introduction of Nurse Practitioner, clinical psychology, and new endoscopic procedures to support IBD Services. He has published over 200 peer reviewed papers and chapters and edited two books. In 2013, he was awarded the Master of the World Gastroenterology Organization, their capstone award.

Emeran A. Mayer has a career long interest in brain gut interactions in health and disease, and is recognized as one of the leading investigators in the world on this topic. He is the director of the Gail and Gerald Oppenheimer Family Center for Neurobiology of Stress, and co-director of the CURE: Digestive Diseases Research Center at UCLA. His work has been continuously funded by the National Institutes of Health since 1989.

Antonina A. Mikocka-Walus is Senior Lecturer and Lead of Psychology in Relation to Health at the University of York, United Kingdom and Visiting Associate Professor of Psychology at the University of Adelaide, Australia. Her main interest is in Psycho-gastroenterology and she has conducted studies on prevalence of co-morbid mental disorders and on psychotherapies and antidepressants for chronic gastrointestinal conditions.

Gregory T. C. Moore completed his Gastroenterology training through Monash University and a PhD in immunology at the University of Melbourne. He heads the IBD Unit at Monash Medical Centre combining clinical practice, trials and investigator initiated research. He is also on the Board of Crohn's and Colitis Australia.

Bjørn Moum is Professor of Gastroenterology with research focus on clinical epidemiology, PRO, genetics and therapies in IBD. He has been President of the Norwegian Gastroenterology Association and National Representative of ECCO and is personal elected member of the IOIBD. He has received national and international research prices and grants.

Reme Mountifield is a Senior Consultant Gastroenterologist at Flinders Medical Centre in South Australia, and Senior Lecturer at Flinders University. The subject of her doctoral thesis is 'Patient Perspectives in Inflammatory Bowel Disease', and her ongoing research interests include reproductive aspects of Inflammatory Bowel Disease, as well as aspects relating to medication taking behaviour.

Randi Opheim is IBD nurse specialist and researcher at Oslo University Hospital, Norway. She has a Master of Philosophy of Health Science and a PhD in Medicine from University of Oslo. Her research interests are within the field of complementary and alternative medicine and psychosocial aspects related to living with chronic illness, particularly among patients with inflammatory bowel disease.

Francesco Pagnini is Assistant Professor in Clinical Psychology at the Catholic University of Milan and collaborate as Postdoc with Harvard University. He has completed his PhD in Clinical Psychology from the University of Bergamo. His primary interest is focused on the improvement of psychological well-being of people with chronic disease, in particular with interventions that improve mindfulness.

xvi Contributors

Marci Reiss is a licensed clinical social worker and Founder of the IBD Support Foundation (IBDSF), a non-profit healthcare foundation devoted to improving the lives of IBD patients and their families. Ms. Reiss has developed innovative psychosocial approaches to reduce the negative impact of IBD. She is currently developing a psychosocial program at University of California San Diego's IBD Center and is developing standardized protocols for psychosocial care, which may be implemented in various settings including IBD Centers and general gastroenterology practices.

Kathryn A. Sexton obtained her MA and PhD in clinical psychology from Concordia University in Montreal, Canada. She is currently a post-doctoral research fellow with the IBD Clinical and Research Centre in the College of Medicine, Faculty of Health Sciences at the University of Manitoba. Her published articles have examined cognitive and behavioural risk factors for anxiety and mood disorders. Her recent work has examined perceived stress and other psychosocial factors in relation to disease activity in inflammatory bowel disease.

Sue Shepherd, Advanced Accredited Practising Dietitian, works as Senior Lecturer and Head of Research at La Trobe University Department of Dietetics and Human Nutrition. She also runs Australia's largest gastrointestinal nutrition specialist dietetic private practice, 'Shepherd Works'. She is recognised internationally as an expert dietitian in gastrointestinal nutrition.

Antonino Spinelli is Head of Colorectal Surgery, Istituto Clinico Humanitas in Milan and Assistant Professor of Surgery in the University of Milano, Italy. He is also Member of the Executive Board of the Italian Society of Colorectal Surgery and has a strong focus on IBD Surgery.

Daniel van Langenberg is a gastroenterologist in public and private practice, is the Head of IBD at Eastern Health and a Senior Lecturer at Monash University (Melbourne, Australia). Since completing his PhD investigating fatigue and muscle dysfunction in Crohn's disease, his ongoing clinical and research interests involve the fields of inflammatory bowel disease and functional GI disorders.

C. Janneke van der Woude is Associate Professor in the department of the Gastroenterology and Hepatology Department of the Erasmus MC, Rotterdam, The Netherlands, Janneke van der Woude is much involved in optimizing care for patients with inflammatory bowel diseases. She leads the clinical unit for inflammatory bowel diseases. Her research focuses on new methods for treatment of IBD, improved quality of life for IBD patients, pregnancy in IBD and colitis related cancer.

Acknowledgements

Simon R. Knowles: I wish to thank all of the contributors to this book. Each of you have significant research and clinical responsibilities and yet have made time to contribute to this edited volume. My own contribution to this volume has been influenced by many individuals, including Dr Diane Bull, Dr William Connell, Dr Edwin Harari, Dr Kaveh Monshet, A/Professor Michael Salzberg, A/Professor Geoff Hebbard, Professor David Castle, Professor Michael Kamm, and Professor Finlay Macrae. To my fellow co-editor, Dr Antonina A. Mikocka-Walus, thank you so much for your expert knowledge of IBD and passion for making the lives of those with gastroenterological conditions better – may this be the first of many collaborative accomplishments. Finally, I wish to thank my patients and the many individuals who have kindly offered their precious time and experiences to give me insight into the complexity of living with IBD.

Antonina A. Mikocka-Walus: I would like to thank all of the contributors for sharing their knowledge and making this book so special. It would not have happened without your time and effort. My own adventure with IBD research would never have started without the help and patient mentorship of two very inspiring women, Professor Jane M. Andrews and Professor Deborah Turnbull. Thank you for your wise guidance and friendship. Thank you to my co-editor, Dr Simon R. Knowles for inviting me to work on this book with him. It has been a great year and a wonderful adventure. Last but certainly not least, I would like to express my warmest thanks to people living with IBD who I have met over the years during research projects and in my clinical practice. We would not know as much as we now do about IBD without your insight and willingness to participate in countless research projects. Thank you for believing in science!

Preface

Thousands of years ago, people believed that mind and body were united and that illness, whether physical or mental, was caused by the presence of evil spirits (Kaplan 1975). Through the centuries, this perspective has changed to eventually reappear in the twentieth century. The ancient philosophers, namely Aristotle and Plato, were the first to separate body from mind. The *dualism* of body and mind was further developed by René Descartes in the seventeenth century (Marx and Hillix 1963). Indeed, the works of Descartes laid the foundation for a contemporary medical approach called the *biomedical model*, which for over 300 years explained illness as an infirmity of body caused by a disturbance of physiological processes (Descartes 1956). Somatic illness in Descartes' theory was, therefore, completely separated from psychosocial processes of the mind. Consequently, the biomedical model has reduced illness to a single-factor problem of biological malfunction, with its greatest flow being ignorance of a patient's attributes as a human being and reducing a person and their psychosocial circumstances to physico-chemical terms (Engel, GL 1960, 1977, 1980).

While the biomedical model may certainly work well in addressing acute health problems, it fails at addressing chronic issues. Thus, responding to the rising incidence of chronic illness worldwide, and thanks to the works of Sigmund Freud (Breuer and Freud 1936; Freud 1922), Flanders Dunbar (Dunbar 1955) and Franz Alexander (Alexander 1952) in the twentieth century, the biomedical concept of illness began to change and the *biopsychosocial model* was born. The new model has implied the interplay of biological, psychological and social factors in causation and experience of an illness (Engel, GL 1977, 1980). It has also emphasised the patient-doctor relationship as an important factor in the therapeutic outcome, and refocused medical care from the doctor to a patient, with the term patient-centred care being coined and the interdisciplinary approach to managing chronic illness promoted, in which the practitioner is expected to be aware of the biopsychosocial factors contributing to illness (Engel, GL 1997). The definition of health and illness has also changed. Health has begun to be understood as something that one achieves through multi-level actions rather than a steady state (Taylor 2006).

At the same time when the biomedical model started losing its glory in favour of the biopsychosocial approach to health, significant changes have happened in the understanding of the gastrointestinal illness. In the common knowledge expressions such as 'butterflies in the stomach' or 'having a gut feeling' had existed long before the concept of the brain-gut-axis (BGA) was developed (Mayer 2011). The term 'nervous diarrhoea' appeared in medical texts in the mid-1800s, while in the early twentieth century Cannon speculated that mental distress may contribute to disturbed digestion (Cannon 1909). Psychological conflict was considered to be at the core of the subtype of inflammatory bowel disease (IBD), ulcerative colitis (UC), in the 1930s, partly thanks to Cecil Murray's published case reports and partly due to the fashion of that time and the development of psychoanalysis. Engel, the father of the biopsychosocial model, also contributed to the psychodynamic view of UC (Engel, GL 1955, 1956; Engel, CC *et al.* 1996; Glaser and Engel 1977). This view has started changing in line with the new developments in immunology and better understanding of the differences between organic (such as IBD) and functional gastrointestinal disorders (FGiDs) [such as irritable bowel syndrome (IBS)]. For some time the psychological aspect of IBD was left afield, while at the same time, thanks to the pioneering work of Douglas Drossmann and colleagues, the role of psychological factors such as life stressors, coping or social support in explaining aetiology and course of FGiDs became appreciated (Drossman 1998; Drossman *et al.* 1999).

There is substantial evidence that stress plays a pervasive role on human psychological and physiological wellbeing and quality of life (QoL). For example, it is well established that stress can both cause and maintain many psychological conditions (American Psychiatric Association, American Psychiatric Association, DSM-5 Task Force 2013; World Health Organization 1992, 1993) and links to many physiological illnesses including cardiovascular disease (Glozier *et al.* 2013; Steptoe and Kivimaki 2012) and immunological conditions such as multiple sclerosis (Artemiadis *et al.* 2011). This has also led to the birth of several new interrelated research fields relevant to gastroenterology, including psychoneuroimmunology and neurogastroenterology. Each of these fields has helped to explore and further clarify the complex process associated with the BGA. Only more recently have we had the ability to explore the complex interplay between psychological processes, diet and microbiota. Despite being in its infancy, this research is showing that the onset of IBD, and the ongoing inflammatory processes involved in IBD, may be due to a complex interplay between genes, gastrointestinal microbiota, diet, psychological process, stress and environmental factors (Bonaz and Bernstein 2013; Mawdsley and Rampton 2006; Nanau and Neuman 2012; Neuman and Nanau 2012).

Evidence for the role of stress and gastrointestinal conditions is now becoming clearly delineated. In 1833, William Beaumont published the first scientific exploration into the influence of stress on the gastrointestinal tract (Beaumont 1833; Beaumont and St. Martin 1834; Myer and Beaumont 1981). In this seminal work, Beaumont observed the changes of gastric secretions in a patient, Alexis St. Martin, who had a gastrocutaneous fistula (due to a gunshot wound). Beaumont identified that when St. Martin experienced strong emotions, such as anger, it resulted in a reduction of gastric secretions. Since this time, there has been a rapid expansion of research exploring stress and its impact on gastrointestinal conditions.

However, as noted earlier, while FGiDs have received significant scientific enquiry in relation to the role of psychological factors, such as stress and mental health processes, much less has been undertaken within the area of IBD. The biopsychosocial approach to inflammatory bowel disease is thus a relatively new area of study.

Of the research conducted to date, there is mixed evidence for the role of stress in IBD activity. For example, while monitoring 62 ulcerative colitis patients in remission for up to 68 months, Levenstein and colleagues (Levenstein *et al.* 2000) found that long-term, but not short-term stress exacerbated the risk of relapse. In contrast, several other studies have found no relationship between stressful events and disease onset or flare-ups in IBD activity (Lerebours *et al.* 2007; Lix *et al.* 2008; Singh *et al.* 2009). Many reviews (Bonaz and Bernstein 2013; Mawdsley and Rampton 2005, 2006; Triantafillidis *et al.* 2013) exploring the role of stress in IBD onset and progression have suggested that while there is anecdotal evidence from both patients and gastroenterologists that stress can play a role in IBD, the evidence is not clear, although there seems to be a growing consensus that stress may play a role. In a review of 11 longitudinal studies exploring the role of stress and depression on IBD, Rampton (Mawdsley and Rampton 2005; Rampton 2009) concluded that most of these studies provided evidence that stress and/or depression did have an adverse impact on IBD activity, although evidence for the possible beneficial role of stress-management for patients with IBD is limited. Given that there is strong evidence for high rate of psychological distress in patients with IBD (Costal and Chaves 2006; Filipovic *et al.* 2007; Graff *et al.* 2006; Jones *et al.* 2006; Knowles *et al.* 2011; Kunzendorf *et al.* 2007; Moser 2006; Porcelli *et al.* 1994, 1996; Walker *et al.* 1996) and that psychological conditions, particularly depression, have been shown to be associated with increased probability of relapses in IBD (Rampton 2009), understanding these processes, and the development of integrated healthcare strategies are essential.

Shifts in the medical curricula worldwide commencing in the 1980s have meant that the latest generations of medical students have become increasingly exposed to the medical humanities (Benbassat *et al.* 2003; Cohen *et al.* 2000; Eaton 1980; Gordon 2005; Jasnoski and Warner 1991; Satterfield *et al.* 2004). Yet, there are few resources available in gastroenterology. Similarly, in psychiatry and psychology the complexity of conditions such as IBD is rarely appreciated yet the incidence is rising and more and more mental health professionals will be faced with opportunities to support GI patients. We hope that with this book we will be able to contribute to professional development of health professionals working with people living with IBD.

The rationale for the book

Due to the significant physical and psychosocial impact of IBD on QoL and the inter-relation between somatic and psychological symptoms, a holistic team-based approach is needed in IBD clinics worldwide. In addition to gastro-enterologists, surgeons, IBD-nurses and stoma-nurses, psychologists, psychiatrists, immunologists, social workers, and dieticians are now often involved in the ongoing support of individuals who live with IBD. Thus, the objective of this book is to bring together world experts who practice an integrated and holistic approach in their care for IBD patients and to provide reviews of the literature across a range of topics associated with the biopsychosocial treatment of IBD. Each chapter will provide an up-to-date comprehensive consolidation and evaluation of the current literature. This review will provide practical recommendations that can then be applied by the reader in their own interaction with IBD patients.

Key themes of this book will include: (i) current understanding of the interrelationship of the neurological (e.g. brain-gut-axis) and biological aspects (e.g. microbiota) of IBD and psychological processes; (ii) identifying the common concerns and issues individuals with IBD face in relation to pre- and post-diagnosis, ongoing medical decisions and interventions; (iii) exploring the differences and challenges associated with IBD across individual life-stages; (iv) reviewing the current evidence for psychosocial interventions associated with IBD; and (v) providing recommendations in relation to future directions of psychosocial work in a multi-team environment and ongoing research in IBD.

The structure of the book

Each chapter in this book is guided by the biopsychosocial approach reviewing the current literature and providing practical recommendations that readers can use within their own profession/IBD treating team. To help delineate and cover the multiple theoretical and practical aspects of the biopsychosocial approach to IBD and patient care, the book has been organised into three key parts.

Chapters 1 to 5 of the book explore the biological and clinical topics consistent with the biological bases of the biopsychosocial model. Chapters 6 to 16 explore the psychosocial dimension of the model through the examination of special IBD populations and exploring various important psychosocial aspects associated with IBD (e.g. sexual health, pregnancy, medical care and surgery, and fatigue). Finally, Chapters 17 to 24 focus on providing solutions and overviews of therapeutic approaches (e.g. psychotherapy, antidepressants, alternative and complementary therapies) and a review of suggested future directions in IBD, including new approaches to overall care delivery (i.e. eHealth and integrated medicine).

The application of common themes and practical recommendations throughout this book as well as the world recognition of the contributing authors ensures it has applicability to treatment, research, and teaching.

Simon R. Knowles and Antonina A. Mikocka-Walus
Melbourne and York, April 2014

References

Alexander, F (1952). *Psychosomatic medicine*. New York: Norton.

American Psychiatric Association, American Psychiatric Association and DSM-5 Task Force (2013). *Diagnostic and statistical manual of mental disorders: DSM-5*, 5th edn. Washington, DC: American Psychiatric Association.

Artemiadis, AK, Anagnostouli, MC and Alexopoulos, EC (2011). Stress as a risk factor for multiple sclerosis onset or relapse: a systematic review. *Neuroepidemiology*, vol. 36, no. 2, pp. 109–20.

Beaumont, W (1833). *Experiments and observations on the gastric juice, and the physiology of digestion*. Plattsburgh: F.P. Allen.

Beaumont, W and St. Martin, A (1834). *Experiments and observations on the gastric juice, and the physiology of digestion*. Boston: Lilly, Wait, and company.

Benbassat, J, Baumal, R, Borkan, JM and Ber, R (2003). Overcoming barriers to teaching the behavioral and social sciences to medical students. *Acad Med*, vol. 78, no. 4, pp. 372–80.

Bonaz, BL and Bernstein, CN (2013). Brain-gut interactions in inflammatory bowel disease. *Gastroenterology*, vol. 144, no. 1, pp. 36–49.

Breuer, J and Freud, S (1936). *Studies in hysteria*. New York: Nervous and Mental Disease Pub. Co.

Cannon, WB (1909). The influence of emotional states on the functions of the alimentary canal. *Am J Med Sci*, vol. 137, pp. 480–6.

Cohen, J, Krackov, SK, Black, ER and Holyst, M (2000). Introduction to human health and illness: a series of patient-centered conferences based on the biopsychosocial model. *Acad Med*, vol. 75, no. 4, pp. 390–6.

Costal, AL and Chaves, EC (2006). [Stress coping strategies and depressive symptoms among ulcerative colitis patients]. *Rev Esc Enferm USP*, vol. 40, no. 4, pp. 507–14. [In Portuguese].

Descartes, R (1956). *Discourse on Method*. New York: Macmillan/Library of Liberal Arts.

Drossman, DA (1998). Gastrointestinal Illness and the biopsychosocial model. *Psychosomatic Medicine*, vol. 60, no. 3, pp. 258–67.

Drossman, D, Creed, F, Olden, K, Svedlund, J, Toner, B and Whitehead, W (1999). Psychosocial aspects of the functional gastrointestinal disorders. *Gut*, vol. 45, (Suppl II), pp. II25–II30.

Dunbar, HF (1955). *Mind and body: psychosomatic medicine*. New York: Random House.

Eaton, JS, Jr. (1980). The biopsychosocial model in education: discussion. *Psychosom Med*, vol. 42, no. 1 (Suppl), pp. 131–3.

Engel, CC, Walker, EA and Katon, WJ (1996). Factors related to dissociation among patients with gastrointestinal complaints. *J Psychosom Res*, vol. 40, pp. 643–53.

Engel, GL (1955). Studies of ulcerative colitis. III. The nature of the psychologic processes. *Am J Med*, vol. 19, no. 2, pp. 231–56.

Engel, GL (1956). Studies of ulcerative colitis. IV. The significance of headaches. *Psychosom Med*, vol. 18, no. 4, pp. 334–46.

Engel, GL (1960). A unified concept of health and disease. *Perspect Biol Med*, vol. 3, pp. 459–85.

Engel, GL (1977). The need for a new medical model: a challenge for biomedicine. *Science*, vol. 196, no. 4286, pp. 129–36.

Engel, GL (1980). The clinical application of the biopsychosocial model. *Am J Psychiatry*, vol. 137, no. 5, pp. 535–44.

Engel, GL (1997). From biomedical to biopsychosocial. Being scientific in the human domain. *Psychosomatics*, vol. 38, no. 6, pp. 521–8.

Filipovic, BR, Filipovic, BF, Kerkez, M, Milinic, N and Randelovic, T (2007). Depression and anxiety levels in therapy-naive patients with inflammatory bowel disease and cancer of the colon. *World J Gastroenterol*, vol. 13, no. 3, pp. 438–43.

Freud, S (1922). *Introductory lectures on psycho-analysis : a course of twenty-eight lectures delivered at the University of Vienna*. London: Allen & Unwin.

Glaser, JP and Engel, GL (1977). Psychodynamics, psychophysiology and gastrointestinal symptomatology. *Clin Gastroenterol*, vol. 6, no. 3, pp. 507–31.

Glozier, N, Tofler, GH, Colquhoun, DM, Bunker, SJ, Clarke, DM, Hare, DL, Hickie, IB, Tatoulis, J, Thompson, DR, Wilson, A and Branagan, MG (2013). Psychosocial risk factors for coronary heart disease. *Med J Aust*, vol. 199, no. 3, pp. 179–80.

Gordon, J (2005). Medical humanities: to cure sometimes, to relieve often, to comfort always. *Med J Aust*, vol. 182, no. 1, pp. 5–8.

Graff, LA, Walker, JR, Lix, L, Clara, I, Rawsthorne, P, Rogala, L, Miller, N, Jakul, L, McPhail, C, Ediger, J and Bernstein, CN (2006). The relationship of inflammatory bowel disease type and activity to psychological functioning and quality of life. *Clin Gastroenterol Hepatol*, vol. 4, no. 12, pp. 1491–501.

Jasnoski, MB and Warner, RM (1991). Graduate and post-graduate medical education with the synchronous systems model. *Behav Sci*, vol. 36, no. 4, pp. 253–73.

Jones, MP, Wessinger, S and Crowell, MD (2006). Coping strategies and interpersonal support in patients with irritable bowel syndrome and inflammatory bowel disease. *Clin Gastroenterol Hepatol*, vol. 4, no. 4, pp. 474–81.

Kaplan, HI (1975). Current psychodynamic concepts in psychosomatic medicine. In: Pasnau, RO (ed). *Consultation-liaison psychiatry*. New York: Grune & Stratton.

Knowles, SR, Wilson, JL, Connell, WR and Kamm, MA (2011). Preliminary examination of the relations between disease activity, illness perceptions, coping strategies, and psychological morbidity in Crohn's disease guided by the common sense model of illness. *Inflamm Bowel Dis*, vol. 17, no. 12, pp. 2551–7.

Kunzendorf, S, Jantschek, G, Straubinger, K, Heberlein, I, Homann, N, Ludwig, D and Benninghoven, D (2007). The Luebeck interview for psychosocial screening in patients with inflammatory bowel disease. *Inflamm Bowel Dis*, vol. 13, no. 1, pp. 33–41.

Lerebours, E, Gower-Rousseau, C, Merle, V, Brazier, F, Debeugny, S, Marti, R, Salomez, JL, Hellot, MF, Dupas, JL, Colombel, JF, Cortot, A and Benichou, J (2007). Stressful life events as a risk factor for inflammatory bowel disease onset: a population-based case-control study. *Am J Gastroenterol*, vol. 102, no. 1, pp. 122–31.

Levenstein, S, Prantera, C, Varvo, V, Scribano, ML, Andreoli, A, Luzi, C, Arca, M, Berto, E, Milite, G and Marcheggiano, A (2000). Stress and exacerbation in ulcerative colitis: a prospective study of patients enrolled in remission. *Am J Gastroenterol*, vol. 95, no. 5, pp. 1213–20.

Lix, LM, Graff, LA, Walker, JR, Clara, I, Rawsthorne, P, Rogala, L, Miller, N, Ediger, J, Pretorius, T and Bernstein, CN (2008). Longitudinal study of quality of life and psychological functioning for active, fluctuating, and inactive disease patterns in inflammatory bowel disease. *Inflamm Bowel Dis*, vol. 14, no. 11, pp. 1575–84.

Marx, MH and Hillix, WA (1963). *Systems and theories in psychology*. New York: McGraw-Hill.

Mawdsley, JE and Rampton, DS (2005). Psychological stress in IBD: new insights into pathogenic and therapeutic implications, *Gut*, vol. 54, no. 10, pp. 1481–91.

Mawdsley, JE and Rampton, DS (2006). The role of psychological stress in inflammatory bowel disease. *Neuroimmunomodulation*, vol. 13, no. 5-6, pp. 327–36.

Mayer, EA (2011). Gut feelings: the emerging biology of gut-brain communication. *Nat Rev Neurosci*, vol. 12, no. 8, pp. 453–66.

Moser, G (2006). Should we incorporate psychological care into the management of IBD? *Nat Clin Pract Gastroenterol Hepatol*, vol. 3, no. 8, pp. 416–7.

Myer, JS and Beaumont, W (1981). *William Beaumont, a pioneer American physiologist: a newly edited and completely reillustrated edition of the Life and letters of Dr. William Beaumont.* St. Louis: Mosby.

Nanau, RM and Neuman, MG (2012). Metabolome and inflammasome in inflammatory bowel disease. *Transl Res*, vol. 160, no. 1, pp. 1–28.

Neuman, MG and Nanau, RM (2012). Inflammatory bowel disease: role of diet, microbiota, life style. *Transl Res*, vol. 160, no. 1, pp. 29–44.

Porcelli, P, Leoci, C and Guerra, V (1996). A prospective study of the relationship between disease activity and psychologic distress in patients with inflammatory bowel disease. *Scand J Gastroenterol*, vol. 31, no. 8, pp. 792–6.

Porcelli, P, Zaka, S, Centonze, S and Sisto, G (1994). Psychological distress and levels of disease activity in inflammatory bowel disease. *Ital J Gastroenterol*, vol. 26, no. 3, pp. 111–5.

Rampton, D (2009). Does stress influence inflammatory bowel disease? The clinical data. *Dig Dis*, vol. 27 (Suppl 1), pp. 76–9.

Satterfield, JM, Mitteness, LS, Tervalon, M and Adler, N (2004). Integrating the social and behavioral sciences in an undergraduate medical curriculum: the UCSF essential core. *Acad Med*, vol. 79, no. 1, pp. 6–15.

Singh, S, Graff, LA and Bernstein, CN (2009). Do NSAIDs, antibiotics, infections, or stress trigger flares in IBD? *Am J Gastroenterol*, vol. 104, no. 5, pp. 1298–313; quiz 314.

Steptoe, A and Kivimaki, M (2012). Stress and cardiovascular disease. *Nat Rev Cardiol*, vol. 9, no. 6, pp. 360–70.

Taylor, SE (2006). *Health Psychology*, 6th edn. New York: McGraw-Hill, Inc.

Triantafillidis, JK, Merikas, E and Gikas, A (2013). Psychological factors and stress in inflammatory bowel disease. *Expert Rev Gastroenterol Hepatol*, vol. 7, no. 3, pp. 225–38.

Walker, EA, Gelfand, MD, Gelfand, AN, Creed, F and Katon, WJ (1996). The relationship of current psychiatric disorder to functional disability and distress in patients with inflammatory bowel disease. *Gen Hosp Psychiatry*, vol. 18, no. 4, pp. 220–9.

World Health Organization (1992). *The ICD-10 classification of mental and behavioural disorders: clinical descriptions and diagnostic guidelines.* Geneva: World Health Organization.

World Health Organization (1993). *The ICD-10 classification of mental and behavioural disorders: diagnostic criteria for research.* Geneva: World Health Organization.

Foreword

There are many unmet needs in the management of patients with inflammatory bowel disease (IBD), with large therapeutic gaps in medical therapy. One unmet need, however, is a reasoned critique of the interface between neural function in its broadest sense and inflammation. No one now believes that ulcerative colitis or Crohn's disease have a psychological cause, but that these chronic inflammatory disorders have psychological consequences is equally beyond dispute. Furthermore, despite years of trying to separate IBD from irritable bowel syndrome (IBS), it is now apparent that the two conditions often overlap in the same patient. How could it be otherwise if the enteric nerves of the gut are involved in inflammation? The extent to which the enteric nervous system influences immune function is intriguing and it is no knight's move in thought to conceive that the enteric nervous system, connected as it is through the spinal cord to the brain, is in turn influenced by higher mental function.

In contrast to work on the pathogenesis and control of inflammation, systematic study of the psychological factors influencing IBD (and vice versa), have been limited. Yet patients intuitively recognise the influence of stress on their symptoms, with evolving evidence that perceived stress is associated with clinical relapse. Patients and their families live daily with the consequences of fatigue, as well as the impact of the disease or treatment on work or recreational life and, so frequently neglected, on sexual function. Too often study into psychosocial factors is dismissed as soft science, although sometimes with justification. This book addresses this deficit.

The editors are to be commended for assembling a group of distinguished, internationally recognised specialists who have written authoritative and well-referenced chapters on a range of fascinating topics. They have risen to the challenge of addressing the biological, psychological and social aspects of IBD. The book should be required reading for IBD specialists and is accessible to informed lay people who may wish to understand the state of the science in the biopsychosocial field. Read on.

Simon Travis DPhil FRCP
Translational Gastroenterology Unit
Nuffield Department of Experimental Medicine
Oxford University Hospital, Oxford UK
President of ECCO 2012–2014

Chapter 1

IBD

What is it and does psyche have anything to do with it?

Jane M. Andrews

Introduction

Inflammatory bowel disease (IBD) is named for its effects on the gut, however, due to the centrality of gastrointestinal (GI) health on the whole person, a purely GI centric view of the illness fails to conceive the full spectrum of the patients' experiences and concerns (Andrews *et al.* 2009). The gut is essential for nutrition and also contributes to the pleasure experienced through taste, food satisfaction, satiety and the emotional, community aspects of shared meals, in addition to serving ritual purposes, both social and religious. Disturbances in GI function and the inability of people to participate fully in this food/meal-based aspect of life that is usually 'taken for granted' can cause much distress. In addition, IBD is a chronic illness, the onset of which is usually before mid-life, meaning that most people affected have a long exposure time, are affected at a time when they expect to be well, and have a long-term illness with an uncertain future, whereas other illnesses affecting this age bracket are usually acute and self-limiting. All of these factors make IBD a difficult disease/illness from a psychological/ societal viewpoint. Hence, the importance of considering the psychological dimension of IBD.

Moreover, it also appears likely that psychological status itself may exert an influence on IBD inflammatory activity/behaviour, although this is an area of contention and is difficult to study. Many patients with IBD are convinced of the relationship, at a personal level, between stress, anxiety, depression and flares. However, due to recall biases, and symptom-based measurement tools, the data to date here is still unclear (Andrews *et al.* 2009; Bernstein *et al.* 2010; Singh *et al.* 2009). Despite the uncertainty in humans, in animals where models of inflammation, stress and depression can be manipulated, there is a clear effect of psychological status (and CNS disturbances) on GI inflammation, moreover, treating these disturbances has been shown to ameliorate GI inflammation (Ghia *et al.* 2009). These data form the basis for the emerging neuro-immune model of inflammation with regard to IBD and provides another major reason we should consider the psychological dimension of IBD.

Current concepts of IBD aetiology, epidemiology and treatment

Aetiology

The precise aetiology of IBD is unknown, although microbial, genetic, dietary and other environmental factors are all implicated. It is generally conceived as a group of autoimmune diseases, as the affected person's own immune system is activated (inappropriately and persistently or recurrently), with a focus on/in GI tissues, which leads to tissue damage. It is, as yet, uncertain whether there is a specific GI tissue/molecular target for the inflammation, although this appears likely due to the relative stability over time of the physical location of the inflammation within an individual. Inflammation can also be seen in other tissues, predominantly the skin and joints; however, the main focus of the disease is GI, which is what distinguishes it from other autoimmune disorders.

The importance of microbial factors will be reviewed in detail in Chapter 4, however, it should be noted here that IBD cannot be induced in germ-free animal models. In humans, luminal disease improves with antibiotics and when luminal contents are diverted (removing the interaction between luminal contents – mainly bacteria – and the mucosa). Genetic risk loci associated with IBD risk and behaviour are now well described, and interestingly, many of these are functional receptors or modulators in pathways that interact with host microbial and immunoregulatory responses and are also noted in other autoimmune diseases (Jostins *et al.* 2012). Despite the large numbers of genes associated with IBD, none of them are either necessary nor sufficient to lead to IBD development in an individual, and concordance, even in identical twins, is not 100 per cent. Significantly, many important genes described in Caucasian populations have not been replicated as risk factors in other racial groups, emphasizing the likelihood that it is the interaction between genes and the environment that lies at the crux of IBD aetiology, rather than a single factor in isolation.

Several environmental factors are also associated with IBD (Gearry *et al.* 2010), and interestingly, these do not always associate with both Crohn's disease (CD) and ulcerative colitis (UC) equally. For example, smoking is more common in CD and has been linked with worse disease behaviour (Lawrance *et al.* 2013), whereas in UC, smokers are less likely to be affected and smoking cessation worsens UC course. Other environmental factors implicated, but not always validated, as either increasing or decreasing risk include: dietary fat and sugar intake, breast feeding in infancy, socioeconomic status, latitude, vitamin D, sun exposure, metropolitan or rural birthplace and having a childhood vegetable garden.

Epidemiology

IBD has increased substantially in incidence since its initial recognition. Both CD and UC became more common in developed countries in the second half of the

1900s and are now rapidly increasing in the developing world (Ng *et al.* 2013). In the developed world, CD is now more common than UC, whereas, in Asia, UC is currently twice as common as UC. Disease onset, in general, is prior to 40 years of age, with ~25 per cent having onset during childhood. While the incidence is low, making them 'uncommon' disorders, they are chronic disorders and their prevalence is much more substantial as each affected person has the disorder 'for life'. Recent prevalence estimates in Western countries sit between 300–480/100,000 (Burisch *et al.* 2013; Rocchi *et al.* 2012), meaning that from an economic and healthcare delivery viewpoint (Access-Economics 2007), this patient group is important to care for well so as to ensure minimal morbidity. As is outlined below, both physical and psychological aspects of care need to be optimal to ensure those affected by IBD are able to enjoy a healthy, productive life.

Treatment

Investigations undertaken to diagnose and evaluate changing symptoms in those with IBD are described in Chapter 5. Here, a brief overview of the logic behind the approach to IBD treatment is presented. The treatment approach to IBD is necessarily tailored, as there are many different clinical scenarios, in terms of diagnosis (CD vs. UC), severity, location in the gut, patient preference, speed of progression of disease, complications and responses to previous therapies (including non-efficacy, allergy and/or side effects). Often, a dichotomy between medical (drug) and surgical therapies is presented, however, in reality, these approaches are often both required, either simultaneously or sequentially. Logically, surgery is the treatment of choice for mechanical complications, especially abscess, perforation, penetrating disease and strictures, whereas medical (anti-inflammatory) therapies are ideal for controlling inflammation. Surgery is discussed further in Chapter 12, however, it is important to emphasise that it should never be presented as a 'last resort', as this imbues the decision with a sense of failure for the patient and physician alike, and moreover, there is clearly a great benefit from proactive surgical management in certain IBD-related clinical scenarios.

Standard medical therapy and particular drug issues with regard to mental health and quality of life are discussed in detail in Chapter 13; here, the principles of therapy are outlined. Although physicians have become more comfortable in recent decades with escalating anti-inflammatory therapies more rapidly to control disease activity, there is still a hierarchy of therapies used. Commencing with those least likely to be associated with side effects, requiring least monitoring, and generally, costing less. When these agents are not sufficiently effective, others of greater potency should be promptly used to control inflammation.

In general, medications are used for two main reasons in IBD. First, they are used to bring new or acute inflammation under control, that is, to induce remission. Second, they are then used to prevent new episodes of inflammation, that is, to maintain remission. Some drugs act as both induction and maintenance agents, whilst others are only properly suited to be used as one or another. As IBD is a chronic disease, it is important that healthcare professionals move away from the out-dated concept that intermittent therapy of acute flares is acceptable management. It is now well accepted that this approach leads to long-term accumulation of damage to the bowel (Pariente *et al.* 2011) and avoidable complications, such as strictures, perforation and even cancer. As all maintenance agents are intended for long-term use, it is important that they are sufficiently safe and effective. It is also important that they are not associated with (or perceived to be) troublesome side effects, or undue risk, from the individual patient's viewpoint.

Treatment, however, is more than simply the prescription of drugs or the performance of an operation (Andrews *et al.* 2009). It additionally involves a longer-term plan, and agreed goals between each patient and their chosen health care professionals (HCPs). Apart from controlling inflammation and preventing relapse, additional foci for longer-term management include minimising infection risk (with a focus on vaccinations and travel risks), bone health, colorectal cancer surveillance (Chapter 11), nutritional review (especially for iron deficiency), skin cancer prevention/surveillance, sexual health and fertility (Chapters 8 and 9) and general preventative health medicine, which is often overlooked in people suffering a chronic disease, presumably due to the distraction of HCPs by acute illness issues. For all these reasons, a chronic care model, wherein patients are seen when they are well, in addition to when needing acute care, is to be recommended in IBD. In this way, chronic disease 'background' issues can be managed without the distraction of acute illness. In the longer-term, this improves health-related quality of life and reduces avoidable morbidity; moreover it also appears to reduce healthcare costs (Sack *et al.* 2012).

Evidence of psychological comorbidity in IBD

It is well documented that any chronic disease leads to a greater burden of psychological stress, anxiety and depression than is seen in the background population and this is no different in IBD. There is also evidence that these are all more prevalent when IBD disease control is worse – with greater rates of psychological comorbidities seen with active disease (Graff *et al.* 2006; Mikocka-Walus *et al.* 2007). As referred to earlier, it is unclear whether this is a unidirectional association from illness leading to psychological problems, or whether there may be a closer inter-relationship between psychological status and inflammatory activity. This possible 'brain-gut' interaction will be more clearly explored in Chapter 3. From a practical clinical viewpoint, what is important about the psychological burden of IBD is that it is highly prevalent in a young patient group. As up to 25 per cent of those with IBD have an onset before 18 years of age, it means they are at risk of psychological disorders from a young age, during a time in which they would often be taking on their first adult roles with regard to education, relationships, sexuality and work. Clearly for this reason alone, it is vital to manage this well.

Many of the psychological issues faced by people with IBD are no different to those faced by others, however, people with IBD do have some particular areas in life where their disease and psychological factors are more likely to interact and are not generally encountered by others without IBD. Therefore, several of these particular issues are dealt with in subsequent chapters: adolescence, Chapter 6; IBD in the elderly, Chapter 7; sexuality and fertility, Chapters 8 and 9; residual – non-inflammatory symptoms (IBS), Chapter 10; cancer risk, Chapter 11; surgery, Chapter 12; and fatigue, Chapter 15. Some of the difficulties in many of these areas arise from the poor match between patients' perceptions of the problem (risk) – which is generally over estimated – and the real risk of a bad outcome. This is particularly shown with regard to family planning decisions (Mountifield *et al.* 2009), where patients overestimate the risks of drugs, yet underestimate the risk of active disease to their pregnancy. The same over-estimation of risk is also noted for colorectal cancer (Mountifield *et al.* 2014). Hence, accurate information may be a useful tool in reducing undue anxiety.

Another important issue to highlight here is the poor match between patients' symptoms (i.e. their perception of their IBD activity) and the actual state of inflammation in the gut (i.e. actual current lesions). This can lead to doctors and patients misunderstanding each other, and create significant stress in the therapeutic relationship. This can worsen psychological health and adherence to therapy as patients may feel they are not believed and their experience is being doubted. Many people with IBD will have ongoing GI symptoms that do not correlate with any visible tissue damage, or are out of proportion to the visible damage. Now that endoscopic and radiologic techniques are better, this is more often appreciated to be the case. While this helps by ensuring people with healed IBD are not given more immunosuppressive drugs, it also leads to them receiving another (perhaps unwelcome) diagnosis of irritable bowel syndrome (IBS). This is common in the general community, and appears to occur at a greater rate in those with IBD, in whom it is associated with a poorer level of psychological health in some studies (Bryant *et al.* 2011). This is dealt with in detail in Chapter 10.

Possible effects of psychological comorbidity of disease course

From the discussion above, it is clear that psychological status can, and does, influence disease course. This may be via direct immunomodulatory effects on the gut or via how each patient engages with the healthcare system due to understandable direct functional impairment resulting from their illness and gut symptoms. The following two chapters will deal with the evidence behind possible direct effects of psychological status on inflammation, whereas later chapters (6–16) will help explore how psychological status influences patients' perception of disease and behaviour in certain specific situations.

An area not dealt with elsewhere is the high rate of opiate use, which is frequently noted in cohort studies of people with IBD (Phan *et al.* 2012).

6   Jane M. Andrews

In general, this surprises most clinicians as well-controlled IBD should not give pain and should certainly not require regular opiate use. The opiates appear to be medicating either poorly controlled disease or psychological distress, and encouragingly, their usage can be substantially reduced simply by implementing a chronic care model. Whether this is due to better IBD control or from patients feeling less distressed as they are better supported is unclear. The concern with opiate use, apart from polypharmacy, worsening GI symptoms and habituation, is that it is independently associated with poor IBD outcomes, including serious infection and death (Lichtenstein *et al.* 2012). This problem is not specific to IBD as community rates of opiate use in most Western countries have also increased hugely in recent decades (Manchikanti *et al.* 2012) and are creating similar social and medical concerns (Bell 1997).

Recommendations for a holistic approach and conclusions

Due to the large and convincing body of evidence that psychological wellbeing is important for people in general, especially those with any chronic disease, and IBD in particular, it is now vital that we heed this evidence and offer a model of care that enables these people to receive holistic care (Mikocka-Walus *et al.* 2012b). In particular, this means being able to offer a team of HCPs who are contactable, responsive and knowledgeable. In addition, there needs to be an acknowledgement of the importance, specifically, of the role of the psyche, and therefore, some psychological assessment and support, if needed, should be made available. This is a challenge in many medical settings, due to cost constraints, but even modest initiatives, such as the provision of specialist IBD nurses and a helpline have been shown to help overall outcomes (Mikocka-Walus *et al.* 2012b; Sack *et al.* 2012). Units around the world have piloted different strategies, with many showing promise (Mikocka-Walus *et al.* 2012a). We feel the time is now right for the WHO recommendations for an integrated model of care to be implemented in the management of people with IBD. We hope that this book helps interested HCPs see how and why they may begin this task in their own practices and institutions.

Current limitations and future considerations

- There is clearly a large interplay between psychological status and each patient's experience of IBD
- Most people with IBD do not get access to holistic care and the psyche is rarely specifically addressed
- This is a lost opportunity to enhance wellbeing and improve outcomes
- It is unclear whether the psyche plays a direct effect on IBD activity
- This is a difficult field to study directly
- There is, as yet, little evidence that specific psychological therapies improve IBD activity
- Better models of care do however improve outcomes in IBD

Practical recommendations

- All those caring for people with IBD should think actively about the potential for IBD to interfere with psychological wellbeing
- Receiving psychological support should be normalised (de-stigmatised), just as one would recommend medications, dietary support or a surgical procedure
- Each person with IBD should be considered for a psychological assessment
- HCPs should have a lower threshold for recommending psychological support in IBD
- Further studies are needed to examine whether specific psychological therapies are effective in IBD, and if so, data gathered regarding cost efficacy to enable them to be provided

Learning points

- IBD is a group of chronic inflammatory gastrointestinal disorders
- IBD – to doctors – is an objective disease
- IBD – to affected patients – is the whole experience of the illness
- People affected by IBD may have both physical and 'non-physical' symptoms
- Both sets of symptoms can equally impair patients and require specific targeted management
- Adequate management over time can only be achieved by a chronic disease model of care
- HCPs need to ensure people with IBD do not become limited/labelled by their disease

References

Access-Economics (2007). The economic costs of Crohn's disease and ulcerative colitis. Available online from www.crohnsandcolitis.com.au/content/Final_IBD_report_9_ June.pdf (accessed 13 May 2014).

Andrews, JM, Mountifield, RE, Van Langenberg, DR, Bampton, PA and Holtmann, GJ (2009). Un-promoted issues in inflammatory bowel disease: opportunities to optimize care. *Intern Med J*, vol. 40, no. 3, pp. 173–82.

Bell, JR (1997). Australian trends in opioid prescribing for chronic non-cancer pain, 1986–1996. *Med J Aust*, vol. 167, no. 1, pp. 26–9.

Bernstein, CN, Singh, S, Graff, LA, Walker, JR, Miller, N and Cheang, M (2010). A prospective population-based study of triggers of symptomatic flares in IBD. *Am J Gastroenterol*, vol. 105, no. 9, pp. 1994–2002.

Bryant, RV, van Langenberg, DR, Holtmann, GJ and Andrews, JM (2011). Functional gastrointestinal disorders in inflammatory bowel disease: impact on quality of life and psychological status. *J Gastroenterol Hepatol*, vol. 26, no. 5, pp. 916–23.

Burisch, J, Jess, T, Martinato, M, Lakatos, PL and EpiCom, E (2013). The burden of inflammatory bowel disease in Europe. *J Crohns Colitis*, vol. 7, no. 4, pp. 322–37.

Gearry, RB, Richardson, AK, Frampton, CM, Dodgshun, AJ and Barclay, ML (2010). Population-based cases control study of inflammatory bowel disease risk factors. *J Gastroenterol Hepatol*, vol. 25, no. 2, pp. 325–33.

Ghia, JE, Blennerhassett, P, Deng, Y, Verdu, EF, Khan, WI and Collins, SM (2009). Reactivation of inflammatory bowel disease in a mouse model of depression. *Gastroenterology*, vol. 136, no. 7, pp. 2280–8.e4.

Graff, LA, Walker, JR, Lix, L, Clara, I, Rawsthorne, P, Rogala, L, Miller, N, Jakul, L, McPhail, C, Ediger, J and Bernstein, CN (2006). The relationship of inflammatory bowel disease type and activity to psychological functioning and quality of life. *Clin Gastroenterol Hepatol*, vol. 4, no. 12, pp. 1491–501.

Jostins, L, Ripke, S, Weersma, RK, Duerr, RH, McGovern, DP, Hui, KY, Lee, JC, Schumm, LP, Sharma, Y, Anderson, CA, Essers, J, Mitrovic, M, Ning, K, Cleynen, I, Theatre, E, Spain, SL, Raychaudhuri, S, Goyette, P, Wei, Z, Abraham, C, Achkar, JP, Ahmad, T, Amininejad, L, Ananthakrishnan, AN, Andersen, V, Andrews, JM, Baidoo, L, Balschun, T, Bampton, PA, Bitton, A, Boucher, G, Brand, S, Buning, C, Cohain, A, Cichon, S, D'Amato, M, De Jong, D, Devaney, KL, Dubinsky, M, Edwards, C, Ellinghaus, D, Ferguson, LR, Franchimont, D, Fransen, K, Gearry, R, Georges, M, Gieger, C, Glas, J, Haritunians, T, Hart, A, Hawkey, C, Hedl, M, Hu, X, Karlsen, TH, Kupcinskas, L, Kugathasan, S, Latiano, A, Laukens, D, Lawrance, IC, Lees, CW, Louis, E, Mahy, G, Mansfield, J, Morgan, AR, Mowat, C, Newman, W, Palmieri, O, Ponsioen, CY, Potocnik, U, Prescott, NJ, Regueiro, M, Rotter, JI, Russell, RK, Sanderson, JD, Sans, M, Satsangi, J, Schreiber, S, Simms, LA, Sventoraityte, J, Targan, SR, Taylor, KD, Tremelling, M, Verspaget, HW, De Vos, M, Wijmenga, C, Wilson, DC, Winkelmann, J, Xavier, RJ, Zeissig, S, Zhang, B, Zhang, CK, Zhao, H, Silverberg, MS, Annese, V, Hakonarson, H, Brant, SR, Radford-Smith, G, Mathew, CG, Rioux, JD, Schadt, EE, Daly, MJ, Franke, A, Parkes, M, Vermeire, S, Barrett, JC and Cho, JH (2012). Host-microbe interactions have shaped the genetic architecture of inflammatory bowel disease. *Nature*, vol. 491, no. 7422, pp. 119–24.

Lawrance, IC, Murray, K, Batman, B, Gearry, RB, Grafton, R, Krishnaprasad, K, Andrews, JM, Prosser, R, Bampton, PA, Cooke, SE, Mahy, G, Radford-Smith, G, Croft, A and Hanigan, K (2013). Crohn's disease and smoking: is it ever too late to quit? *J Crohns Colitis*, vol. 7, no. 12, pp. e665–71.

Lichtenstein, GR, Feagan, BG, Cohen, RD, Salzberg, BA, Diamond, RH, Price, S, Langholff, W, Londhe, A and Sandborn, WJ (2012). Serious infection and mortality in patients with Crohn's disease: more than 5 years of follow-up in the TREAT registry. *Am J Gastroenterol*, vol. 107, no. 9, pp. 1409–22.

Manchikanti, L, Helm, S, 2nd, Fellows, B, Janata, JW, Pampati, V, Grider, JS and Boswell, MV (2012). Opioid epidemic in the United States. *Pain Physician*, vol. 15, no. 3 (Suppl), pp. ES9–38.

Mikocka-Walus, AA, Andrews, JM, Bernstein, CN, Graff, LA, Walker, JR, Spinelli, A, Danese, S, van der Woude, CJ, Goodhand, J, Rampton, D and Moser, G (2012a). Integrated models of care in managing inflammatory bowel disease: a discussion. *Inflamm Bowel Dis*, vol. 18, no. 8, pp. 1582–7.

Mikocka-Walus, AA, Turnbull, D, Holtmann, G and Andrews, JM (2012b). An integrated model of care for inflammatory bowel disease sufferers in Australia: development and the effects of its implementation. *Inflamm Bowel Dis*, vol. 18, no. 8, pp. 1573–81.

Mikocka-Walus, AA, Turnbull, DA, Moulding, NT, Wilson, IG, Andrews, JM and Holtmann, GJ (2007). Controversies surrounding the comorbidity of depression and anxiety in inflammatory bowel disease patients: a literature review. *Inflamm Bowel Dis*, vol. 13, no. 2, pp. 225–34.

Mountifield, R, Bampton, P, Prosser, R, Mikocka-Walus, A and Andrews, JM (2014). Colon cancer surveillance in inflammatory bowel disease: unclear gain but no psychological pain? *Intern Med J*, vol. 44, no. 2, pp. 131–8.

Mountifield, R, Bampton, P, Prosser, R, Muller, K and Andrews, JM (2009). Fear and fertility in inflammatory bowel disease: a mismatch of perception and reality affects family planning decisions. *Inflamm Bowel Dis*, vol. 15, no. 5, pp. 720–5.

Ng, SC, Tang, W, Ching, JY, Wong, M, Chow, CM, Hui, AJ, Wong, TC, Leung, VK, Tsang, SW, Yu, HH, Li, MF, Ng, KK, Kamm, MA, Studd, C, Bell, S, Leong, R, de Silva, HJ, Kasturiratne, A, Mufeena, MN, Ling, KL, Ooi, CJ, Tan, PS, Ong, D, Goh, KL, Hilmi, I, Pisespongsa, P, Manatsathit, S, Rerknimitr, R, Aniwan, S, Wang, YF, Ouyang, Q, Zeng, Z, Zhu, Z, Chen, MH, Hu, PJ, Wu, K, Wang, X, Simadibrata, M, Abdullah, M, Wu, JC, Sung, JJ, Chan, FK and Asia–Pacific Crohn's and Colitis Epidemiologic Study (ACCESS) Study Group (2013). Incidence and phenotype of inflammatory bowel disease based on results from the Asia-pacific Crohn's and colitis epidemiology study. *Gastroenterology*, vol. 145, no. 1, pp. 158–65 e2.

Pariente, B, Cosnes, J, Danese, S, Sandborn, WJ, Lewin, M, Fletcher, JG, Chowers, Y, D'Haens, G, Feagan, BG, Hibi, T, Hommes, DW, Irvine, EJ, Kamm, MA, Loftus, EV, Jr., Louis, E, Michetti, P, Munkholm, P, Oresland, T, Panes, J, Peyrin-Biroulet, L, Reinisch, W, Sands, BE, Schoelmerich, J, Schreiber, S, Tilg, H, Travis, S, van Assche, G, Vecchi, M, Mary, JY, Colombel, JF and Lemann, M (2011). Development of the Crohn's disease digestive damage score, the Lemann score. *Inflamm Bowel Dis*, vol. 17, no. 6, pp. 1415–22.

Phan, VA, van Langenberg, DR, Grafton, R and Andrews, JM (2012). A dedicated inflammatory bowel disease service quantitatively and qualitatively improves outcomes in less than 18 months: a prospective cohort study in a large metropolitan centre. *Frontline Gastroenterology*, vol. 3, no. 3, pp. 137–42.

Rocchi, A, Benchimol, EI, Bernstein, CN, Bitton, A, Feagan, B, Panaccione, R, Glasgow, KW, Fernandes, A and Ghosh, S (2012). Inflammatory bowel disease: a Canadian burden of illness review. *Can J Gastroenterol*, vol. 26, no. 11, pp. 811–7.

Sack, C, Phan, VA, Grafton, R, Holtmann, G, van Langenberg, DR, Brett, K, Clark, M and Andrews, JM (2012). A chronic care model significantly decreases costs and healthcare utilisation in patients with inflammatory bowel disease. *J Crohns Colitis*, vol. 6, no. 3, pp. 302–10.

Singh, S, Graff, LA and Bernstein, CN (2009). Do NSAIDs, antibiotics, infections, or stress trigger flares in IBD? *Am J Gastroenterol*, vol. 104, no. 5, pp. 1298–313; quiz 314.

Chapter 2

Stress, distress and IBD

Kathryn A. Sexton and Charles N. Bernstein

Stress and distress in IBD

An accumulating body of research has explored the prevalence of stress and distress in inflammatory bowel disease (IBD) and their roles in the disease course. Three main questions have been explored: Is psychological distress elevated among individuals with active IBD? Does the presence of stress or distress have long-term implications for the course of the disease? And if so, what are the mechanisms by which stress and disease activity may be associated?

The nature of stress

Stress is conceptualized not just as the presence of an environmental stressor, but as the feeling of being overwhelmed by a threatening event or an evolving situation (Lazarus and Folkman 1984; Selye 1975). Appraisals of the threat potential of a stressor and of one's capacity to cope are therefore key to understanding the experience of stress (Lazarus and Folkman 1984). In the context of IBD, the assessment of *perceived stress* is currently the method of choice for evaluating stress and its role in health (Keefer *et al.* 2008; Singh *et al.* 2009).

Emotional distress: stress, anxiety, and mood disorders in IBD

Stress has been shown to exacerbate or interact with predisposing genetic, biological, environmental, and psychosocial vulnerabilities to result in emotional distress and potentially in the onset of health disorders, both mental and physical (Taylor 2010). Stress has been identified as a risk factor for anxiety and depression. In IBD populations, several studies have demonstrated significant associations between perceived stress and anxiety or depression, whether the latter are treated as continuous symptoms (Camara *et al.* 2011) or as anxiety and mood disorders (Goodhand *et al.* 2012; Walker *et al.* 2008). Perceived stress, anxiety, and depression symptoms are best conceptualized as related and continuous variables that vary in severity throughout the population. As these reach a critical level of severity, anxiety, or mood disorders may be diagnosed and conceptualized as categorical variables. The effects of stress, depression, and anxiety overlap and are associated with symptom exacerbations in IBD (Camara *et al.* 2011).

Conceptually, perceived stress may represent the core of these emotional distress variables and perhaps capture a broader vulnerability.

The association between stress or distress and IBD disease activity appears to operate bidirectionally (Camara *et al.* 2011; Graff *et al.* 2009), with IBD resulting in stress and perceived stress resulting in acute IBD flare-ups. The chronicity of IBD is also a stress factor. Perceived stress (Levenstein *et al.* 2000) and distress (Mittermaier *et al.* 2004) have also been observed to be generally stable over long periods of time in IBD. This chronicity may be particularly relevant to IBD progression. Acute stress may also have a different, potentially heightened, effect when experienced in the context of chronic stress (Levenstein *et al.* 2000; Mawdsley and Rampton 2005).

Epidemiology of stress and distress in IBD: who is stressed?

Several independent studies document a higher level of perceived stress reported by those with active symptoms of IBD than by individuals with IBD who are not experiencing active symptoms or by healthy non-IBD comparison groups (Graff *et al.* 2009). Higher levels of distress (e.g. anxiety and depression symptoms) have also been observed among IBD patients with active symptoms compared both to the general population and to individuals with IBD in remission (Hauser *et al.* 2011). A significantly higher number of individuals with active IBD symptoms (Bernstein, MT *et al.* 2013, 2014; Singh *et al.* 2011) do report IBD as a significant source of stress as symptoms continue over time; however, stress is not solely related to IBD. We recently reported that individuals with active symptoms are more likely to endorse significant stress regarding their work/school, interpersonal relationships and their finances (Bernstein, MT *et al.* 2013; Singh *et al.* 2011). The possibility that increased stress in these broader life areas may precede the re-occurrence of IBD disease activity is currently being explored (Bernstein, MT *et al.* 2014).

Several studies have found a higher prevalence of distress, at a level that meets criteria for anxiety or mood disorders, among individuals diagnosed with IBD compared to healthy controls (Graff *et al.* 2009; Kurina *et al.* 2001; Walker *et al.* 2008). A higher rate of documented anxiety and mood disorders has also been observed among IBD patients presenting at hospital or specialty clinics, compared to patients presenting to hospital for minor health complaints or minor surgical care (Kurina *et al.* 2001). Comorbid mood and anxiety disorders were more prevalent both preceding and following the diagnosis of IBD (Kurina *et al.* 2001; Walker *et al.* 2008), potentially reflecting the important consequence that these chronic illnesses pose to patients' wellbeing.

Stress, distress, and disease activity: a two-way street?

Perceived stress and distress predict symptom re-occurrence

While stress and distress are common consequences of more symptomatic or severe disease, they are also implicated in the course of IBD. However, when stress is defined as a universal response to an event (e.g. loss of a job) that is assumed to have the same impact across all individuals, prospective findings on the association between major life events or daily hassles and future IBD symptom flares have been mixed. A majority of studies on life events show inconclusive or null findings, and studies of daily hassles have shown weak associations with future IBD symptom flares (see Keefer *et al.* 2008; Mawdsley and Rampton 2006). In contrast, a range of prospective studies evaluating an individual's *perceived stress* (see Mawdsley and Rampton 2006; Rampton 2009; Singh *et al.* 2009; Triantafillidis *et al.* 2013) with few exceptions (Mikocka-Walus *et al.* 2008) suggests that individuals with higher levels of perceived stress experience a greater likelihood of symptom re-occurrence as much as 3 months (Bernstein, CN *et al.* 2010; Langhorst *et al.* 2013 to 4 years later (Levenstein *et al.* 2000), and more frequent IBD symptoms over a period of 5 years (Sexton *et al.* 2013).

A similar, if less consistent (Mikocka-Walus *et al.* 2008), trend has been observed in prospective studies on the role of depression in exacerbations of IBD disease activity (Mardini *et al.* 2004; Mittermaier *et al.* 2004) as much as 18 months later (see Mittermaier *et al.* 2004; Maunder and Levenstein 2008; Mawdsley and Rampton 2006; Rampton 2009, for reviews). Major depression disorder and generalized anxiety disorder have also been associated with an increased risk of surgery in IBD (Ananthakrishnan *et al.* 2013a). Anxiety has been studied less frequently but has also been associated with IBD symptoms concurrently and prospectively (see Camara *et al.* 2009; Triantafillidis *et al.* 2013 for reviews).

Stress and distress in the onset of IBD

Prospectively, the question of whether stress, anxiety, or depressed mood has an impact on the onset of IBD has been explored in only a handful of studies. Li and colleagues (2004) assessed the incidence of the adverse experience of the death of a child among >21,000 parents, and prospectively identified those who later developed Crohn's disease or ulcerative colitis. No significant differences in the subsequent incidence of IBD were observed, compared to a matched subset of the general population. In contrast, the incidence and severity of a mood disorder showed a linear association with subsequent onset of Crohn's disease in two cohorts of nurses (n > 66,000, n > 85,000; Ananthakrishnan *et al.* 2013b). In the population-based Manitoba IBD cohort study, Walker and colleagues (2008) similarly found that mood disorders antedated the IBD diagnosis by several years. Further, those with a lifetime history of anxiety or mood disorder presented with IBD at a younger age compared to those without (Walker *et al.* 2008). There are as of yet no prospective studies that have assessed perceived stress in relation to the onset of IBD.

The impact of stress and distress on quality of life in IBD

One consistent finding is the impact of stress on quality of life. Several reviews have observed that the presence of significant disease activity in IBD is a consistent predictor of poorer quality of life (Graff *et al.* 2009; Graff *et al.* 2006; Guthrie *et al.* 2002; Moradkhani *et al.* 2013; Zhang *et al.* 2013; see also Mikocka-Walus *et al.*, 2007, for a review). In addition, persons reporting significant perceived stress (Moradkhani *et al.* 2013) or distress (Graff *et al.* 2009; Zhang *et al.* 2013) or experiencing comorbid psychiatric symptoms (Guthrie *et al.* 2002) show significantly greater decrements in their quality of life. Attention to stress and mental health, unfortunately, may be overlooked while clinicians focus on intestinal related symptoms in encounters with patients with IBD (Graff *et al.* 2009).

Potential pathways linking stress and IBD

The biological basis of the association between stress and IBD

Stress has known modulatory effects on the key communication methods between the neuroendocrine and immune systems, namely on both the hypothalamic-pituitary-adrenal (HPA) axis and the hypothalamic-autonomic nervous system (HANS) axes (and their bidirectional communication functions between the central and enteric nervous systems). Both axes are sensitive to stress and play a role in the regulation of the physiological stress response. Both are also implicated in immunoinflammatory responses in the gastrointestinal tract.

The regulatory function of these axes affects several processes and substances known or hypothesized to be relevant to IBD. Mast cells, for instance, are activated via the sympathetic nervous system (Bonaz and Bernstein 2013; Farhadi *et al.* 2007; Gareau *et al.* 2008; Mackner *et al.* 2011). Mast cells prompt changes in intestinal permeability, resulting in a phagocytic uptake of bacteria, and increase colonic water and ion secretion. Intestinal barrier dysfunction can thus be influenced by mast cells, and also by neurotransmitters such as acetylcholine, corticotropin-releasing factor (CRF), and nerve growth factor, all of which are affected by stress (Farhadi *et al.* 2007). Tumour necrosis factor-α (TNF-α), which is known to play a role in IBD, is also in part regulated by the action of these axes (Mawdsley and Rampton 2005). Gut microbiota also communicate with the sympathetic nervous system via the brain-gut axis (Bonaz and Bernstein 2013; Collins and Bercik 2009), and their role in IBD pathogenesis and their potential susceptibility to stress is being explored (Collins and Bercik 2009).

Recent evidence implicates the vagus nerve, intermediary between the autonomic system and the gut, in the mechanism of association between stress and IBD (Bonaz and Bernstein 2013). Much of this research comes from animal models (Ghia *et al.* 2008), where induced depression behaviours in mice have been shown to promote intestinal inflammation via vagus nerve inhibition on dendritic cells. This inflammation was shown to be improved with the use of tricyclic antidepressants.

Few studies have explored how IBD systems, pathways, and inflammatory mediators may be affected by stress in human populations, in part because of the difficulty in conducting experimental studies on stress in humans and the challenges involved in designing an experimental paradigm to reflect the effects of *chronic* stress. A handful of preliminary findings in the context of IBD, however, do point to dysregulation of the HPA and HNAS axes and the systems they affect. The most consistent finding is one of a decoupling between the HPA-axis and the sympathetic nervous system. Sympathetic tone and HPA-axis stimulation are normally positively correlated in healthy populations; however, in the context of IBD these have shown either no association or a negative correlation (Straub *et al.* 2002). This may reflect either greater activation in the sympathetic autonomic nervous system, or reduced HPA-axis stimulation; both have been observed (Collins and Bercik 2009). Some indicators of sympathetic nervous system functioning have also demonstrated abnormal function in IBD samples; a lack of a heart rate variability, for instance, has been observed in a subset of individual with ulcerative colitis, and has been associated with disease activity (Maunder *et al.* 2006), albeit inconsistently (Mawdsley and Rampton 2006). Functioning of the HPA is also altered in IBD: under conditions of experimental stress, for instance, individuals with IBD have shown evidence of heightened HPA responsiveness (Farhadi *et al.* 2005).

Single molecules with diverse effects across systems: putative emissaries at the intersection of the stress response and immune function that warrant further study

Understanding the role of stress on IBD immunopathogenesis is limited by our lack of definite understanding of the pathogenesis of IBD (Maunder 2000). Plausible mediating substances include: substance P, vasoactive intestinal proteins, TNF-α, glucocorticoids and glucocorticoid receptors, nitric oxide and heat shock proteins (Maunder 2000). At the molecular level, CRF and its regulation of glucocorticoid levels appears to be a likely candidate in the stress-IBD interaction (Larauche *et al.* 2009), as does substance P (Rosenkranz 2007) and TNF-α (Mawdsley *et al.* 2006). At the cellular level, accumulating evidence implicates mast cells as relevant players in the effect of stress on IBD (Bonaz and Bernstein 2013; Farhadi *et al.* 2005; Mackner *et al.* 2011). The role of the vagus nerve in downregulating inflammation supports the possibility that cholinomimetics may be of some value in IBD (Ghia *et al.* 2008).

Conclusions

For many individuals with IBD, stress is an important part of the experience. Particularly when disease is active, high perceived stress is more likely to be present in the form of heightened concern about both the disease itself and a range of other important life areas. Several neural pathways as well as substances at the molecular and cellular levels that are both implicated in IBD and responsive to stress have been identified. These suggest a likely role for stress in the regulation of the HPA and HNAS-axes, in their communication with the enteric nervous system via the vagus nerve and in the functioning of the immune and endocrine systems. The effects of stress on CRF, on TNF-α, on mast cells, on substance P, on intestinal permeability, on the immune response, and on colonic motility in the context of IBD warrant further exploration.

Current limitations and future considerations

- Stress has too often been conceptualized as a static occurrence rather than a dynamic and idiographic (individual-specific) process that changes over time
- To date, research has paid insufficient attention to the distinct influence of chronic stress in IBD
- Many existing studies on the epidemiology of anxiety and mood disorders or perceived stress in IBD are cross-sectional, making it difficult to isolate the role of anxiety and depression in IBD
- Studies on transactional models of stress in the context of IBD are lacking. Evaluation of this more detailed conceptualization of perceived stress requires the assessment of events, contextual factors, cognitive appraisals, and coping strategies to model their interactions over time

Practical recommendations

- When symptoms of IBD are active, evaluate patient stress and emotional distress
- *Perceived stress* should be evaluated, rather than just situations or events, to more adequately conceptualize the context and meaning of the situation for the person
- When significant perceived stress is present (whether or not disease is active), consider a referral for psychological or counseling services. Evidence-based therapies to improve coping and stress management are available
- Anxiety and mood disorders co-occurring with IBD should be treated, with either or both pharmacological or psychological interventions, given the potential benefits to disease course and quality of life

Learning points

- Higher rates of anxiety and mood disorders have been observed in IBD, particularly in the early years following IBD onset
- Perceived stress, anxiety, and depression have been associated in some studies with the onset of IBD
- Perceived stress and distress have been associated with IBD disease activity both cross-sectionally and prospectively
- Perceived stress/distress and active disease symptoms are independently associated with poorer quality of life

- Plausible pathways have been proposed regarding the influence of stress on disease course via the HPA axis and its central and peripheral effects, or through the vagus nerve connecting the autonomic and enteric nervous systems; these merit further investigation

References

Ananthakrishnan, AN, Gainer, VS, Perez, RG, Cai, T, Cheng, SC, Savova, G, Chen, P, Szolovits, P, Xia, Z, De Jager, PL, Shaw, SY, Churchill, S, Karlson, EW, Kohane, I, Perlis, RH, Plenge, RM, Murphy, SN and Liao, KP (2013a). Psychiatric co-morbidity is associated with increased risk of surgery in Crohn's disease. *Aliment Pharmacol Ther*, vol. 37, no. 4, pp. 445–54.

Ananthakrishnan, AN, Khalili, H, Pan, A, Higuchi, LM, de Silva, P, Richter, JM, Fuchs, CS and Chan, AT (2013b). Association between depressive symptoms and incidence of Crohn's disease and ulcerative colitis: results from the Nurses' Health Study. *Clin Gastroenterol Hepatol*, vol. 11, no. 1, pp. 57–62.

Bernstein, CN, Singh, S, Graff, LA, Walker, JR, Miller, N and Cheang, M (2010). A prospective population-based study of triggers of symptomatic flares in IBD. *Am J Gastroenterol*, vol. 105, no. 9, pp. 1994–2002.

Bernstein, MT, Sexton, KA, Targownik, LE, Graff, LA, Miller, N, Rogala, L and Walker, JR (2013). Sources of stress in IBD and relation to disease activity. *Gastroenterology*, vol. 144, no. 5, pp. S632–3.

Bernstein, MT, Sexton, KA, Targownik, LE, Graff, LA, Miller, N, Rogala, L and Walker, JR (2014). A prospective study of the complex relationship between symptomatic disease activity and stress in persons with IBD. *Can J Gastro*, vol. 28 (Suppl A), p. 272A.

Bonaz, BL and Bernstein, CN (2013). Brain-gut interactions in inflammatory bowel disease. *Gastroenterology*, vol. 144, no. 1, pp. 36–49.

Camara, RJ, Schoepfer, AM, Pittet, V, Begre, S, von Kanel, R and Swiss Inflammatory Bowel Disease Cohort Study Group (2011). Mood and nonmood components of perceived stress and exacerbation of Crohn's disease. *Inflamm Bowel Dis*, vol. 17, no. 11, pp. 2358–65.

Camara, RJ, Ziegler, R, Begre, S, Schoepfer, AM, von Kanel, R and Swiss Inflammatory Bowel Disease Cohort Study Group (2009). The role of psychological stress in inflammatory bowel disease: quality assessment of methods of 18 prospective studies and suggestions for future research. *Digestion*, vol. 80, no. 2, pp. 129–39.

Collins, SM and Bercik, P (2009). The relationship between intestinal microbiota and the central nervous system in normal gastrointestinal function and disease. *Gastroenterology*, vol. 136, no. 6, pp. 2003–14.

Farhadi, A, Fields, JZ and Keshavarzian, A (2007). Mucosal mast cells are pivotal elements in inflammatory bowel disease that connect the dots: stress, intestinal hyperpermeability and inflammation. *World J Gastroenterol*, vol. 13, no. 22, pp. 3027–30.

Farhadi, A, Keshavarzian, A, Van de Kar, LD, Jakate, S, Domm, A, Zhang, L, Shaikh, M, Banan, A and Fields, JZ (2005). Heightened responses to stressors in patients with inflammatory bowel disease. *Am J Gastroenterol*, vol. 100, no. 8, pp. 1796–804.

Gareau, MG, Silva, MA and Perdue, MH (2008). Pathophysiological mechanisms of stress-induced intestinal damage. *Curr Mol Med*, vol. 8, no. 4, pp. 274–81.

Ghia, JE, Blennerhassett, P and Collins, SM (2008). Impaired parasympathetic function increases susceptibility to inflammatory bowel disease in a mouse model of depression. *J Clin Invest*, vol. 118, no. 6, pp. 2209–18.

Goodhand, JR, Wahed, M, Mawdsley, JE, Farmer, AD, Aziz, Q and Rampton, DS (2012). Mood disorders in inflammatory bowel disease: relation to diagnosis, disease activity, perceived stress, and other factors. *Inflamm Bowel Dis*, vol. 18, no. 12, pp. 2301–9.

Graff, LA, Walker, JR and Bernstein, CN (2009). Depression and anxiety in inflammatory bowel disease: a review of comorbidity and management. *Inflamm Bowel Dis*, vol. 15, no. 7, pp. 1105–18.

Graff, LA, Walker, JR, Lix, L, Clara, I, Rawsthorne, P, Rogala, L, Miller, N, Jakul, L, McPhail, C, Ediger, J and Bernstein, CN (2006). The relationship of inflammatory bowel disease type and activity to psychological functioning and quality of life. *Clin Gastroenterol Hepatol*, vol. 4, no. 12, pp. 1491–501.

Guthrie, E, Jackson, J, Shaffer, J, Thompson, D, Tomenson, B and Creed, F (2002). Psychological disorder and severity of inflammatory bowel disease predict health-related quality of life in ulcerative colitis and Crohn's disease. *Am J Gastroenterol*, vol. 97, no. 8, pp. 1994–9.

Hauser, W, Janke, KH, Klump, B and Hinz, A (2011). Anxiety and depression in patients with inflammatory bowel disease: comparisons with chronic liver disease patients and the general population. *Inflamm Bowel Dis*, vol. 17, no. 2, pp. 621–32.

Keefer, L, Keshavarzian, A and Mutlu, E (2008). Reconsidering the methodology of "stress" research in inflammatory bowel disease. *J Crohns Colitis*, vol. 2, no. 3, pp. 193–201.

Kurina, LM, Goldacre, MJ, Yeates, D and Gill, LE (2001). Depression and anxiety in people with inflammatory bowel disease. *J Epidemiol Community Health*, vol. 55, no. 10, pp. 716–20.

Langhorst, J, Hofstetter, A, Wolfe, F and Hauser, W (2013). Short-term stress, but not mucosal healing nor depression was predictive for the risk of relapse in patients with ulcerative colitis: a prospective 12-month follow-up study. *Inflamm Bowel Dis*, vol. 19, no. 11, pp. 2380–6.

Larauche, M, Kiank, C and Tache, Y (2009). Corticotropin releasing factor signaling in colon and ileum: regulation by stress and pathophysiological implications. *J Physiol Pharmacol*, vol. 60 (Suppl 7), pp. 33–46.

Lazarus, RS and Folkman, S (1984). *Stress, appraisal, and coping*. New York: Springer Publishing Company.

Levenstein, S, Prantera, C, Varvo, V, Scribano, ML, Andreoli, A, Luzi, C, Arca, M, Berto, E, Milite, G and Marcheggiano, A (2000). Stress and exacerbation in ulcerative colitis: a prospective study of patients enrolled in remission. *Am J Gastroenterol*, vol. 95, no. 5, pp. 1213–20.

Li, J, Norgard, B, Precht, DH and Olsen, J (2004). Psychological stress and inflammatory bowel disease: a follow-up study in parents who lost a child in Denmark. *Am J Gastroenterol*, vol. 99, no. 6, pp. 1129–33.

Mackner, LM, Clough-Paabo, E, Pajer, K, Lourie, A and Crandall, WV (2011). Psychoneuroimmunologic factors in inflammatory bowel disease. *Inflamm Bowel Dis*, vol. 17, no. 3, pp. 849–57.

Mardini, HE, Kip, KE and Wilson, JW (2004). Crohn's disease: a two-year prospective study of the association between psychological distress and disease activity. *Dig Dis Sci*, vol. 49, no. 3, pp. 492–7.

Maunder, R (2000). Mediators of stress effects in inflammatory bowel disease: not the usual suspects. *J Psychosom Res*, vol. 48, no. 6, pp. 569–77.

Maunder, RG, Greenberg, GR, Nolan, RP, Lancee, WJ, Steinhart, AH and Hunter, JJ (2006). Autonomic response to standardized stress predicts subsequent disease activity in ulcerative colitis. *Eur J Gastroenterol Hepatol*, vol. 18, no. 4, pp. 413–20.

Maunder, RG and Levenstein, S (2008). The role of stress in the development and clinical course of inflammatory bowel disease: epidemiological evidence. *Curr Mol Med*, vol. 8, no. 4, pp. 247–52.

Mawdsley, JE, Macey, MG, Feakins, RM, Langmead, L and Rampton, DS (2006). The effect of acute psychologic stress on systemic and rectal mucosal measures of inflammation in ulcerative colitis. *Gastroenterology*, vol. 131, no. 2, pp. 410–9.

Mawdsley, JE and Rampton, DS (2005). Psychological stress in IBD: new insights into pathogenic and therapeutic implications. *Gut*, vol. 54, no. 10, pp. 1481–91.

Mawdsley, JE and Rampton, DS (2006). The role of psychological stress in inflammatory bowel disease. *Neuroimmunomodulation*, vol. 13, no. 5-6, pp. 327–36.

Mikocka-Walus, AA, Turnbull, DA, Moulding, NT, Wilson, IG, Andrews, JM, and Holtmann, GJ (2007). Controversies surrounding the comorbidity of depression and anxiety in inflammatory bowel disease patients: a literature review. *Inflamm Bowel Dis*, vol. 13, no. 2, pp. 225–34.

Mikocka-Walus, AA, Turnbull, DA, Moulding, NT, Wilson, IG, Holtmann, GJ and Andrews, JM (2008). Does psychological status influence clinical outcomes in patients with inflammatory bowel disease (IBD) and other chronic gastroenterological diseases: an observational cohort prospective study. *Biopsychosoc Med*, vol. 2, pp. 11–19.

Mittermaier, C, Dejaco, C, Waldhoer, T, Oefferlbauer-Ernst, A, Miehsler, W, Beier, M, Tillinger, W, Gangl, A and Moser, G (2004). Impact of depressive mood on relapse in patients with inflammatory bowel disease: a prospective 18-month follow-up study. *Psychosom Med*, vol. 66, no. 1, pp. 79–84.

Moradkhani, A, Beckman, LJ and Tabibian, JH (2013). Health-related quality of life in inflammatory bowel disease: psychosocial, clinical, socioeconomic, and demographic predictors. *J Crohns Colitis*, vol. 7, no. 6, pp. 467–73.

Rampton, D (2009). Does stress influence inflammatory bowel disease? The clinical data. *Dig Dis*, vol. 27 (Suppl 1), pp. 76–9.

Rosenkranz, MA (2007). Substance P at the nexus of mind and body in chronic inflammation and affective disorders. *Psychol Bull*, vol. 133, no. 6, pp. 1007–37.

Selye, H (1975). Confusion and controversy in the stress field. *J Human Stress*, vol. 1, no. 2, pp. 37–44.

Sexton, KA, Walker, JR, Graff, LA, Clara, I, Lix, L, Targownik, LE, Carr, R, Rogala, L, Miller, N and Bernstein, CN (2013). The Manitoba IBD Cohort Study: disease characteristics, personal characteristics, and perceived stress as predictors of disease activity over five years. *Gastroenterology*, vol. 144, no. 5 (Suppl 1), pp. S-763–S-764.

Singh, S, Blanchard, A, Walker, JR, Graff, LA, Miller, N and Bernstein, CN (2011). Common symptoms and stressors among individuals with inflammatory bowel diseases. *Clin Gastroenterol Hepatol*, vol. 9, no. 9, pp. 769–75.

Singh, S, Graff, LA and Bernstein, CN (2009). Do NSAIDs, antibiotics, infections, or stress trigger flares in IBD? *Am J Gastroenterol*, vol. 104, no. 5, pp. 1298–313; quiz 314.

Straub, RH, Herfarth, H, Falk, W, Andus, T and Scholmerich, J (2002). Uncoupling of the sympathetic nervous system and the hypothalamic-pituitary-adrenal axis in inflammatory bowel disease? *J Neuroimmunol*, vol. 126, no. 1-2, pp. 116–25.

Taylor, SE (2010). Mechanisms linking early life stress to adult health outcomes. *Proc Natl Acad Sci U S A*, vol. 107, no. 19, pp. 8507–12.

Triantafillidis, JK, Merikas, E and Gikas, A (2013). Psychological factors and stress in inflammatory bowel disease. *Expert Rev Gastroenterol Hepatol*, vol. 7, no. 3, pp. 225–38.

Walker, JR, Ediger, JP, Graff, LA, Greenfeld, JM, Clara, I, Lix, L, Rawsthorne, P, Miller, N, Rogala, L, McPhail, CM and Bernstein, CN (2008). The Manitoba IBD cohort study: a population-based study of the prevalence of lifetime and 12-month anxiety and mood disorders. *Am J Gastroenterol*, vol. 103, no. 8, pp. 1989–97.

Zhang, CK, Hewett, J, Hemming, J, Grant, T, Zhao, H, Abraham, C, Oikonomou, I, Kanakia, M, Cho, JH and Proctor, DD (2013). The influence of depression on quality of life in patients with inflammatory bowel disease. *Inflamm Bowel Dis*, vol. 19, no. 8, pp. 1732–9.

Chapter 3

The brain-gut axis and psychological processes in IBD

Emeran A. Mayer, Sylvie Bradesi, Arpana Gupta and David J. Katibian

Introduction

Despite a wealth of preclinical data on the acute and persistent effects of gut inflammation on the innervation of the gut (reviewed in Vergnolle 2008), the role of chronic intestinal inflammation on symptoms, comorbidities and brain responses in human patients with inflammatory bowel diseases (IBD), such as ulcerative colitis (UC) and Crohn's disease (CD) are poorly understood.

A major scientific breakthrough in understanding the interaction of the nervous system with the digestive system occurred with the discovery of the so-called "enteric nervous system (ENS)" in the middle of the nineteenth century (Furness 2006). Even before the discovery of the ENS, the importance of interactions between the brain and the digestive system in health and disease has been recognized for many centuries, and has been studied by prominent psychologists, psychiatrists and physiologists during the latter part of the nineteenth and earlier part of the twentieth century (reviewed in Mayer and Brunnhuber 2012). Both top down modulation of gastrointestinal (GI) function by stress and emotions, as well as bottom signaling from visceral afferents to the brain in abdominal pain syndromes, and possible emotion regulation has been reported by early investigators. This topic has received increased attention during the past two decades, largely due to a series of independent, yet converging, scientific discoveries from various fields of research, including enteric neuroscience (Furness 2006), neuroimaging (Mayer *et al.* 2009), intestinal microbiology and host microbial interactions (Round and Mazmanian 2009), and most recently, microbial gut brain signaling (Rhee *et al.* 2009) and neuroinflammation (D'Mello and Swain 2011).

In the following chapter, we will briefly review current concepts of the bidirectional brain gut interactions with an emphasis on the role of immune related pathways, both in the healthy organism, and in changes occurring at each level of the brain gut axis during chronic gut inflammation. We will discuss the possible influence of these alterations on IBD symptoms, including pain, disease related quality of life, psychological comorbidity and possibly disease trajectory.

The brain gut microbiome axis

The brain communicates to the GI tract, its immune system and its microbiome via multiple parallel pathways, including the two branches of the autonomic nervous system (ANS) (modulating a wide range of GI target cells), the hypothalamic pituitary adrenal (HPA) and sympatho-adrenal axis [modulating the gut associated lymphoid tissue (GALT)], and descending monoaminergic pathways (modulating gain of spinal reflexes and dorsal horn excitability). This system of parallel outflows from cortico-limbic-pontine networks, which are engaged by distinct homeostatic states has been referred to as the emotional motor system (EMS), and consists of integrated motor autonomic, neuroendocrine and pain modulatory components (Holstege *et al.* 1996). The output from the EMS to the GI tract can be altered due to primary central factors (depression, anxiety, and enhanced stress sensitivity) or it can be altered as a consequence of chronic inflammatory conditions in the periphery.

Brain to gut signalling

The sympathetic innervation of the GI tract and its role in the modulation of GI function has extensively been reviewed elsewhere (Furness 2006). It has been divided into subclasses of functional specific postganglionic neurons, including immune modulatory neurons. While the best experimental evidence for such communication between the sympathetic nervous system (SNS), lymphocytes and macrophages comes from the spleen, evidence for sympathetically mediated immune modulation in the gut has been demonstrated both in Peyer's patches, but also in the non-follicular mucosa in close proximity to different classes of immune cells, including dendritic cells, mast cells and B lymphocytes (Lyte *et al.* 2010). The parasympathetic innervation of the GI tract is comprised of the vagal and sacral parasympathetic divisions, which innervate foregut and hindgut structures respectively (Powley *et al.* 1991). Vagal modulation of macrophage activation via nicotinic acetylcholine receptors has been reported as part of a vago-vagal anti-inflammatory reflex (Pavlov and Tracey 2005). Prolonged alterations in ANS output to the gut is likely to induce changes in peripheral target cells, such as downregulation of adrenergic receptors on immune cells, reduced expression of TLRs on epithelial cells, or changes in primary afferent neurons, changing chronically the gain of gut to brain signaling, and possibly resulting in remodeling of brain regions receiving this enhanced input. Such lasting changes in brain-gut signaling may be associated with tonic ANS dysfunction related to altered emotional states including trait anxiety, anxiety disorders or depression.

Gut to brain signalling

Seventy to eighty percent of the body's immune cells are contained within the GALT, reflecting the unique challenge of this part of the immune system to maintain a homeostatic balance between tolerance and immunity in the intestine. The physical constraints that the undisturbed epithelial layer imparts on sampling the luminal space are overcome by specialized lymphoid structures (including small intestinal Peyer's patches) which are embedded in the lamina propria throughout the intestine (Artis 2008). Subsets of vagal afferent nerve terminals are in close proximity to mucosal immune cells and contain receptors for signaling molecules released from these cells, including mast cell products (proteases, histamine, serotonin, corticotropin-releasing factor) (Barbara *et al.* 2007) and cytokines released from macrophages. Immune cell products can indirectly influence the functional properties of enteroendocrine cells.

Even though the continuous stream of interoceptive signals from the gut is enormous, only a small fraction of this information in the healthy person is consciously perceived, in general only those for which a conscious behavioral response (ingestive behaviors, defecation) is required. However, recent evidence suggests that various forms of subliminal interoceptive inputs from the gut, including those associated with chronic gut inflammation and those generated by intestinal microbes, may influence memory formation, emotional arousal, and affective behaviors (Berntson *et al.* 2003). The human insula (INS) and related brain networks (including the saliency network), has emerged as a crucial brain region supporting this integration.

Inflammation and the brain gut axis

Based on the close interactions of communication systems within the entire brain gut axis (BGA), chronic gut inflammation would be expected to affect multiple peripheral and central components of the BGA. This is shown from alterations in gastrointestinal motility (mediated by direct effects on smooth muscle and indirect, ENS mediated effects) to changes in central control systems (ANS and HPA axis) to changes in brain structure and function.

Effects of chronic inflammation on gastrointestinal motility

Smooth muscle

Multiple mechanisms have been involved in the effect of intestinal inflammation on gastrointestinal motility, including changes in smooth muscle function, ENS activity and secretory and cellular mediators activity. Inflammation-related shift in the activity of resident immune cells and infiltration of new cells, and the resulting cytokine profile, is a strong determinant in the effect of inflammation on smooth muscle contractility (Shea-Donohue *et al.* 2012). Reported molecular smooth muscle changes associated with gut inflammation include changes in the activity of muscarinic receptors, alterations in the expression of various ion channels, or inflammation-induced changes in contractile proteins (Shea-Donohue *et al.* 2012). In addition, chronic inflammation can induce structural remodeling of smooth muscles (Burke *et al.* 2007). More recently, proteases and proteolytic pathways involved in immune cells recruitment have been involved in the smooth muscle response to inflammation and represent a new mechanism by which inflammation may affect smooth muscle contractility (Moore *et al.* 2011).

Enteric nervous system

There has been an increasing interest in the role of ENS neuroglial interactions in the modulation of the gut immune system and in GI dysfunction in inflammation. Alterations of the ENS morphology in IBD have been reported in previous reviews (De Giorgio *et al.* 2004) and subtle changes in the neurophysiology of enteric microcircuits, also called enteric neuroplasticity, have been reported in animal models of intestinal inflammation (Lomax *et al.* 2005). The direct or neuronal-mediated role of enteric glial cells in this plasticity remains to be determined.

Changes in Enterochromaffin cells (ECC) number and their serotonin (5HT) content, as well as a decrease in the expression level of the epithelial 5HT reuptake transporter (SERT), have been reported clinically in both CD and UC, suggesting a potential role of 5HT in gut inflammation (Mawe and Hoffman 2013). The role of enteric 5HT from ECC in intestinal inflammation was further confirmed by experimental studies in transgenic mice lacking SERT showing increased chemically-induced intestinal inflammation or mice depleted with tryptophan hydroxylase 1 (TPH1) exhibiting reduced intestinal inflammation when challenged chemically (Mawe and Hoffman 2013).

Effects of chronic inflammation on the brain

Abdominal pain

Inflammatory changes in the viscera, including the liver and the gut can result in cytokine mediated activation of vagal afferent pathways (including Tumor necrosis factor-α (TNFα), IL-1 and IL-6 receptors) signaling to the hypothalamus and related limbic brain regions. This vagally mediated brain modulation has been implicated in pain and behavioral responses characterized by hyperalgesia and social withdrawal ("sickness behavior") (Watkins and Maier 2005). Additional non-vagal mechanisms by which peripheral cytokines can reach the central nervous system (CNS) have been reported (D'Mello and Swain 2009; Dunn 2002). Mucosal release of cytokines and other inflammatory mediators, including bradykinin, histamine, and proteases, can also result in sensitization and activation of spinal afferent terminals, resulting in visceral hyperalgesia. Multiple effects of such inflammation or toxin-induced changes in afferent terminals have been reported, including release of neuropeptides such as substance P and calcitonin gene-related peptide, from afferent nerve terminals, development of mechanosensitivity of previously unresponsive afferents and development of peripheral and central sensitization resulting in greatly increased signaling of visceral afferent information to the CNS (Gold and Gebhart 2010).

Several studies performed in IBD patients are consistent with the concept that the majority of IBD patients are able to effectively downregulate chronic visceral hyperalgesia despite the presence of chronic inflammation (Chang *et al.* 2000). The effective engagement of peripheral (Verma-Gandhu *et al.* 2007) as well as central (Chang *et al.* 2004) pain inhibition systems have been proposed as plausible mechanisms for this paucity of pain symptoms in the majority of IBD patients.

Emotional and cognitive function

Chronic inflammatory diseases such as rheumatoid arthritis or inflammatory bowel disease are often associated with fatigue, altered cognitive and emotional functions (Gunnarsson *et al.* 2012). Even though the precise mechanisms and signaling pathways underlying those changes remain poorly understood, a human equivalent of the "sickness behavior" identified in rodent models has been implicated (Dantzer and Kelley 2007), including the involvement of peripheral pro-inflammatory cytokines in brain dysfunction. This hypothesis is further supported by evidence that treatment with cytokine antagonists (anti-TNF for IBD patients) often provides immediate symptomatic improvement of affective and cognitive dysfunction in human patients (Raison *et al.* 2013), as well as an improvement of altered emotional behaviors in animal models (Hess *et al.* 2011; Peyrin-Biroulet 2010). The pathways that have been identified linking the effect of peripheral cytokines to the brain include activation of vagal afferents, signaling via cerebral endothelial cells, and infiltration of circulating immune cells across the blood brain barrier (D'Mello *et al.* 2013). In the brain, glia is a major source of cytokines and increasing amount of data from experimental studies indicate that centrally produced cytokines are important in mediating the behavioral effect of cytokines from peripheral origin (Capuron and Miller 2011). Cytokines interact with neurotransmitters, receptors and enzymes important in behavior and pain modulation such as noradrenaline, excitatory/inhibitory amino acid such as glutamate or dopamine. Cytokines also affect neuronal excitability through interactions with neurotransmitters. It has been suggested that altered neuro-immune regulation in specific neuronal circuits may be involved in altered behaviors such as "sickness behavior" or altered cognitive function in chronic inflammatory disease (Capuron and Miller 2011).

Brain structure, function, and receptors

Multimodal brain imaging provides a unique opportunity to identify the effects of chronic inflammation on the human brain and to probe for possible correlation of these brain changes with biological, behavioral, and clinical parameters. A limited number of brain imaging studies have revealed both structural changes, functional changes to provocative stimuli, and altered functional connectivities between distinct brain regions in patients with CD and UC (Agostini *et al.* 2011, 2013a, 2013b; Hong *et al.* 2014).

Structural brain alterations

Morphological alterations in several brain regions have been identified in patients suffering from persistent pain disorders, with the most common being a decrease in grey matter (GM) in the insula, frontal and cingulate cortices ("pain matrix"). Similar GM abnormalities have been observed in patients with CD when compared to healthy control subjects (HCs), including decreased GM volumes in the dorso-lateral prefrontal cortex and anterior midcingulate cortex (Agostini *et al.* 2013a). In another study, UC patients showed greater cortical thickness in sub-regions of the cingulate cortex and in the left primary somatosensory cortex, as well as cortical thickness reductions in prefrontal and insular cortical subregions (Hong *et al.* 2014). The mechanisms underlying these structural changes of the brain in IBD patients are poorly understood but they may include the consequences of regional neuroinflammation (triggered by peripheral cytokines as mentioned above). Furthermore, studies have also demonstrated neurological complications in IBD patients, resulting in an increased risk of developing demyelinating diseases (Stovicek *et al.* 2014).

Functional brain alterations

Using functional magnetic resonance imaging (fMRI), Agostini *et al.* (2013b) reported altered brain responses of affective brain regions (incl. the amygdala) during habituation to stress, which may play a role in the connection between stress and symptom flares in CD (Agostini *et al.* 2013b). In another study, UC patients displayed a reduced response of certain brain regions when exposed to positive emotional stimuli (Agostini *et al.* 2011). The authors speculated that chronic intestinal inflammation may result in a decreased sensitivity to positive emotions.

Using positron emission tomography (PET) to study brain responses in response to aversive rectal distension in patients with UC and IBS and HCs, our group showed that UC patients displayed more activation in brain regions concerned with endogenous pain inhibition compared to IBS patients. In contrast, IBS patients showed greater activation of emotion related regions, including the amygdala. The authors speculated that UC patients may activate corticopontine pain inhibition systems to diminish visceral pain perception, whereas IBS patients activate limbic regions that facilitate perceptual responses to the stimulus (Mayer *et al.* 2005). Similarly, Bernstein *et al.* (2002) used fMRI to study differences in the effects of aversive visceral distension on brain activation between IBD and IBS patients, and identified group differences in ACC and somatosensory cortical responses (Bernstein *et al.* 2002). Jarcho *et al.* (2013) used positron emission tomography (PET) with [18F]SPA-RQ to measure substance P receptor

(NK-1R) availability in HCs and patients with IBD and IBS (Jarcho *et al.* 2013). Compared to HCs, IBD patients had NK-1R binding potential deficits across a widespread network of cortical and subcortical regions. IBS patients had similar, but less pronounced deficits. Binding potential in a subset of these regions was robustly related to discrete clinical parameters in each patient population.

Conclusions

There is growing evidence to support the involvement of the brain in the pathophysiology of IBD. Recent neuroimaging studies in IBD patients have identified functional and structural brain changes that may be the neurobiological correlate of often reported symptoms of depression, fatigue and impaired quality of life. A better characterization of the role of central factors in IBD pathophysiology and clinical course may provide the basis for effective adjuvant therapies, including centrally acting medications, mind based therapies and electrical vagal stimulation.

Current limitations and future considerations

- Carefully designed studies in well characterized large patient populations (male versus female, remission versus flare, disease duration, etc.) are required to better characterize the role of the nervous system in the pathophysiology of inflammatory bowel disorders in subsets of IBD patients
- Studies should aim at characterizing the distinct structural and functional brain changes, and determine possible correlations of these changes with symptoms, as well as mucosal and systemic immune mediators
- Longitudinal studies and intervention studies are required to determine possible causalities between brain alterations, peripheral immune activation and clinical symptoms
- Reverse translational studies should aim at identifying molecular mechanisms and potential therapeutic targets involved in these brain changes

Practical recommendations

- Alterations in brain gut interactions should be evaluated in every IBD patient, in particular the presence of "brain-related" comorbities, such as depression, cognitive impairments and fatigue
- Such patients are likely to benefit from a combination of centrally targeted therapies (mind-based and/or pharmacological) in addition to their primary anti-inflammatory therapy

Learning points

- The BGA is a bidirectional communication system between the gut and the brain that aims to maintain homeostasis of the organism in the face of

external (psychological stress) and internal (food intake, gut inflammation) perturbations
- In rodent models, chronic peripheral inflammation is associated with well-characterized changes at multiple levels of the BGA including neuroinflammation at the level of CNS. Neuroinflammation may affect responsiveness of brain circuits and lead to neuroplastic remodeling of brain circuits
- Human brain imaging studies have revealed alterations in the responsiveness of the brain to acute psychological and gut related stressors, as well as neuroplastic gray matter changes, and changes in regional receptor expression of the neurokinin signaling system. These brain changes may play a role in the commonly reported symptoms of depression, fatigue and cognitive impairment, and may mediate the effect of psychosocial stressors on disease flares

References

Agostini, A, Benuzzi, F, Filippini, N, Bertani, A, Scarcelli, A, Farinelli, V, Marchetta, C, Calabrese, C, Rizzello, F, Gionchetti, P, Ercolani, M, Campieri, M and Nichelli, P (2013a). New insights into the brain involvement in patients with Crohn's disease: a voxel-based morphometry study. *Neurogastroenterol Motil*, vol. 25, no. 2, pp. 147–e82.

Agostini, A, Filippini, N, Benuzzi, F, Bertani, A, Scarcelli, A, Leoni, C, Farinelli, V, Riso, D, Tambasco, R, Calabrese, C, Rizzello, F, Gionchetti, P, Ercolani, M, Nichelli, P and Campieri, M (2013b). Functional magnetic resonance imaging study reveals differences in the habituation to psychological stress in patients with Crohn's disease versus healthy controls. *J Behav Med*, vol. 36, no. 5, pp. 477–87.

Agostini, A, Filippini, N, Cevolani, D, Agati, R, Leoni, C, Tambasco, R, Calabrese, C, Rizzello, F, Gionchetti, P, Ercolani, M, Leonardi, M and Campieri, M (2011). Brain functional changes in patients with ulcerative colitis: a functional magnetic resonance imaging study on emotional processing. *Inflamm Bowel Dis*, vol. 17, no. 8, pp. 1769–77.

Artis, D (2008). Epithelial-cell recognition of commensal bacteria and maintenance of immune homeostasis in the gut. *Nat Rev Immunol*, vol. 8, no. 6, pp. 411–20.

Barbara, G, Wang, B, Stanghellini, V, De Giorgio, R, Cremon, C, Di Nardo, G, Trevisani, M, Campi, B, Geppetti, P, Tonini, M, Bunnett, NW, Grundy, D and Corinaldesi, R (2007). Mast cell-dependent excitation of visceral-nociceptive sensory neurons in irritable bowel syndrome. *Gastroenterology*, vol. 132, no. 1, pp. 26–37.

Bernstein, CN, Frankenstein, UN, Rawsthorne, P, Pitz, M, Summers, R and McIntyre, MC (2002). Cortical mapping of visceral pain in patients with GI disorders using functional magnetic resonance imaging. *Am J Gastroenterol*, vol. 97, no. 2, pp. 319–27.

Berntson, GG, Sarter, M and Cacioppo, JT (2003). Ascending visceral regulation of cortical affective information processing. *Eur J Neurosci*, vol. 18, no. 8, pp. 2103–9.

Burke, JP, Mulsow, JJ, O'Keane, C, Docherty, NG, Watson, RW and O'Connell, PR (2007). Fibrogenesis in Crohn's disease. *Am J Gastroenterol*, vol. 102, no. 2, pp. 439–48.

Capuron, L and Miller, AH (2011). Immune system to brain signaling: neuropsychopharmacological implications. *Pharmacol Ther*, vol. 130, no. 2, pp. 226–38.

Chang, L, Berman, SM, Suyenobu, B, Gordon, WA, Mandelkern, MA, Naliboff, BD and Mayer, EA (2004). Differences in brain responses to rectal distension between patients with inflammatory and functional GI disorders. *Gastroenterology*, vol. 126, no. 4 (Suppl 2), pp. A–106.

Chang, L, Munakata, J, Mayer, EA, Schmulson, MJ, Johnson, TD, Bernstein, CN, Saba, L, Naliboff, B, Anton, PA and Matin, K (2000). Perceptual responses in patients with inflammatory and functional bowel disease. *Gut*, vol. 47, no. 4, pp. 497–505.

D'Mello, C and Swain, MG (2011). Liver-brain inflammation axis. *Am J Physiol Gastrointest Liver Physiol*, vol. 301, no. 5, pp. G749–61.

D'Mello, C, Le, T and Swain, MG (2009). Cerebral microglia recruit monocytes into the brain in response to tumor necrosis factoralpha signaling during peripheral organ inflammation. *J Neurosci*, vol. 29, no. 7, pp. 2089–102.

D'Mello, C, Riazi, K, Le, T, Stevens, KM, Wang, A, McKay, DM, Pittman, QJ and Swain, MG (2013). P-selectin-mediated monocyte-cerebral endothelium adhesive interactions link peripheral organ inflammation to sickness behaviors. *J Neurosci*, vol. 33, no. 37, pp. 14878–88.

Dantzer, R and Kelley, KW (2007). Twenty years of research on cytokine-induced sickness behavior. *Brain Behav Immun*, vol. 21, no. 2, pp. 153–60.

De Giorgio, R, Guerrini, S, Barbara, G, Stanghellini, V, De Ponti, F, Corinaldesi, R, Moses, PL, Sharkey, KA and Mawe, GM (2004). Inflammatory neuropathies of the enteric nervous system. *Gastroenterology*, vol. 126, no. 7, pp. 1872–83.

Dunn, AJ (2002). Mechanisms by which cytokines signal the brain. *Int Rev Neurobiol*, vol. 52, pp. 43–65.

Furness, JB (2006). *The Enteric Nervous System*, 1st edn. Oxford: Blackwell.

Gold, MS and Gebhart, GF (2010). Nociceptor sensitization in pain pathogenesis. *Nat Med*, vol. 16, no. 11, pp. 1248–57.

Gunnarsson, C, Chen, J, Rizzo, JA, Ladapo, JA and Lofland, JH (2012). Direct health care insurer and out-of-pocket expenditures of inflammatory bowel disease: evidence from a US national survey. *Dig Dis Sci*, vol. 57, no. 12, pp. 3080–91.

Hess, A, Axmann, R, Rech, J, Finzel, S, Heindl, C, Kreitz, S, Sergeeva, M, Saake, M, Garcia, M, Kollias, G, Straub, RH, Sporns, O, Doerfler, A, Brune, K and Schett, G (2011). Blockade of TNF-alpha rapidly inhibits pain responses in the central nervous system. *Proc Natl Acad Sci U S A*, vol. 108, no. 9, pp. 3731–6.

Holstege, G, Bandler, R, Saper, CB, Holstege, G, Bandler, R and Saper, CB (1996). The emotional motor system. In: *Progress in brain research*. Amsterdam: Elsevier.

Hong, JY, Labus, JS, Jiang, Z, Ashe-McNalley, C, Dinov, I, Gupta, A, Shi, Y, Stains, J, Heendeniya, N, Smith, SR, Tillisch, K and Mayer, EA (2014). Regional neuroplastic brain changes in patients with chronic inflammatory and non-inflammatory visceral pain. *Plos One*, vol. 9, no. 1, p. e84564.

Jarcho, JM, Feier, NA, Bert, A, Labus, JA, Lee, M, Stains, J, Ebrat, B, Groman, SM, Tillisch, K, Brody, AL, London, ED, Mandelkern, MA and Mayer, EA (2013). Diminished neurokinin-1 receptor availability in patients with two forms of chronic visceral pain. *Pain*, vol. 154, no. 7, pp. 987–96.

Lomax, AE, Fernandez, E and Sharkey, KA (2005). Plasticity of the enteric nervous system during intestinal inflammation. *Neurogastroenterol Motil*, vol. 17, no. 1, pp. 4–15.

Lyte, M, Vulchanova, L and Brown, DR (2010). Stress at the intestinal surface: catecholamines and mucosa-bacteria interactions. *Cell Tissue Res*, vol. 343, no. 1, pp. 23–32.

Mawe, GM and Hoffman, JM (2013). Serotonin signalling in the gut—functions, dysfunctions and therapeutic targets. *Nat Rev Gastroenterol Hepatol*, vol. 10, no. 8, pp. 473–86.

Mayer, EA, Aziz, Q, Coen, S, Kern, M, Labus, JS, Lane, R, Kuo, B, Naliboff, B and Tracey, I (2009). Brain imaging approaches to the study of functional GI disorders: a Rome working team report. *Neurogastroenterol Motil*, vol. 21, no. 6, pp. 579–96.

Mayer, EA, Berman, S, Suyenobu, B, Labus, J, Mandelkern, MA, Naliboff, BD and Chang, L (2005). Differences in brain responses to visceral pain between patients with irritable bowel syndrome and ulcerative colitis. *Pain*, vol. 115, no. 3, pp. 398–409.

Mayer, EA and Brunnhuber, S (2012). Gastrointestinal disorders. In: *Handbook of clinical neurology, 3rd series*, vol. 106, pp. 607–31.

Moore, BA, Manthey, CL, Johnson, DL and Bauer, AJ (2011). Matrix metalloproteinase-9 inhibition reduces inflammation and improves motility in murine models of postoperative ileus. *Gastroenterology*, vol. 141, no. 4, pp. 1283–92, 92.e1–4.

Pavlov, VA and Tracey, KJ (2005). The cholinergic anti-inflammatory pathway. *Brain Behav Immun*, vol. 19 no. 6, pp. 493–9.

Peyrin-Biroulet, L (2010). Anti-TNF therapy in inflammatory bowel diseases: a huge review. *Minerva Gastroenterol Dietol*, vol. 56, no. 2, pp. 233–43.

Powley, TL, Berthoud, HR, Prechtl, JC and Fox, EA (1991). Fibers of the vagus nerve regulating gastrointestinal function. In: Tache, Y and Wingate, D (eds). *Brain-gut interactions*. Boston: CRC Press, vol. 1, pp. 73–82.

Raison, CL, Rutherford, RE, Woolwine, BJ, Shuo, C, Schettler, P, Drake, DF, Haroon, E and Miller, AH (2013). A randomized controlled trial of the tumor necrosis factor antagonist infliximab for treatment-resistant depression: the role of baseline inflammatory biomarkers. *JAMA Psychiatry*, vol. 70, no. 1, pp. 31–41.

Rhee, SH, Pothoulakis, C and Mayer, EA (2009). Principles and clinical implications of the brain-gut-enteric microbiota axis. *Nat Rev Gastroenterol Hepatol*, vol. 6, no. 5, pp. 306–14.

Round, JL and Mazmanian, SK (2009). The gut microbiota shapes intestinal immune responses during health and disease. *Nat Rev Immunol*, vol. 9, no. 5, pp. 313–23.

Shea-Donohue, T, Notari, L, Sun, R and Zhao, A (2012). Mechanisms of smooth muscle responses to inflammation. *Neurogastroenterol Motil*, vol. 24, no. 9, pp. 802–11.

Stovicek, J, Liskova, P, Lisy, J, Hlava, S and Keil, R (2014). Crohn's disease: is there a place for neurological screening? *Scand J Gastroenterol*, vol. 49, no. 2, pp. 173–6.

Vergnolle, N (2008). Postinflammatory visceral sensitivity and pain mechanisms. *Neurogastroenterol Motil*, vol. 20 (Suppl 1), pp. 73–80.

Verma-Gandhu, M, Verdu, EF, Bercik, P, Blennerhassett, PA, Al-Mutawaly, N, Ghia, JE and Collins, SM (2007). Visceral pain perception is determined by the duration of colitis and associated neuropeptide expression in the mouse. *Gut*, vol. 56, no. 3, pp. 358–64.

Watkins, LR and Maier, SF (2005). Immune regulation of central nervous system functions: from sickness responses to pathological pain. *J Intern Med*, vol. 257, no. 2, pp. 139–55.

Chapter 4

Microbiota and psychological processes and IBD

Peter De Cruz

Introduction

Inflammatory bowel diseases (IBD) are thought to develop as a result of an exaggerated immune response to the gut microbiota. Animal models of inflammation require bacteria to produce inflammation (Sartor 2004). Antibiotics are effective in Crohn's disease (CD), pouchitis and ulcerative colitis (UC), and probiotics have therapeutic efficacy in pouchitis and UC (Sartor 2004). Diversion of the faecal stream from the inflamed gut induces healing in CD, while re-infusion of intestinal content into surgically excluded ileum triggers early disease recurrence (D'Haens *et al.* 1998). These findings have helped establish that the gut microbiota is a key contributor to IBD pathogenesis, with disease more prevalent in genetically susceptible individuals (Jostins *et al.* 2012).

The gut microbiota is a complex ecological environment, with each human harbouring up to a 100 trillion (10^{14}) bacteria (Turnbaugh *et al.* 2007). Man can be considered a 'supra-organism' – a composite of human and microbial genes (the microbiome) (Turnbaugh *et al.* 2007). The microbiome is estimated to encode 100-fold more genes than the human genome (Turnbaugh *et al.* 2007). Seventy per cent of the gut microbiota have not been cultured by standard, culture-based techniques (Turnbaugh *et al.* 2007). Metagenomics, the study of microbiota using culture-independent techniques (Turnbaugh *et al.* 2007) has advanced our understanding of the role of the gut microbiota in health and IBD. Central to metagenomics is the bacterial 16S ribosomal (r)RNA gene that has revolutionised bacterial taxonomy enabling the identification of both known and novel bacteria based on sequence similarity to previously identified bacteria.

Characterisation of the gut microbiota in health and IBD has been complicated by large person-to-person variation with the 'normal' human bowel community yet to be defined (Turnbaugh *et al.* 2007). Nonetheless, there are 50–100 bacterial species that are shared by many individuals and are referred to as the 'phylogenetic core' (Qin *et al.* 2010). The phylogenetic core describes which bacteria are commonly 'present' in the gut between individuals whereas the 'functional core microbiome' refers to what the microbiota are 'doing' at a gene expression level and relates to the products and effects of the microbiota (Qin *et al.* 2010).

Host-bacterial mutualism

A tightly regulated and finely balanced relationship has evolved between man and microbiota that has been referred to as host-bacterial mutualism (Backhed *et al.* 2005). The host plays a role in determining the nature and activity of the microbiota and the microbiota plays a role in determining aspects of host immunity.

Host control of the microbiota in IBD

The importance of host microbe interaction in the aetiology of IBD has been highlighted in a recent study that demonstrated that the majority of genes increasing susceptibility to IBD are associated with pathways responsible for detecting, responding to and processing microbiota (Jostins *et al.* 2012). Mutations in a number of genes involved in innate immunity including NOD2, ATG16L1, IRGM and IL23R have been implicated in the development of CD (Jostins *et al.* 2012), suggesting that the pathogenesis of IBD is driven by the interaction between the microbiota and specific gene polymorphisms associated with IBD.

Microbiota control of host immunity in IBD

The gut microbiota plays a role in the development and regulation of the host immune system. A key mediator of the effect of the gut microbiota on host immunity are dendritic cells (DC), which sample and respond to luminal microbiota via pattern recognition and therefore modify the nature of subsequent T-cell responses (Stagg *et al.* 2004). Commensal microbiota, such as segmented filamentous bacteria (SFB), have also been shown to regulate the balance between T helper 17 (Th17) and regulatory T cells, contributing to the influence that microbiota composition has on intestinal immunity, tolerance, and susceptibility to IBD (Ivanov *et al.* 2008).

The concept that elements of the microbiota may have a modifying effect on inflammation in IBD was introduced by the finding that a lower abundance of *Faecalibacterium prausnitzii* in the ileal mucosa of patients with CD was associated with recurrent disease 6 months after surgery (Sokol *et al.* 2008). Furthermore, *F. prausnitzii*, induced IL-10 production *in vitro* and had anti-inflammatory effects in mouse models of colitis (Sokol *et al.* 2008). *F. prausnitzii* has therefore become the target of ongoing research as a potential probiotic in the management of IBD (Sokol *et al.* 2008).

Characterisation of the gut microbiota in IBD

The role of the microbiota in IBD has been characterised using two main approaches. Characterisation of the microbial community as a whole has been referred to as the 'global description strategy'. It has led to the concept of 'dysbiosis', which refers to an imbalance between beneficial and harmful bacteria. The alternate approach has focused on the identification of single specific microorganisms that are thought to be pathogenic and has been called the 'candidate microorganism strategy'.

'Global description strategy'

IBD is characterised by an overall reduction in microbiota diversity. The composition and abundance of the gut microbiota differs between disease subtype (CD vs UC), inflamed versus non-inflamed mucosa (Walker *et al.* 2011) and phenotype (colonic vs ileal CD) (Willing *et al.* 2010).

Dysbiosis in CD is associated with a reduction in the diversity of the phylum Firmicutes (Walker *et al.* 2011), particularly *Faecalibacterium prausznitzii* (Sokol *et al.* 2008; Walker *et al.* 2011), and an increase in *Enterobacteriaceae*, especially *Escherichia coli* (Darfeuille-Michaud *et al.* 2004). Studies have confirmed a lower prevalence of *F. prausnitzii* in adults with both CD (Joossens *et al.* 2011) and UC (Varela *et al.* 2013), however, a reduced abundance of *F. prausnitzii* does not appear essential for the development of IBD and may simply represent a marker of a disordered microbiota. CD has also been found to be associated with an increased abundance of the mucolytic species *Ruminococcus torques* and *Ruminococcus gnavus* (Joossens *et al.* 2011).

Dysbiosis in UC is associated with a reduction in the Firmicutes, particularly the C. coccoides group (Walker *et al.* 2011). A significantly lower abundance of *Roseburia hominis* and *F. prausnitzii* has been found in UC patients compared with controls (Machiels *et al.* 2013). Differences in the bacterial communities between CD and UC suggest that the microbiota plays different roles in these disease subtypes.

'Candidate microorganism strategy'

The search for a single specific pathogen associated with the development of CD has largely focused on two organisms, MAP and *E.coli*.

MAP

The hypothesis of a single specific pathogen was initially driven by the assumption that CD was caused by *Mycobacterium. avium* subsp. *paratuberculosis* (MAP) due to the clinical similarity of Johne's disease in cattle, caused by MAP, and CD in humans (Dalsiel 1913). MAP has been identified in CD using molecular methods, however, the results have been inconsistent (Abubakar *et al.* 2008). The evidence against MAP being the causative agent in CD comes from the lack of efficacy that anti-MAP therapy had in the induction of remission of CD in the largest randomised controlled trial to date (Selby *et al.* 2007).

E. coli

E. coli is a commensal organism that plays a role in maintaining intestinal homeostasis. *Adherent invasive E. coli* (AIEC) is a pathogenic strain of *E coli* that has developed virulence factors that allows it to adapt, survive and colonize the intestinal mucosa of approximately a third of patients with ileal CD and is associated with early postoperative recurrence of CD (Darfeuille-Michaud *et al.* 2004). AIEC is able to resist phagocytosis, replicate within macrophages and upregulate ileal CEACAM-6 receptors to which it binds, allowing it to create an amplification loop of colonization and inflammation (Darfeuille-Michaud *et al.* 2004).

Other organisms

Other bacteria, including Pseudomonas and Campylobacter, have also been linked to IBD, however, no definitive pathophysiological role has been identified. It also remains unclear as to what role viruses and fungi may play in the aetiology of IBD.

The microbiota gut brain axis and IBD

An emerging hypothesis is that interaction between the gut microbiota and the gut-brain axis (GBA) plays a role in the pathogenesis of IBD (Collins and Bercik 2009). The GBA refers to a communication network that integrates neural, hormonal and immunological signalling between the gut and brain (Collins and Bercik 2009). The GBA is thought to provide the gut microbiota and its metabolites a route by which to access the nervous system (Collins and Bercik 2009). The microbiota-GBA is thought to be a bidirectional communication system that enables the brain to influence the composition of the intestinal microbiota, whereby the microbiota influences brain and behaviour (Collins and Bercik 2009).

Inflammatory bowel diseases are associated with an increased prevalence of depression (Walker *et al.* 2008). Symptoms of irritable bowel syndrome (IBS) may co-exist in patients with IBD and the natural history of both conditions is influenced by emotional factors such as stress and depression (Mawdsley and Rampton 2005). Evidence supporting a role for the microbiota-GBA in mental health is expanding and has been recently reviewed (Bested *et al.* 2013).

The microbiota-GBA is considered to be one of several mechanisms by which stress and depression mediate their effects in IBD. In mouse models, stress has been shown to: (i) increase intestinal permeability; (ii) alter microbiota composition and function; (iii) increase circulating cytokine levels; and (iv) increase susceptibility to infections (Bonaz and Bernstein 2013). Furthermore, stress induced changes in the sympathetic nervous system with catecholamine release into the gut may alter microbiota community structure via interference with inter-bacterial signalling (Bonaz and Bernstein 2013). Based on the experimental evidence that perturbation of the microbiota alters behaviour and the association of IBD and IBS with dysbiosis, it has been speculated that dysbiosis may be a contributing factor to the behavioural changes that are reported in some patients with IBD and IBS (Collins and Bercik 2009). In concert, these observations provide preliminary evidence of a relationship between the brain, gut microbiota and behaviour in the pathogenesis of IBD.

Therapeutic manipulation of the gut microbiota in IBD

Microbial ecology within the gut can be modulated with pharmacological or nutritional interventions that aim to ameliorate the effects of dysbiosis.

Probiotics

Probiotics refer to 'live organism(s), which in adequate quantities provide a benefit to the host' (Sartor 2004). Probiotics mediate their effect via exclusion of pathogens, maintenance of epithelial barrier function and induction of adaptive immunity. Probiotics have demonstrated efficacy in induction and maintenance of remission in UC, and maintenance of remission in pouchitis (Sartor 2004). However, the current repertoire of probiotics available are limited in their potency. To date there has been no evidence of any benefit from probiotics in active CD or prevention of CD recurrence after surgery (Sartor 2004).

Prebiotics

Prebiotics are non-digestible food ingredients that are fermented by intestinal bacteria in a selective manner and promote changes in the gut ecosystem that benefit the host (Sartor 2004). Inulin and oligofructose stimulate saccharolysis in the colonic lumen, favouring the growth of indigenous lactobacilli and bifidobacteria, which have been associated with reduced mucosal inflammation in animal models of IBD (Sartor 2004). However, the results of two recent large randomised controlled trials in CD have been conflicting in relation to the impact of oligofructose-enriched inulin supplementation on disease activity and *Bifidobacterium* counts (Benjamin *et al.* 2011; Joossens *et al.* 2012).

Antibiotics

In CD, antibiotics have proven efficacy in the induction and maintenance of remission, prevention of post-operative recurrence and perianal CD (Sartor 2004). In contrast, the evidence for antibiotic therapy in UC is relatively lacking except in the setting of acute colitis and pouchitis (Sartor 2004). Despite their efficacy in IBD, antibiotics are limited by drug intolerance, the risk of antibiotic resistance and the lack of durability of response upon treatment cessation.

Faecal microbiota transplantation

Faecal microbiota transplantation (FMT) aims to re-establish normal colonisation resistance in patients with a persistently altered microbiota. A recent systematic review of FMT in IBD found nine reports (but no controlled trials) that demonstrated promising results (Anderson *et al.* 2012). However, controlled trials of FMT with molecular microbiologic correlation are required to establish which patients with IBD might most benefit.

Diet and the gut microbiota

Dietary intake has a major impact on microbiota composition (David *et al.* 2013; Wu *et al.* 2011). The microbiota metabolize fibre and starch to the short chain fatty acids (SCFAs) butyrate, acetate and propionate, which serve as a major energy source for colonocytes, and have been implicated in the prevention of colitis (Macfarlane and Macfarlane 2003). IBD is associated with reduced numbers of butyrate producing bacteria (including *F. prausnitzii*), and accordingly, reduced concentrations of SCFAs (Sokol *et al.* 2008). Dietary interventions in IBD have largely been restricted to the use of enteral and total parenteral nutrition with the aim of providing bowel rest. Exclusive enteral nutrition (EEN) is effective in paediatric CD in inducing clinical remission, mucosal healing and improving nutritional status and growth (Critch *et al.* 2012). A lack of efficacy and palatability has limited EEN use in adult CD. Preliminary reports suggest that EEN may have restorative effects on gut ecology but larger studies are required to confirm these findings.

Conclusions

Characterisation of the gut microbiota using emerging molecular techniques has opened up the prospect of identifying novel diagnostic and therapeutic targets to enable personalised medicine in IBD. Exploration of the interaction between the gut microbiota and the gut-brain axis has the potential to establish the link between the gut microbiota, systemic immunity and the neuro-psychiatric comorbidities that accompany IBD. Understanding the complex interaction between the host and gut microbiome in both form and function will be required to inform strategies on how to manipulate the gut microbiota for optimal therapeutic benefit.

Current limitations and future considerations

- Due to large inter-individual variation the normal spectrum of gut microbiota composition in healthy individuals is still unknown
- It remains unclear whether compositional changes in the microbiota contribute to the development of IBD or instead are a consequence of inflammatory disease
- Compositional changes in the microbiota associated with IBD are yet to be linked to gene expression, transcript activity and metabolism which is required to understand the relationship between the microbiome and IBD
- The mechanism of action, optimal dosing and treatment duration of current therapeutic regimens to modulate the microbiota is unclear and requires well designed trials with concurrent molecular characterisation of the microbiota

- Microbiota-GBA interactions may play a role in the development of psychological symptoms associated with IBD and suggest that interventions targeting the gut microbiota may be of psychological benefit to IBD patients

Practical recommendations

- Current evidence supports a key role of the microbiota in the pathogenesis of IBD
- The potential link between the gut, brain and behaviour in IBD provides a framework to direct ongoing research and educate patients about the potential relationship between stress, depression and dysbiosis in IBD
- Therapeutic strategies to manipulate the microbiota in IBD are evolving with evidence currently supporting a role for antibiotics, probiotics and EEN for specific indications

Learning points

- The gut microbiota plays a key role in the pathogenesis of inflammatory bowel disease (IBD)
- IBD is associated with an overall reduction in microbiota diversity, a relative reduction in abundance of the phylum Firmicutes and dysbiosis
- Interplay between the microbiota and the gut-brain axis represents a potential pathway via which dysbiosis, stress and depression mediate their effects in IBD
- Therapeutic manipulation of the microbiota is possible but the efficacy of current treatments is variable and the durability of treatment response is uncertain

References

Abubakar, I, Myhill, D, Aliyu, SH and Hunter, PR (2008). Detection of Mycobacterium avium subspecies paratuberculosis from patients with Crohn's disease using nucleic acid-based techniques: a systematic review and meta-analysis. *Inflamm Bowel Dis*, vol. 14, no. 3, pp. 401–10.

Anderson, JL, Edney, RJ and Whelan, K (2012). Systematic review: faecal microbiota transplantation in the management of inflammatory bowel disease. *Aliment Pharmacol Ther*, vol. 36, no. 6, pp. 503–16.

Backhed, F, Ley, RE, Sonnenburg, JL, Peterson, DA and Gordon, JI (2005). Host-bacterial mutualism in the human intestine. *Science*, vol. 307, no. 5717, pp. 1915–20.

Benjamin, JL, Hedin, CR, Koutsoumpas, A, Ng, SC, McCarthy, NE, Hart, AL, Kamm, MA, Sanderson, JD, Knight, SC, Forbes, A, Stagg, AJ, Whelan, K and Lindsay, JO (2011). Randomised, double-blind, placebo-controlled trial of fructo-oligosaccharides in active Crohn's disease. *Gut*, vol. 60, no. 7, pp. 923–9.

Bested, AC, Logan, AC and Selhub, EM (2013). Intestinal microbiota, probiotics and mental health: from Metchnikoff to modern advances: part I – autointoxication revisited. *Gut Pathogens*, vol. 5:5, doi:10.1186/1757-4749-5-5.

Bonaz, BL and Bernstein, CN (2013). Brain-gut interactions in inflammatory bowel disease. *Gastroenterology*, vol. 144, no. 1, pp. 36–49.

Collins, SM and Bercik, P (2009). The relationship between intestinal microbiota and the central nervous system in normal gastrointestinal function and disease. *Gastroenterology*, vol. 136, no. 6, pp. 2003–14.

Critch, J, Day, AS, Otley, A, King-Moore, C, Teitelbaum, JE and Shashidhar, H (2012). Use of enteral nutrition for the control of intestinal inflammation in pediatric Crohn disease. *J Pediatr Gastroenterol Nutr*, vol. 54, no. 2, pp. 298–305.

D'Haens, GR, Geboes, K, Peeters, M, Baert, F, Penninckx, F and Rutgeerts, P (1998). Early lesions of recurrent Crohn's disease caused by infusion of intestinal contents in excluded ileum. *Gastroenterology*, vol. 114, no. 2, pp. 262–7.

Dalsiel, TK (1913). Chronic intestinal enteritis. *Br Med J*, vol. 2, pp. 1068–70.

Darfeuille-Michaud, A, Boudeau, J, Bulois, P, Neut, C, Glasser, AL, Barnich, N, Bringer, MA, Swidsinski, A, Beaugerie, L and Colombel, JF (2004). High prevalence of adherent-invasive Escherichia coli associated with ileal mucosa in Crohn's disease. *Gastroenterology*, vol. 127, no. 2, pp. 412–21.

David, LA, Maurice, CF, Carmody, RN, Gootenberg, DB, Button, JE, Wolfe, BE, Ling, AV, Devlin, AS, Varma, Y, Fischbach, MA, Biddinger, SB, Dutton, RJ and Turnbaugh, PJ (2013). Diet rapidly and reproducibly alters the human gut microbiome. *Nature*, vol. 505, no. 7484, pp. 559–63.

Ivanov, II, Frutos Rde, L, Manel, N, Yoshinaga, K, Rifkin, DB, Sartor, RB, Finlay, BB and Littman, DR (2008). Specific microbiota direct the differentiation of IL-17-producing T-helper cells in the mucosa of the small intestine. *Cell Host Microbe*, vol. 4, no. 4, pp. 337–49.

Joossens, M, De Preter, V, Ballet, V, Verbeke, K, Rutgeerts, P and Vermeire, S (2012). Effect of oligofructose-enriched inulin (OF-IN) on bacterial composition and disease activity of patients with Crohn's disease: results from a double-blinded randomised controlled trial. *Gut*, vol. 61, no. 6, p. 958.

Joossens, M, Huys, G, Cnockaert, M, De Preter, V, Verbeke, K, Rutgeerts, P, Vandamme, P and Vermeire, S (2011). Dysbiosis of the faecal microbiota in patients with Crohn's disease and their unaffected relatives. *Gut*, vol. 60, no. 5, pp. 631–7.

Jostins, L, Ripke, S, Weersma, RK, Duerr, RH, McGovern, DP, Hui, KY, Lee, JC, Schumm, LP, Sharma, Y, Anderson, CA, Essers, J, Mitrovic, M, Ning, K, Cleynen, I, Theatre, E, Spain, SL, Raychaudhuri, S, Goyette, P, Wei, Z, Abraham, C, Achkar, JP, Ahmad, T, Amininejad, L, Ananthakrishnan, AN, Andersen, V, Andrews, JM, Baidoo, L, Balschun, T, Bampton, PA, Bitton, A, Boucher, G, Brand, S, Buning, C, Cohain, A, Cichon, S, D'Amato, M, De Jong, D, Devaney, KL, Dubinsky, M, Edwards, C, Ellinghaus, D, Ferguson, LR, Franchimont, D, Fransen, K, Gearry, R, Georges, M, Gieger, C, Glas, J, Haritunians, T, Hart, A, Hawkey, C, Hedl, M, Hu, X, Karlsen, TH, Kupcinskas, L, Kugathasan, S, Latiano, A, Laukens, D, Lawrance, IC, Lees, CW, Louis, E, Mahy, G, Mansfield, J, Morgan, AR, Mowat, C, Newman, W, Palmieri, O, Ponsioen, CY, Potocnik, U, Prescott, NJ, Regueiro, M, Rotter, JI, Russell, RK, Sanderson, JD, Sans, M, Satsangi, J, Schreiber, S, Simms, LA, Sventoraityte, J, Targan, SR, Taylor, KD, Tremelling, M, Verspaget, HW, De Vos, M, Wijmenga, C, Wilson, DC, Winkelmann, J, Xavier, RJ, Zeissig, S, Zhang, B, Zhang, CK, Zhao, H, Silverberg, MS, Annese, V, Hakonarson, H, Brant, SR, Radford-Smith, G, Mathew, CG, Rioux, JD, Schadt, EE, Daly, MJ, Franke, A, Parkes, M, Vermeire, S, Barrett, JC and Cho, JH (2012). Host-microbe interactions have shaped the genetic architecture of inflammatory bowel disease. *Nature*, vol. 491, no. 7422, pp. 119–24.

Macfarlane, S and Macfarlane, GT (2003). Regulation of short-chain fatty acid production. *Proc Nutr Soc*, vol. 62, no. 1, pp. 67–72.

Machiels, K, Joossens, M, Sabino, J, De Preter, V, Arijs, I, Eeckhaut, V, Ballet, V, Claes, K, Van Immerseel, F, Verbeke, K, Ferrante, M, Verhaegen, J, Rutgeerts, P and Vermeire, S (2013). A decrease of the butyrate-producing species Roseburia hominis and Faecalibacterium prausnitzii defines dysbiosis in patients with ulcerative colitis. *Gut*, doi: 10.1136/gutjnl-2013-304833.

Mawdsley, JE and Rampton, DS (2005). Psychological stress in IBD: new insights into pathogenic and therapeutic implications. *Gut*, vol. 54, no. 10, pp. 1481–91.

Qin, J, Li, R, Raes, J, Arumugam, M, Burgdorf, KS, Manichanh, C, Nielsen, T, Pons, N, Levenez, F, Yamada, T, Mende, DR, Li, J, Xu, J, Li, S, Li, D, Cao, J, Wang, B, Liang, H, Zheng, H, Xie, Y, Tap, J, Lepage, P, Bertalan, M, Batto, JM, Hansen, T, Le Paslier, D, Linneberg, A, Nielsen, HB, Pelletier, E, Renault, P, Sicheritz-Ponten, T, Turner, K, Zhu, H, Yu, C, Jian, M, Zhou, Y, Li, Y, Zhang, X, Qin, N, Yang, H, Wang, J, Brunak, S, Dore, J, Guarner, F, Kristiansen, K, Pedersen, O, Parkhill, J, Weissenbach, J, Bork, P and Ehrlich, SD (2010). A human gut microbial gene catalogue established by metagenomic sequencing. *Nature*, vol. 464, no. 7285, pp. 59–65.

Sartor, RB (2004). Therapeutic manipulation of the enteric microflora in inflammatory bowel diseases: antibiotics, probiotics, and prebiotics. *Gastroenterology*, vol. 126, no. 6, pp. 1620–33.

Selby, W, Pavli, P, Crotty, B, Florin, T, Radford-Smith, G, Gibson, P, Mitchell, B, Connell, W, Read, R, Merrett, M, Ee, H and Hetzel, D (2007). Two-year combination antibiotic therapy with clarithromycin, rifabutin, and clofazimine for Crohn's disease. *Gastroenterology*, vol. 132, no. 7, pp. 2313–9.

Sokol, H, Pigneur, B, Watterlot, L, Lakhdari, O, Bermudez-Humaran, LG, Gratadoux, JJ, Blugeon, S, Bridonneau, C, Furet, JP, Corthier, G, Grangette, C, Vasquez, N, Pochart, P, Trugnan, G, Thomas, G, Blottiere, HM, Dore, J, Marteau, P, Seksik, P and Langella, P (2008). Faecalibacterium prausnitzii is an anti-inflammatory commensal bacterium identified by gut microbiota analysis of Crohn disease patients. *Proc Natl Acad Sci USA*, vol. 105, no. 43, pp. 16731–6.

Stagg, AJ, Hart, AL, Knight, SC and Kamm, MA (2004). Microbial-gut interactions in health and disease. Interactions between dendritic cells and bacteria in the regulation of intestinal immunity. *Best Pract Res Clin Gastroenterol*, vol. 18, no. 2, pp. 255–70.

Turnbaugh, PJ, Ley, RE, Hamady, M, Fraser-Liggett, CM, Knight, R and Gordon, JI (2007). The human microbiome project. *Nature*, vol. 449, no. 7164, pp. 804–10.

Varela, E, Manichanh, C, Gallart, M, Torrejon, A, Borruel, N, Casellas, F, Guarner, F and Antolin, M (2013). Colonisation by Faecalibacterium prausnitzii and maintenance of clinical remission in patients with ulcerative colitis. *Aliment Pharmacol Ther*, vol. 38, no. 2, pp. 151–61.

Walker, AW, Sanderson, JD, Churcher, C, Parkes, GC, Hudspith, BN, Rayment, N, Brostoff, J, Parkhill, J, Dougan, G and Petrovska, L (2011). High-throughput clone library analysis of the mucosa-associated microbiota reveals dysbiosis and differences between inflamed and non-inflamed regions of the intestine in inflammatory bowel disease. *BMC Microbiol*, vol. 11, p. 7.

Walker, JR, Ediger, JP, Graff, LA, Greenfeld, JM, Clara, I, Lix, L, Rawsthorne, P, Miller, N, Rogala, L, McPhail, CM and Bernstein, CN (2008). The Manitoba IBD cohort study: a population-based study of the prevalence of lifetime and 12-month anxiety and mood disorders. *Am J Gastroenterol*, vol. 103, no. 8, pp. 1989–97.

Willing, B, Dicksved, J, Halfvarson, J, Andersson, A, Lucio, M, Zeng, Z, Jarnerot, G, Tysk, C, Jansson, JK and Engstrand, L (2010). A pyrosequencing study in twins shows that GI microbial profiles vary with inflammatory bowel disease phenotypes. *Gastroenterology*, vol. 139, no. 6, pp. 1844–54.

Wu, GD, Chen, J, Hoffmann, C, Bittinger, K, Chen, YY, Keilbaugh, SA, Bewtra, M, Knights, D, Walters, WA, Knight, R, Sinha, R, Gilroy, E, Gupta, K, Baldassano, R, Nessel, L, Li, H, Bushman, FD and Lewis, JD (2011). Linking long-term dietary patterns with gut microbial enterotypes. *Science*, vol. 334, no. 6052, pp. 105–8.

Chapter 5

Diagnostic procedures in IBD
Addressing common client concerns

Gregory T. C. Moore

Introduction

Inflammatory bowel disease (IBD) is a term used to encompass a heterogeneous group of conditions that involve ongoing inflammatory damage to the intestines, classified as ulcerative colitis (UC), Crohn's disease (CD) or indeterminate colitis (IC), where a clear distinction between UC and CD affecting the colon cannot be made. The forms of IBD have overlapping genetic, immunological and histopathological features, but using a combination of clinical, endoscopic, histopathological and radiological features, a definitive diagnosis can usually be made (Baumgart and Sandborn 2012). The therapy of IBD is largely determined by not just the type of IBD, but also the severity, extent, behaviour and complications of the disease, the presence or absence of extraintestinal manifestations, the age of the patient and prior responsiveness to therapy. In order to accurately determine this information, an array of diagnostic tests and procedures are often required. Some of these tests are familiar to most people, such as blood testing, however, others are less well understood and have particular fears, such as diagnostic imaging procedures involving radiation or a stigma attached to them, such as colonoscopy. The aim of this chapter is to describe the common diagnostic procedures from the perspective of the patient.

Common diagnostic procedures in IBD

Diagnostic procedures are used throughout the course of a patient's journey with IBD for different reasons. Initially, testing is used to establish a diagnosis, assess severity and the risk of complications and progression. Once therapy is established, some procedures are required to assess the response to treatment in order to optimise the patient's health and long-term prognosis. Frequent testing of blood is required to monitor for potential complications from either the disease or some of the therapies used to treat it. This section will outline common diagnostic tests and reasons for their use.

Physical examination

While strictly not a diagnostic test, physical examination is included here as it can be a cause for patient concerns and anxieties. Physical examination in patients with IBD includes the common process of abdominal palpation, auscultation and percussion but also involves a thorough assessment of the region around the anus, and of the anus itself, with a digital rectal examination. Crohn's disease, but not UC, can cause anal skin tags, ulcers in the lining of the anal skin, narrowing or stenosis of the anal canal, and fistulas (burrowing tracts) communicating from abscesses and the internal lining of the bowel. An initial thorough inspection of this area is made, and where signs of CD are present, periodic examination of this region is important to assess the progress of the disease and the response to therapy. In the presence of perianal Crohn's disease, a more detailed examination with potential therapeutic drainage of abscesses may be required; therefore, this is performed by colorectal surgeons in the operating theatre and is known as examination under anaesthesia (EUA).

Blood tests

Blood testing is where a fine needle is inserted into the vein and a small volume of blood (usually around 20ml) is withdrawn. Blood is analysed for red and white blood cell number and appearance, for salts and electrolytes, liver enzyme levels, nutritional parameters such as iron and specific vitamins such as vitamin D and B12. Markers of inflammation and immune status that may help to determine prior exposure to vaccinations or infectious diseases, or help in determining the IBD type are also analysed. Blood testing is repeated on a regular basis for patients who require common immunosuppressive agents such as azathioprine or 6-mercaptopurine or methotrexate to monitor for white blood cell numbers and liver function. Similarly, tests of inflammation and nutritional markers are repeated regularly to assess disease severity and response to therapy and to prevent complications.

Faecal tests

Samples of faeces are assessed at times of disease diagnosis or a flare in activity to exclude the presence of an infectious cause. Faeces are now also used to assess the degree of inflammation present using faecal biomarkers, such as calprotectin or lactoferrin, typically at times of quiescent disease (Sipponen 2013).

Endoscopy

Endoscopy is the collective term for using flexible tubes with fibre optics to visualise inside the digestive tract and is a mainstay of investigations in IBD (Simpson and Papadakis 2008). An endoscopic examination by the mouth is known as an oesophago-gastro-duodenoscopy as it typically reaches as far distally as the duodenum. Colloquially, these are often referred to as OGD, gastroscopy, upper GI endoscopy or just endoscopy. Endoscopic examination through the anus into the lower gastrointestinal tract is referred to as ileo-colonoscopy (where the procedure reaches as far proximally as the terminal ileum) or colonoscopy. Procedures navigating just into the distal colon are referred to as flexible sigmoidoscopy. On occasion, some patients with structuring disease of the bile ducts known as primary sclerosing cholangitis (PSC) may require a specialised endoscopic procedure via the mouth where a cannula is inserted from the duodenum into the bile ducts to obtain x-ray imaging and sometimes to dilate strictures. This procedure is known as endoscopic retrograde cholangiopancreatography (ERCP). A long endoscope can be passed further into the small bowel than standard procedures. This is known as enteroscopy and may be either standard or push enteroscopy where just a long tube is used, or passage through the small intestine is achieved using one or two inflatable balloons attached to the endoscope, which is called balloon enteroscopy. A newer form of endoscopy where a tube is not inserted into the body is capsule endoscopy. This is where a swallowed capsule containing a camera, light and image recording equipment is swallowed and passes through the patient's intestines, either transmitting the images or recording them for later retrieval. This is particularly useful for obtaining images of the small intestines, beyond the reach of standard endoscopes.

In a typical diagnostic workup for someone suspected of having IBD, oesophago-gastro-duodenoscopy and ileo-colonosocpy with biopsy samples of the intestinal mucosa (lining) are undertaken. Subsequent endoscopic testing may be undertaken to assess response to therapy, with the presence of mucosal healing now a therapeutic goal in IBD management. If a patient develops increasing symptoms, a repeat procedure may be undertaken to assess for inflammation or the presence of a narrowing or stricture. In IBD with long standing colonic disease, frequent, sometimes yearly, colonoscopy is required to look for dysplasia, a precursor to colorectal cancer.

Diagnostic imaging

Diagnostic imaging is a collective term that encompasses all modalities that capture an image that can define the patient's anatomy and determine whether it is of a normal healthy appearance; it can also describe abnormal features and what type of process may be causing the altered appearance. Diagnostic imaging modalities include plain x-ray or radiographs, computerised tomography (CT) scanning using x-rays to obtain cross sectional and reconstructed 3-dimensional imaging, ultrasound (typically from a probe applied to the skin but sometimes via the rectum, vagina or attached to an endoscope), magnetic resonance imaging (MRI) and nuclear medicine, where radioactive tracers that highlight certain processes or anatomy are injected or ingested and delayed images are obtained. Similar to the other diagnostic procedures described, diagnostic imaging modalities are used to establish the diagnosis of IBD, determine the disease extent and behaviour and the presence of complications. There is also a trend to use diagnostic imaging to assess long-term response to therapy.

Common concerns about diagnostic procedures in IBD

Many of the concerns patients have about diagnostic procedures in IBD are directly related to the location of the disease within their body. By necessity, examinations need to target the digestive tract, which can result in the patient feeling embarrassment at being required to expose the ano-genital region. These negative feelings can also include fear of abnormal findings. Concerns about inadequate hygiene due to the effects of the disease process are often expressed. There are no specific studies looking at the experiences of IBD patients with physical examination but research into female pelvic examinations has shown that careful explanation by the clinician of exactly how the examination is to be conducted and the likely sensations that the patient will experience, along with trust and confidence in the clinician, can reduce the negative experiences patients may have (Oscarsson and Benzein 2002).

Similarly, patients can experience embarrassment and express disgust at being required to collect a stool sample for analysis, however, in a study of patient preferences for types of examinations, having to obtain a sample of their own stool was preferred to undergoing colonoscopy or being exposed to radiation (Nelson *et al.* 2001).

Blood testing is associated with a small degree of pain but some patients have significant anxiety regarding these tests. Explanation of the reason for requiring blood testing and the safety implications of missing tests can help to reduce feelings of repeated unnecessary testing that some patients express, especially when they feel well.

Colonoscopy is frequently required in the management of IBD. Non-IBD patients report colonoscopy has a stigma attached, is embarrassing, and they feel anxiety from a range of factors, including a perceived lack of control and unequal relationship with their doctor. The bowel preparation to clean the large bowel of faeces prior to the endoscopic examination can induce anxiety and discomfort (Mikocka-Walus *et al.* 2012). IBD patients have higher levels of embarrassment and report greater difficulty with bowel preparation and more discomfort from the procedure compared with non-IBD patients (Denters *et al.* 2013). In addition, IBD patients undergoing colonoscopy have higher levels of visceral sensitivity, and increased pain with bowel preparation. These further increase in patients with more active disease, however, it has been noted to decrease with the greater number of colonoscopies the patient has previously undergone (Bessissow *et al.* 2013). Higher levels of gastrointestinal specific anxiety and co-morbid anxiety were shown to be associated with increased level of pain and nausea during the bowel preparation, potentially making measures that can reduce anxiety effective, improving the tolerance of bowel preparation and colonoscopy.

The main concerns expressed by patients regarding diagnostic imaging procedures are whether the test will be uncomfortable and whether there is a long-term risk to exposure to radiation that could have longer-term health implications. It is known that exposure to ionising radiation can slightly increase the lifetime risk of developing subsequent cancer, and there is a recognition that where possible, other forms of imaging that do not use ionising radiation should be used where practical and safe. Several studies have demonstrated that around 1 in 10 IBD patients may be cumulatively exposed to potentially harmful levels of radiation (Chatu *et al.* 2012, 2013; Hou *et al.* 2014; Swanson *et al.* 2013). Such exposures have been associated with a small but significant increase in the incidence of cancers ranging from 0.6–1.8 per cent (Berrington de Gonzalez and Darby 2004). Alternative imaging techniques, such as MRI, are available but often not in a time critical acute setting and their cost is significantly higher, resulting in limited access for many patients depending on where they live. Some authors have suggested that MR enterography may be cost effective when compared with CT enterography (Cipriano *et al.* 2012).

Another concern patients have with MRI is claustrophobia. This relates to the design of the machine that requires the patient to lie in an enclosed tunnel. This was more of an issue with older style machines and is less common with abdominal or pelvic imaging compared with imaging of the head. Rates of anxiety are also further reduced by lying prone but in some cases sedation is required (Dewey *et al.* 2007; Eshed *et al.* 2007; Munn and Jordan 2013).

Future directions in diagnostics in IBD

While the mainstays of clinical assessment of patients with IBD shall remain clinical history and examination. However, in the future, the landscape of available technologies for diagnostics and how we use them will certainly change. In time, it is to be expected that there will be an increased utilisation of MRI with a reduction in CT scanning. As the paradigm of management of IBD has shifted so that clinicians now aim not just for resolution of clinical symptoms but achieving healing of the gut mucosa, so too will the need increase for accurate and non-invasive biomarkers that can assess the degree of inflammation in a patient at a given time without the need for repeated endoscopy. These tests will likely remain based on blood and faecal markers.

The importance of personalised medicine with tailoring of therapy to individual patients will require tests that can accurately predict a patient's disease phenotype as well as the likely response to specific therapeutic agents. This is an area still in its infancy but the use of genetic markers to not only define likely disease behaviour but also the likely efficacy of medications in an individual will increase, along with the potential for associated anxiety about the use and interpretation of these tests. Some research has shown that despite our increased awareness of susceptibility genes, beyond that of simply having an IBD affected family member, communication of such information may not actually influence the behaviour in the at risk individual in terms of modifying their risk behaviour, such as continuing to smoke (Hollands *et al.* 2012).

Conclusions

The heterogeneous nature of IBD and the varied diseases that patients may experience requires extensive assessment and investigation to accurately determine the individual patient's appropriate therapy and ongoing monitoring. This may include blood testing, physical examination, faecal testing, endoscopy or diagnostic imaging, but the unifying factor in reducing patient concerns is having a trusting therapeutic relationship with the patient and explaining exactly why the testing is recommended, and the potential risks and benefits from undertaking it.

Current limitations and future considerations

- There is a paucity of IBD specific research assessing patient concerns regarding investigations in IBD
- Changes in the goals of treatment will be accompanied by changes in the utilisation of diagnostic procedures in IBD

Practical recommendations

- Take the time to explain the rationale for undertaking a series of diagnostic tests to help the patient understand their need and how they will change their management and potential future disease course
- Recognize the burden that diagnostic testing places on the patient
- Minimise testing wherever possible
- Maintain a trusting and open relationship with the patient
- Minimise exposure to ionising radiation, particularly if an alternative diagnostic imaging test is available and appropriate

Learning points

- Understand the variety of diagnostic procedures that an IBD patient may undergo
- Recognise the common concerns and experiences that patients have
- Recognise the burden that diagnostic procedures place upon patients
- Be conscious of keeping diagnostic procedures to a necessary minimum
- Develop an empathetic approach to guide a patient through this processes

References

Baumgart, DC and Sandborn, WJ (2012). Crohn's disease. *Lancet*, vol. 380, no. 9853, pp. 1590–605.

Berrington de Gonzalez, A and Darby, S (2004). Risk of cancer from diagnostic x-rays: estimates for the UK and 14 other countries. *Lancet*, vol. 363, no. 9406, pp. 345–51.

Bessissow, T, Van Keerberghen, CA, Van Oudenhove, L, Ferrante, M, Vermeire, S, Rutgeerts, P and Van Assche, G (2013). Anxiety is associated with impaired tolerance of colonoscopy preparation in inflammatory bowel disease and controls. *J Crohns Colitis*, vol. 7, no. 11, pp. e580–7.

Chatu, S, Poullis, A, Holmes, R, Greenhalgh, R and Pollok, RC (2013). Temporal trends in imaging and associated radiation exposure in inflammatory bowel disease. *Int J Clin Pract*, vol. 67, no. 10, pp. 1057–65.

Chatu, S, Subramanian, V and Pollok, RC (2012). Meta-analysis: diagnostic medical radiation exposure in inflammatory bowel disease. *Aliment Pharmacol Ther*, vol. 35, no. 5, pp. 529–39.

Cipriano, LE, Levesque, BG, Zaric, GS, Loftus, EV, Jr. and Sandborn, WJ (2012). Cost-effectiveness of imaging strategies to reduce radiation-induced cancer risk in Crohn's disease. *Inflamm Bowel Dis*, vol. 18, no. 7, pp. 1240–8.

Denters, MJ, Schreuder, M, Depla, AC, Mallant-Hent, RC, van Kouwen, MC, Deutekom, M, Bossuyt, PM, Fockens, P and Dekker, E (2013). Patients' perception of colonoscopy: patients with inflammatory bowel disease and irritable bowel syndrome experience the largest burden. *Eur J Gastroenterol Hepatol*, vol. 25, no. 8, pp. 964–72.

Dewey, M, Schink, T and Dewey, CF (2007). Claustrophobia during magnetic resonance imaging: cohort study in over 55,000 patients. *J Magn Reson Imaging*, vol. 26, no. 5, pp. 1322–7.

Eshed, I, Althoff, CE, Hamm, B and Hermann, KG (2007). Claustrophobia and premature termination of magnetic resonance imaging examinations. *J Magn Reson Imaging*, vol. 26, no. 2, pp. 401–4.

Hollands, GJ, Whitwell, SC, Parker, RA, Prescott, NJ, Forbes, A, Sanderson, J, Mathew, CG, Lewis, CM, Watts, S, Sutton, S, Armstrong, D, Kinmonth, AL, Prevost, AT and Marteau, TM (2012). Effect of communicating DNA based risk assessments for Crohn's disease on smoking cessation: randomised controlled trial. *BMJ*, vol. 345, p. e4708.

Hou, JK, Malaty, HM and Thirumurthi, S (2014). Radiation exposure from diagnostic imaging studies among patients with inflammatory bowel disease in a safety-net healthcare system. *Dig Dis Sci*, vol. 59, no. 3, pp. 546–53.

Mikocka-Walus, AA, Moulds, LG, Rollbusch, N and Andrews, JM (2012). "It's a tube up your bottom; it makes people nervous": the experience of anxiety in initial colonoscopy patients. *Gastroenterol Nurs*, vol. 35, no. 6, pp. 392–401.

Munn, Z and Jordan, Z (2013). Interventions to reduce anxiety, distress and the need for sedation in adult patients undergoing magnetic resonance imaging: a systematic review. *Int J Evid Based Healthc*, vol. 11, no. 4, pp. 265–74.

Nelson, RL, Schwartz, A and Pavel, D (2001). Assessment of the usefulness of a diagnostic test: a survey of patient preference for diagnostic techniques in the evaluation of intestinal inflammation. *BMC Med Res Methodol*, vol. 1, p. 5.

Oscarsson, M and Benzein, E (2002). Women's experiences of pelvic examination: an interview study. *J Psychosom Obstet Gynaecol*, vol. 23, no. 1, pp. 17–25.

Simpson, P and Papadakis, KA (2008). Endoscopic evaluation of patients with inflammatory bowel disease. *Inflamm Bowel Dis*, vol. 14, no. 9, pp. 1287–97.

Sipponen, T (2013). Diagnostics and prognostics of inflammatory bowel disease with fecal neutrophil-derived biomarkers calprotectin and lactoferrin. *Dig Dis*, vol. 31, no. 3-4, pp. 336–44.

Swanson, G, Behara, R, Braun, R and Keshavarzian, A (2013). Diagnostic medical radiation in inflammatory bowel disease: how to limit risk and maximize benefit. *Inflamm Bowel Dis*, vol. 19, no. 11, pp. 2501–8.

Chapter 6

Psychosocial aspects of IBD in paediatric and adolescent patients

The impact of transition

James Lindsay

Introduction

The incidence of inflammatory bowel disease (IBD) presenting in children is increasing, more than 25 per cent cases are now diagnosed under the age of 18 (Sawczenko *et al.* 2001). IBD presenting at this age is more extensive and severe than in adults (Van Limbergen *et al.* 2008; Vernier-Massouille *et al.* 2008). It interferes with growth, education and employment as well as psychosocial and sexual development. Young people with IBD have lower self-reported health related quality of life, although data on the impact of IBD on self-esteem, depression and anxiety, impaired social competence and behavioural problems in this age group are conflicting. This chapter reviews differences in the course of disease between adolescents and adults with IBD focusing on the impact of IBD on physical as well as psycho-social development. Finally, the evidence that supports the role of transition for patients with IBD will be discussed and different models of care for patients in this age group will be reviewed.

Childhood compared with adult onset IBD

There are important differences in the incidence, presentation, clinical phenotype and management of IBD between children and adults. Overall more than 25 per cent of cases of IBD are now diagnosed under the age of 18 (Sawczenko *et al.* 2001). The paediatric incidence of ulcerative colitis (UC) in the UK is 1.3/100,000, and in contrast to adults, Crohn's disease is more common with 2.5/100,000 new diagnoses per year (Armitage *et al.* 2001). However, more recent studies report a much higher incidence in paediatric IBD (Muller *et al.* 2013). Although adult incidence rates appear to be stable, incidence rates in children are increasing. For example, there has been a 71 per cent increase in the incidence of Crohn's disease in the 10–19 year old age group in northern France from 6.5/100,000 (1988–1990) to 11.1/100,000 (2006–2007) (Chouraki *et al.* 2011).

Studies indicate that children and adolescents with IBD are more likely to have Crohn's disease than ulcerative colitis (Goodhand, J *et al.* 2010; Van Limbergen et al. 2008). Both diseases tend to be more extensive and severe when diagnosed at a young age and are more likely to extend in the first 3 years after diagnosis than in adults (Van Limbergen et al. 2008; Vernier-Massouille et al. 2008). Upper gastrointestinal (GI) involvement is reported more commonly in paediatric IBD (Vernier-Massouille et al. 2008), although this may reflect the routine performance of upper GI endoscopy in paediatric patients diagnosed with IBD (a practice that is not common in adults).

One of the most important differences between adults and children with IBD is the potential for growth failure and/or pubertal delay. At presentation, 10–40 per cent of children have evidence of growth failure that may result from anorexia and malabsorption, as well as a direct effect of intestinal inflammation (Heuschkel, R et al. 2008; Sanderson and Croft 2005). Subsequent use of corticosteroids to induce remission has been shown to have a significant negative impact on growth velocity (Heuschkel, RB et al. 2000).

These factors drive management strategies that are specific to patients in this age group. In Europe, an exclusive liquid diet is recommended as induction therapy for Crohn's disease to avoid the negative impact of steroids on growth (Van Assche et al. 2010). The extensive disease at presentation and the potential long duration of IBD in adolescents may mandate early use of combination therapy (e.g. thiopurine and anti-tumour necrosis factor) (Van Assche et al. 2010). The long-term side effects of this strategy in paediatric cohorts are not known, although hepato-splenic T cell lymphoma is more likely to occur in young men with CD who are receiving combination therapy (Thai and Prindiville 2010). In addition, medical and surgical strategies may impact on both fertility and fecundity, which has particular relevance to adolescent patients later in life (van der Woude et al. 2010). Thus, both the benefits and the risks of individual therapeutic strategies are different in the adolescent compared to the adult patient.

Psychosocial aspects of IBD in adolescents

IBD diagnosed during childhood leads to behavioural as well as physical adaptations that can interfere with psychosocial and sexual development, education and employment. The psychosocial adjustment of adolescents with IBD has been investigated in multiple studies and summarised in a recent review article (Mackner et al. 2013). Among studies that included a comparison group, all but one reported that children with IBD had significantly more behavioural/emotional symptoms overall and more internalising symptoms than healthy children. In contrast, there were few differences between children with IBD and children with other chronic illnesses.

Reported rates of psychiatric disorders reported in adolescents with IBD vary from 10 per cent to 73 per cent (Mackner et al. 2013). Studies that include larger sample sizes (>20) and employ robust methodologies report rates of current depression vary from 10 per cent to 25 per cent [reviewed in Mackner et al.

(2013)]. Likewise, adolescents with IBD report poorer quality of life (QOL) scores and a higher prevalence of psychological distress than unaffected peers (Szigethy *et al.* 2009). A recent meta-analysis based upon 19 studies ($n = 1,167$ patients with IBD, mean age 14.33) indicated that young patients with IBD had higher rates of depressive disorders and internalizing disorders than those with other chronic conditions (Greenley *et al.* 2010). In addition, young patients with IBD had higher parent-reported internalising symptoms, lower parent- and youth-reported QoL, and lower youth-reported social functioning compared to healthy controls. Clearly, the processes underlying psychological and psychosocial development in children and adolescents with IBD is complex and that further research, especially longitudinal studies, is needed (Persoons *et al.* 2005).

Adolescence and transition to adulthood[1]

The understanding of a chronic disease and level of engagement with health care services will vary according to a patient's developmental stage. In early adolescence (10–12 years), patients should be able to describe their disease and name medications (Blum *et al.* 1993; Christie and Viner 2005). They may or may not feel confident to discuss the role of their family, teachers, peer groups and themselves in their care. Likewise, their appreciation of the impact of disease on school attendance and academic aspirations may vary. At the end of adolescence, patients should be capable of making informed decisions about therapeutic strategy; to maintain an awareness of their sexual fecundity and the need for contraception; and to plan ahead and use healthcare services in a flexible way. In addition, they are expected to take on the administrative roles previously carried out by their parents, which will include the ability to book and attend appointments and investigations.

Transition and transfer of medical care

Introduction

Transition, in the context of healthcare, can be defined as the purposeful, planned movement of adolescents with chronic physical and medical conditions to adult-orientated healthcare systems (Blum *et al.* 1993). Ideally, transition is an uninterrupted, coordinated process that is matched to the developmental abilities of the individual. Transfer is the point of handover to the adult healthcare team, and should be considered part of, not necessarily the end of, transition.

Consequence of failed transition

Transition aims to educate both the patient and their parents so that they are ready for transfer to adult services and to ensure that the ongoing healthcare provider is sufficiently informed about the past and current problems to provide continuity of care (Blum *et al.* 1993). An inadequate transition process may result in delayed or inappropriate care, improper timing of transfer, and undue emotional stress for patients and their families. Non-specific measures such as lost to follow-up, admission and medication non-adherence rates can be used as surrogate markers to assess the efficacy of transition services. Much of the evidence for the benefit of a structured transition process comes from other chronic diseases that affect this age group, such as congenital heart disease, diabetes and arthritis.

Thus, up to 75 per cent of patients with congenital heart disease are lost to follow up on transfer to adult cardiology clinics (Reid *et al.* 2004). In addition, there is an increase in admission rates at the point of transfer in both congenital heart disease and diabetes (Gurvitz *et al.* 2007; Nakhla *et al.* 2009). Individuals who were transferred after a coordinated transition were 20 per cent less likely to be hospitalised than those who were transferred to a new physician without transition support (Nakhla *et al.* 2009). A study of the outpatient non-attendance rates from our institution revealed that adolescents with IBD were significantly more likely to miss appointments than a matched cohort of adults (Goodhand, J *et al.* 2010).

There is evidence from several chronic diseases affecting adolescents that adherence to medication during transition is variable, which may lead to adverse health outcome (Danne *et al.* 2001; Dobbels *et al.* 2005). The factors underpinning adherence to IBD medications are complex and poorly understood. We assessed adherence to thiopurines in 140 adolescents and adults with IBD (Goodhand, JR *et al.* 2013). Overall 12 per cent of patients were non-adherent. Multivariate analysis confirmed that being a young adult of lower socioeconomic status and reporting higher HADS-D scores were associated with non-adherence. Non-adherence resulted in more frequent escalation in therapy, hospital admission and surgery in the subsequent 6 months of follow-up (Goodhand, JR *et al.* 2013).

Supportive evidence for structured transition

Structured transition programs may reduce unnecessary admissions, improve adherence and enhance physical and psychosocial wellbeing. However, no large-scale prospective study has compared outcomes of transfer, with or without a structured transition program in IBD. A pilot educational program for adolescent liver transplant recipients reported a significant reduction in the previously documented variation of serum immunosuppressant levels in association with a reduction in elevated liver enzymes (Annunziato *et al.* 2008). Likewise, structured transition in diabetes has been reported to improve glycaemic control and the number of admissions to hospital (Holmes-Walker *et al.* 2007). Finally, an age-adjusted structured transition program improved QoL in both patients with juvenile arthritis and their parents (McDonagh *et al.* 2007).

Approaches to transition in IBD

In order to develop a successful model for transition in IBD, one must take account of differences in maturity, disease phenotype between childhood onset and adult onset IBD, as well as variability in the structure and geographical organization of health care provision (Sebastian *et al.* 2012). Unfortunately, the lack of comparative studies means that no specific model can yet be recommended (Baldassano *et al.* 2002).

Types of transition reported in IBD

The simplest method of transfer is the use of a detailed handover letter or discharge summary. Although inexpensive, anecdotal reports suggest that this form of abrupt transfer leads to a lack of confidence on ongoing care by patients and their parents as well as frustration in the adult gastroenterologist. Limited uncontrolled data suggest that a single 1-hour joint clinic where paediatricians introduce the adolescent to the adult team and handover care in detail is sufficient with 85 per cent of patients and 74 per cent of parents being ready to transfer (Dabadie *et al.* 2008). Similar positive feedback has been reported by patients attending several joint-run clinics (Van Pieterson *et al.* 2007). The final option is to have dedicated adolescent IBD clinics where paediatricians and adult gastroenterologists provide joint care for adolescent with IBD in conjunction with a full multidisciplinary team (Goodhand, J *et al.* 2011). However, there are relatively few paediatric gastroenterologists and most are clustered together in city teaching hospitals. One solution might be to create a managed clinical network ensuring that clinicians can have the appropriate training and facilities to care for this age group as close to home as possible. In order to improve lines of communication between different treating physicians and as part of the 'The Good 2 Go Transition Program' established at the Hospital for Sick Children in Toronto, a handheld synopsis of their condition, called the MyHealth passport, has been developed for adolescents (Benchimol *et al.* 2011). This simple card details the pertinent IBD history and fits into a wallet, it remains to be seen whether adolescents will use these or other (e.g. electronic) reminders and whether they improve knowledge, drug adherence, or clinic attendance.

Timing of transfer

Not all patients psychologically adapt to IBD in the same way, some will be mature enough to transfer at 16, but others may need to stay in transition care much longer. Wherever possible the timing of transfer to adult services should be adjusted to the maturity of the individual. Unfortunately, not all healthcare providers allow this flexibility and insist upon transfer at a predefined chronological age. As in juvenile rheumatological disorders, independence/self-efficacy scales have been developed, but not yet validated in paediatric IBD ('IBD-yourself')

(Zijlstra *et al.* 2009). In the future, these psychometric tools may allow an objective measurement of maturity to determine when transfer is most appropriate.

Current limitations and future considerations

- Studies assessing the impact of IBD on mood and behaviour in adolescents are often underpowered and the data is conflicting. Studies that compare adolescents with IBD to adults are lacking
- The impact of healthcare transfer on patients with IBD has not been formally studied – data is extrapolated from other chronic diseases
- No controlled trial has assessed the relative benefit of different modes of transition in patients with IBD

Practical recommendations

- All adolescents with IBD should be managed in experienced clinics as their disease is often more severe than in adults. Optimum care is provided by a multidisciplinary team
- The health care team should consider the impact of disease on psychosocial as well as physical development
- A clear process for transition to adult healthcare systems should be defined and implemented

Learning points

- IBD frequently presents in adolescents and is often more extensive in this age group than in adults
- Disease impacts on physical and well as psychosocial development
- Transfer to adult care can be associated with reduced engagement in health care
- Appropriate transition is designed to improve physical and psychosocial outcome for patients

Endnote

1 Adulthood is defined by the acquisition of secondary sexually characteristics and fecundity; it usually occurs between 11 and 15 years of age. Psychologically, the onset of adulthood is more difficult to define and may differ according to gender with girls maturing at a younger age than boys. Adolescence describes the period of physical, emotional and cognitive development that occurs between the onset of puberty and adulthood. Early adolescence (10–12 years) is characterised by pubertal development, middle adolescence (13–15 years) by psychosocial independence and late adolescence (16–18 years) by the development of personal identity, life aspirations and goals, as well as ethical and moral value (Goodhand, JR *et al.* 2013). However, there are no absolute age cut-offs and different adolescent developmental milestones may be reached at different times.

References

Annunziato, RA, Emre, S, Shneider, BL, Dugan, CA, Aytaman, Y, McKay, MM and Shemesh, E (2008). Transitioning health care responsibility from caregivers to patient: a pilot study aiming to facilitate medication adherence during this process. *Pediatr Transplant*, vol. 12, no. 3, pp. 309–15.

Armitage, E, Drummond, HE, Wilson, DC and Ghosh, S (2001). Increasing incidence of both juvenile-onset Crohn's disease and ulcerative colitis in Scotland. *Eur J Gastroenterol Hepatol*, vol. 13, no. 12, pp. 1439–47.

Baldassano, R, Ferry, G, Griffiths, A, Mack, D, Markowitz, J and Winter, H (2002). Transition of the patient with inflammatory bowel disease from pediatric to adult care: recommendations of the North American Society for Pediatric Gastroenterology, Hepatology and Nutrition. *J Pediatr Gastroenterol Nutr*, vol. 34, no. 3, pp. 245–8.

Benchimol, EI, Walters, TD, Kaufman, M, Frost, K, Fiedler, K, Chinea, Z and Zachos, M (2011). Assessment of knowledge in adolescents with inflammatory bowel disease using a novel transition tool. *Inflamm Bowel Dis*, vol. 17, no. 5, pp. 1131–7.

Blum, RW, Garell, D, Hodgman, CH, Jorissen, TW, Okinow, NA, Orr, DP and Slap, GB (1993). Transition from child-centered to adult health-care systems for adolescents with chronic conditions. A position paper of the Society for Adolescent Medicine. *J Adolesc Health*, vol. 14, no. 7, pp. 570–6.

Chouraki, V, Savoye, G, Dauchet, L, Vernier-Massouille, G, Dupas, JL, Merle, V, Laberenne, JE, Salomez, JL, Lerebours, E, Turck, D, Cortot, A, Gower-Rousseau, C and Colombel, JF (2011). The changing pattern of Crohn's disease incidence in northern France: a continuing increase in the 10- to 19-year-old age bracket (1988–2007). *Aliment Pharmacol Ther*, vol. 33, no. 10, pp. 1133–42.

Christie, D and Viner, R (2005). Adolescent development. *BMJ*, vol. 330, no. 7486, pp. 301–4.

Dabadie, A, Troadec, F, Heresbach, D, Siproudhis, L, Pagenault, M and Bretagne, JF (2008). Transition of patients with inflammatory bowel disease from pediatric to adult care. *Gastroenterol Clin Biol*, vol. 32, no. 5 (Pt 1), pp. 451–9.

Danne, T, Mortensen, HB, Hougaard, P, Lynggaard, H, Aanstoot, HJ, Chiarelli, F, Daneman, D, Dorchy, H, Garandeau, P, Greene, SA, Hoey, H, Holl, RW, Kaprio, EA, Kocova, M, Martul, P, Matsuura, N, Robertson, KJ, Schoenle, EJ, Sovik, O, Swift, PG, Tsou, RM, Vanelli, M and Aman, J (2001). Persistent differences among centers over 3 years in glycemic control and hypoglycemia in a study of 3,805 children and adolescents with type 1 diabetes from the Hvidore Study Group. *Diabetes Care*, vol. 24, no. 8, pp. 1342–7.

Dobbels, F, Van Damme-Lombaert, R, Vanhaecke, J and De Geest, S (2005). Growing pains: non-adherence with the immunosuppressive regimen in adolescent transplant recipients. *Pediatr Transplant*, vol. 9, no. 3, pp. 381–90.

Goodhand, J, Dawson, R, Hefferon, M, Tshuma, N, Swanson, G, Wahed, M, Croft, NM and Lindsay, JO (2010). Inflammatory bowel disease in young people: the case for transitional clinics. *Inflamm Bowel Dis*, vol. 16, no. 6, pp. 947–52.

Goodhand, J, Hedin, CR, Croft, NM and Lindsay, JO (2011). Adolescents with IBD: the importance of structured transition care. *J Crohns Colitis*, vol. 5, no. 6, pp. 509–19.

Goodhand, JR, Kamperidis, N, Sirwan, B, Macken, L, Tshuma, N, Koodun, Y, Chowdhury, FA, Croft, NM, Direkze, N, Langmead, L, Irving, PM, Rampton, DS and Lindsay, JO (2013). Factors associated with thiopurine non-adherence in patients with inflammatory bowel disease. *Aliment Pharmacol Ther*, vol. 38, no. 9, pp. 1097–108.

Greenley, RN, Hommel, KA, Nebel, J, Raboin, T, Li, SH, Simpson, P and Mackner, L (2010). A meta-analytic review of the psychosocial adjustment of youth with inflammatory bowel disease. *J Pediatr Psychol*, vol. 35, no. 8, pp. 857–69.

Gurvitz, MZ, Inkelas, M, Lee, M, Stout, K, Escarce, J and Chang, RK (2007). Changes in hospitalization patterns among patients with congenital heart disease during the transition from adolescence to adulthood. *J Am Coll Cardiol*, vol. 49, no. 8, pp. 875–82.

Heuschkel, R, Salvestrini, C, Beattie, RM, Hildebrand, H, Walters, T and Griffiths, A (2008). Guidelines for the management of growth failure in childhood inflammatory bowel disease. *Inflamm Bowel Dis*, vol. 14, no. 6, pp. 839–49.

Heuschkel, RB, Menache, CC, Megerian, JT and Baird, AE (2000). Enteral nutrition and corticosteroids in the treatment of acute Crohn's disease in children. *J Pediatr Gastroenterol Nutr*, vol. 31, no. 1, pp. 8–15.

Holmes-Walker, DJ, Llewellyn, AC and Farrell, K (2007). A transition care programme which improves diabetes control and reduces hospital admission rates in young adults with Type 1 diabetes aged 15–25 years. *Diabet Med*, vol. 24, no. 7, pp. 764–9.

Mackner, LM, Greenley, RN, Szigethy, E, Herzer, M, Deer, K and Hommel, KA (2013). Psychosocial issues in pediatric inflammatory bowel disease: report of the North American Society for Pediatric Gastroenterology, Hepatology, and Nutrition. *J Pediatr Gastroenterol Nutr*, vol. 56, no. 4, pp. 449–58.

McDonagh, JE, Southwood, TR, Shaw, KL and British Society of Paediatric and Adolescent Rheumatology (2007). The impact of a coordinated transitional care programme on adolescents with juvenile idiopathic arthritis. *Rheumatology (Oxford)*, vol. 46, no. 1, pp. 161–8.

Muller, KE, Lakatos, PL, Arato, A, Kovacs, JB, Varkonyi, A, Szucs, D, Szakos, E, Solyom, E, Kovacs, M, Polgar, M, Nemes, E, Guthy, I, Tokodi, I, Toth, G, Horvath, A, Tarnok, A, Csoszanszki, N, Balogh, M, Vass, N, Bodi, P, Dezsofi, A, Gardos, L, Micskey, E, Papp, M, Cseh, A, Szabo, D, Voros, P, Veres, G and Hungarian IBD Registry Group (HUPIR) (2013). Incidence, Paris classification, and follow-up in a nationwide incident cohort of pediatric patients with inflammatory bowel disease. *J Pediatr Gastroenterol Nutr*, vol. 57, no. 5, pp. 576–82.

Nakhla, M, Daneman, D, To, T, Paradis, G and Guttmann, A (2009). Transition to adult care for youths with diabetes mellitus: findings from a Universal Health Care System. *Pediatrics*, vol. 124, no. 6, pp. e1134–41.

Persoons, P, Vermeire, S, Demyttenaere, K, Fischler, B, Vandenberghe, J, Van Oudenhove, L, Pierik, M, Hlavaty, T, Van Assche, G, Noman, M and Rutgeerts, P (2005). The impact of major depressive disorder on the short- and long-term outcome of Crohn's disease treatment with infliximab. *Aliment Pharmacol Ther*, vol. 22, no. 2, pp. 101–10.

Reid, GJ, Irvine, MJ, McCrindle, BW, Sananes, R, Ritvo, PG, Siu, SC and Webb, GD (2004). Prevalence and correlates of successful transfer from pediatric to adult health care among a cohort of young adults with complex congenital heart defects. *Pediatrics*, vol. 113, no. 3 (Pt 1), pp. e197–205.

Sanderson, IR and Croft, NM (2005). The anti-inflammatory effects of enteral nutrition. *JPEN J Parenter Enteral Nutr*, vol. 29, no. 4 (Suppl), pp. S134–8; discussion S8–40, S84–8.

Sawczenko, A, Sandhu, BK, Logan, RF, Jenkins, H, Taylor, CJ, Mian, S and Lynn, R (2001). Prospective survey of childhood inflammatory bowel disease in the British Isles. *Lancet*, vol. 357, no. 9262, pp. 1093–4.

Sebastian S, Jenkins H, McCartney S, Ahmad T, Arnott I, Croft N, Russell R and Lindsay JO. (2012). The requirements and barriers to successful transition of adolescents with inflammatory bowel disease: differing perceptions from a survey of adult and paediatric gastroenterologists. *J Crohns Colitis*, vol. 6, no. 8, pp. 830–44.

Szigethy, E, Craig, AE, Iobst, EA, Grand, RJ, Keljo, D, DeMaso, D and Noll, R (2009). Profile of depression in adolescents with inflammatory bowel disease: implications for treatment. *Inflamm Bowel Dis*, vol. 15, no. 1, pp. 69–74.

Thai, A and Prindiville, T (2010). Hepatosplenic T-cell lymphoma and inflammatory bowel disease. *J Crohns Colitis*, vol. 4, no. 5, pp. 511–22.

Van Assche, G, Dignass, A, Reinisch, W, van der Woude, CJ, Sturm, A, De Vos, M, Guslandi, M, Oldenburg, B, Dotan, I, Marteau, P, Ardizzone, A, Baumgart, DC, D'Haens, G, Gionchetti, P, Portela, F, Vucelic, B, Soderholm, J, Escher, J, Koletzko, S, Kolho, KL, Lukas, M, Mottet, C, Tilg, H, Vermeire, S, Carbonnel, F, Cole, A, Novacek, G, Reinshagen, M, Tsianos, E, Herrlinger, K, Oldenburg, B, Bouhnik, Y, Kiesslich, R, Stange, E, Travis, S, Lindsay, J and European Crohn's and Colitis Organisation (ECCO) (2010). The second European evidence-based consensus on the diagnosis and management of Crohn's disease: special situations. *J Crohns Colitis*, vol. 4, no. 1, pp. 63–101.

van der Woude, CJ, Kolacek, S, Dotan, I, Oresland, T, Vermeire, S, Munkholm, P, Mahadevan, U, Mackillop, L, Dignass, A and European Crohn's and Colitis Organisation (ECCO) (2010). European evidenced-based consensus on reproduction in inflammatory bowel disease. *J Crohns Colitis*, vol. 4, no. 5, pp. 493–510.

Van Limbergen, J, Russell, RK, Drummond, HE, Aldhous, MC, Round, NK, Nimmo, ER, Smith, L, Gillett, PM, McGrogan, P, Weaver, LT, Bisset, WM, Mahdi, G, Arnott, ID, Satsangi, J and Wilson, DC (2008). Definition of phenotypic characteristics of childhood-onset inflammatory bowel disease. *Gastroenterology*, vol. 135, no. 4, pp. 1114–22.

Van Pieterson, M, van der Roorn, P, van der Woude, CJ and Escher, JC (2007). Transition of care in IBD: expectations and outcomes in adolescents and young adults. *J Pediatr Gastroenterol Nutr*, vol. 44, p. e95.

Vernier-Massouille, G, Balde, M, Salleron, J, Turck, D, Dupas, JL, Mouterde, O, Merle, V, Salomez, JL, Branche, J, Marti, R, Lerebours, E, Cortot, A, Gower-Rousseau, C and Colombel, JF (2008). Natural history of pediatric Crohn's disease: a population-based cohort study. *Gastroenterology*, vol. 135, no. 4, pp. 1106–13.

Zijlstra, M, Breij, L, van der Woude, J, de Ridder, L, van Pieterson, M and Escher, JC (2009). Assessment of self-efficacy during transition in adolescents with IBD. *J Crohns Colitis*, vol. 3, no. 1, p. S87.

Chapter 7

IBD in the elderly

Marci Reiss and Sunanda Kane

Introduction

There are several key considerations in terms of diagnosis, treatment and management for inflammatory bowel disease (IBD) patients over 65. Those who have had disease for a long time may have better and more developed coping skills; therefore, attention can be focused on other aspects of care. Approximately 10–30 percent of incident IBD cases are over the age of 60, and of these, 10 percent are in their 80s (Grimm and Friedman 1990; Jones and Hoare 1988; Piront *et al.* 2002). For those with new onset disease, coping with a chronic illness that often manifests as pain or diarrhea, usually accompanied by fatigue, is much harder. The concept of "Fit vs. Frail" when considering the older patient may drive treatment decisions. Certainly, a 75-year-old patient who still plays tennis three times a week should not be regarded as the same as one who has multiple co-morbidities and is confined to their home.

Other physical considerations in the elderly include a diagnosis that may be delayed secondary to a broader differential diagnosis, along with the lack of awareness or appreciation that IBD can and does occur in patients over 65. Visual impairment can make it difficult to comply with injectable therapies; arthritis can make it difficult to maneuver injections, breaking pills in half, or self-administering enemas. Diminished anal sphincter tone can be troublesome for application of topical therapies, as well as confound the assessment for pathologic diarrhea. Dementia can also have an impact on trying to assess patients for active symptoms, as many treatment decisions are based on symptom reporting. Active gastrointestinal symptoms can also lead to other complications, such as rushing to the washroom may provoke a fall and subsequent hip fracture. Abdominal pain or nausea can lead to decreased oral intake and result in worse malnutrition or dehydration.

Other practical aspects include the possibility of poly-pharmacy, as older patients tend to have more co-morbidities, and thus, take more medications. The likelihood of drug interactions is small but not non-existent (Katz *et al.* 2013). An older retrospective chart review study by Shapiro *et al.* with a review of medical charts of patients with Crohn's disease over the age of 60 admitted to a single tertiary referral hospital from 1966 to 1979 found that these Crohn's patients were likely to be on a mean of 6.6 medications/day (Shapiro *et al.* 1981). Over the counter medications, such as non-steroidal anti-inflammatories, commonly used for arthritic pain in the older population, are also a special concern as these have been associated in some studies to exacerbate disease (Takeuchi *et al.* 2006). However, the introduction of selective inhibitors suggest a more favorable side effect profile in a randomized controlled trial conducted specifically in the IBD population (Sandborn *et al.* 2006). Additionally, as finances may be more limited in the elderly, deciding which therapy will be effective needs to be balanced with which therapies the patients can afford (Ha, CY and Katz, S 2013). This chapter will thus explore the relevance of psychosocial care in the elderly IBD population and make recommendations for further research.

Formula for the best outcomes in IBD

Defining best outcomes for IBD patients has been an issue of recent debate (see Figure 7.1). Should the best outcome be defined by mucosal healing? One could argue in the elderly population that the goal should be symptom control as pushing to mucosal healing could be associated with more aggressive immunosuppression and risk. Should best outcomes be defined as symptom resolution? Perhaps the right way to define best outcomes is to include a combination of mucosal improvement rather than true healing, with resolution of the clinical symptoms including diarrhea, pain, and fatigue (Rogler *et al.* 2013).

Psychosocial care

Psychosocial care in the healthcare setting may be defined as the provision of psychological and emotional support and practical advocacy, as it relates to patients adapting to their medical condition, as well as accessing and adhering to care and treatment. It requires an understanding that patients will adapt and react to their disease and related treatments based on their unique psychological makeup and interaction with their social environment.

The "psychosocial world" of a patient involves the patient's personality, their family and friends, their work and/or school environments, their finances, their religion and culture, and their relationship with their doctor and the broader health system in which they get their care. All of these facets impact the patient's ability to adapt to their disease, accept, access and be compliant with treatment and influences their ability to continue with their lives in a successful and

Figure 7.1 Formula for best outcomes in inflammatory bowel disease.

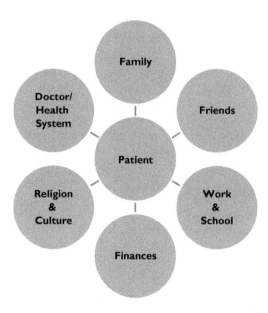

Figure 7.2 Psychosocial world of a patient.

productive manner. All of these facets are also impacted by the age and life stage of the patient.

Psychosocial care in variable #1

According to the formula, the first step in achieving best outcomes is proper utilization of best medical therapies (Lichtenstein *et al.* 2009). In the absence of treatment, inflammation in the gastrointestinal tract will not heal. Therefore, appropriate therapy is an obvious first variable in the formula. However, in the elderly, there is a higher risk of adverse events from standard immunosuppressant medications (Cottone *et al.* 2011; Ha, C and Katz, S 2013; Toruner *et al.* 2008). Assuming physicians recommend best therapies, what might prevent patients from following through with the recommendations? Barriers to treatment are often psychosocial in nature and differ depending on the individual's particular circumstances, which are unique in the elderly patient.

Barriers to treatment include both practical access to therapies and psychological barriers to treatment. In variable #1, this discussion is focused on decreasing or eliminating the psychosocial barriers to accepting, accessing and maintaining best therapies in those patients over 65.

Studies show that patients with supportive networks of friends and family are more likely to accept therapies and be adherent (Selinger *et al.* 2013). Yet, the literature also shows that social isolation is associated with IBD (Kemp *et al.*

2012), which would seem to work against the need for supportive networks. Studies additionally show that elderly patients who live alone may not do as well in maintaining remission in addition to having overall increased morbidity and mortality (Udell *et al.* 2012). Reduction in work life and losing social contacts due to illness or death are common issues facing the elderly. The reduction in social support that is age and life stage related should be recognized as an additional barrier to treatment.

Work settings for IBD patients may not be supportive of time off required for necessary care, including doctor visits, procedures, and medication infusions, leading patients to be non-compliant with necessary components of care. While legally employees cannot be discriminated against in this manner, in a non-supportive work environment, patients may recognize and feel the impact that their medical condition is having on their job. Over time, patients can learn to deal with these added challenges but these challenges might prevent patients from accepting or following through with appropriate components of treatment. For the elderly, work settings can be difficult in the absence of IBD, where they may face obstacles related to task difficulty, problems with coworkers and management, lack of self-confidence, ageism, and stereotyping (Unson and Richardson 2013). Additionally, for the elderly, employment opportunities are generally less robust. Therefore, any threat to the security of their job setting, such as needing time off to take care of illness related issues, may result in a significant barrier to treatment (Gunnarsson *et al.* 2013; Netjes and Rijken 2013).

Therapies in an era of biologics often mean significant financial hardships and sometimes patients simply cannot afford care (Holubar *et al.* 2012; Kane *et al.* 2008; Tang *et al.* 2013). Co-pays may be insurmountable, and government based insurance coverage is not always adequate for the more expensive, newer therapies. Additionally, where prior authorizations are required, patients may not be able to navigate the insurance world, especially when therapies or diagnostic tests or procedures are denied. Even if the patient might ultimately be able to find their way through the insurance maze, oftentimes, patients simply do not have the ability to spend hours during their workday to make or receive the necessary related phone calls. Elderly IBD patients need to be very cognizant of their spending and their limited income, therefore, substantial medical costs may pose a heavy financial strain.

Religion and cultural perspectives may pose barriers to treatment as well. Religion may influence a patient's ability to adapt to their disease (Cotton *et al.* 2009) and influence their medical decisions (Sheppe *et al.* 2013). Different cultures view illness as more or less stigmatic. In cultures where illness is stigmatized, patients can become ostracized and isolated (Engebretson 2013), potentially compromising their willingness to accept a diagnosis or follow through with a treatment plan. Religious and cultural perspectives of the elderly life stage may impact a patient's feelings of self-worth. Where the elderly life stage is viewed negatively, increased isolation and depression may result. For the elderly IBD patient, religious or cultural perspectives may prove to be additional barriers to care, therefore, these should be given adequate consideration.

At times, even the doctor-patient relationship can be a barrier to treatment. This relationship is a crucial element in enabling patients to trust their physician and be able to overcome their concerns and accept treatment (Kane *et al.* 2008). Some elderly patients have difficulty establishing the trust relationship for various reasons. First, some feel their physicians have incorrect perceptions of them as a result of general societal ageism and attempt to find ways to manage their physician's impressions of them as worthy patients (Clarke *et al.* 2013). Additionally, for all patients, a lack of time with their physician, insufficient access, and insufficient communication all have the potential to damage the therapeutic relationship, lessening the patient's willingness to trust their doctor's treatment recommendations. This may be particularly relevant in the case of elderly patients who may feel uniquely vulnerable. In addition, if there is a significant age differences between the patients and their doctors, there may be perceived or actual issues related to mutual respect. All of these issues may pose unintended barriers to treatment and should be recognized.

By using the psychosocial world radial in Figure 7.2, it seems that psychosocial support in the healthcare setting plays a significant role in each area of acceptance, access and adherence to therapies. Studies are needed to evaluate the significance of that impact.

With regard to a lack of supportive social networks that can be a barrier to adherence (Selinger *et al.* 2013), psychosocial support decreases feelings of isolation and increases empowering social supports. Whether the psychosocial care is in the form of a single trained provider or the psychosocial support is provided in the context of a social patient community, patients will feel less isolated, less different and more supported, and may ultimately lead to improved treatment acceptance and compliance.

Where barriers to care are a result of non-supportive work environments, psychosocial support can involve solution focused problem solving or direct advocacy. For example, with non-supportive work environments, psychosocial care providers can assist patients in determining best methods of disclosure of disease related issues and best methods for requesting accommodations. With regard to financial barriers to care, psychosocial support can assist patients in navigating through insurance denials or appeals processes, and copay or patient assistance programs. Support here can also involve direct phone calls on the patient's behalf to obtain information, enroll patients in appropriate programs or connect patients with other helpful resources.

Psychosocial care plays a significant role in improving the doctor-patient relationship. Patients will often tell social workers or psychologists things that they will not tell their physicians. When the psychosocial services provider is able to convey to the treating physician the specific patient concerns or barriers to treatment that the patient is facing, the physician is able to provide more individualized therapy and is more able to effectively utilize the time with the patient to discuss relevant issues. This may improve communication and trust between the patient and their provider, potentially leading to improved treatment acceptance.

Additionally, navigating the broader health system can be complicated for all patients, and in particular, the elderly. With psychosocial care, this population would be far more able to successfully work with their doctor's offices, their insurance companies, and the broader health system to access the care they need.

Psychosocial care in variable #2

What additional role does psychosocial care play if the best outcomes are defined as a resolution of clinical symptoms and feelings of psychological wellness?

In variable #2, psychosocial care may be defined as individualized therapy, which can decrease anxiety and depression and the clinical symptoms that are driven by these non-inflammatory etiologies. Modalities of therapy that have shown some efficacy in decreasing anxiety and depression in chronic disease populations include cognitive behavioral therapy (Knowles *et al.* 2013c; Mikocka-Walus *et al.* 2012; Mussell *et al.* 2003) and solution focused therapy (Vogelaar *et al.* 2011).

It is well recognized that clinical symptoms can manifest in the absence of objective evidence of inflammation (Sandborn 2009). In the elderly IBD patient population, there are numerous stressors related to personal circumstances in this life stage that can potentially cause anxiety and depression, and contribute to clinical symptoms in the absence of inflammation. Therefore, individualized therapy may reduce or eliminate symptoms driven by non-inflammatory etiologies, ultimately leading to reduced symptoms and increased physical and psychological wellness.

Conclusions

Psychosocial care is a significant part of care for an IBD patient. Unique challenges in the older population make this form of care even more important to ensure best outcomes. Physical, financial, cognitive, and social limitations for the elderly patient make treatment decisions more challenging but recognizing these challenges goes a long way towards maximizing outcomes.

Current limitations and future considerations

- The relative small number (but now ever increasing) of elderly patients makes generalizing management decisions difficult
- The relative inexperience of most gastroenterologists to care for IBD patients over the age of 65 makes optimizing disease difficult
- Future population based natural history studies are needed to understand the unique risks to this population

Practical recommendations

- Consider IBD in the differential diagnosis of any patient, regardless of age, that presents with bloody diarrhea, chronic diarrhea with pain, or other signs or symptoms consistent with that diagnosis

- Remember the physical, psychological, social, cultural and financial issues unique to an older population when making treatment choices
- Engage the help of a social worker or psychologist early in the care of an elderly patient

Learning points

- Good data are lacking in regards to the natural history of IBD in patients diagnosed after the age of 65
- Patients with an established diagnosis of IBD have unique challenges for disease management after the age of 65
- Psychosocial care may be even more important in this population as the elderly have unique challenges related to their support systems and social environment

Bibliography

Clarke, LH, Bennett, EV and Korotchenko, A (2013). Negotiating vulnerabilities: how older adults with multiple chronic conditions interact with physicians. *Can J Aging*, vol. Nov 4, pp. 1–12.

Cotton, S, Kudel, I, Roberts, YH, Pallerla, H, Tsevat, J, Succop, P and Yi, MS (2009). Spiritual well-being and mental health outcomes in adolescents with or without inflammatory bowel disease. *J Adolesc Health*, vol. 44, no. 5, pp. 485–92.

Cottone, M, Kohn, A, Daperno, M, Armuzzi, A, Guidi, L, D'Inca, R, Bossa, F, Angelucci, E, Biancone, L, Gionchetti, P, Ardizzone, S, Papi, C, Fries, W, Danese, S, Riegler, G, Cappello, M, Castiglione, F, Annese, V and Orlando, A (2011). Advanced age is an independent risk factor for severe infections and mortality in patients given anti-tumor necrosis factor therapy for inflammatory bowel disease. *Clin Gastroenterol Hepatol*, vol. 9, no. 1, pp. 30–5.

Engebretson, J (2013). Understanding stigma in chronic health conditions: implications for nursing. *J Am Assoc Nurse Pract*, vol. 25, no. 10, pp. 545–50.

Fuller-Thomson, E and Sulman, J (2006). Depression and inflammatory bowel disease: findings from two nationally representative Canadian surveys. *Inflamm Bowel Dis*, vol. 12, no. 8, pp. 697–707.

Grimm, IS and Friedman, LS (1990). Inflammatory bowel disease in the elderly. *Gastroenterol Clin North Am*, vol. 19, no. 2, pp. 361–89.

Gunnarsson, C, Chen, J, Rizzo, JA, Ladapo, JA, Naim, A and Lofland, JH (2013). The employee absenteeism costs of inflammatory bowel disease: evidence from US National Survey Data. *J Occup Environ Med*, vol. 55, no. 4, pp. 393–401.

Ha, C and Katz, S (2013). Management of inflammatory bowel disease in the elderly: do biologicals offer a better alternative? *Drugs Aging*, vol. 30, no. 11, pp. 871–6.

Ha, CY and Katz, S (2013). Clinical outcomes and management of inflammatory bowel disease in the older patient. *Curr Gastroenterol Rep*, vol. 15, no. 2, p. 310.

Hauser, W, Janke, KH, Klump, B and Hinz, A (2011). Anxiety and depression in patients with inflammatory bowel disease: comparisons with chronic liver disease patients and the general population. *Inflamm Bowel Dis*, vol. 17, no. 2, pp. 621–32.

IBD in the elderly 63

Holubar, SD, Pendlimari, R, Loftus, EV, Jr., Moriarty, JP, Larson, D, O'Byrne, M, Pemberton, JH and Cima, RR (2012). Drivers of cost after surgical and medical therapy for chronic ulcerative colitis: a nested case-cohort study in Olmsted County, Minnesota. *Dis Colon Rectum*, vol. 55, no. 12, pp. 1258–65.

Jones, HW and Hoare, AM (1988). Does ulcerative colitis behave differently in the elderly? *Age Ageing*, vol. 17, no. 6, pp. 410–4.

Kane, SV, Brixner, D, Rubin, DT and Sewitch, MJ (2008). The challenge of compliance and persistence: focus on ulcerative colitis. *J Manag Care Pharm*, vol. 14, no. 1 (Suppl A), pp. s2–12; quiz s3–5.

Katz, S, Surawicz, C and Pardi, DS (2013). Management of the elderly patients with inflammatory bowel disease: practical considerations. *Inflamm Bowel Dis*, vol. 19, no. 10, pp. 2257–72.

Keefer, L, Kiebles, JL, Martinovich, Z, Cohen, E, Van Denburg, A and Barrett, TA (2011). Behavioral interventions may prolong remission in patients with inflammatory bowel disease. *Behav Res Ther*, vol. 49, no. 3, pp. 145–50.

Kemp, K, Griffiths, J and Lovell, K (2012). Understanding the health and social care needs of people living with IBD: a meta-synthesis of the evidence. *World J Gastroenterol*, vol. 18, no. 43, pp. 6240–9.

Knowles, SR, Cook, SI and Tribbick, D (2013a). Relationship between health status, illness perceptions, coping strategies and psychological morbidity: a preliminary study with IBD stoma patients. *J Crohns Colitis*, vol. 7, no. 10, pp. e471–8.

Knowles, SR, Gass, C and Macrae, F (2013b). Illness perceptions in IBD influence psychological status, sexual health and satisfaction, body image and relational functioning: a preliminary exploration using structural equation modeling. *J Crohns Colitis*, vol. 7, no. 9, pp. e344–50.

Knowles, SR, Monshat, K and Castle, DJ (2013c). The efficacy and methodological challenges of psychotherapy for adults with inflammatory bowel disease: a review. *Inflamm Bowel Dis*, vol. 19, no. 12, pp. 2704–15.

Lichtenstein, GR, Hanauer, SB and Sandborn, WJ (2009). Management of Crohn's disease in adults. *Am J Gastroenterol*, vol. 104, no. 2, pp. 465–83; quiz 4, 84.

McCormick, M, Reed-Knight, B, Lewis, JD, Gold, BD and Blount, RL (2010). Coping skills for reducing pain and somatic symptoms in adolescents with IBD. *Inflamm Bowel Dis*, vol. 16, no. 12, pp. 2148–57.

Mikocka-Walus, AA, Turnbull, D, Holtmann, G and Andrews, JM (2012). An integrated model of care for inflammatory bowel disease sufferers in Australia: development and the effects of its implementation. *Inflamm Bowel Dis*, vol. 18, no. 8, pp. 1573–81.

Morrison, G, Van Langenberg, DR, Gibson, SJ and Gibson, PR (2013). Chronic pain in inflammatory bowel disease: characteristics and associations of a hospital-based cohort. *Inflamm Bowel Dis*, vol. 19, no. 6, pp. 1210–7.

Mussell, M, Bocker, U, Nagel, N, Olbrich, R and Singer, MV (2003). Reducing psychological distress in patients with inflammatory bowel disease by cognitive-behavioural treatment: exploratory study of effectiveness. *Scand J Gastroenterol*, vol. 38, no. 7, pp. 755–62.

Netjes, JE and Rijken, M (2013). Labor participation among patients with inflammatory bowel disease. *Inflamm Bowel Dis*, vol. 19, no. 1, pp. 81–91.

Piront, P, Louis, E, Latour, P, Plomteux, O and Belaiche, J (2002). Epidemiology of inflammatory bowel diseases in the elderly in the province of Liege. *Gastroenterol Clin Biol*, vol. 26, no. 2, pp. 157–61.

Rogler, G, Vavricka, S, Schoepfer, A and Lakatos, PL (2013). Mucosal healing and deep remission: what does it mean? *World J Gastroenterol*, vol. 19, no. 43, pp. 7552–60.

Sandborn, WJ (2009). How to avoid treating irritable bowel syndrome with biologic therapy for inflammatory bowel disease. *Dig Dis*, vol. 27 (Suppl 1), pp. 80–4.

Sandborn, WJ, Stenson, WF, Brynskov, J, Lorenz, RG, Steidle, GM, Robbins, JL, Kent, JD and Bloom, BJ (2006). Safety of celecoxib in patients with ulcerative colitis in remission: a randomized, placebo-controlled, pilot study. *Clin Gastroenterol Hepatol*, vol. 4, no. 2, pp. 203–11.

Selinger, CP, Eaden, J, Jones, DB, Katelaris, P, Chapman, G, McDonald, C, Smith, P, Lal, S, Leong, RW, McLaughlin, J and Robinson, A (2013). Modifiable factors associated with nonadherence to maintenance medication for inflammatory bowel disease. *Inflamm Bowel Dis*, vol. 19, no. 10, pp. 2199–206.

Shapiro, PA, Peppercorn, MA, Antoniolo, DA, Joffe, N and Goldman, H (1981). Crohn's disease in the elderly. *Am J Gastroenterol*, vol. 76, no. 2, pp. 132–7.

Sheppe, AH, Nicholson, RF, 3rd, Rasinski, KA, Yoon, JD and Curlin, FA (2013). Providing guidance to patients: physicians' views about the relative responsibilities of doctors and religious communities. *South Med J*, vol. 106, no. 7, pp. 399–406.

Takeuchi, K, Smale, S, Premchand, P, Maiden, L, Sherwood, R, Thjodleifsson, B, Bjornsson, E and Bjarnason, I (2006). Prevalence and mechanism of nonsteroidal anti-inflammatory drug-induced clinical relapse in patients with inflammatory bowel disease. *Clin Gastroenterol Hepatol*, vol. 4, no. 2, pp. 196–202.

Tang, DH, Harrington, AR, Lee, JK, Lin, M and Armstrong, EP (2013). A systematic review of economic studies on biological agents used to treat Crohn's disease. *Inflamm Bowel Dis*, vol. 19, no. 12, pp. 2673–94.

Thompson, RD, Craig, A, Crawford, EA, Fairclough, D, Gonzalez-Heydrich, J, Bousvaros, A, Noll, RB, DeMaso, DR and Szigethy, E (2012). Longitudinal results of cognitive behavioral treatment for youths with inflammatory bowel disease and depressive symptoms. *J Clin Psychol Med Settings*, vol. 19, no. 3, pp. 329–37.

Toruner, M, Loftus, EV, Jr., Harmsen, WS, Zinsmeister, AR, Orenstein, R, Sandborn, WJ, Colombel, JF and Egan, LJ (2008). Risk factors for opportunistic infections in patients with inflammatory bowel disease. *Gastroenterology*, vol. 134, no. 4, pp. 929–36.

Udell, JA, Steg, PG, Scirica, BM, Smith, SC, Jr., Ohman, EM, Eagle, KA, Goto, S, Cho, JI and Bhatt, DL (2012). Living alone and cardiovascular risk in outpatients at risk of or with atherothrombosis. *Arch Intern Med*, vol. 172, no. 14, pp. 1086–95.

Unson, C and Richardson, M (2013). Insights into the experiences of older workers and change: through the lens of selection, optimization, and compensation. *Gerontologist*, vol. 53, no. 3, pp. 484–94.

Vogelaar, L, Van't Spijker, A, Vogelaar, T, van Busschbach, JJ, Visser, MS, Kuipers, EJ and van der Woude, CJ (2011). Solution focused therapy: a promising new tool in the management of fatigue in Crohn's disease patients psychological interventions for the management of fatigue in Crohn's disease. *J Crohns Colitis*, vol. 5, no. 6, pp. 585–91.

Chapter 8

Sexual function, contraception and IBD

Reme Mountifield

Introduction

Inflammatory bowel disease (IBD) is often diagnosed during the reproductive years; psychological adjustment to the disease often coinciding with the formation of partner relationships and the making of reproductive decisions. Sexuality and contraception are important considerations, and these topics can be especially difficult to discuss with patients in the setting of physician patient gender mismatch and where acute disease or new disease onset are the focus of care. The traditional reactive model of IBD care is particularly poorly suited to addressing sexuality, which can be best managed in a chronic disease management setting (Andrews *et al.* 2010). IBD care teams must identify and address sexual concerns as part of optimising quality of life (QoL), and provide information and assistance before family planning decisions are made.

The chapter will address the impact of IBD on emotional and physical aspects of sexuality. Studies looking at body image, relationships, psychological factors, and the specific effects of medical and surgical IBD treatments, as well as the disease itself will be reviewed. Planned conception and careful contraception are important aspects of sexuality in IBD, and controversial data regarding the oral contraceptive pill (OCP) in women will be reviewed. Other methods of contraception will be briefly addressed.

Sexual function and IBD

Sexual dysfunction is very common in IBD, with a reported prevalence of up to 75 per cent in women and 44 per cent of men (Moody *et al.* 1992; Timmer *et al.* 2007a, 2007b). In an Australian survey of 217 IBD patients, frequency of sexual activity was reportedly decreased by IBD in 57.6 per cent as a result of multifactorial problems with sex, with more females (66.3 per cent) reporting a negative impact than males (40.5 per cent, $p < 0.0001$) (Muller *et al.* 2010).

Emotional aspects of sexuality: are body image, relationships and libido affected by IBD?

It is intuitive that IBD has a negative effect on body image. Contributors to negative body image include the presence of visible disease, such as anal fistulae and fissures, effects of corticosteroids causing weight gain and acne, stomas, extraintestinal manifestations, such as skin lesions and pallor. In the Australian IBD cohort described above, 66.8 per cent reported impaired body image, more so in female patients (74.8 per cent vs 51.4 per cent, $p = 0.0007$) and those with previous surgery (81.4 per cent vs 51.3 per cent, $p = 0.0003$) (Muller *et al.* 2010), and older data confirm this observation (Joachim and Milne 1987). IBD surgery can be detrimental to body image, and it is controversial whether laparoscopic technique produces better outcomes than open surgery (Larson *et al.* 2008).

Regarding partner relationships, more than half of all IBD patients report a negative effect of IBD (Muller *et al.* 2010; Trachter *et al.* 2002). This may be driven by fear of sexual rejection, which is highly prevalent amongst IBD patients, especially women (Basson 1998). An online study of 74 subjects found that sexual satisfaction had a positive relationship with marital functioning and family functioning (Knowles *et al.* 2013). Interestingly, a recent Swedish study of 74 IBD and 81 subjects with irritable bowel syndrome (IBS) reported that although women and men with IBD were at risk of impaired relationship function, they compared favourably to patients with IBS in having less anxiety in close relationships, and higher self-esteem (Bengtsson *et al.* 2013).

Libido was reduced by IBD in 58.5 per cent of respondents in the Australian cohort (Muller *et al.* 2010), risk factors again being female (67.1 per cent vs 41.9 per cent, $p = 0.0005$), and having had previous IBD surgery (67.4 per cent vs 52.6 per cent, $p = 0.035$) (Muller *et al.* 2010). Reduced desire was particularly associated with active disease in a German study of 336 women (Timmer *et al.* 2008), and the online survey described above reported that 53.9 per cent of males and 83.6 per cent of females with IBD identified a lack of sexual interest (Knowles *et al.* 2013).

Effect of depression and anxiety on sexual function

Depression is more common in IBD than in the general population, as is the use of antidepressant medication (Chapter 21). Depression in IBD patients has been reported as the most important predictor of low sexual function in a large German survey of men and women with matched controls, involving 334 matched pairs in total (Timmer *et al.* 2007a). Further German data demonstrated that mood disturbances and social environment amongst women were more impacting on sexual function than disease specific factors (Timmer *et al.* 2008). Females with depression reported decreased desire, impaired orgasm and reduced intercourse frequency (Timmer *et al.* 2008). This finding is not restricted to women, depressed mood decreasing sexual satisfaction was shown in a survey of 280 men with IBD (Timmer *et al.* 2007b). The recent online study showed that depression in IBD was related to adverse body image and self-consciousness during intimacy, sexual problems and poorer family functioning (Knowles *et al.* 2013). Anxiety has also been shown to have a deleterious effect on sexual function in IBD but not to the same extent as depressive symptoms (Timmer *et al.* 2008).

Are 'mechanical' aspects of sexuality affected by IBD and its treatments?

A cross-sectional analysis of 280 IBD men found that 44 per cent felt severely sexually compromised by the disease itself, and that erectile dysfunction was associated with disease activity [odds ratio (OR) 2.5, 95 per cent confidence interval (CI) 1.3–4.9] (Timmer *et al.* 2007b). Mechanical sexual difficulties differ for women with IBD, 60 per cent reporting dyspareunia (Moody *et al.* 1992), especially with perianal disease, and this is increased by vaginal candidiasis.

Medications used to treat IBD may cause additional sexual problems. Nearly 10 per cent of subjects in the Australian survey omitted medications citing perception of negative effects on sexual function (Muller *et al.* 2010). Minimal data exist regarding the actual effect of IBD medications on sexuality. Methotrexate has been associated with impotence, and a Spanish case control study (Marin *et al.* 2013) found that corticosteroid use was an independent predictor of sexual dysfunction in women, as was the use of biological agents in men with IBD. Overall, however, IBD medications are not associated with high rates of sexual dysfunction.

Pelvic dissection involved in many types of IBD surgery can damage autonomic nerves needed for normal sexual function. The main problems for men are erectile dysfunction and retrograde ejaculation, and for women dyspareunia and reduced sexual satisfaction. Results of individual studies vary markedly. In a systematic review investigating the effect of restorative proctocolectomy (RPC) on sexuality in 1,852 women, the incidence of sexual dysfunction was 8 per cent pre and 25 per cent post operatively (Cornish, JA *et al.* 2007). More recent case control data, however, found that RPC does not adversely affect sexual function in women (Cornish, J *et al.* 2012), and other data suggest that sexual function improves after surgery (Davies *et al.* 2008). Amongst men, rates of erectile dysfunction after RPC are partly age determined, 1.8 per cent under the age of 50 years and 3.8 per cent over the age of 50 years, and a smaller rate of retrograde ejaculation was reported in one study of 156 men (Lindsey *et al.* 2001).

Contraception and inflammatory bowel disease

Effective, low-risk contraception needs to be discussed with IBD patients early in their disease course. Although fertility and pregnancy outcomes are very good, best outcomes are achieved when conception is deliberately planned during disease remission. A recent chart review of 100 IBD patients identified that only 1 per cent of patients were noted to have had discussion of family planning as part of the IBD consultation (Gawron *et al.* 2014), but that 82 per cent of patients with IBD were using contraception (Marri *et al.* 2007). It is also important to consider that this discussion may need to take place early in a patient's illness, as up to 25 per cent of people developing IBD have onset at less than 18 years of age, and hence, those dealing with paediatric/adolescent groups need to be comfortable with and cognisant of sexual and contraceptive issues. Whilst there are no studies evaluating the safety and efficacy of contraceptive methods in men with IBD, women use the same options as the general population, the most popular being the OCP and barrier methods (Marri *et al.* 2007).

The OCP for women: does it cause or exacerbate IBD?

The role of hormones in the pathogenesis of IBD remains controversial. It has long been postulated that oestrogen and progesterone have a thrombogenic, proinflammatory effect on intestinal microvasculature. As early, individual reports were not convincing, a 2008 meta-analysis of 14 studies examining 36,797 OCP exposed subjects up to 2007 was performed (Cornish, JA *et al.* 2008). Current OCP users were found to have a relative risk (RR) of 1.46 (95 per cent CI 1.26–1.70) for developing Crohn's disease (CD) and 1.28 (95 per cent CI 1.06–1.54) for ulcerative colitis (UC), adjusted for smoking. The risk increased with increasing length of exposure, and improved upon OCP cessation. The included studies were small, OCP formulations were often not specified, or they used higher doses and different progestogens than are used today.

Subsequently a large, prospective cohort study was performed to further clarify the association between IBD onset and OCP use, adjusted for potential confounding variables such as smoking, body mass index, parity, age at menarche and endometriosis (Khalili *et al.* 2013). This study examined the Nurses' Health Cohort of 232,000 women with no prior IBD, finding 315 cases of CD and 392 of UC over 5 million person years of follow-up. Current OCP users had a hazard ratio (HR) of 2.82 (95 per cent CI 1.65–4.82) for CD compared with never users, and amongst previous OCP users HR of 1.39 (CI 1.05–1.85). An increase in UC was only seen in OCP users in the context of smoking (Khalili *et al.* 2013).

For women already diagnosed with IBD, a recent review of five cohort studies (fair to good evidence) examining contraceptive use suggested no convincing increase in relapse frequency and severity, nor post-operative recurrence amongst women who take the OCP [Centers for Disease Control and Prevention (CDC) 2010; Bitton *et al.* 2001; Sutherland *et al.* 1992; Timmer *et al.* 1998; Zapata *et al.* 2010].

Does the OCP further increase the risk of venous thromboembolism (VTE) in women with IBD?

The risk of VTE is known to be increased in IBD, especially when the disease is active and in the setting of extensive IBD (Miehsler *et al.* 2004; Nguyen and Sam 2008). Oestrogenic OCP formulations are also pro-thrombotic, but there are no prospective data examining the potential synergistic risks of OCP use in IBD. Consensus group recommendations suggest patients with both thrombotic risk factors of IBD and OCP use who require major elective surgery cease their

OCP 4 weeks prior to surgery and recommence after, using other contraception in the meanwhile [Thromboembolic Risk Factors (THRIFT) Consensus Group 1992]. In the absence of surgery, World Health Organisation (WHO) guidelines recommend continuing the OCP in women with mild disease, but choosing alternative contraception in those with active or extensive disease, immobilisation, corticosteroid use, vitamin deficiencies or fluid depletion [Centers for Disease Control and Prevention (CDC) 2010].

Is the OCP adequately absorbed in women with IBD?

Two small pharmacokinetic studies examining OCP absorption in women with mild UC, those with a stoma after proctocolectomy with limited ileal resection, and healthy women demonstrated no differences (Grimmer *et al.* 1986; Nilsson *et al.* 1985; Zapata *et al.* 2010). However, women with Crohn's and extensive small intestinal disease have not been studied, and hormone doses in these studies were higher than OCP formulations used today, limiting generalizability of these findings. Progesterone only injectables, intrauterine methods or subcutaneous implants are alternatives where malabsorption is suspected.

Other contraceptive options for women with IBD

Barrier methods of contraception have not been studied specifically in IBD and are acceptable, although a higher failure rate than other methods make these agents less appropriate for women taking potential teratogens such as methotrexate. Laparoscopic sterilisation for women with a previous history of abdominal surgery is twice as likely to result in complications (RCOG 1999) and is less favoured for women with IBD.

Progesterone only preparations, such as the progesterone only pill (POP), injectable, implants and intrauterine preparations are not associated with increased VTE risk (WHO 2000). The levonorgestrel intrauterine device (IUD) is acceptable although two case reports describe exacerbation of IBD after insertion (Cox *et al.* 2002; Wakeman 2003). The nondrug-eluting IUD also appears safe in IBD, as the increased risk of infection in immunosuppressed patients was not seen in studies of women with HIV or SLE (Browne *et al.* 2008).

Conclusions

Sexual function is compromised in men and women with IBD, affecting personal relationships and quality of life. Psychological influences on sexuality, such as depression and anxiety, must be sought and treated. Contraceptive advice for female IBD patients is similar to that for the general population, although the OCP may be substituted for other options during active disease due to an increased risk of VTE. No data exist regarding contraceptive safety and efficacy amongst males with IBD.

Current limitations and future considerations

- Problems with sexual function in IBD have both emotional and physical components, where the most important predictor is the presence of depression. Research is limited, however, and these issues are often neglected in clinical consultation
- Whilst the OCP does not appear to cause relapse of IBD, larger studies are needed using modern OCP formulations and standardised dosing
- The OCP probably compounds the already increased VTE risk in IBD, but current evidence to substantiate clinical guidelines is insufficient
- Absorption of the OCP amongst women with small intestinal Crohn's disease has not been investigated
- Currently, there is no data that addresses the safety and efficacy of contraceptive options in men with IBD

Practical recommendations

- Depression has a major influence on sexual function and should be identified and treated, as an important opportunity to improve QoL in IBD
- The OCP may be associated with an increased risk of developing Crohn's disease, and women with a strong family history of the disease should be counselled regarding possible contraceptive alternatives
- For women with IBD, the World Health Organisation recommends avoiding the OCP whilst IBD is active or if the disease is extensive to reduce VTE risk
- Other methods of contraception seem well tolerated in IBD women but data are limited

Learning points

- Difficulties in sexual function are common in both women and men with IBD, the disease influencing both emotional and physical aspects of sexuality, possibly in a bidirectional fashion
- Depression and anxiety have a very important negative effect on sexual function and deserve attention in both research and clinical settings
- Effective contraception is important particularly for women with IBD as all women deserve access to safe and effective contraception if they choose, and pregnancy outcomes in IBD are best when disease is in remission at conception
- The OCP is the most widely used contraceptive method amongst women with IBD, but has been associated with an increased risk of developing IBD
- Further studies are required to accurately assess the additional risk of VTE posed by OCP use in women already at higher risk due to active IBD

References

Andrews, JM, Mountifield, RE, Van Langenberg, DR, Bampton, PA and Holtmann, GJ (2010). Un-promoted issues in inflammatory bowel disease (IBD): opportunities to optimize care. *Intern Med J*, vol. 40, no. 3, pp. 173–82.

Basson, R (1998). Sexual health of women with disabilities. *CMAJ*, vol. 159, no. 4, pp. 359–62.

Bengtsson, M, Sjoberg, K, Candamio, M, Lerman, A and Ohlsson, B (2013). Anxiety in close relationships is higher and self-esteem lower in patients with irritable bowel syndrome compared to patients with inflammatory bowel disease. *Eur J Intern Med*, vol. 24, no. 3, pp. 266–72.

Bitton, A, Peppercorn, MA, Antonioli, DA, Niles, JL, Shah, S, Bousvaros, A, Ransil, B, Wild, G, Cohen, A, Edwardes, MD and Stevens, AC (2001). Clinical, biological, and histologic parameters as predictors of relapse in ulcerative colitis. *Gastroenterology*, vol. 120, no. 1, pp. 13–20.

Browne, H, Manipalviratn, S and Armstrong, A (2008). Using an intrauterine device in immunocompromised women. *Obstet Gynecol*, vol. 112, no. 3, pp. 667–9.

Centers for Disease Control and Prevention (CDC) (2010). US medical eligibility criteria for contraceptive use, 2010. *MMWR Recomm Rep*, vol. 59, no. RR-4, pp. 1–86.

Cornish, J, Wooding, K, Tan, E, Nicholls, RJ, Clark, SK and Tekkis, PP (2012). Study of sexual, urinary, and fecal function in females following restorative proctocolectomy. *Inflamm Bowel Dis*, vol. 18, no. 9, pp. 1601–7.

Cornish, JA, Tan, E, Simillis, C, Clark, SK, Teare, J and Tekkis, PP (2008). The risk of oral contraceptives in the etiology of inflammatory bowel disease: a meta-analysis. *Am J Gastroenterol*, vol. 103, no. 9, pp. 2394–400.

Cornish, JA, Tan, E, Teare, J, Teoh, TG, Rai, R, Darzi, AW, Paraskevas, P, Clark, SK and Tekkis, PP (2007). The effect of restorative proctocolectomy on sexual function, urinary function, fertility, pregnancy and delivery: a systematic review. *Dis Colon Rectum*, vol. 50, no. 8, pp. 1128–38.

Cox, M, Tripp, J and Blacksell, S (2002). Clinical performance of the levonorgestrel intrauterine system in routine use by the UK Family Planning and Reproductive Health Research Network: 5-year report. *J Fam Plann Reprod Health Care*, vol. 28, no. 2, pp. 73–7.

Davies, RJ, O'Connor, BI, Victor, C, MacRae, HM, Cohen, Z and McLeod, RS (2008). A prospective evaluation of sexual function and quality of life after ileal pouch-anal anastomosis. *Dis Colon Rectum*, vol. 51, no. 7, pp. 1032–5.

Gawron, LM, Hammond, C and Keefer, L (2014). Documentation of reproductive health counseling and contraception in women with inflammatory bowel diseases. *Patient Educ Couns*, vol. 94, no. 1, pp. 134–7.

Grimmer, SF, Back, DJ, Orme, ML, Cowie, A, Gilmore, I and Tjia, J (1986). The bioavailability of ethinyloestradiol and levonorgestrel in patients with an ileostomy. *Contraception*, vol. 33, no. 1, pp. 51–9.

Joachim, G and Milne, B (1987). Inflammatory bowel disease: effects on lifestyle. *J Adv Nurs*, vol. 12, no. 4, pp. 483–7.

Khalili, H, Higuchi, LM, Ananthakrishnan, AN, Richter, JM, Feskanich, D, Fuchs, CS and Chan, AT (2013). Oral contraceptives, reproductive factors and risk of inflammatory bowel disease. *Gut*, vol. 62, no. 8, pp. 1153–9.

Knowles, SR, Gass, C and Macrae, F (2013). Illness perceptions in IBD influence psychological status, sexual health and satisfaction, body image and relational functioning: a preliminary exploration using structural equation modeling. *J Crohns Colitis*, vol. 7, no. 9, pp. e344–50.

Larson, DW, Davies, MM, Dozois, EJ, Cima, RR, Piotrowicz, K, Anderson, K, Barnes, SA, Harmsen, WS, Young-Fadok, TM, Wolff, BG and Pemberton, JH (2008). Sexual function, body image, and quality of life after laparoscopic and open ileal pouch-anal anastomosis. *Dis Colon Rectum*, vol. 51, no. 4, pp. 392–6.

Lindsey, I, George, BD, Kettlewell, MG and Mortensen, NJ (2001). Impotence after mesorectal and close rectal dissection for inflammatory bowel disease. *Dis Colon Rectum*, vol. 44, no. 6, pp. 831–5.

Marin, L, Manosa, M, Garcia-Planella, E, Gordillo, J, Zabana, Y, Cabre, E and Domenech, E (2013). Sexual function and patients' perceptions in inflammatory bowel disease: a case-control survey. *J Gastroenterol*, vol. 48, no. 6, pp. 713–20.

Marri, SR, Ahn, C and Buchman, AL (2007). Voluntary childlessness is increased in women with inflammatory bowel disease. *Inflamm Bowel Dis*, vol. 13, no. 5, pp. 591–9.

Miehsler, W, Reinisch, W, Valic, E, Osterode, W, Tillinger, W, Feichtenschlager, T, Grisar, J, Machold, K, Scholz, S, Vogelsang, H and Novacek, G (2004). Is inflammatory bowel disease an independent and disease specific risk factor for thromboembolism? *Gut*, vol. 53, no. 4, pp. 542–8.

Moody, G, Probert, CS, Srivastava, EM, Rhodes, J and Mayberry, JF (1992). Sexual dysfunction amongst women with Crohn's disease: a hidden problem. *Digestion*, vol. 52, no. 3-4, pp. 179–83.

Muller, KR, Prosser, R, Bampton, P, Mountifield, R and Andrews, JM (2010). Female gender and surgery impair relationships, body image, and sexuality in inflammatory bowel disease: patient perceptions. *Inflamm Bowel Dis*, vol. 16, no. 4, pp. 657–63.

Nguyen, GC and Sam, J (2008). Rising prevalence of venous thromboembolism and its impact on mortality among hospitalized inflammatory bowel disease patients. *Am J Gastroenterol*, vol. 103, no. 9, pp. 2272–80.

Nilsson, LO, Victor, A, Kral, JG, Johansson, ED and Kock, NG (1985). Absorption of an oral contraceptive gestagen in ulcerative colitis before and after proctocolectomy and construction of a continent ileostomy. *Contraception*, vol. 31, no. 2, pp. 195–204.

RCOG (1999). Male and female sterilisation (National Evidence-based Clinical Guidelines). London: RCOG Press, vol. 4.

Sutherland, LR, Ramcharan, S, Bryant, H and Fick, G (1992). Effect of oral contraceptive use on reoperation following surgery for Crohn's disease. *Dig Dis Sci*, vol. 37, no. 9, pp. 1377–82.

Thromboembolic Risk Factors (THRIFT) Consensus Group (1992). Risk of and prophylaxis for venous thromboembolism in hospital patients. *BMJ*, vol. 305, no. 6853, pp. 567–74.

Timmer, A, Bauer, A, Dignass, A and Rogler, G (2007a). Sexual function in persons with inflammatory bowel disease: a survey with matched controls. *Clin Gastroenterol Hepatol*, vol. 5, no. 1, pp. 87–94.

Timmer, A, Bauer, A, Kemptner, D, Furst, A and Rogler, G (2007b). Determinants of male sexual function in inflammatory bowel disease: A survey-based cross-sectional analysis in 280 men. *Inflamm Bowel Dis*, vol. 13, no. 10, pp. 1236–43.

Timmer, A, Kemptner, D, Bauer, A, Takses, A, Ott, C and Furst, A (2008). Determinants of female sexual function in inflammatory bowel disease: a survey based cross-sectional analysis. *BMC Gastroenterol*, vol. 8, p. 45.

Timmer, A, Sutherland, LR and Martin, F (1998). Oral contraceptive use and smoking are risk factors for relapse in Crohn's disease. The Canadian Mesalamine for Remission of Crohn's Disease Study Group. *Gastroenterology*, vol. 114, no. 6, pp. 1143–50.

Trachter, AB, Rogers, AI and Leiblum, SR (2002). Inflammatory bowel disease in women: impact on relationship and sexual health. *Inflamm Bowel Dis*, vol. 8, no. 6, pp. 413–21.

Wakeman, J (2003). Exacerbation of Crohn's disease after insertion of a levonorgestrel intrauterine system: a case report. *J Fam Plann Reprod Health Care*, vol. 29, no. 3, p. 154.

WHO (2000). Improving access to quality care in family planning. Medical eligibility criteria for contraceptive use, 2nd edn. Geneva: WHO.

Zapata, LB, Paulen, ME, Cansino, C, Marchbanks, PA and Curtis, KM (2010). Contraceptive use among women with inflammatory bowel disease: a systematic review. *Contraception*, vol. 82, no. 1, pp. 72–85.

Chapter 9

Fertility and pregnancy in patients with IBD

C. Janneke van der Woude

Introduction

Trying to conceive and being pregnant is an emotional period for those involved. There are many uncertainties that arise, especially among those patients receiving maintenance treatment for inflammatory bowel disease (IBD) or with a newly diagnosed IBD or flare that needs intervention during pregnancy. As many IBD patients are diagnosed between 20–40 years of age, their reproductive plan should be part of the treatment strategy. However, management of a pregnant IBD patient presents an even bigger challenge for health care providers. The current US Food and Drug Administration (FDA) (Boothby and Doering 2001) classifications do not fully address the fact that the benefits of treatment of some chronic conditions might outweigh the risk of foetal drug exposure. In this chapter, the effect of IBD drugs on fertility and pregnancy outcomes will be discussed. However, as large studies are lacking in most situations, risks, even if small, must be discussed with the patients, preferably during preconception clinics as advocated by the European Crohn's and Colitis (ECCO) consensus on reproduction in patients with inflammatory bowel disease (van der Woude *et al.* 2010) in order to focus on delivering a new healthy life.

Fertility

Fertility is defined as the capacity to produce offspring (Practice Committee of American Society for Reproductive Medicine in collaboration with Society for Reproductive Endocrinology and Infertility 2008) and is different from fecundability, which is the probability of becoming pregnant per month by unprotected intercourse. Aside from physiological factors that may limit fertility, such as abstinence or reduced sexual activity because of pain, fear of incontinence and diarrhoea or a negative body image (Muller *et al.* 2010), IBD drugs do not affect fertility, although this remains a major concern for IBD patients. It has been shown that in general, IBD patients with a quiescent disease are equally fertile compared to the non-IBD patients, but patients with Crohn's disease (CD) have fewer children as a result of voluntary childlessness (Marri *et al.* 2007). Fear of the effect of drugs on the child is an important factor in this voluntary childlessness

(Mountifield *et al.* 2009). It has been observed that drug adherence during pregnancy is suboptimal (Nielsen, MJ *et al.* 2010) and this is related to the above-mentioned fear. Disease activity at conception and pregnancy negatively impacts the outcome of the child and disease activity might be associated with subfertility (Abhyankar *et al.* 2013; Hudson *et al.* 1997; Manosa *et al.* 2013). As it seems that IBD females are inadequately educated about reproduction (Selinger *et al.* 2012, 2013), counselling may improve knowledge and prevent the cessation of maintenance drugs that, in turn, results in fewer relapses during pregnancy.

Although voluntary childlessness is common in CD patients, in female patients with ulcerative colitis (UC), a systematic review from 2013 showed no evidence of decreased fertility (Tavernier *et al.* 2013). Several studies, as evidenced by the meta-analysis, showed that surgery impacts fertility in UC females with reported rates of fecundability around 30 per cent in patients that underwent ileal pouch-anal anastomosis (IPAA) (Cornish, JA *et al.* 2007; Ording Olsen *et al.* 2002; Rajaratnam *et al.* 2011; Waljee *et al.* 2006). However, more recent studies have reported the fertility outcome after laparoscopy-assisted IPAA and this significantly differs from the open IPAA techniques (Bartels *et al.* 2012; Beyer-Berjot *et al.* 2013), which may be due to less damage to the pelvis in the laparoscopic procedure, although the precise mechanism that leads to decreased fecundability remains unknown.

In males, it was shown that before the diagnosis of CD, patients had more children when compared to the number of children after the CD diagnosis, however, these studies did not report involuntary childlessness and are therefore difficult to interpret (Tavernier *et al.* 2013). Only one study, including 70 males, showed that none of the IBD drugs led to infertility (Burnell *et al.* 1986). However, from the literature it is known that sulphasalazine and methotrexate influence sperm quality, which in the case of sulphasalazine is reversible. In the case of methotrexate, although also reversible, its use is contraindicated 3–6 months before conception, and therefore, should not be taken (Moody *et al.* 1997). Studies on UC males show no increased risk for infertility (Tavernier *et al.* 2013).

Men who undergo ileoanal pouch surgery for UC may experience retrograde ejaculation and erectile dysfunction (Damgaard *et al.* 1995; Davies *et al.* 2008; Johnson *et al.* 2001; Tiainen *et al.* 1999). However, these studies have shown that overall, there is no change or even an improvement in sexual function post-surgery.

Drugs for inflammatory bowel disease and pregnancy outcomes

Conception and early pregnancy

As discussed above, education of IBD patients is of utmost importance to limit the risk of disease relapse during pregnancy with subsequent negative child outcome. Part of this education is discussing pivotal time points in pregnancy such as placental development and the development of the organs. Theoretically, disease activity negatively impacts placenta development leading to preterm birth and low birth weight, and although the exact mechanism is not elucidated for

IBD, in patients with diabetes mellitus uncontrolled disease is associated with poor outcome and may be related to poor placental development (Feig and Palda 2002). If the patient is aware of this important period for placental development, maintaining drugs may seem more logical to them, and together with the knowledge that most IBD drugs are not related to congenital malformations will lead to drug adherence during pregnancy. If congenital malformations related to IBD itself remains uncertain, a large cohort study in 1,703 children of mothers with IBD and 384,811 children of mothers without IBD showed no increased risk in IBD patients compared to non-IBD patients (Ban *et al.* 2014; Cornish, J *et al.* 2007; Norgard *et al.* 2003).

Congenital malformations are related to the use of methotrexate and thalidomide (Kozlowski *et al.* 1990; Smithells and Newman 1992). Although their use is prohibited, undeliberate use of methotrexate does not immediately indicate therapeutic abortion in case of pregnancy (Martinez Lopez *et al.* 2009; Viktil *et al.* 2012). The couple should be adequately counselled in collaboration with therapeutic abortion experts. Data on paternal use of methotrexate and the outcome of children show limited risks of major congenital malformation (Beghin *et al.* 2011; Viktil *et al.* 2012). Therefore, the following approach seems appropriate in the case of methotrexate use: stop methotrexate, start with high dose folic acid, inform the parents-to-be that methotrexate may lead to congenital malformations and, in the case when the parents wish to continue the pregnancy, perform detailed foetal ultrasound to rule out major congenital malformations.

Most studies have shown thiopurines to be safe in females and males, with no increased risk of malformations in the newborn (Angelberger *et al.* 2011; Casanova *et al.* 2013; Coelho *et al.* 2011; Hutson *et al.* 2013; Shim *et al.* 2011). Although a recent meta-analysis has shown an increased risk of preterm birth (Akbari *et al.* 2013), it is advised to continue on thiopurines during conception and pregnancy.

Anti-TNF alpha agents during conception and pregnancy are not related to an increased risk of congenital malformations, however, data are still limited (Nielsen *et al.* 2013). Although the use of corticosteroids in the first trimester has been reported to be associated with an increased risk of orofacial malformations (Park-Wyllie *et al.* 2000), a recent population-based study showed no increased risk (Hviid and Molgaard-Nielsen 2011).

Pregnancy

Physiologic changes of pregnancy affect the pharmacokinetics of medications used by pregnant women. This mechanism is well illustrated for thiopurines where 6MMP and 6TG levels change. During pregnancy, the median 6-TGN concentration decreases, while 6-MMP levels increase. This alteration in thiopurine metabolism does not lead to biochemical toxicity or adverse events in the mothers. After delivery, both 6-TGN and 6-MMP levels return to the baseline levels (Jharap *et al.* 2014).

In order for a drug to cause a teratogenic or pharmacological effect on the foetus, it must cross from maternal circulation to foetal circulation through the placenta by diffusion. The rate of transfer depends on the chemical properties of the drug, such as protein binding, pH difference, lipid solubility and molecular weight of the drug. Transplacental transfer of drugs increases in the third trimester due to increased maternal and placental blood flow, decreased thickness and increased surface area of the placenta (Zelinkova *et al.* 2011). In addition, IBD drugs pass the placenta. The foetus is exposed to 6-TGN and the levels found in the cord blood correlate with maternal 6-TGN levels (Jharap *et al.* 2014), although whether these levels are associated with clinically relevant anaemia in the newborns needs to be elucidated.

Infliximab (IFX) and adalimumab (ADA) are IgG1 antibodies, and cross the placenta (Mahadevan, U. *et al.* 2013; Marchioni and Lichtenstein 2013). Several studies suggest that IFX is of low risk in pregnancy, at least in terms of short-term outcomes, and does not seem to be teratogenic (Marchioni and Lichtenstein 2013; Nielsen *et al.* 2013; Schnitzler *et al.* 2011). For ADA, the data available are limited, but also show no increase in the rate of adverse pregnancy outcomes (Mahadevan *et al.* 2012; Zelinkova *et al.* 2013). The long-term effect of biologics on the developing immune system and the risk of infectious disease in the newborn remains unknown. Therefore, discontinuation of the treatment around gestational week 22–24 may be considered in order to limit the intra-uterine exposure to these agents; this strategy showed no increased incidence of relapse in a small prospective cohort (Zelinkova *et al.* 2013), but should only be applied when the female is in remission and there are no other indications to continue anti-TNF.

All corticosteroids (systemic, oral, topical) can cross the placenta but are rapidly converted by placental 11-hydroxygenase to less active metabolites, resulting in low foetal blood concentration. As short-acting prednisone, prednisolone and methylprednisolone are more efficiently metabolized by the placenta, and therefore, reach lower concentrations in the foetus than the longer-acting dexamethasone and betamethasone, the former molecules are preferred for the treatment of maternal conditions necessitating glucocorticosteroids. Neonatal adrenal suppression due to the use of corticosteroids in late pregnancy of woman with IBD has been reported, therefore, a paediatrician should check infants after birth. Furthermore, corticosteroids are known to increase the risk of hypertension and diabetes mellitus in patients because the pregnant female is at risk for gestational hypertension and gestational diabetes mellitus. A stringent follow-up is warranted when corticosteroids are prescribed (Homar *et al.* 2008).

IBD and preconceptional care

As stated in the introduction, in every patient with a (future) reproductive wish, this wish should become part of the therapeutic strategy, and more importantly, all IBD patients should be properly counselled preconceptionally to increase knowledge, and consequently, improve drug adherence. Illustrated in Figure 9.1

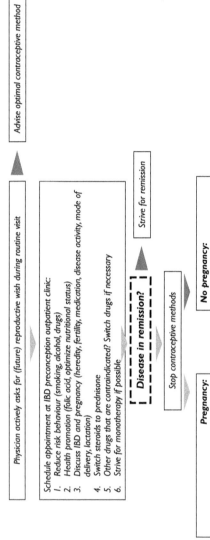

Figure 9.1 Rotterdam preconceptional pregnancy IBD care, pale arrow head indicates 'proceed', dark arrow head indicates 'adjust current strategy'. IBD: inflammatory bowel disease. OBGYN: obstetrician, gynaecology (author's own figure).

Fertility and pregnancy in IBD 79

is the Rotterdam preconceptional pregnancy IBD care. In short, IBD patients with a reproductive wish are counselled as follows:

- A general counselling including: reduction of risk behaviour (alcohol, smoking, drug abuse), health promotion (start folic acid, optimize nutritional status)
- A specific and individual counselling including: increasing knowledge of IBD and IBD drugs on fertility, child outcome, mode of delivery and breastfeeding.

The patient receives a letter summarising the important points discussed during this consultation. All patients are referred to the obstetrician for follow-up during pregnancy and the female IBD patients are seen every 2 months at the out-patient clinic when in remission. For measuring disease activity, clinical indices are not always helpful during pregnancy and also faecal calprotectin is not yet vali-dated, therefore, a combination of these indices are used to assess activity, however, endoscopy remains an important tool for assessing disease activity and extensiveness. Although endoscopy is not necessary in patients with mild disease relapse that do not require major therapeutic changes, in pregnant females with more active disease treatment with corticosteroids or anti-TNF alpha agents must be fully justified. In case of relapse, patients are followed-up at least every other week.

Conclusion

Pregnancy is a unique state and can be affected by multiple factors leading to a worse outcome for both mother and child. In a pregnant woman suffering from a chronic illness, there are even more risk factors that can lead to a worse out-come. This chapter has provided some guidance for clinicians to counsel patients with a wish to conceive while being treated for inflammatory bowel disease.

Current limitations and future considerations

- The impact of preconceptional counselling on pregnancy outcome remains unknown and should be investigated to establish preconceptional care in IBD patients
- Although regarded as relatively safe, data on anti-TNF alpha agents in rela-tion to pregnancy outcome and child development are limited, therefore, long-term prospective studies are needed
- The exact impact of transplacental passage of thiopurines is unknown as yet and should receive further attention in research

Practical recommendations

- In every IBD patient at reproductive age, child wish must be discussed and should be part of the treatment strategy

- Physicians should be aware of voluntary childlessness in CD patients
- IBD patients with an active reproductive wish should receive preconceptional counselling to optimize patients' knowledge

Learning points

- Knowledge on fertility and pregnancy in IBD patients is inadequate
- Amongst patients with Crohn's disease there is a high rate of voluntary childlessness
- IBD and IBD drugs do not lead to infertility
- IBD drugs, with the exception of methotrexate and thalidomide, are not related to a negative pregnancy outcome
- Preconceptional counselling is advocated for all IBD patients with a wish to conceive

References

Abhyankar, A, Ham, M and Moss, AC (2013). Meta-analysis: the impact of disease activity at conception on disease activity during pregnancy in patients with inflammatory bowel disease. *Aliment Pharmacol Ther*, vol. 38, no. 5, pp. 460–6.

Akbari, M, Shah, S, Velayos, FS, Mahadevan, U and Cheifetz, AS (2013). Systematic review and meta-analysis on the effects of thiopurines on birth outcomes from female and male patients with inflammatory bowel disease. *Inflamm Bowel Dis*, vol. 19, no. 1, pp. 15–22.

Angelberger, S, Reinisch, W, Messerschmidt, A, Miehsler, W, Novacek, G, Vogelsang, H and Dejaco, C (2011). Long-term follow-up of babies exposed to azathioprine in utero and via breastfeeding. *J Crohns Colitis*, vol. 5, no. 2, pp. 95–100.

Ban, L, Tata, LJ, Fiaschi, L and Card, T (2014). Limited risks of major congenital anomalies in children of mothers with IBD and effects of medications. *Gastroenterology*, vol. 146, no. 1, pp. 76–84.

Bartels, SA, D'Hoore, A, Cuesta, MA, Bensdorp, AJ, Lucas, C and Bemelman, WA (2012). Significantly increased pregnancy rates after laparoscopic restorative proctocolectomy: a cross-sectional study. *Ann Surg*, vol. 256, no. 6, pp. 1045–8.

Beghin, D, Cournot, MP, Vauzelle, C and Elefant, E (2011). Paternal exposure to methotrexate and pregnancy outcomes. *J Rheumatol*, vol. 38, no. 4, pp. 628–32.

Beyer-Berjot, L, Maggiori, L, Birnbaum, D, Lefevre, JH, Berdah, S and Panis, Y (2013). A total laparoscopic approach reduces the infertility rate after ileal pouch-anal anastomosis: a 2-center study. *Ann Surg*, vol. 258, no. 2, pp. 275–82.

Boothby, LA and Doering, PL (2001). FDA labeling system for drugs in pregnancy. *Ann Pharmacother*, vol. 35, no. 11, pp. 1485–9.

Burnell, D, Mayberry, J, Calcraft, BJ, Morris, JS and Rhodes, J (1986). Male fertility in Crohn's disease. *Postgrad Med J*, vol. 62, no. 726, pp. 269–72.

Casanova, MJ, Chaparro, M, Domenech, E, Barreiro-de Acosta, M, Bermejo, F, Iglesias, E, Gomollon, F, Rodrigo, L, Calvet, X, Esteve, M, Garcia-Planella, E, Garcia-Lopez, S, Taxonera, C, Calvo, M, Lopez, M, Ginard, D, Gomez-Garcia, M, Garrido, E, Perez-Calle, JL, Beltran, B, Piqueras, M, Saro, C, Botella, B, Duenas, C, Ponferrada, A, Manosa, M, Garcia-Sanchez, V, Mate, J and Gisbert, JP (2013). Safety of thiopurines and anti-TNF-alpha drugs during pregnancy in patients with inflammatory bowel disease. *Am J Gastroenterol*, vol. 108, no. 3, pp. 433–40.

Coelho, J, Beaugerie, L, Colombel, JF, Hebuterne, X, Lerebours, E, Lemann, M, Baumer, P, Cosnes, J, Bourreille, A, Gendre, JP, Seksik, P, Blain, A, Metman, EH, Nisard, A, Cadiot, G, Veyrac, M, Coffin, B, Dray, X, Carrat, F, Marteau, P and CESAME Pregnancy Study Group (France) (2011). Pregnancy outcome in patients with inflammatory bowel disease treated with thiopurines: cohort from the CESAME Study. *Gut*, vol. 60, no. 2, pp. 198–203.

Cornish, J, Tan, E, Teare, J, Teoh, TG, Rai, R, Clark, SK and Tekkis, PP (2007). A meta-analysis on the influence of inflammatory bowel disease on pregnancy. *Gut*, vol. 56, no. 6, pp. 830–7.

Cornish, JA, Tan, E, Teare, J, Teoh, TG, Rai, R, Darzi, AW, Paraskevas, P, Clark, SK and Tekkis, PP (2007). The effect of restorative proctocolectomy on sexual function, urinary function, fertility, pregnancy and delivery: a systematic review. *Dis Colon Rectum*, vol. 50, no. 8, pp. 1128–38.

Damgaard, B, Wettergren, A and Kirkegaard, P (1995). Social and sexual function following ileal pouch-anal anastomosis. *Dis Colon Rectum*, vol. 38, no. 3, pp. 286–9.

Davies, RJ, O'Connor, BI, Victor, C, MacRae, HM, Cohen, Z and McLeod, RS (2008). A prospective evaluation of sexual function and quality of life after ileal pouch-anal anastomosis. *Dis Colon Rectum*, vol. 51, no. 7, pp. 1032–5.

Feig, DS and Palda, VA (2002). Type 2 diabetes in pregnancy: a growing concern. *Lancet*, vol. 359, no. 9318, pp. 1690–2.

Homar, V, Grosek, S and Battelino, T (2008). High-dose methylprednisolone in a pregnant woman with Crohn's disease and adrenal suppression in her newborn. *Neonatology*, vol. 94, no. 4, pp. 306–9.

Hudson, M, Flett, G, Sinclair, TS, Brunt, PW, Templeton, A and Mowat, NA (1997). Fertility and pregnancy in inflammatory bowel disease. *Int J Gynaecol Obstet*, vol. 58, no. 2, pp. 229–37.

Hutson, JR, Matlow, JN, Moretti, ME and Koren, G (2013). The fetal safety of thiopurines for the treatment of inflammatory bowel disease in pregnancy. *J Obstet Gynaecol*, vol. 33, no. 1, pp. 1–8.

Hviid, A and Molgaard-Nielsen, D (2011). Corticosteroid use during pregnancy and risk of orofacial clefts. *CMAJ*, vol. 183, no. 7, pp. 796–804.

Jharap, B, de Boer, NK, Stokkers, P, Hommes, DW, Oldenburg, B, Dijkstra, G, van der Woude, CJ, de Jong, DJ, Mulder, CJ, van Elburg, RM, van Bodegraven, AA and Dutch Initiative on Crohn and Colitis (2014). Intrauterine exposure and pharmacology of conventional thiopurine therapy in pregnant patients with inflammatory bowel disease. *Gut*, vol. 63, no. 3, pp. 451–7.

Johnson, E, Carlsen, E, Nazir, M and Nygaard, K (2001). Morbidity and functional outcome after restorative proctocolectomy for ulcerative colitis. *Eur J Surg*, vol. 167, no. 1, pp. 40–5.

Kozlowski, RD, Steinbrunner, JV, MacKenzie, AH, Clough, JD, Wilke, WS and Segal, AM (1990). Outcome of first-trimester exposure to low-dose methotrexate in eight patients with rheumatic disease. *Am J Med*, vol. 88, no. 6, pp. 589–92.

Mahadevan, U, Martin, CF, Sandler, RS, Kane, SV, Dubinsky, M, Lewis, JD, Sandborn, WJ and Sands, BE (2012). 'PIANO: a 1000 patient prospective registry of pregnancy outcomes in women with IBD exposed to immunomodulators and biologic therapy. *Gastroenterology*, vol. 142, no. 5 (Suppl 1), pp. S–149.

82 C. Janneke van der Woude

Mahadevan, U, Wolf, DC, Dubinsky, M, Cortot, A, Lee, SD, Siegel, CA, Ullman, T, Glover, S, Valentine, JF, Rubin, DT, Miller, J and Abreu, MT (2013). Placental transfer of anti-tumor necrosis factor agents in pregnant patients with inflammatory bowel disease. *Clin Gastroenterol Hepatol*, vol. 11, no. 3, pp. 286–92; quiz e24.

Manosa, M, Navarro-Llavat, M, Marin, L, Zabana, Y, Cabre, E and Domenech, E (2013). Fecundity, pregnancy outcomes, and breastfeeding in patients with inflammatory bowel disease: a large cohort survey. *Scand J Gastroenterol*, vol. 48, no. 4, pp. 427–32.

Marchioni, RM and Lichtenstein, GR (2013). Tumor necrosis factor-alpha inhibitor therapy and fetal risk: a systematic literature review. *World J Gastroenterol*, vol. 19, no. 17, pp. 2591–602.

Marri, SR, Ahn, C and Buchman, AL (2007). Voluntary childlessness is increased in women with inflammatory bowel disease. *Inflamm Bowel Dis*, vol. 13, no. 5, pp. 591–9.

Martinez Lopez, JA, Loza, E and Carmona, L (2009). Systematic review on the safety of methotrexate in rheumatoid arthritis regarding the reproductive system (fertility, pregnancy, and breastfeeding). *Clin Exp Rheumatol*, vol. 27, no. 4, pp. 678–84.

Moody, GA, Probert, C, Jayanthi, V and Mayberry, JF (1997). The effects of chronic ill health and treatment with sulphasalazine on fertility amongst men and women with inflammatory bowel disease in Leicestershire. *Int J Colorectal Dis*, vol. 12, no. 4, pp. 220–4.

Mountifield, R, Bampton, P, Prosser, R, Muller, K and Andrews, JM (2009). Fear and fertility in inflammatory bowel disease: a mismatch of perception and reality affects family planning decisions. *Inflamm Bowel Dis*, vol. 15, no. 5, pp. 720–5.

Muller, KR, Prosser, R, Bampton, P, Mountifield, R and Andrews, JM (2010). Female gender and surgery impair relationships, body image, and sexuality in inflammatory bowel disease: patient perceptions. *Inflamm Bowel Dis*, vol. 16, no. 4, pp. 657–63.

Nielsen, MJ, Norgaard, M, Holland-Fisher, P and Christensen, LA (2010). Self-reported antenatal adherence to medical treatment among pregnant women with Crohn's disease. *Aliment Pharmacol Ther*, vol. 32, no. 1, pp. 49–58.

Nielsen, OH, Loftus, EV, Jr. and Jess, T (2013). Safety of TNF-alpha inhibitors during IBD pregnancy: a systematic review. *BMC Med*, vol. 11, p. 174.

Norgard, B, Puho, E, Pedersen, L, Czeizel, AE and Sorensen, HT (2003). Risk of congenital abnormalities in children born to women with ulcerative colitis: a population-based, case-control study. *Am J Gastroenterol*, vol. 98, no. 9, pp. 2006–10.

Ording Olsen, K, Juul, S, Berndtsson, I, Oresland, T and Laurberg, S (2002). Ulcerative colitis: female fecundity before diagnosis, during disease, and after surgery compared with a population sample. *Gastroenterology*, vol. 122, no. 1, pp. 15–9.

Park-Wyllie, L, Mazzotta, P, Pastuszak, A, Moretti, ME, Beique, L, Hunnisett, L, Friesen, MH, Jacobson, S, Kasapinovic, S, Chang, D, Diav-Citrin, O, Chitayat, D, Nulman, I, Einarson, TR and Koren, G (2000). Birth defects after maternal exposure to corticosteroids: prospective cohort study and meta-analysis of epidemiological studies. *Teratology*, vol. 62, no. 6, pp. 385–92.

Practice Committee of American Society for Reproductive Medicine in collaboration with Society for Reproductive Endocrinology and Infertility (2008). Optimizing natural fertility. *Fertil Steril*, vol. 90, no. 5 (Suppl), pp. S1–6.

Rajaratnam, SG, Eglinton, TW, Hider, P and Fearnhead, NS (2011). Impact of ileal pouch-anal anastomosis on female fertility: meta-analysis and systematic review. *Int J Colorectal Dis*, vol. 26, no. 11, pp. 1365–74.

Schnitzler, F, Fidder, H, Ferrante, M, Ballet, V, Noman, M, Van Assche, G, Spitz, B, Hoffman, I, Van Steen, K, Vermeire, S and Rutgeerts, P (2011). Outcome of pregnancy in women with inflammatory bowel disease treated with antitumor necrosis factor therapy. *Inflamm Bowel Dis*, vol. 17, no. 9, pp. 1846–54.

Selinger, CP, Eaden, J, Selby, W, Jones, DB, Katelaris, P, Chapman, G, McDonald, C, McLaughlin, J, Leong, RW and Lal, S (2012). Patients' knowledge of pregnancy-related issues in inflammatory bowel disease and validation of a novel assessment tool ('CCPKnow'). *Aliment Pharmacol Ther*, vol. 36, no. 1, pp. 57–63.

Selinger, CP, Eaden, J, Selby, W, Jones, DB, Katelaris, P, Chapman, G, McDondald, C, McLaughlin, J, Leong, RW and Lal, S (2013). Inflammatory bowel disease and pregnancy: lack of knowledge is associated with negative views. *J Crohns Colitis*, vol. 7, no. 6, pp. e206–13.

Shim, L, Eslick, GD, Simring, AA, Murray, H and Weltman, MD (2011). The effects of azathioprine on birth outcomes in women with inflammatory bowel disease (IBD). *J Crohns Colitis*, vol. 5, no. 3, pp. 234–8.

Smithells, RW and Newman, CG (1992). Recognition of thalidomide defects. *J Med Genet*, vol. 29, no. 10, pp. 716–23.

Tavernier, N, Fumery, M, Peyrin-Biroulet, L, Colombel, JF and Gower-Rousseau, C (2013). Systematic review: fertility in non-surgically treated inflammatory bowel disease. *Aliment Pharmacol Ther*, vol. 38, no. 8, pp. 847–53.

Tiainen, J, Matikainen, M and Hiltunen, KM (1999). Ileal J-pouch–anal anastomosis, sexual dysfunction, and fertility. *Scand J Gastroenterol*, vol. 34, no. 2, pp. 185–8.

van der Woude, CJ, Kolacek, S, Dotan, I, Oresland, T, Vermeire, S, Munkholm, P, Mahadevan, U, Mackillop, L, Dignass, A and European Crohn's Colitis Organisation (ECCO) (2010). European evidenced-based consensus on reproduction in inflammatory bowel disease. *J Crohns Colitis*, vol. 4, no. 5, pp. 493–510.

Viktil, KK, Engeland, A and Furu, K (2012). Outcomes after anti-rheumatic drug use before and during pregnancy: a cohort study among 150,000 pregnant women and expectant fathers. *Scand J Rheumatol*, vol. 41, no. 3, pp. 196–201.

Waljee, A, Waljee, J, Morris, AM and Higgins, PD (2006). Threefold increased risk of infertility: a meta-analysis of infertility after ileal pouch anal anastomosis in ulcerative colitis. *Gut*, vol. 55, no. 11, pp. 1575–80.

Zelinkova, Z, de Haar, C, de Ridder, L, Pierik, MJ, Kuipers, EJ, Peppelenbosch, MP and van der Woude, CJ (2011). High intra-uterine exposure to infliximab following maternal anti-TNF treatment during pregnancy. *Aliment Pharmacol Ther*, vol. 33, no. 9, pp. 1053–8.

Zelinkova, Z, van der Ent, C, Bruin, KF, van Baalen, O, Vermeulen, HG, Smalbraak, HJ, Ouwendijk, RJ, Hoek, AC, van der Werf, SD, Kuipers, EJ, van der Woude, CJ and Dutch Delta IBD Group (2013). Effects of discontinuing anti-tumor necrosis factor therapy during pregnancy on the course of inflammatory bowel disease and neonatal exposure. *Clin Gastroenterol Hepatol*, vol. 11, no. 3, pp. 318–21.

Chapter 10

IBS in IBD and psychological implications

Anil K. Asthana and Peter R. Gibson

Introduction

Irritable bowel syndrome (IBS) is a functional gastrointestinal disorder character-ised by abdominal pain, bloating and alteration in bowel frequency. The diagnosis is based upon symptom duration of at least 12 consecutive weeks of the preceding 12 months; these include abdominal pain or discomfort that is relieved with defe-cation and/or has an onset associated with a change in frequency of stool and/or in its form (appearance). Point prevalence of IBS in the developed world has been estimated to be approximately 10.5 per cent (6.6 per cent of men and 14 per cent of women) (Wilson *et al.* 2004). There is significant morbidity associated with IBS; quality of life is reduced and mental component scores have been found to be worse than in patients with a stroke or heart failure (Wilson *et al.* 2004).

Many patients with inflammatory bowel disease (IBD) continue to report symptoms, such as abdominal pain and diarrhoea, even when biochemically and endoscopically in remission. This cohort of patients is challenging to manage; stepping-up therapy by initiating or increasing steroids, immunomodulators or biologic therapy, or labelling such patients as having refractory IBD may not be appropriate. There are no universally accepted guidelines regarding their man-agement and it is these groups who are labelled as having 'IBD-IBS'.

Much data have been published in the last 5 years regarding the epidemiology of IBD-IBS. Its overall prevalence has been estimated to be about 40 per cent, using data pooled from 13 studies that included 1,703 IBD patients (Halpin and Ford 2012). The likelihood of having IBS-like symptoms in patients with IBD was more than fourfold than in controls, whether the disease was active or in remission (Halpin and Ford 2012).

Pathophysiology

The essential question, that only recently has begun to be addressed, is whether the IBD-IBS phenomenon is due to the coexistence of two separate conditions (IBD and IBS) or whether the IBS symptoms are a manifestation of occult or continued low-grade mucosal inflammation, or the effects of previous inflamma-tion. Examining for genetic clues, assessing the function of the enteric nervous

IBS and psychological implications   85

system, looking for evidence of occult inflammation and dissection of psychological factors can help address this critical question.

Genetics

Few studies have addressed the issue of genetic versus environmental factors in patients having IBD-IBS. However, clues have derived from a prevalence study of IBS among first-degree relatives of patients with IBD (Aguas *et al.* 2011). The overall prevalence of IBS amongst first-degree relatives of patients with IBD was nearly 50 per cent according to Rome I criteria. It was higher in first-degree relatives than in spouses of patients and was not dependent on whether relatives were living with the index case (Aguas *et al.* 2011). This suggests that the aetiology may have a genetic component in addition to an environmental one.

Function and structure of the enteric nervous system

Lessons can be gleaned from addressing whether the common pathophysiological features identified in patients with IBS are also present specifically in patients having IBD-IBS. While there is a body of data that reveals gut sensory and motor function to be abnormal in patients with active IBD, few studies have addressed the issues in patients in remission with and without IBS-like symptoms. Those studies have, however, indicated that similar underlying pathophysiological mechanisms may be present in patients having IBD in remission, with some having specificity to those with IBS-like symptoms, as shown in Table 10.1. Lessons may also be learnt from examining the features of IBS in those where the precipitant was a self-limited gut inflammatory event, the so-called *post-infectious IBS*. However, the pathophysiological importance of the inflammation in terms of symptom genesis (as best shown by abolishing the inflammation) has not been established.

Occult inflammation

It is possible that IBS symptoms are mostly a manifestation of ongoing inflammation in the intestinal wall, despite clinical assessment that the inflammation is under control and the patient is in remission. This relationship can be addressed by examining the association of heightened intestinal inflammation (using non-conventional but sensitive markers) with IBS-like symptoms. The ultimate demonstration of the pathogenic importance of inflammation will lie in randomised controlled trials of aggressive anti-inflammatory agents in such patient groups, but this approach has yet to be reported.

Calprotectin is a neutrophil-associated protein that is resistant to degradation by bacteria and proteases (Voganatsi *et al.* 2001). Neutrophils migrate from inflamed intestinal wall into the lumen where they undergo death and release calprotectin. Hence, during inflammation, the calprotectin content of faeces

86 Anil K. Asthana and Peter R. Gibson

Table 10.1 Pathophysiological changes described in the function and structure of the enteric nervous system in patients with inflammatory bowel disease (IBD) in remission with or without irritable bowel syndrome (IBS)-like symptoms

Indices	Abnormalities described
Visceral hypersensitivity	Increased rectal sensitivity patients with IBS-like symptoms: • Adults with ulcerative colitis in remission (Motomura *et al.* 2008) and • Children with quiescent Crohn's disease (Wang *et al.* 2007) Neurobiological correlates in patients with IBS-like symptoms and IBD in remission: • Elevated expression of tryptophan hydroxylase (TpH)-1 in ileal and colonic biopsies (Wheatcroft *et al.* 2005) • Four-fold increase in density of transient receptor potential vanilloid type 1 (TRPV1)-immunoreactive nerve fibres in the rectosigmoid biopsies (Akbar *et al.* 2010) • Greater transcription of TRPV1 and concentration of neuropeptides in sigmoid mucosal samples (Keohane *et al.* 2010)
Motility and/or its response to stimuli	In patients with IBD in remission, subtle differences in motor responses to lipids and acid compared with those in controls (but not specific to IBS-like symptoms) (Berrill *et al.* 2013) Low amplitude propagated manometric activity in the colon of patients with ulcerative colitis in remission tended to show IBS-like patterns (but specificity ot IBS-like symptoms not tested) (Bassotti *et al.* 2006)
Lessons from post-infectious irritable bowel syndrome	Persistent structural and functional changes in the enteric nervous system post-infection even once the acute inflammation has settled down and mucosa has healed (Motomura *et al.* 2008; Wang *et al.* 2007; Wheatcroft *et al.* 2005), including: • Enterochromaffin cell hyperplasia • Dysmotility • Elevated mast cell density around nerve endings • Evidence for persisting low-grade inflammation

will rise. Indeed, it is elevated in conditions such as IBD, non-steroidal anti-inflammatory enteropathy as well as in colorectal adenomas and carcinoma. Faecal calprotectin may be, therefore, a useful non-invasive and sensitive marker of intestinal inflammation that potentially can differentiate between inflammatory and non-inflammatory conditions of the gut, particularly as it has a high negative predictive value (Sydora *et al.* 2012). Recently, there have been many studies in patients with IBD-IBS to assess for occult inflammation using faecal calprotectin and these are summarised in Table 10.2. There is heterogeneity of findings, presumably related to the clinicians' ability to determine whether patients are truly in remission. However, the results do highlight the fact that

IBS and psychological implications   87

Table 10.2 Studies comparing levels of faecal calprotectin (FC) in inflammatory bowel disease (IBD) patients with and without irritable bowel syndrome (IBS)-like symptoms

Reference	Year	Country	Number studied	Design	FC levels in patients with vs without IBS-like symptoms
Akbar et al.	2010	UK	68	Open-trial	No difference
Keohane et al.	2010	Ireland	106	Cross-sectional	Higher levels of FC in IBS-positive patients
Berrill et al.	2013	UK	169	Cross-sectional	No difference
Jelsness-Jorgensen et al.	2013	Norway	144	Cross-sectional	Higher levels of FC in IBS-positive patients
Jonefjäll et al.	2013	Sweden	94	Longitudinal	No difference

IBS-like symptoms might reflect unsuspected intestinal inflammation in a proportion of patients.

Another way to address occult inflammation is to study the bowel at the mucosal level. In the only study to specifically address these issues, changes in the expression of tight junction proteins and paracellular permeability in Ussing chambers in colonic and terminal ileal biopsies of patients with IBD-IBS, but not IBD in remission without symptoms, closely mimicked those in an IBS population. Those with symptoms had more than threefold higher mucosal TNF-α expression. Thus, the conclusion was made that IBS-like symptoms in quiescent IBD may be a result of low-grade inflammation leading to structural changes similarly shown in IBS patients (Vivinus-Nébot *et al.* 2014).

Psychological factors

There is robust evidence regarding the interaction of psychological factors with the activity of IBD (Ghia *et al.* 2009). The Manitoba IBD cohort study illustrated that IBD patients have twofold increased risk of developing a lifetime diagnosis of depression compared to controls (Walker *et al.* 2008). Having a previous mental disorder increases the chances of a relapse in chronic conditions, including IBD (Kessler *et al.* 2003), and depression has been shown to adversely affect the natural course of intestinal inflammation in mice models (Ghia *et al.* 2009). Stress is also thought to contribute to disease exacerbation rather than to the aetiology *per se* (Grover *et al.* 2009). Furthermore, the autonomic nervous system is known to mediate stress-related increase in gut permeability as well as reactivation of inflammatory mucosal changes (Taylor and Keely 2007).

There is also robust evidence that patients with IBD-IBS have higher levels of anxiety and depression than those without (Berrill *et al.* 2013; Jonefjäll *et al.* 2013). Furthermore, anxiety was an independent predictor of IBS-like symptoms

88   Anil K. Asthana and Peter R. Gibson

that affected almost one-half of a cohort of patients with IBD in remission (Simren *et al.* 2002). Such data suggest that psychological factors may be important in the genesis of IBS-like symptom in patients with IBD, as they are believed to be in patients with IBS.

Overview

It appears that there is evidence for involvement in IBD-IBS of factors independent of the mucosal inflammation (possibly genetic), psychological factors, factors associated with the aftermath of inflammation and changes to the enteric nervous system, and active inflammation itself. Thus, a complex, multifactorial pathogenesis with likely heterogeneity across individuals seems likely.

Biopsychosocial model

With such a diversity of factors that might influence the complex interplay between disease inflammatory activity and functional gut symptoms, a biopsychosocial model is a useful way of approaching IBD patients with functional symptoms rather than categorising the symptoms in a dualistic manner such as IBD and IBS (Long and Drossman 2010). Evidence supporting this model includes the adverse link between stress and mucosal permeability, inflammatory response and the hypothalamic-pituitary-adrenal axis (HPA) (Grover *et al.* 2009). Viewing IBD patients with functional symptoms as part of a spectrum rather than as distinct pathologies (organic vs functional) would be a more accurate reflection of the underlying pathophysiology and would provide a better framework for designing management strategies. It is reasonable to view psychological disorders in patients with IBD in a similar way that smoking is viewed in patients with Crohn's disease – their management should be mandatory in any therapeutic approach.

Treatment

Management of functional symptoms in IBD patients' needs to be individualised. Treatment of a patient having ongoing gut symptoms despite endoscopic remission primarily consists of excluding ongoing inflammation by using non-invasive tests with a high negative predictive value, such as faecal calprotectin. In the instance of an elevated level, stepping-up anti-inflammatory medications would be the obvious treatment option. However, if the symptoms appear to be out-of-step with the degree of inflammation present, or if the faecal calprotectin is normal or in the equivocal range, attention to other differentials, such as celiac disease, pancreatic insufficiency, small intestinal bacterial overgrowth or bile salt malabsorption, ought to be considered by specific tests (celiac serology, faecal elastase-1) or by therapeutic trials (pancreatic enzyme replacement, antibiotics or cholestyramine). Functional gut symptoms should be actively managed, but there

IBS and psychological implications   89

is a dearth of controlled trials specifically addressing the question of treating IBS symptoms in IBD patients to guide the choice of therapeutic approach.

A multifaceted, biopsychosocial approach would be advisable (Mikocka-Walus *et al.* 2012), as per the literature for managing IBS patients (Gibson 2012). This may include:

- Harnessing the placebo. The counselling and physician's skills of listening, explaining and reassuring, with appropriate attention to psychosocial issues is a key to successful management.
- Specific dietary measures. Dietary interventions form part of first-line management with the expert assistance of an experienced dietician in some parts of the world. This is largely related to the provision of high quality evidence for the efficacy of restricting poorly absorbed short-chain carbohydrates (FODMAP) (Gibson *et al.* 2013; Halmos *et al.* 2014; Muir and Gibson 2013). There is also some evidence for efficacy of the low FODMAP diet in patients with IBD (Grover *et al.* 2009) (see also Chapter 14). Hypolactasia is common in patients with ulcerative colitis. Fructose malabsorption, as defined by a positive breath hydrogen test after challenge with 35 g fructose, is very common in patients with Crohn's disease, especially involving the terminal ileum (Barrett 2013).
- Pharmacotherapy. Antidepressants may have outcome benefit in patients with IBD as they do in IBS (Chao and Zhang 2013). The use of symptom-directed pharmacotherapy has received little quality attention in patients with IBD-IBS, but the use of therapy to reduce diarrhoea (e.g. loperamide) is commonly used, and to treat constipation in patients with distal ulcerative colitis in remission (e.g. iso-osmotic laxatives) is not an unreasonable option.
- Specific psychological measures. There is now increasing evidence that specific psychological therapies such as cognitive behaviour therapy or gut-directed hypnotherapy (Gerson *et al.* 2013) may be of therapeutic benefit in patients with IBS. Their specific application in patients with IBD-IBS has not been reported. However, patients with IBD and chronic pain have poor coping skills and heightened catastrophisation (Morrison *et al.* 2013) both potentially amenable to cognitive behavioural therapy (see Chapter 20).

Thus, judicious escalation of anti-inflammatory therapy where evidence for clinically significant gut inflammation is present, combined with interventions utilised in patients with pure IBS are warranted in patients with IBD-IBS. Good quality interventional trials are needed to better guide therapy in this challenging group of patients.

Current limitations and future considerations

- At present, functional symptoms in IBD patients in remission are attributed to the coexistence of IBS. Some recent studies have highlighted the presence of occult inflammation in such patients by elevated levels of faecal calprotectin, thus dismissing the presence of IBS as a distinct co-entity with IBD. Further controlled studies are required to assess the degree by which continued low-grade inflammation contributes to functional symptoms in IBD patients. In particular, the efficacy of resolution of that inflammation using more aggressive anti-inflammatory therapy is warranted

- Neuroinflammation may play a salient role in understanding the pathophysiology of functional symptoms in IBD patients. Further mechanistic studies would be required to potentially identify therapeutic targets
- There is no current serum or faecal biochemical marker to diagnose or differentiate IBS from IBD
- The efficacy of specific therapies for IBS, including dietary and psychological therapies, in patients with IBD-IBS requires elucidation to permit their rational integration into routine practice

Practical recommendations

- Evidence-based strategies for IBS should be adopted in patients with IBD in remission who have apparent functional gastrointestinal symptoms. In the presence of positive objective markers for inflammation, escalation of anti-inflammatory medications is advisable
- The biopsychosocial model is a useful approach to managing functional symptoms – it is particularly important to assess for a psychological component and remember to use a multi-disciplinary approach (such as physician, psychologist, dietician)
- A trial of low FODMAP diet should be given to IBD patients with the aid of a dedicated dietician who has expertise in this area
- As no current guidelines on the management of these patients exist, it is reasonable to follow existing high-quality evidence for IBS

Learning points

- The priority in investigation of IBS-like symptoms in IBD patients is exclusion of ongoing inflammation with the aid of a faecal calprotectin
- The pathophysiology of functional symptoms in IBD patients is multifactorial consisting of dysmotility, occult mucosal inflammation, neuroinflammation and strong psychological associations
- A trial of a low-FODMAP diet has been shown to benefit these patients. A biopsychosocial model in management of such symptoms is advisable

References

Aguas, M, Garrigues, V, Bastida, G, Nos, P, Ortiz, V, Fernandez, A and Ponce, J (2011). Prevalence of irritable bowel syndrome (IBS) in first-degree relatives of patients with inflammatory bowel disease (IBD). *J Crohns Colitis*, vol. 5, no. 3, pp. 227–33.

IBS and psychological implications 91

Barrett, JS (2013). Extending our knowledge of fermentable, short-chain carbohydrates for managing gastrointestinal symptoms. *Nutr Clin Pract*, vol. 28, no. 3, pp. 300–6.

Berrill, JW, Green, JT, Hood, K and Campbell, AK (2013). Symptoms of irritable bowel syndrome in patients with inflammatory bowel disease: examining the role of sub-clinical inflammation and the impact on clinical assessment of disease activity. *Aliment Pharmacol Ther*, vol. 38, no. 1, pp. 44–51.

Chao, GQ and Zhang, S (2013). A meta-analysis of the therapeutic effects of amitriptyline for treating irritable bowel syndrome. *Intern Med*, vol. 52, no. 4, pp. 419–24.

Gerson, CD, Gerson, J and Gerson, MJ (2013). Group hypnotherapy for irritable bowel syndrome with long-term follow-up. *Int J Clin Exp Hypn*, vol. 61, no. 1, pp. 38–54.

Ghia, JE, Blennerhassett, P, Deng, Y, Verdu, EF, Khan, WI and Collins, SM (2009). Reactivation of inflammatory bowel disease in a mouse model of depression. *Gastroenterology*, vol. 136, no. 7, pp. 2280–8.e1–4.

Gibson, PR (2012). How to treat: irritable bowel syndrome. *Australian Doctor* vol. 133, pp. 27–41.

Gibson, PR, Barrett, JS and Muir, JG (2013). Functional bowel symptoms and diet. *Intern Med J*, vol. 43, no. 10, pp. 1067–74.

Grover, M, Herfarth, H and Drossman, DA (2009). The functional-organic dichotomy: postinfectious irritable bowel syndrome and inflammatory bowel disease-irritable bowel syndrome. *Clin Gastroenterol Hepatol*, vol. 7, no. 1, pp. 48–53.

Halmos, EP, Power, VA, Shepherd, SJ, Gibson, PR and Muir, JG (2014). A diet low in FODMAPs reduces symptoms of irritable bowel syndrome. *Gastroenterology*, vol. 146, no. 1, pp. 67–75.e5.

Halpin, SJ and Ford, AC (2012). Prevalence of symptoms meeting criteria for irritable bowel syndrome in inflammatory bowel disease: systematic review and meta-analysis. *Am J Gastroenterol*, vol. 107, no. 10, pp. 1474–82.

Jonefjäll, B, Strid, H, Ohman, L, Svedlund, J, Bergstedt, A and Simren, M (2013). Characterization of IBS-like symptoms in patients with ulcerative colitis in clinical remission. *Neurogastroenterol Motil*, vol. 25, no. 9, pp. 756–e578.

Kessler, RC, Merikangas, KR, Berglund, P, Eaton, WW, Koretz, DS and Walters, EE (2003). Mild disorders should not be eliminated from the DSM-V. *Arch Gen Psychiatry*, vol. 60, no. 11, pp. 1117–22.

Long, MD and Drossman, DA (2010). Inflammatory bowel disease, irritable bowel syndrome, or what?: A challenge to the functional-organic dichotomy. *Am J Gastroenterol*, vol. 105, no. 8, pp. 1796–8.

Mikocka-Walus, AA, Gordon, AL, Stewart, BJ and Andrews, JM (2012). The role of antidepressants in the management of inflammatory bowel disease (IBD): a short report on a clinical case-note audit. *J Psychosom Res*, vol. 72, no. 2, pp. 165–7.

Morrison, G, Van Langenberg, DR, Gibson, SJ and Gibson, PR (2013). Chronic pain in inflammatory bowel disease: characteristics and associations of a hospital-based cohort. *Inflamm Bowel Dis*, vol. 19, no. 6, pp. 1210–7.

Muir, JG and Gibson, PR (2013). The low FODMAP diet for treatment of irritable bowel syndrome and other gastrointestinal disorders. *Gastroenterol Hepatol (N Y)*, vol. 9, no. 7, pp. 450–2.

Simren, M, Axelsson, J, Gillberg, R, Abrahamsson, H, Svedlund, J and Bjornsson, ES (2002). Quality of life in inflammatory bowel disease in remission: the impact of IBS-like symptoms and associated psychological factors. *Am J Gastroenterol*, vol. 97, no. 2, pp. 389–96.

Sydora, MJ, Sydora, BC and Fedorak, RN (2012). Validation of a point-of-care desk top device to quantitate fecal calprotectin and distinguish inflammatory bowel disease from irritable bowel syndrome. *J Crohns Colitis*, vol. 6, no. 2, pp. 207–14.

Taylor, CT and Keely, SJ (2007). The autonomic nervous system and inflammatory bowel disease. *Auton Neurosci*, vol. 133, no. 1, pp. 104–14.

Vivinus-Nébot, M, Frin-Mathy, G, Bzioueche, H, Dainese, R, Bernard, G, Anty, R, Filippi, J, Saint-Paul, MC, Tulic, MK, Verhasselt, V, Hébuterne, X and Piche, T (2014). Functional bowel symptoms in quiescent inflammatory bowel diseases: role of epithelial barrier disruption and low-grade inflammation. *Gut*, vol. 63, no. 5, pp. 744–52.

Voganatsi, A, Panyutich, A, Miyasaki, KT and Murthy, RK (2001). Mechanism of extracellular release of human neutrophil calprotectin complex. *J Leukoc Biol*, vol. 70, no. 1, pp. 130–4.

Walker, JR, Ediger, JP, Graff, LA, Greenfeld, JM, Clara, I, Lix, L, Rawsthorne, P, Miller, N, Rogala, L, McPhail, CM and Bernstein, CN (2008). The Manitoba IBD cohort study: a population-based study of the prevalence of lifetime and 12-month anxiety and mood disorders. *Am J Gastroenterol*, vol. 103, no. 8, pp. 1989–97.

Wilson, S, Roberts, L, Roalfe, A, Bridge, P and Singh, S (2004). Prevalence of irritable bowel syndrome: a community survey. *Br J Gen Pract*, vol. 54, no. 504, pp. 495–502.

Chapter 11

IBD, cancer, and its psychosocial impact

Simon R. Knowles and Finlay A. Macrae

Introduction

A recent study involving 271 inflammatory bowel disease (IBD) patents indicated that within the first 2 months of diagnosis, 78 per cent identified attaining information about the risk of developing cancer as 'very important'. However 73 per cent of this cohort identified receiving 'none or little' information about cancer and cancer risk associated with IBD, and only 8 per cent of patients perceived receiving the 'right' amount of information (Wong *et al.* 2012). Even after 10 years of diagnosis, 53 per cent of the cohort identified that they had not received or attained helpful information in relation to the risk of developing cancer associated with IBD (Wong *et al.* 2012). This chapter will review the rates of cancer and mortality associated with IBD, predictive and protective factors associated with cancer in IBD, and the psychosocial distress and common psychosocial concerns raised by individuals, partners and family members in relation to cancer and IBD.

Cancer and mortality in IBD

Hutfless *et al.* (2007) evaluated rates of mortality in a large US IBD cohort between 1996–2003 and found that patients with IBD had a 20 per cent increased rate of mortality compared to the general population. Standardized mortality ratio in Crohn's disease (CD) cohorts due to cancer were due to small intestinal cancer 48.1 [95 per cent confidence interval (CI) 5.8–17.4], colorectal cancer 1.9 (95 per cent CI 0.9–3.7), lymphatic and hematopoietic cancer 1.0 (95 per cent CI 0.3–2.3), and other neoplasms 0.9 (95 per cent CI 0.7–1.3). Mortality in ulcerative colitis (UC) cohorts due to cancer were due to colorectal cancer 1.6 (95 per cent CI 0.9–2.8), neoplasms 0.9 (95 per cent CI 0.7–1.2), and lymphatic and hematopoietic cancer 0.8 (95 per cent CI 0.3–1.6).

Based on a series of meta-analyses of six population-based CD cohorts, Jess *et al.* (2005) reported that the overall risk, measured using a standardized incidence ratio (SIR), of developing colorectal cancer (CRC) was 1.9 (95 per cent CI 1.4–2.5). Further analyses by Jess *et al.* (2005) using four studies identified that the risk of colon cancer and rectal cancer was 2.5 (95 per cent CI 1.7–3.5) and

1.4 (95 per cent CI 0.8–2.6), respectively. SIR risk of small bowel cancer was found to be 27.1 (95 per cent CI 14.9–49.2) based on five population-based cohort studies.

Eaden *et al.* (2001) explored the risk of CRC in UC patients using a total of 116 studies ($n = 54,748$ patients). The pooled prevalence estimate of any patient with UC having CRC was 3.7 per cent (95 per cent CI 3.2–4.2) and while non-significant, incidence rates increased with disease duration: 2 per cent by 10 years, 8 per cent by 20 years, and 18 per cent by 30 years. Eaden *et al.* (2001) also identified that there were geographical differences, with higher CRC rates found in the US and UK (5 and 4/1,000 person years duration respectively) versus Scandinavia, Iran, Israel, Oman, Czechoslovakia, and Turkey (2/1,000 person years duration).

Predictive factors associated with cancer in IBD

Multiple risk factors have been identified for cancer development in IBD cohorts. These include a long history of colitis, extensive colonic involvement, severity of inflammation, primary sclerosing cholangitis (PSC), evidence of previous dysplasia, a family history of CRC, colonic strictures (UC only), having a shortened colon, and/or multiple post-inflammatory pseudopolyps, inadequate IBD pharmacological therapy, inadequate surveillance, folate deficiency and non-smoking (Farraye *et al.* 2010; Itzkowitz *et al.* 2005; Pohl *et al.* 2000; Rutter *et al.* 2004; Triantafillidis *et al.* 2009). Several other risk factors have also been identified although the evidence is based on only a limited number of studies or has been conflicting; these include earlier age of diagnosis/onset and backwash ileitis (Itzkowitz and Harpaz 2004).

Despite the lack of randomised controlled studies, the American Gastroenterology Association position statement recommends that surveillance begins when there is either an 8-year history of IBD or evidence of PSC (Farraye *et al.* 2010). Surveillance examination should occur every 1–3 years and involve a careful inspection of the colorectal mucosa with extensive biopsies of all anatomic segments (Farraye *et al.* 2010). Chromoendoscopy has more recently been shown to be equivalent if not better than extensive (>32) biopsies (Marion *et al.* 2008; Repici *et al.* 2012).

Protective factors associated with cancer in IBD

Several protective factors have been identified to reduce the risk of cancer, specifically CRC in IBD cohorts. These include compliance with cancer surveillance guidelines, compliance with IBD treatment and folic acid use in patients with PSC (Mattar *et al.* 2011). Engaging in positive-health related behaviours such as having a healthy diet (Yusof *et al.* 2012) and exercise (Quadrilatero and Hoffman-Goetz 2003) are also recommended. Other suggested chemoprevention strategies include the administration of ursodeoxycholic acid, and possibly statins and

NSAIDs, although further research is needed (Dube *et al.* 2007; Rostom *et al.* 2007; Triantafillidis *et al.* 2009; Velayos *et al.* 2006). Although smoking may act as an anti-inflammatory, and in-turn lower the risk of CRC (Velayos *et al.* 2006), it is not recommended due to its recognised adverse impact on human health. NSAIDs can also trigger exacerbations of IBD (Ananthakrishnan 2013). A growing body of research indicates that ongoing 5-ASA use may reduce the risk of colorectal cancer by reducing inflammation via several molecular pathways, although this is not fully understood (Cheng and Desreumaux 2005; Lopez and Peyrin-Biroulet 2013; Lyakhovich and Gasche 2010; Munkholm *et al.* 2006).

IBD medication and mortality

In a nested case control study involving 387 CD and 355 UC patients, Long *et al.* (2010) explored the risk of non-melanoma skin cancer (NMSC) (per 100,000 person-years) compared to matched non-IBD controls. Results indicated that the risk ratio of NMSC was slightly higher in IBD patients compared to controls (1.64; 95 per cent, CI: 1.51–1.78). Adjusted odds ratio for NMSC for recent thiopurine or biologic use (≤90 days) were 3.56 (95 per cent, CI: 2.81–4.50) and 2.07 (95 per cent, CI: 1.28–3.33), respectively. Persistent thiopurine or biologic use (>365 days) adjusted odds ratio for NMSC were 4.27 (95 per cent, CI: 3.08–5.92) and 2.18 (95 per cent, CI: 1.07–4.46), respectively.

Beaugerie *et al.* (2009) conducted a large cohort observational study ($n = 19,486$; followed for a total of 49,713 person-years) and identified only 23 cases of lymphoma, with 17 of these associated with thiopurine exposure (indicating a risk ratio of 1:1,146 patients with IBD and being treated with thiopurine exposure versus 1:3248 risk in patient with IBD and thiopurine naive). Incidence rates of lymphoproliferative disorder in patents who never received thiopurines, received thiopurines, and who discontinued its use in patient years were 0.26/1,000 (0.10–0.57), 0.90 per 1,000 (95 per cent CI 0.50–1.49), 0.20/1,000 (0.02–0.72), respectively.

Siegel *et al.* (2009) conducted a meta-analysis exploring the risk of lymphoma associated with combination anti-tumour necrosis factor (TNF) and immuno-modulator therapy for the treatment of Crohn's disease. Based on 26 studies involving 8,905 patients with 21,178 patient-years of follow-up, the total number of cases of non-Hodgkin's lymphoma was 6.1 per 10,000 patient-years, compared to a baseline of 1.9 per 10,000 patient-years.

As concluded by Mason and Siegel (2013), the outlined studies provide evidence that while combination therapy (immunomodulator and anti-TNF) may increase NMSC and lymphoma, the absolute incidence rates are low. In practice, patients will naturally be concerned about any increased risk; however, they should be counselled to understand how these risk rates compare to the known risk rates of developing cancer. For example, in Australia, the risk of colorectal cancer is 1 in 10 for males, by aged 85 years, and 1 in 15 for females, orders of magnitude more than the treatment related risks in IBD (Cancer Council Australia 2014).

Psychosocial distress and the common psychosocial concerns raised by individuals, partners and family members in relation to cancer and IBD

Despite IBD being associated with an increased risk of cancer, particularly CRC, there has been limited research exploring the prevalence and forms of distress associated with cancer in IBD cohorts. In the only study published to date, Rini *et al.* (2008) explored the levels of CRC-specific distress in 223 IBD patients. Interestingly, they found that 78 per cent of IBD patients reported no CRC-specific distress, 16 per cent reported mild-to-moderate CRC-specific distress, and only 6 per cent reported severe CRC-specific distress as measured by a modified version of the Impact of Events Scale (Horowitz *et al.* 1979). Further analysis indicated that the level of distress was not related to years since diagnosed, generalised distress, partial or complete removal of colon, or social support. Having a first-degree history of CRC and/or second-degree or more distant relatives with a history of CRC was found to be associated with increased CRC-specific distress. Based on these findings, Rini *et al.* (2008) concluded that while IBD cohorts are at a greater risk of CRC, they actually have low levels of CRC-specific distress. Rini *et al.* (2008) explain this inconsistency between greater risk, but lower concern, as being due to more immediate concerns, such as managing active symptoms or avoiding thoughts associated with CRC-risk when the disease is in a quiescent phase.

In the recent study involving 139 IBD patients, Mountifield *et al.* (2014) compared the differences between a colon cancer surveillance group (56 per cent of sample) versus a control group, who did not meet the surveillance criteria. No significant differences were found across quality of life (as measured by the SF-36), anxiety, depression, curiosity or anger. Further, both groups reported that the lifetime risk of developing CRC was 50 per cent, a significant overestimation of the real relative risk as identified previously. These findings suggest that irrespective of whether patients receive CRC surveillance, perceived risk is still overestimated.

It should be noted that often concerns relating to cancer are not limited to individuals with IBD, but also other individuals who play an integral part in their life, including family and friends – especially when they are caregivers. To date, there are no studies of psycho-oncological interventions addressing cancer risk distress in IBD; however, for patients actually affected with cancer in general, small to medium improvements in emotional distress and quality of life have been seen (Faller *et al.* 2013; Galway *et al.* 2012; Meijer *et al.* 2013; Meijer *et al.* 2011; Shimizu 2013).

From anecdotal clinical practice experience, common cancer-related concerns raised by patients with IBD and their families include the increased risk of developing cancer due to their disease and treatment methods (especially pharmacological therapy) associated with IBD management. At times, patients with IBD are required to make decisions in relation to their disease management that may mean taking a medication known to increase the risk of cancer (e.g. immunomodulators). Given this, it is important that patients themselves have an active role in the decision making relating to their care. In relation to cancer screening, patients should be provided with options of screening and their relative advantages and disadvantages (Winawer *et al.* 2003).

Conclusions

Given that patients with IBD are at a greater risk of developing some malignancies, especially colorectal cancer (CRC), lymphomas and non melanotic skin cancers, identifying effective strategies to manage patient concerns about cancer and enabling protective behaviours to reduce cancer risk in these cohorts (e.g. compliance with treatments, engaging in a healthy lifestyle) are needed. Screening for distress and subsequent referral in subgroups who experience severe cancer risk related stress is needed, and their information and psycho-oncological needs addressed. To date, there is a lack of research exploring the psychosocial impact of cancer risk perception in IBD cohorts and the form of psychosocial interventions that may be of benefit. This is in contrast to the evidence that IBD cohorts themselves indicate that further information and support in this area is needed.

Current limitations and future considerations

- There is a lack of research exploring the concerns and psychosocial impact of cancer risk information, a diagnosis of cancer or ongoing treatment for cancer in IBD cohorts
- IBD clinicians should be alert to identifying subgroups of IBD who experience high levels of cancer-risk related distress and should consider referral to clinical psychology services
- However, there is a lack of research exploring the efficacy of psychosocial interventions to target psychological distress in IBD cohorts at risk of, or with cancer
- Further research is needed to evaluate the cancer risks associated with independent or combined biologic and immunomodulatory medications in both Crohn's disease and ulcerative colitis cohorts, accommodating for underlying IBD disease activity which often confounds studies of drug use and cancer in IBD

Practical recommendations

- Several national bodies produce guidelines in relation to screening for cancer in IBD cohorts (e.g. Cairns *et al.* 2010; Farraye *et al.* 2010). These should be made part of any medical treatment plan for patients with IBD
- Patients should be offered information and advice regarding concerns about the risk of cancer in IBD including associated with IBD therapies. Patients should be provided with options of screening and their relative advantages and disadvantages. The discussion should be balanced in the context of the

efficacy of treatment for IBD, which itself may reduce cancer risk through controlling inflammation, and placed in the context of cancer risks in the general population

- Where cancer develops, National Comprehensive Cancer Network (NCCN) guidelines on distress management provide practical recommendations and procedures for helping manage distress in cancer cohorts (Holland *et al.* 2013)
- Other government and non-government cancer-specific sites can also be helpful. These include The Cancer Council Australia (http://www.cancer.org.au/), and the American Cancer Society (http://www.cancer.org/)
- Patients with IBD should be encouraged to reduce the risk of cancer by complying with agreed IBD treatment, and engaging in a healthy diet and regular exercise
- Upon diagnosis of cancer or as part of ongoing treatment for cancer, patients (and their families) should be screened for psychological distress and offered, where relevant, psychological support

Learning points

- Patients with IBD are at an increased risk of developing cancer, especially colorectal cancer
- Patients should be informed of the relative risks of developing cancer associated with having IBD, its ongoing management, and also provided with strategies that attenuate the risk of cancer (e.g., disease remission, surveillance screening, 5ASA-based medications, exercise, and healthy diet). Risk information, however, should be balanced with information on efficacy of therapy
- Surveillance should occur when there is an 8-year history of IBD and/or evidence of primary sclerosing cholangitis. Surveillance examination should occur every 1–3 years and involve a careful inspection of the colorectal mucosa with extensive biopsies of all anatomic segments or with image enhancing technologies such as chromoendoscopy
- Medications designed to suppress inflammation likely reduce colorectal cancer risk, but some increase the risk of lymphoma (i.e. immunosuppressants)
- Psychological distress should be assessed and managed using interdisciplinary teams

References

Ananthakrishnan, AN (2013). Environmental triggers for inflammatory bowel disease. *Curr Gastroenterol Rep*, vol. 15, no. 1, p. 302.

Beaugerie, L, Brousse, N, Bouvier, AM, Colombel, JF, Lemann, M, Cosnes, J, Hebuterne, X, Cortot, A, Bouhnik, Y, Gendre, JP, Simon, T, Maynadie, M, Hermine, O, Faivre, J, Carrat, F and CESAME Study Group (2009). Lymphoproliferative disorders in patients receiving thiopurines for inflammatory bowel disease: a prospective observational cohort study. *Lancet*, vol. 374, no. 9701, pp. 1617–25.

Cairns, SR, Scholefield, JH, Steele, RJ, Dunlop, MG, Thomas, HJ, Evans, GD, Eaden, JA, Rutter, MD, Atkin, WP, Saunders, BP, Lucassen, A, Jenkins, P, Fairclough, PD, Woodhouse, CR, British Society of Gastroenterology and Association of Coloproctology for Great Britain and Ireland (2010). Guidelines for colorectal cancer screening and surveillance in moderate and high risk groups (update from 2002). *Gut*, vol. 59, no. 5, pp. 666–89.

Cancer Council Australia (2014). Bowel cancer. Available online from www.cancer.org. au/about-cancer/types-of-cancer/bowel-cancer.

Cheng, Y and Desreumaux, P (2005). 5-aminosalicylic acid is an attractive candidate agent for chemoprevention of colon cancer in patients with inflammatory bowel disease. *World J Gastroenterol*, vol. 11, no. 3, pp. 309–14.

Dube, C, Rostom, A, Lewin, G, Tsertsvadze, A, Barrowman, N, Code, C, Sampson, M, Moher, D and US Preventive Services Task Force (2007). The use of aspirin for primary prevention of colorectal cancer: a systematic review prepared for the U.S. Preventive Services Task Force. *Ann Intern Med*, vol. 146, no. 5, pp. 365–75.

Eaden, JA, Abrams, KR and Mayberry, JF (2001). The risk of colorectal cancer in ulcerative colitis: a meta-analysis. *Gut*, vol. 48, no. 4, pp. 526–35.

Faller, H, Schuler, M, Richard, M, Heckl, U, Weis, J and Kuffner, R (2013). Effects of psycho-oncologic interventions on emotional distress and quality of life in adult patients with cancer: systematic review and meta-analysis. *J Clin Oncol*, vol. 31, no. 6, pp. 782–93.

Farraye, FA, Odze, RD, Eaden, J, Itzkowitz, SH, McCabe, RP, Dassopoulos, T, Lewis, JD, Ullman, TA, James, T, 3rd, McLeod, R, Burgart, LJ, Allen, J, Brill, JV and AGA Institute Medical Position Panel on Diagnosis and Management of Colorectal Neoplasia in Inflammatory Bowel Disease (2010). AGA medical position statement on the diagnosis and management of colorectal neoplasia in inflammatory bowel disease. *Gastroenterology*, vol. 138, no. 2, pp. 738–45.

Galway, K, Black, A, Cantwell, M, Cardwell, CR, Mills, M and Donnelly, M (2012). Psychosocial interventions to improve quality of life and emotional wellbeing for recently diagnosed cancer patients. *Cochrane Database Syst Rev*, vol. 11, p. CD007064.

Holland, JC, Andersen, B, Breitbart, WS, Buchmann, LO, Compas, B, Deshields, TL, Dudley, MM, Fleishman, S, Fulcher, CD, Greenberg, DB, Greiner, CB, Handzo, GF, Hoofring, L, Hoover, C, Jacobsen, PB, Kvale, E, Levy, MH, Loscalzo, MJ, McAllister-Black, R, Mechanic, KY, Palesh, O, Pazar, JP, Riba, MB, Roper, K, Valentine, AD, Wagner, LI, Zevon, MA, McMillian, NR and Freedman-Cass, DA (2013). Distress management. *J Natl Compr Canc Netw*, vol. 11, no. 2, pp. 190–209.

Horowitz, M, Wilner, N and Alvarez, W (1979). Impact of Event Scale: a measure of subjective stress. *Psychosom Med*, vol. 41, no. 3, pp. 209–18.

Hutfless, SM, Weng, X, Liu, L, Allison, J and Herrinton, LJ (2007). Mortality by medication use among patients with inflammatory bowel disease, 1996–2003. *Gastroenterology*, vol. 133, no. 6, pp. 1779–86.

Itzkowitz, SH and Harpaz, N (2004). Diagnosis and management of dysplasia in patients with inflammatory bowel diseases. *Gastroenterology*, vol. 126, no. 6, pp. 1634–48.

Itzkowitz, SH, Present, DH and Crohn's and Colitis Foundation of America Colon Cancer in IBD Study Group (2005). Consensus conference: colorectal cancer screening and surveillance in inflammatory bowel disease. *Inflamm Bowel Dis*, vol. 11, no. 3, pp. 314–21.

Jess, T, Gamborg, M, Matzen, P, Munkholm, P and Sorensen, TI (2005). Increased risk of intestinal cancer in Crohn's disease: a meta-analysis of population-based cohort studies. *Am J Gastroenterol*, vol. 100, no. 12, pp. 2724–9.

Long, MD, Herfarth, HH, Pipkin, CA, Porter, CQ, Sandler, RS and Kappelman, MD (2010). Increased risk for non-melanoma skin cancer in patients with inflammatory bowel disease. *Clin Gastroenterol Hepatol*, vol. 8, no. 3, pp. 268–74.

Lopez, A and Peyrin-Biroulet, L (2013). 5-Aminosalicylic acid and chemoprevention: does it work? *Dig Dis*, vol. 31, no. 2, pp. 248–53.

Lyakhovich, A and Gasche, C (2010). Systematic review: molecular chemoprevention of colorectal malignancy by mesalazine. *Aliment Pharmacol Ther*, vol. 31, no. 2, pp. 202–9.

Marion, JF, Waye, JD, Present, DH, Israel, Y, Bodian, C, Harpaz, N, Chapman, M, Itzkowitz, S, Steinlauf, AF, Abreu, MT, Ullman, TA, Aisenberg, J, Mayer, L and Chromoendoscopy Study Group at Mount Sinai School of Medicine (2008). Chromoendoscopy-targeted biopsies are superior to standard colonoscopic surveillance for detecting dysplasia in inflammatory bowel disease patients: a prospective endoscopic trial. *Am J Gastroenterol*, vol. 103, no. 9, pp. 2342–9.

Mason, M and Siegel, CA (2013). Do inflammatory bowel disease therapies cause cancer? *Inflamm Bowel Dis*, vol. 19, no. 6, pp. 1306–21.

Mattar, MC, Lough, D, Pishvaian, MJ and Charabaty, A (2011). Current management of inflammatory bowel disease and colorectal cancer. *Gastrointest Cancer Res*, vol. 4, no. 2, pp. 53–61.

Meijer, A, Roseman, M, Delisle, VC, Milette, K, Levis, B, Syamchandra, A, Stefanek, ME, Stewart, DE, de Jonge, P, Coyne, JC and Thombs, BD (2013). Effects of screening for psychological distress on patient outcomes in cancer: a systematic review. *J Psychosom Res*, vol. 75, no. 1, pp. 1–17.

Meijer, A, Roseman, M, Milette, K, Coyne, JC, Stefanek, ME, Ziegelstein, RC, Arthurs, E, Leavens, A, Palmer, SC, Stewart, DE, de Jonge, P and Thombs, BD (2011). Depression screening and patient outcomes in cancer: a systematic review. *PLoS ONE*, vol. 6, no. 11, p. e27181.

Mountifield, R, Bampton, P, Prosser, R, Mikocka-Walus, A and Andrews, JM (2014). Colon cancer surveillance in inflammatory bowel disease: unclear gain but no psychological pain? *Intern Med J*, vol. 44, no. 2, pp. 131–8.

Munkholm, P, Loftus, EV, Jr., Reinacher-Schick, A, Kornbluth, A, Mittmann, U and Esendal, B (2006). Prevention of colorectal cancer in inflammatory bowel disease: value of screening and 5-aminosalicylates. *Digestion*, vol. 73, no. 1, pp. 11–9.

Pohl, C, Hombach, A and Kruis, W (2000). Chronic inflammatory bowel disease and cancer. *Hepatogastroenterology*, vol. 47, no. 31, pp. 57–70.

Quadrilatero, J and Hoffman-Goetz, L (2003). Physical activity and colon cancer. A systematic review of potential mechanisms. *J Sports Med Phys Fitness*, vol. 43, no. 2, pp. 121–38.

Repici, A, Laterra, MA, Cisaro, F, Pellicano, R, Fini, L and Ishaq, S (2012). Unveiling cancer in IBD: screening colonoscopy or chromoendoscopy. *Curr Drug Targets*, vol. 13, no. 10, pp. 1268–72.

Rini, C, Jandorf, L, Valdimarsdottir, H, Brown, K and Itzkowitz, SH (2008). Distress among inflammatory bowel disease patients at high risk for colorectal cancer: a preliminary investigation of the effects of family history of cancer, disease duration, and perceived social support. *Psycho-Oncology*, vol. 17, no. 4, pp. 354–62.

Rostom, A, Dube, C and Lewin, G (2007). *Use of Aspirin and NSAIDs to Prevent Colorectal Cancer*. Rockville: Agency for Healthcare Research and Quality (US), Report No.: 07-0596-EF-1. Available online at www.ncbi.nlm.nih.gov/pubmed/20722142.

Rutter, MD, Saunders, BP, Wilkinson, KH, Rumbles, S, Schofield, G, Kamm, MA, Williams, CB, Price, AB, Talbot, IC and Forbes, A (2004). Cancer surveillance in long-standing ulcerative colitis: endoscopic appearances help predict cancer risk. *Gut*, vol. 53, no. 12, pp. 1813–6.

Shimizu, K (2013). Effects of integrated psychosocial care for distress in cancer patients. *Jpn J Clin Oncol*, vol. 43, no. 5, pp. 451–7.

Siegel, CA, Marden, SM, Persing, SM, Larson, RJ and Sands, BE (2009). Risk of lymphoma associated with combination anti-tumor necrosis factor and immunomodulator therapy for the treatment of Crohn's disease: a meta-analysis. *Clin Gastroenterol Hepatol*, vol. 7, no. 8, pp. 874–81.

Triantafillidis, JK, Nasioulas, G and Kosmidis, PA (2009). Colorectal cancer and inflammatory bowel disease: epidemiology, risk factors, mechanisms of carcinogenesis and prevention strategies. *Anticancer Res*, vol. 29, no. 7, pp. 2727–37.

Velayos, FS, Loftus, EV, Jr., Jess, T, Harmsen, WS, Bida, J, Zinsmeister, AR, Tremaine, WJ and Sandborn, WJ (2006). Predictive and protective factors associated with colorectal cancer in ulcerative colitis: a case-control study. *Gastroenterology*, vol. 130, no. 7, pp. 1941–9.

Winawer, S, Fletcher, R, Rex, D, Bond, J, Burt, R, Ferrucci, J, Ganiats, T, Levin, T, Woolf, S, Johnson, D, Kirk, L, Litin, S, Simmang, C and Gastrointestinal Consortium Panel (2003). Colorectal cancer screening and surveillance: clinical guidelines and rationale—update based on new evidence. *Gastroenterology*, vol. 124, no. 2, pp. 544–60.

Wong, S, Walker, JR, Carr, R, Graff, LA, Clara, I, Promislow, S, Rogala, L, Miller, N, Rawsthorne, P and Bernstein, CN (2012). The information needs and preferences of persons with longstanding inflammatory bowel disease. *Can J Gastroenterol*, vol. 26, no. 8, pp. 525–31.

Yusof, AS, Isa, ZM and Shah, SA (2012). Dietary patterns and risk of colorectal cancer: a systematic review of cohort studies (2000–2011). *Asian Pac J Cancer Prev*, vol. 13, no. 9, pp. 4713–7.

Chapter 12

Patients and IBD surgery
Rightful fears and preconceptions

Antonino Spinelli and Francesco Pagnini

Introduction

While people with inflammatory bowel disease (IBD) have normal life expectancy when adequately treated (van der Eijk *et al.* 2000), quality of life (QoL) may be significantly poorer than in the general population, in both the physical and psychological meaning (Keefer *et al.* 2012). Common IBD symptoms such as diarrhea, constipation, bloating, abdominal and perianal discomfort or pain, ulcers, and bleeding may lead to significant psychosocial impairment. Ulcerative colitis (UC) and Crohn's disease (CD) share symptoms, however, people who suffer from CD report more disease-related concerns and psychological distress and lower levels of QoL (Vogelaar *et al.* 2009).

Surgery may provide a permanent cure in case of UC and a way to effectively induce remission in CD. The intervention can reduce or eliminate the need for ongoing medication and intensive medical follow-up in most UC patients, while patients affected by CD can experience a significant improvement in their QoL. However, despite generally positive outcomes of surgery, people with IBD often perceive surgical intervention as the end of the road, the failure of their therapy. For various reasons, surgery is sometimes perceived with extreme discomfort by patients, convinced that their goal is to try to avoid it at all costs (Muller *et al.* 2010). Most people focus their attention on potential risks of complications or side effects of surgery, but appear to be much less concerned by the side effects of medications, even when they are not negligible. This attitude may prevent or delay the achievement of a long-term symptom relief. People's attitudes may also play an important role during post-operative recovery (Langer *et al.* 1975).

On both clinical and psychological sides, the decision to proceed with surgery is highly important for IBD patients as it will impact their overall QoL. Decision making should ideally be a collaborative effort between the patient and their managing gastroenterologist and surgeon (Siegel 2009). With the exclusion of emergency conditions, caused by complications of the disease, there is often enough time to take an aware and mindful decision. This decision-making process may sometimes benefit from the assistance of a psychologist that may help the patient in exploring possible psychological issues and fears around surgery.

Positive outcomes in patient's wellbeing are often associated with mindful decisions preceding surgery, which are sensitive of patient's attitudes and the information received (Phillips and Pagnini 2014). The latter are influenced by the relationship with the physician. Effective physicians' interpersonal and communication competencies, such as the ability to perceive, use, understand, and manage emotions (Pagnini *et al.* 2009), are often underestimated as predictive factors in a positive clinical outcome after surgery and mastering them should be promoted. Sometimes it is not easy for the physician to completely understand the subjective experience of their patients (Kane *et al.* 2008). For example, previous studies indicated that gastroenterologists tend to underestimate occurrence and impact of IBD on the daily life of patients (Rubin *et al.* 2009), namely resulting physical and functional impairments as well as psychological aspects (Calkins *et al.* 1991; Stephens *et al.* 1997). Even when discussing surgery, which probably represents the most biologically grounded intervention in the era of biological medicine, psychological and relational issues can influence the outcomes. Therefore, considering the surgical operation as a mechanical procedure only, without relational and psychological components, would lead to a lower success rate. Clinicians and surgeons should be aware of patients' expectations and fears, be able to take them into account, and should then be prompted to help patients cope with them. This chapter explores the psychological impact of surgery in the hope of alerting clinicians to the importance of psychological variables in surgery-related decision-making.

Fears and beliefs

Surgical intervention is one of the main fears of those who receive a diagnosis of IBD (Irvine 2004). It is often perceived as a sword of Damocles hanging over their head, and thus, something highly undesirable. It is also often perceived as the "end of the road" where all other avenues for treatment have failed. Common beliefs that surround this fear deal with the lack of control, the post-operative pain, possible complications, and consequences to the body image. Most of these fears have roots in the reality, referring to real risks. For example, one of the highest rated concerns of people with IBD is requiring an ostomy bag (Jelsness-Jørgensen *et al.* 2011). However, sometimes people tend to unnecessarily exaggerate the risk, developing severe anxiety. In fact, anxiety related to the surgical intervention is not uncommon in the general population. People with an already-existing anxiety disorder may be more prone to surgical anxiety and fear than the average person. Nonetheless, many patients first experience it when preparing for surgery. Reasons for anxiety vary from fear of the unknown to having a bad experience with previous surgeries (Keefer *et al.* 2012).

Among IBD patients, the hospitalization itself is associated with a significant risk for depression and anxiety, even in the absence of foreseen surgery (Ananthakrishnan *et al.* 2013). Being hospitalized represents an important event for people with IBD, as it is full of mental representations, fantasies, expectations, and worries. Physicians and care operators should be aware of the possible psychological implications of the hospitalization, dealing with a chronic condition that is highly responsive to stress (Maunder and Levenstein 2008).

One of the main fears related to surgery is lack of control over what will happen during the operation. While under anesthesia, patients are not aware of what is being done to them. Many people become nervous just imagining this situation (Pritchard 2009). Even if the control during the intervention is in most cases not obtainable, a common way to cope with this issue is the improvement of knowledge about the intervention and its implications. Previous findings indicate that patients' concerns were strongly correlated with their information level about the illness (Velanovich 2000) and the treatment (Räsänen *et al.* 2001).

Learning about the treatment and its effects has a positive influence on patients' levels of anxiety and fear, by projecting into the future, when the benefits of the surgery will improve the person's QoL. Informed patients report a better psychological wellbeing and are actively motivated to do everything they can that can improve the outcome (Weinstein *et al.* 2007).

Quality of life outcomes after surgery

Although life expectancy of people with IBD approximates that of the general population, the illness may substantially impair QoL (Casellas *et al.* 2002). QoL has been defined as "a broad ranging concept affected in a complex way by the person's physical health, psychological state, level of independence, social relationships, personal beliefs and their relationship to salient features of their environment" (WHOQOL Group 1998, p. 1570). The decision to undergo surgery is commonly an attempt to improve QoL impaired by IBD. The impact of surgical intervention does not only affect the body, but extends to the mind level, impacting on psychological wellbeing.

Previous studies have indicated that overall QoL tends to improve after surgery (Blondel-Kucharski *et al.* 2001). There are, however, variations in the pattern of convalescence in the 3–6 months after intervention. While, in general, there is a positive effect of the overall wellbeing right after surgery, sometimes the post-operative period may be characterized by a reduction of QoL. However, even if recent surgery might temporarily decrease QOL in the immediate postoperative period, it thereafter rapidly improves over the following months (Blondel-Kucharski *et al.* 2001). In fact, long-term analyses indicate that after 12 months, the QOL is comparable with that of the general population (Ko *et al.* 2001).

The clinical experience, supported by the literature, suggests that there are differences in the pattern of recovery, which should be taken into account according to an idiographic approach, with a strong commitment to the individual patient. This approach tests rather than assumes that each individual will have similar characteristics. For example, whereas the experience of discomfort and loss of vitality may vanish soon after successful surgery, bowel problems and sexual activity may be restored more slowly.

While surgery itself leads most of the time to a positive QoL outcome, the installation of a stoma may cause a stressful and depressive effect. Right after surgery, the stoma affects a patient's lifestyle considerably. There are physical and psychological changes in the body image that may lead to a lack of self-confidence and, sometimes, to social isolation. Moreover, there may be a reduction of personal hygiene associated with stoma-related complications such as leakage, ballooning of bags, and skin rashes (Nugent *et al.* 1999). However, as well as for other surgical patients, *time heals all wounds*, as there is a positive adaptation to the stoma through time, leading to a "normal" QoL (Silva *et al.* 2003). Preoperative counseling, a positive patient-physician relationship, and close contact with a stoma nurse during the postoperative period, as well as a postoperative counseling, if needed, can significantly accelerate recovery (El-Tawil and Nightingale 2013).

One of the most reported problems after surgery that affects QoL is the suppression of sexual desires. That happens after many surgical operations (Irani and Lowry 2011) and is sometimes related to the change in body image, the interference of the eventual stoma and its appliance during sexual intercourse (Silva *et al.* 2003). Correct education and counseling may be useful to face this problem, which is often perceived as a taboo. Appropriate interventions addressed to patients and their partners may play a significant role towards better acceptance and coping (El-Tawil and Nightingale 2013).

Anxiety, depression and other psychological variables after surgery

Despite the general improvement in QoL, people with IBD who underwent surgery are at a greater risk of depression and anxiety than the general population (Mikocka-Walus *et al.* 2007). Excluding those who received a diagnosis of depression before surgery, after surgery IBD patients have a 10–15 percent risk of receiving a diagnosis of depression within 5 years, with a similar substantial risk of anxiety (Ananthakrishnan *et al.* 2013). Furthermore, despite surgery for UC being considered curative, a similar risk between CD and UC has been observed with respect to the development of depression or anxiety (Ananthakrishnan *et al.* 2013).

In the latter case, causes of distress include frequent bowel movements that may continue even after an ileal-pouch is installed, including the need for nocturnal bowel movements, which could in turn lead to depressive symptoms (Ananthakrishnan *et al.* 2013). Risk factors for anxiety and depression from epidemiological studies further include fluctuations in disease activity (Ananthakrishnan *et al.* 2013), female gender (Hauser *et al.* 2011), perianal disease (Mahadev *et al.* 2012), and early surgery (Ananthakrishnan *et al.* 2013).

Conclusions

Surgery represents a valid and efficient option for treating IBD in the presence of a correct indication, resulting in a relevant improvement in quality of life, as reported by patients themselves and by most studies. In referral centers the outcomes of surgery have greatly improved over the last 20 years with the introduction of innovations such as minimally invasive surgery and enhanced-recovery protocols; consequently, complication rates have decreased compared to earlier times. Nevertheless, patients' perception of IBD surgery remains generally poor.

Surgery is often perceived as the last resort, the enemy to avoid at all costs, even when medical therapies are becoming clearly ineffective and do not offer acceptable quality of life anymore. This negative perception, even if understandable, has important consequences on the attitude towards surgery. Furthermore, these preconceptions may delay the acceptance of surgery, often resulting in suboptimal management of IBD and delayed timing of the procedure. Delay of surgery is generally associated with a worse general condition and, in many cases, with a more complex disease with a higher risk for complications.

Surgeons, on their side, are sometimes too worried about technical issues, forgetting to answer important questions from their patients. Moreover, surgery planning rarely considers patients' timing requirements regarding studies, work, and family needs. The promotion of the patient's engagement and the cultivation of a positive relationship between the patient and the physician are important for the experience and outcomes of surgery. For that reason, physicians and surgeons should be aware of the possible psychological issues related to the intervention. The healthcare team should be ready to provide adequate support, not limited to biomedical issues.

Current limitations and future considerations

- Studies that investigated psychological variables related to surgery in IBD are mainly cross sectional, with only little longitudinal research available
- Very few papers about psychological interventions around surgery have been found
- Few studies have investigated gastroenterologists' and surgeons' psychological issues with IBD patients or physicians' perspective on the patient-physician relationship in IBD

Practical recommendations

- Physicians should pay particular attention to psychological issues of IBD patients before and after surgery and take into account patients' needs and attitudes, whenever possible, when planning surgery
- It is important to engage patients in discussion from the beginning of the decisional process related to surgery
- Time investment in clear and objective patients' information before surgery could result in better compliance in the perioperative phase, and probably impact (at least on the perception) of the final surgery outcome

Learning points

- Surgery is negatively perceived by IBD patients, despite strong evidence of positive effects on quality of life
- Patients' fears and misconceptions should be addressed by the physicians in the consultation phase
- Patients should be involved in the decision-making process. Physicians should do their best to increase patients' engagement

References

Ananthakrishnan, AN, Gainer, VS, Cai, T, Perez, RG, Cheng, S-C, Savova, G, Chen, P, Szolovits, P, Xia, Z and De Jager, PL (2013). Similar risk of depression and anxiety following surgery or hospitalization for Crohn's disease and ulcerative colitis. *Am J Gastroenterol*, vol. 108, no. 4, pp. 594–601.

Blondel-Kucharski, F, Chircop, C, Marquis, P, Cortot, A, Baron, F, Gendre, JP and Colombel, JF (2001). Health-related quality of life in Crohn's disease: a prospective longitudinal study in 231 patients. *Am J Gastroenterol*, vol. 96, no. 10, pp. 2915–20.

Calkins, DR, Rubenstein, LV, Cleary, PD, Davies, AR, Jette, AM, Fink, A, Kosecoff, J, Young, RT, Brook, RH and Delbanco, TL (1991). Failure of physicians to recognize functional disability in ambulatory patients. *Ann Intern Med*, vol. 114, no. 6, pp. 451–4.

Casellas, F, Lopez-Vivancos, J, Casado, A and Malagelada, JR (2002). Factors affecting health related quality of life of patients with inflammatory bowel disease. *Qual Life Res*, vol. 11, no. 8, pp. 775–81.

El-Tawil, A and Nightingale, P (2013). Living with stoma: long-term effects on patients' quality of life. *J Clin Cell Immunol*, vol. 4, no. 145, p. 2.

Hauser, G, Tkalčić, M, Štimac, D, Milić, S and Mijandrušić Sinčić, B (2011). Gender related differences in quality of life and affective status in patients with inflammatory bowel disease. *Coll Antropol*, vol. 35, no. 2, pp. 203–7.

Irani, JL and Lowry, AC (2011). Postoperative sexual function. *Semin Colon Rectal Surg*, vol. 22, no. 4, pp. 243–8.

Irvine, E (2004). Patients' fears and unmet needs in inflammatory bowel disease. *Aliment Pharmacol Ther*, vol. 20, no. s4, pp. 54–9.

Jelsness-Jørgensen, LP, Moum, B and Bernklev, T (2011). Worries and concerns among inflammatory bowel disease patients followed prospectively over one year. *Gastroenterol Res Pract*, vol. 2011, 492034.

Kane, SV, Loftus Jr, EV, Dubinsky, MC and Sederman, R (2008). Disease perceptions among people with Crohn's disease. *Inflamm Bowel Dis*, vol. 14, no. 8, pp. 1097–101.

Keefer, L, Taft, TH and Kiebles, JL (2012). Gastrointestinal diseases. *Handbook of Psychology*, 2nd edn. Hoboken: John Wiley & Sons.

Ko, CY, Rusin, LC, Schoetz Jr, DJ, Moreau, L, Coller, JC, Murray, JJ, Roberts, PL and Marcello, PW (2001). Long-term outcomes of the ileal pouch anal anastomosis: the association of bowel function and quality of life 5 years after surgery. *J Surg Res*, vol. 98, no. 2, pp. 102–7.

Langer, EJ, Janis, IL and Wolfer, JA (1975). Reduction of psychological stress in surgical patients. *J Exp Soc Psychol*, vol. 11, no. 2, pp. 155–65.

Mahadev, S, Young, JM, Selby, W and Solomon, MJ (2012). Self-reported depressive symptoms and suicidal feelings in perianal Crohn's disease. *Colorectal Dis*, vol. 14, no. 3, pp. 331–5.

Maunder, RG and Levenstein, S (2008). The role of stress in the development and clinical course of inflammatory bowel disease: epidemiological evidence. *Curr Mol Med*, vol. 8, no. 4, pp. 247–52.

Mikocka-Walus, AA, Turnbull, DA, Moulding, NT, Wilson, IG, Andrews, JM and Holtmann, GJ (2007). Controversies surrounding the comorbidity of depression and anxiety in inflammatory bowel disease patients: a literature review. *Inflamm Bowel Dis*, vol. 13, no. 2, pp. 225–34.

Muller, KR, Prosser, R, Bampton, P, Mountifield, R and Andrews, JM (2010). Female gender and surgery impair relationships, body image, and sexuality in inflammatory bowel disease: patient perceptions. *Inflamm Bowel Dis*, vol. 16, no. 4, pp. 657–63.

Nugent, KP, Daniels, P, Stewart, B, Patankar, R and Johnson, CD (1999). Quality of life in stoma patients. *Dis Colon Rectum*, vol. 42, no. 12, pp. 1569–74.

Pagnini, F, Manzoni, GM and Castelnuovo, G (2009). Emotional intelligence training and evaluation in physicians. *JAMA*, vol. 301, no. 6, p. 600; author reply, p. 601.

Phillips, D and Pagnini, F (2014). A mindful approach to chronic illness. In: Le, A, Ngnoumen, CT and Langer, E (eds). *The Wiley-Blackwell Handbook of Mindfulness*. London: Wiley-Blackwell, pp. 852–63.

Pritchard, MJ (2009). Managing anxiety in the elective surgical patient. *Br J Nurs*, vol. 18, no. 7, pp. 416–9.

Räsänen, JV, Niskanen, MM, Miettinen, P, Sintonen, H and Alhava, E (2001). Health-related quality of life before and after gastrointestinal surgery. *Eur J Surg*, vol. 167, no. 6, pp. 419–25.

Rubin, DT, Siegel, CA, Kane, SV, Binion, DG, Panaccione, R, Dubinsky, MC, Loftus, EV and Hopper, J (2009). Impact of ulcerative colitis from patients' and physicians' perspectives: results from the UC: NORMAL survey. *Inflamm Bowel Dis*, vol. 15, no. 4, pp. 581–8.

Siegel, CA (2009). Making therapeutic decisions in IBD: the role of patients. *Curr Opin Gastroenterol*, vol. 25, no. 4, p. 334.

Silva, MA, Ratnayake, G and Deen, KI (2003). Quality of life of stoma patients: temporary ileostomy versus colostomy. *World J Surg*, vol. 27, no. 4, pp. 421–4.

Stephens, R, Hopwood, P, Girling, D and Machin, D (1997). Randomized trials with quality of life endpoints: are doctors' ratings of patients' physical symptoms interchangeable with patients' self-ratings? *Qual Life Res*, vol. 6, no. 3, pp. 225–36.

van der Eijk, I, Stockbrügger, R and Russel, M (2000). Influence of quality of care on quality of life in inflammatory bowel disease (IBD): literature review and studies planned. *Eur J Intern Med*, vol. 11, no. 4, pp. 228–34.

Velanovich, V (2000). Laparoscopic vs open surgery: a preliminary comparison of quality-of-life outcomes. *Surg Endosc*, vol. 14, no. 1, pp. 16–21.

Vogelaar, L, Spijker, AV and van der Woude, CJ (2009). The impact of biologics on health-related quality of life in patients with inflammatory bowel disease. *Clin Exp Gastroenterol*, vol. 2, p. 101–9.

Weinstein, JN, Clay, K and Morgan, TS (2007). Informed patient choice: patient-centered valuing of surgical risks and benefits. *Health Aff (Millwood)*, vol. 26, no. 3, pp. 726–30.

WHOQOL Group (1998). The World Health Organization quality of life assessment (WHOQOL): development and general psychometric properties. *Soc Sci Med*, vol. 46, no. 12, pp. 1569–85.

Chapter 13

Standard medical care, side effects and compliance

Philip Hendy, Yoram Inspector and Ailsa Hart

Introduction

The inflammatory bowel diseases (IBD), ulcerative colitis (UC) and Crohn's disease (CD), are relapsing remitting chronic diseases with no cure. They tend to present in the young, who are faced with lifelong medication and monitoring. The medications in IBD carry a risk of adverse effects. This chapter is divided into two sections. The first addresses the potential psychological impact of IBD medical treatment. The second section explores the effect of psychological factors upon medication adherence, and techniques that the physician may use to improve adherence.

The effects of standard medical care for IBD upon psychological wellbeing

Positive effects

Whilst discussing side effect profiles of IBD medications, and their impact upon psychological wellbeing, it is important to remember that many patients do not suffer from significant side effects, and that the enhanced disease control gained by treatment can lead to dramatic improvements in quality of life (QOL). For example, studies comparing infliximab with placebo show a significant benefit in health related QOL in the treatment group. This benefit is seen in both physical and mental health (Feagan *et al.* 2007). Patients with perianal Crohn's disease also report an enhanced QOL, as measured by improved IBD questionnaire (IBDQ) scores while on anti-TNF drugs (Tozer *et al.* 2012). Steroids have also been show to rapidly and significantly improve IBDQ scores (Irvine *et al.* 2000).

Negative effects

There is an acknowledged negative correlation between IBD and psychological wellbeing, and longstanding debate over whether this is cause or effect (Aberra and Lewis 2013; Ananthakrishnan *et al.* 2013; Sajadinejad *et al.* 2012). Treatment for IBD may contribute to deterioration of usual psychological wellbeing in a number of ways, including physical and psychiatric side effects (Cross *et al.* 2008). Below, the physical, psychiatric and psychological adverse effects of IBD medication have been separated for ease of review, but in clinical practice, they must be considered together (Figure 13.1). Physical symptoms can contribute to psychological distress (Sajadinejad *et al.* 2012), whilst disturbed psychological wellbeing frequently exacerbates disease symptoms and reduces treatment compliance (Cross *et al.* 2008; Goodhand *et al.* 2013).

General psychological sequelae of IBD treatment

Treatment for IBD may disrupt the normal daily routine of the sufferer in a number of unexpected ways. The physician should be mindful of the potential impact on the life of the patient and tailor the treatment plan to the individual. Below are a number of common psychosocial consequences of IBD treatment.

Deviation from social normality

IBD most commonly presents at an early age. The young are particularly keen to observe the social norms of their peer group in order to consolidate their own sense of identity and self-worth. Missed lessons and lectures whilst attending the clinic, radiology, endoscopy and phlebotomy appointments required to monitor treatment mark the young patient out as different. This can impact on their confidence and ability to develop friendships and relationships.

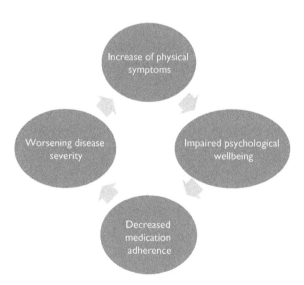

Figure 13.1 The cycle of deteriorating psychological wellbeing, disease activity and medication adherence.

Taking a medication admits poor health

The regular use of medication is a daily reminder of being ill and some patients develop the rationale 'if I'm not taking the medication, then it means that I'm not ill'.

Topical treatment carries social stigma

The use of enemas and suppositories can be efficacious for the treatment of proctitis and left sided disease. Applying rectal therapy carries social stigma and causes patients to feel self-conscious (Frei *et al.* 2012). It can act as a psychological barrier to forming new relationships and, for patients already in a relationship, it can decrease self-esteem and make sexual intimacy more difficult.

Fear

Patients are faced with the continued threat of disease flares, medication side effects, surgery and an increased risk of colon and other cancers, which can lead to anxiety and fears around every day issues.

Reproductive issues

The peak incidence of IBD overlaps with the reproductive years (see Chapters 8 and 9). Patients worry about the effect of chronic disease on fertility. If pregnancy is considered then it is important to discuss the potential risks of drug-induced teratogenicity. The hallmark of management here is to give accurate counselling regarding fertility and pregnancy outcomes so that the patient can make an informed decision. Fear that the disease and/or the treatment is harmful has been shown to lead to unjustified voluntary childlessness (Mountifield *et al.* 2009).

Physical side effects of IBD medication

The medications listed below (Table 13.1) are those most commonly used to treat IBD, however, the list is not exhaustive. The physical side effects cited represent just a small percentage of possible reactions, but include some of the most common and some of the most serious. The purpose of highlighting these physical side effects is to emphasise how disruptive treatment for IBD can be, to explore the fears that may hinder patient uptake of medication and to demonstrate that psychological sequelae in this context are often a normal response to an abnormal situation.

When reviewing the list of potential adverse effects, it is important to do so through the eyes of the patient. From the clinician's viewpoint, every drug prescribed has potential adverse effects, and it is easy to dismiss a patient's fear about

Table 13.1 A review of both the important and the common adverse effects of inflammatory bowel disease (IBD) medications

Medication	Common or important adverse effects						
	Nausea and vomiting	Susceptible to infections	Pancreatitis, hepatitis or both	Renal failure	Blood dyscrasias	Increased Malignancy risk	Hyper-sensitivity reactions
5-ASA	✓		✓	✓	✓		✓
Thiopurine	✓	✓	✓	✓	✓	✓	✓
Steroids		✓	✓				✓
Methotrexate	✓	✓	✓	✓	✓		✓
Cyclosporine	✓	✓	✓	✓	✓		✓
Anti-TNF	✓	✓	✓		✓	✓	✓

drug commencement. As a patient, however, each adverse effect listed has the potential to reduce quality of life, thus appearing more significant.

Specific direct psychiatric and psychological drug related effects

Steroids may have an acute, deleterious effect on mental health. Steroid-induced psychosis, a contraindication to further therapy, may be florid and occur even at low doses. Depression, suicidal ideation, psychological dependence, mood swings, mania, insomnia and exacerbation of schizophrenia are all psychiatric symptoms associated with steroids. Close monitoring is imperative when initiating treatment in a patient with a known mental health diagnosis. Encephalopathy is a known adverse effect of cyclosporine, alongside anorexia and extreme fatigue. Tacrolimus is associated with psychosis, depression, confusion, anxiety and mood changes, whilst infliximab and adalimumab have been implicated in agitation, confusion, sleep disturbance and anxiety.

The impact of psychiatric and psychological factors on treatment adherence in IBD

Kubler Ross stages of grief

In order for a patient to accept and adhere to a treatment regime, they must first accept their diagnosis of IBD. A diagnosis of chronic disease, no matter its aetiology, inevitably results in a series of psychological reactions. This is particularly the case with IBD, which may be associated with extremes of variability in the clinical course. There are five sequential stages named by Elisabeth Kubler-Ross in the mourning process (Kubler-Ross *et al.* 1972), which have also been applied to chronic disease (Isla Pera *et al.* 2008). These five stages are denial followed by anger, bargaining, depression, and finally, acceptance. Thus, the patient will sway from:

- 'I feel fine, this cannot be happening to me' (denial) to;
- 'Why me? It's not fair; how can this happen to me? Who is to blame?' (anger) to;
- 'I can still do something to change the situation' (bargaining) to;
- 'I'm so sad, why bother with anything?' (depression) to;
- 'I can't fight it, I may as well prepare for it; It's going to be okay' (acceptance).

Acceptance of the diagnosis cannot be reached without first going through the other stages. Therefore, the clinician must be patient in allowing time for this normal process to take place. If rushed, the patient may not be ready, psychologically, for the ramifications of their disease management. This so-called 'pseudo-acceptance', with the patient trying to please the clinician by a false early acceptance, will eventually result in poor adherence to therapy. Some patients may never gain a true acceptance of their disease, and it is important to closely monitor adherence to treatment in this group.

Patients with impaired mental or emotional resilience can have difficulty implementing effective strategies to cope with a chronic illness such as IBD, and this may lead to maladjustment. Mohr's recent study highlighted the role of insufficient coping behaviour as a risk factor for both physical and mental health problems (Mohr *et al.* 2014).

Depressive disorders

Depression is common in patients with Crohn's disease (Helzer *et al.* 1984; Walker *et al.* 2008). IBD is characterised by feelings of being helpless, worthless and hopeless – the cognitive triad at the core of depression. These negative thoughts and feelings may significantly impact upon the patient's ability to adhere to treatment.

'If I feel that there is no *hope* for a remission of this disease then why should I engage with such a complex therapy (I am *hopeless*)? If living with IBD is not a life *worth* living then why make the effort to tolerate the unpleasant side effects of immunosuppressant therapy (I am *worthless*)? If there is no effective curative treatment, why take medications that cannot cure? (I am *helpless*)'.

Depression adversely affects motivation, which is key to adherence with long-term medical treatment. Depression has also been shown to diminish the response to treatment (Katon 1996).

Overcoming psychological issues to improve adherence

i. The doctor's approach – 'I-Thou.'

An old Chinese proverb says 'tell me something and I will forget, show me something and I will learn, involve me and I will understand.' Involvement of the patient in the management of their IBD is key to optimising therapy and results in improved adherence to drug regimens and a more honest discussion between a physician and patient. A transparent, supportive, respectful and empathic relationship reassures the patient that they are an important member of the team treating the disease. It allows for a key adjustment of the physician's approach to the patient. Instead of focusing on 'an object' (the disease to be treated), there is a change in emphasis to the individual who is a patient with 'an object' that needs treating. This point is emphasised by the philosopher Martin Buber. He made the distinction between what he called the 'I-It' and the 'I-Thou' relationships (Ennis 1990). When the patient is treated as an object, with a disease to be treated, this is within the 'I-It' relationship. However, if a clinician is sensitive and attuned to the individuality and human uniqueness of their patients, and remain open to meet the patients' internal psychic world, then the 'I-Thou' relationship will flourish. Such a relationship is likely to improve adherence to treatment (Schaurich 2011).

ii. The patient's approach - ownership

'You know how they say that people get Crohn's – well I feel that Crohn's got me (sic).' is a quote from the book 'Working therapeutically with clients with inflammatory bowel disease' by Dr G. Thomas. It is this feeling that acts as a bar to benefiting from the array of therapeutic interventions available. If the mind-set of the patient can be changed to one where they consider themselves as a person who happens to have IBD then they will develop a sense of ownership over the disease. This is the core issue in the psychological support for these patients. Thus, the patient is more likely to take responsibility for, and be actively involved in, complex medical regimens and, consequently, adherence to treatment will improve. A surprisingly upbeat expression of the ownership principal can be found in the contemporary rap song 'Got that IBD' written and sung by K-Dub, a rapper who has IBD. The song ends 'IBD might be a disease that you have, but it doesn't define you.' It is the physician's challenge to guide the patient to a position where they can own their disease and not let it define them.

Conclusions

The interplay in IBD between symptoms, mood, treatment adherence and treatment side effects is complex, and it can be difficult to assign causality. Some patients have difficulty accepting a diagnosis of IBD and clinicians should be aware that this may affect their ability to become fully involved in their own treatment. The psychosocial wellbeing of the patient is sometimes, unwittingly, ignored by the clinician, who focuses on treating the disease, but this may be at the expense of patient health-related quality of life and treatment compliance. A bespoke treatment regimen must be devised for patients that recognises their individuality, and this may help empower the patient and improve therapy compliance.

Current limitations and future considerations

- Adherence to medical treatment in IBD is poor. There is a paucity of data supporting psychological interventions to aid adherence
- Prospective studies are needed to evaluate strategies for improving poor adherence relating to psychosocial issues

Practical recommendations

- Ideally we would be able to introduce the idea of medical therapy a while before we intend to prescribe it, to give patients time to adjust to the idea. Practically, however, we often need to start medication without delay, and in

these cases it is valuable to have access to nurse specialists who can give extra time and further explanations to the patient
- Knowledge of the Kubler-Ross grief stages, and recognising those patients who are struggling to come to terms with their diagnosis, can help improve medication adherence
- Involvement of the patient in key decision making, and treating them as part of an 'I-Thou' relationship can improve adherence to medical therapy

Learning points

- Medical therapy for IBD may be associated with significant physical and psychological comorbidity
- Adherence rates with IBD medications are low
- Patients with IBD have high rates of psychiatric illness
- Psychiatric illness may interfere further with medication adherence
- Doctors should be vigilant to the psychological wellbeing of the patient, as medication adherence and quality of life status depend upon this

References

Aberra, FN and Lewis, JD (2013). As in the chicken or the egg: stress or inflammatory bowel disease? *Clin Gastroenterol Hepatol*, vol. 11, no. 1, pp. 63–4.

Ananthakrishnan, AN, Khalili, H, Pan, A, Higuchi, LM, de Silva, P, Richter, JM, Fuchs, CS and Chan, AT (2013). Association between depressive symptoms and incidence of Crohn's disease and ulcerative colitis: results from the Nurses' Health Study. *Clin Gastroenterol Hepatol*, vol. 11, no. 1, pp. 57–62.

Cross, RK, Lapshin, O and Finkelstein, J (2008). Patient subjective assessment of drug side effects in inflammatory bowel disease. *J Clin Gastroenterol*, vol. 42, no. 3, pp. 244–51.

Ennis, JH (1990). The physician-patient relationship: a patient-physician's view. *Can Fam Physician*, vol. 36, pp. 2215–20.

Feagan, BG, Reinisch, W, Rutgeerts, P, Sandborn, WJ, Yan, S, Eisenberg, D, Bala, M, Johanns, J, Olson, A and Hanauer, SB (2007). The effects of infliximab therapy on health-related quality of life in ulcerative colitis patients. *Am J Gastroenterol*, vol. 102, no. 4, pp. 794–802.

Frei, P, Biedermann, L, Manser, CN, Wilk, M, Manz, M, Vavricka, SR and Rogler, G (2012). Topical therapies in inflammatory bowel disease. *Digestion*, vol. 86 (Suppl 1), pp. 36–44.

Goodhand, JR, Kamperidis, N, Sirwan, B, Macken, L, Tshuma, N, Koodun, Y, Chowdhury, FA, Croft, NM, Direkze, N, Langmead, L, Irving, PM, Rampton, DS and Lindsay, JO (2013). Factors associated with thiopurine non-adherence in patients with inflammatory bowel disease. *Aliment Pharmacol Ther*, vol. 38, no. 9, pp. 1097–108.

Helzer, JE, Chammas, S, Norland, CC, Stillings, WA and Alpers, DH (1984). A study of the association between Crohn's disease and psychiatric illness. *Gastroenterology*, vol. 86, no. 2, pp. 324–30.

Irvine, EJ, Greenberg, GR, Feagan, BG, Martin, F, Sutherland, LR, Thomson, AB, Nilsson, LG and Persson, T (2000). Quality of life rapidly improves with budesonide therapy for active Crohn's disease. Canadian Inflammatory Bowel Disease Study Group. *Inflamm Bowel Dis*, vol. 6, no. 3, pp. 181–7.

Isla Pera, P, Moncho Vasallo, J, Guasch Andreu, O and Torras Rabasa, A (2008). Alignment of the Kubler-Ross grief cycle phases with the process of adaptation to type 1 diabetes mellitus. *Endocrinol Nutr*, vol. 55, no. 2, pp. 78–83.

Katon, W (1996). The impact of major depression on chronic medical illness. *Gen Hosp Psychiatry*, vol. 18, no. 4, pp. 215–9.

Kubler-Ross, E, Wessler, S and Avioli, LV (1972). On death and dying. *JAMA*, vol. 221, no. 2, pp. 174–9.

Mohr, C, Braun, S, Bridler, R, Chmetz, F, Delfino, JP, Kluckner, VJ, Lott, P, Schrag, Y, Seifritz, E and Stassen, HH (2014). Insufficient coping behavior under chronic stress and vulnerability to psychiatric disorders. *Psychopathology*, doi:10.1159/000356398.

Mountifield, R, Bampton, P, Prosser, R, Muller, K and Andrews, JM (2009). Fear and fertility in inflammatory bowel disease: a mismatch of perception and reality affects family planning decisions. *Inflamm Bowel Dis*, vol. 15, no. 5, pp. 720–5.

Sajadinejad, MS, Asgari, K, Molavi, H, Kalantari, M and Adibi, P (2012). Psychological issues in inflammatory bowel disease: an overview. *Gastroenterol Res Pract*, vol. 2012, p. 106502.

Schaurich, D (2011). I-THOU eternal relationship in the life of caregivers of children with AIDS: study based on Martin Buber philosophy. *Rev Bras Enferm*, vol. 64, no. 4, pp. 651–7. [In Portugese].

Tozer, P, Ng, SC, Siddiqui, MR, Plamondon, S, Burling, D, Gupta, A, Swatton, A, Tripoli, S, Vaizey, CJ, Kamm, MA, Phillips, R and Hart, A (2012). Long-term MRI-guided combined anti-TNF-alpha and thiopurine therapy for Crohn's perianal fistulas. *Inflamm Bowel Dis*, vol. 18, no. 10, pp. 1825–34.

Walker, JR, Ediger, JP, Graff, LA, Greenfeld, JM, Clara, I, Lix, L, Rawsthorne, P, Miller, N, Rogala, L, McPhail, CM and Bernstein, CN (2008). The Manitoba IBD cohort study: a population-based study of the prevalence of lifetime and 12-month anxiety and mood disorders. *Am J Gastroenterol*, vol. 103, no. 8, pp. 1989–97.

Chapter 14

Diet, nutrition and mental health in IBD

Sue Shepherd

Introduction

Definitive data about the role of nutrition in the aetiology of inflammatory bowel disease (IBD) are lacking. Therefore, this chapter will examine the role of nutrition as a therapy, with the goal of alleviating symptoms of IBD, correcting any nutritional deficiencies, achieving and preserving healthy body weight and promoting the growth and development in children. This chapter will explore the dietary and nutritional issues of IBD and some of the mental health issues that can be associated with these.

Dietary management of IBD

Nutrition should be a priority for the patient and practitioner in the setting of IBD. The overriding objective of nutrition as a therapy is to attain and maintain normal nutritional status. This includes prevention or treatment of malnutrition and micro-nutritional deficiencies, prevention of osteoporosis, promotion of growth and development in children and optimising quality of life by minimising symptoms where possible. The setting for this is a healthy, balanced eating pattern, which is particularly important for normal growth and development in children. While there is no special diet for IBD, some people may need to modify their eating pattern at various times according to disease activity and/or any disease-associated implications.

Malnutrition in IBD is common, particularly in active Crohn's disease (CD). The severity and scope depends on many factors, including the age of onset and disease activity. Possible nutritional consequences of IBD include weight loss, growth failure/delayed puberty, hypoalbuminaemia, anaemia (e.g. iron, B12, folate deficiencies), trace element deficiency (e.g. zinc, copper, selenium), vitamin deficiency (e.g. B12, A, B, C, D, E), fat malabsorption, fluid and electrolyte losses and lactose malabsorption (usually temporary) (Hartman *et al.* 2009).

Factors contributing to malnutrition in IBD

There are many factors that contribute to the malnutrition frequently observed in IBD, many of these are entwined and are described in Table 14.1 (Hartman *et al.* 2009).

Diet, nutrition and mental health in IBD 119

Table 14.1 Contributions to malnutrition in inflammatory bowel disease (IBD)

Factor contributing to malnutrition	Related issues
Inadequate oral intake	Anorexia
	Chronic illness
	Abdominal pain
	Nausea
	Diarrhoea
	Restricted diets, therapeutic fasting
	Alterations in taste
	Reduced food intake to avoid gastrointestinal symptoms
	Drug interactions
Reduced absorption of nutrients	Active disease, e.g. inflammation, fistulae
	Resection
	Bypass
	Bacterial overgrowth, blind loops
Enteric nutrient losses	Protein losing (exudative) enteropathy
	Chronic occult blood loss
	Diarrhoea leading to increased losses of zinc, potassium, magnesium
	Steatorrhoea leading to increased losses of fat soluble vitamins (ADEK) and cations: magnesium, zinc, calcium, copper
Increased nutritional requirements	Inflammation
	Fistulae
	Abscesses
	Infection/sepsis
	Fever
	Post-surgery
	Repletion of body stores
	Growth (children)
Drug-nutrient interactions	Corticosteroids: reduce intestinal calcium absorption, alter protein catabolism
	Sulphasalazine: competitive inhibition of folate absorption
	Methotrexate: folic acid antagonist
	Cholestyramine: bile acid binding resin used to reduce diarrhoea in patients with ileal resection. Can accelerate fat soluble vitamin depletion
	Antimicrobials: can reduce vitamin K production

Nutritional status

Body weight

Body weight can be useful as a guide of nutritional adequacy. Weight loss (and/or an inability to gain weight) can be exacerbated by increased resting energy expenditure (inflammation, fever), infectious complications and increased nutritional needs post-surgery. Anorexia, which can be a symptom of disease flare-up, will also contribute to weight loss. Weight loss has been reported to occur in 70–80 per cent of hospitalised Crohn's disease patients (20–40 per cent of outpatient Crohn's disease patients) and in 18–62 per cent of patients with ulcerative colitis (UC) (Hartman *et al.* 2009). Therefore, nutritional supplementation can be useful. Weight gain and increased appetite may be a nutritional issue for some patients on steroid therapy.

Growth and development in children

Delayed growth in children is a frequently observed manifestation of IBD. It is reported to affect 75 per cent of children with Crohn's disease and 10 per cent of children with ulcerative colitis (Lucendo and De Rezende 2009). Growth failure in children can be the result of energy and nutrient deficiencies, influence of pro-inflammatory cytokines (anorexia, bone metabolism disturbance, increased catabolism), disease severity and location, drugs (e.g. corticosteroids), delayed onset of sexual maturation (hypogonadism) and abnormal bone metabolism (pro-inflammatory cytokines, GH-IGF1 axis dysfunction) (Hartman *et al.* 2009).

Nutritional therapy

The type and intensity of nutritional intervention will depend on the site and severity of disease and any related issues, for example, side effects of treatment. In situations where a patient is acutely unwell and hospitalised, enteral feeding (as a primary treatment or supplement to oral intake) may be necessary if they are unable to obtain adequate oral intake. If enteral feeding is not tolerated (e.g. severe disease), total parenteral nutrition may be indicated, although this is not common. In well-nourished patients, maintenance of good nutritional status is the primary nutritional management goal. A nutritionally balanced and well-varied diet is recommended for all patients with IBD, including foods from all food groups.

Enteral nutrition therapy

Enteral nutrition may assist in improving nutritional status and body composition. In CD, enteral nutrition appears to alter the inflammatory response; however, there is no indication for enteral nutrition therapy in ulcerative colitis. It is usually administered to CD patients for 3–6 weeks and is effective for inducing remission in children (60–80 per cent) (National Collaborating Centre for Acute Care 2006). Therefore, in children, it is an alternative to corticosteroids, where avoidance of steroid therapy is desirable (growth and development issues). There is no difference in efficacy of elemental vs polymeric enteral feeds in children. Evidence suggests enteral nutrition therapy seems to be less effective than corticosteroids in adults; however, this may be due to tolerability issues (National

Collaborating Centre for Acute Care 2006). Psychologically, nasogastric feeding is not well accepted; as many as 26 of 39 (66 per cent) home enteral feeding cancer patients wanted the tube removed after only 3 weeks of feeding, and 33 per cent expressed negative perceptions regarding body image (Roberge *et al.* 2000). Although research has supported the potential of enteral nutrition in inducing remission, there is little evidence suggesting enteral nutrition has a role in maintenance therapy (National Collaborating Centre for Acute Care 2006).

Food avoidance

It may be appropriate that a patient avoids foods that are thought to provoke symptoms. However, this should generally only be considered a short-term measure. Any food avoidance should be managed in consultation with a dietitian, and if the food avoidance is due to food fears, a psychologist will offer valuable counselling. As whole food groups (e.g. dairy) are often avoided, and in many instances unnecessarily, a dietitian can assist to prevent over-restriction, to achieve a nutritionally adequate diet and advise on how to reintroduce food (or find suitable alternatives). There is now limitless access to all sorts of dietary regimens via the internet, and most of these are not scientifically sound. The low fermentable oligosaccharides, disaccharide, monosaccharide and polyols (FODMAP) diet (described below) has good evidence in reducing abdominal symptoms in IBD patients with inactive disease (Shepherd *et al.* 2013b).

Fluid intake

Adequate fluid intake is encouraged (approx. 1.5–2L day), and additional fluid may be required to compensate for increased fluid losses, for example, diarrhoea.

Nutrients – vitamins and minerals

Deficiencies of folate, vitamin B12 and iron are common (50 per cent, 20–60 per cent, 40 per cent respectively) in the IBD population (Hartman *et al.* 2009). Well established links between depression and deficiencies of these nutrients (and also calcium, selenium and zinc) have been found, consequently, monitoring these is warranted with the view of optimising management of the patient's psychological health (Leung and Kaplan 2009). Additionally, as oxidative stress can contribute to the inflammatory response in IBD (Lucendo and De Rezende 2009), adequate intake of antioxidant nutrients including vitamins A, C, and E and also selenium are recommended. It has been shown that plasma levels of these nutrients are inversely correlated with pro-inflammatory agents (Lucendo and De Rezende 2009).

Vitamin and mineral supplementation is not always required for every patient with IBD. However, there are many common situations where vitamin and/or mineral supplementation is warranted. For example, during long periods of flare-ups with poor food intake; with any identified nutritional deficiency (e.g. folate, iron, B12, vitamin D, other fat soluble vitamins, zinc, calcium); with prolonged corticosteroid therapy (calcium); with disease/resection of the terminal ileum (vitamin B12); with excessive diarrhoea (zinc, potassium, magnesium and copper); and with long term sulphasalazine therapy (folate).

Probiotics

Probiotics are used as a therapy with the goal of changing the endogenous flora. VSL#3 (Sigma-tau Pharmaceuticals Inc., Gaithersburg, MD, USA) has been reported to be effective in preventing pouchitis and may assist in maintenance and treatment of UC (Haller *et al.* 2010). Additionally, in UC, *Escherichia coli* Nissle (200mg/daily) has been shown to be equivalent in efficacy in maintaining remission to standard doses of mesalazine. This may pose a suitable alternative to UC patients unable/unwilling to use mesalazine. There is no evidence supporting the use of probiotics in maintenance of remission in CD (National Collaborating Centre for Acute Care 2006).

Low residue diet

A 'low residue' diet may be helpful to control diarrhoea during a flare-up and may also assist with minimising pain and nausea in people with strictures. In a prospective controlled study involving seventy patients with non-stenosing Crohn's who were allocated to either low residue or normal diet for 29 months, there was no difference in outcomes including symptoms, need for hospitalisation or surgery, nutritional status, new complications or post-operative recurrence (Levenstein *et al.* 1985). Specific guidelines regarding a low residue diet vary from institution to institution. Depending on the reason for the low residue diet, some additional foods may be included or the diet may be quite restricted. The general principles are to avoid legumes, wholegrains and wholegrain products, nuts and seeds and most fruits and vegetables (some peeled, non-fibrous or juiced varieties may be permitted) (Levenstein *et al.* 1985). Due to the risk of nutritional inadequacy, it is recommended for patients to take a multi vitamin/mineral supplement and for weight to be monitored. Patients should be encouraged to return to a normal diet as early as possible, which will also reduce the psychological burden associated with following a restrictive diet (Levenstein *et al.* 1985).

Lactose intolerance

Approximately 40 per cent of IBD patients experience lactose intolerance (often temporary, relating to disease activity, however it may also be permanent) (Barrett *et al.* 2009b). In such instances, it is recommended to follow a low lactose diet. See section below regarding FODMAPs for details on lactose restriction.

The low FODMAP diet

It is well documented that patients with inactive (quiescent) IBD are two to three times more likely to develop IBS-like symptoms (including excessive wind, abdominal bloating, pain, changes in bowel habits) than people without IBD (Mikocka-Walus *et al.* 2008). This concept of IBS 'overlapping' with IBD can offer an explanation for ongoing gastrointestinal (GI) symptoms in people in remission of their IBD. The low FODMAP diet has extensive proven efficacy as the primary dietary management for IBS (Gibson and Shepherd 2010; Ong *et al.* 2010; Shepherd *et al.* 2008) and data also suggest it is effective for reducing symptoms in quiescent IBD (Croagh *et al.* 2007; Gearry *et al.* 2009).

In a pilot study, Gearry *et al.* (2009) retrospectively evaluated the symptoms and dietary habits of 52 consecutive Crohn's disease and 20 ulcerative colitis patients in regards to a prior low FODMAP dietary intervention taught at least 3 months earlier. Approximately half of the patients who were compliant to the low FODMAP diet reported improvements in overall abdominal symptoms, abdominal pain, bloating, wind and diarrhoea ($p < 0.02$ for all), however, constipation did not improve. A trend was observed where the greater efficacy was observed in those who had better compliance to the diet (Gearry *et al.* 2009).

Additionally, a randomised cross-over, single-blinded intervention study of 10 ileostomates with high output (two CD, eight UC) found improvements in ileostomy output (quantity and quality) on a low FODMAP diet compared with a high FODMAP diet [mean 95ml (22 per cent) reduction in volume per day] (Barrett *et al.* 2009a).

Although apparently beneficial in the above groups of patients, the low FODMAP diet may not be suitable for all IBD patients, in particular, for those patients with low ileostomy output. Such patients may be at risk of a bowel obstruction on a low FODMAP diet as the osmotic activity that FODMAPs illicit is reduced.

FODMAPs are a family of sugars that are potentially poorly absorbed in the small intestine and arrive into the large intestine where they act as a food source for the bacteria that reside in the large bowel. FODMAPs cause the bowel to distend by drawing in more fluid and rapidly generating gas when they are fermented by bacteria in the bowel. The acronym FODMAP is described below (Shepherd *et al.* 2013b).

Fermentable – referring to the fermentation (breaking down) by bacteria in the large bowel
Oligo-saccharides – oligo means few and saccharide means sugar. These are chains of sugars and include fructans and galacto-oligosaccharides (GOS)
Disaccharide – a double sugar, in particular lactose
Monosaccharide – a single sugar, in particular fructose. However, fructose is only potentially malabsorbed if it is present in foods in amounts greater than glucose
And
Polyols – sugar alcohols, including sorbitol, mannitol, xylitol, maltitol

There are two steps to the low FODMAP diet.

Step one:

- Restrict all high FODMAP foods or eat them in only very small amounts for about 6–8 weeks
- Enjoy the low FODMAP foods
- Symptoms should improve during this trial time

Step two:

- Continue eating low FODMAP foods
- Slowly introduce some of the high FODMAP foods back into your diet
- The goal: experiment with the high FODMAP foods, one by one, until you reach and understand your own tolerance level

See Table 14.2 for examples of high and low FODMAP foods.

Fat malabsorption

Some people with Crohn's disease may experience steatorrhoea. In such instances, the first approach to manage symptoms is to decrease high fat foods from the diet (e.g. pies, pastries, fried foods, potato crisps, fatty meats, full fat dairy products) and encourage low fat alternatives. It is important to note that fat is a valuable source of energy, and any restriction should be considered carefully in patients prone to weight loss and children (due to growth and developmental needs). In severe cases, a low fat diet may not be sufficient to manage symptoms, and medium chain triglyceride (MCT) supplementation may be necessary. Although MCT improves fat absorption in many people with steatorrhoea, in some, it may induce osmotic diarrhoea, and thus, monitoring is required.

Mental health in relation to optimising nutritional status

Patients with IBD are conservatively estimated to be at least twice as likely to suffer from depression and anxiety than the general public, which is not uncommon for chronic diseases; similar rates have been seen in those with rheumatoid arthritis and diabetes (Graff *et al.* 2009). A population-based cohort study of 388 individuals with IBD diagnosed within the previous 7 years found those with active disease to have increased levels of distress, health anxiety, perceived stress, perceived lower social support, wellbeing and disease-specific quality of life compared to those with inactive disease (Graff *et al.* 2006). These findings were consistent with those in a recent review, where at times of active disease, stress can intensify symptoms of anxiety and depression (Graff *et al.* 2009).

Table 14.2 Examples of high FODMAP foods (adapted from Shepherd 2013)

Fruit and fruit products	Vegetables and vegetable products	Milk products	Grain and starch foods	Legumes, nuts and seeds	Others
Apples	Artichoke – globe	Cow's milk (full fat, low fat, skim)	Barley-, rye-, and wheat-based: bread, crackers, pasta, couscous, gnocchi, noodles, croissants, muffins, crumpets	Cashews	Agave
Apricots	Artichoke – Jerusalem	Custard		Chickpeas	Chicory-based drinks
Blackberries	Asparagus	Dairy desserts		Legumes (eg. red kidney beans, soy beans, borlotti beans)	Fructo-oligosaccharides
Boysenberry	Cauliflower	Evaporated milk			High fructose corn syrup
Custard apples	Garlic	Goat's milk (full fat, low fat, skim)	Cracker*	Lentils	Honey
Fruit juices (apple, pear, mango, tropical)	Leek	Ice cream	Buckwheat	Pistachios	Inulin
	Mushroom	Milk powder	Corn	Almonds*	Salts – onion, garlic, vegetable
Fruit leathers (strap bars)	Onion	Sheep's milk (full fat, low fat, skim)	Gluten-free bread and cereal products	Chia seeds	Sweeteners: sorbitol (420),
Fruit-based muesli-bars	Shallot	Sweetened condensed milk		Hazelnuts*	mannitol (421),
	Snow peas			Linseed (flaxseed), Poppy seeds,	xylitol (967),
Mango	Spring onion (white part)	Hard cheeses, e.g. Blue vein, Brie, Cheddar, Colby, Edam, Feta, Gouda, Mozzarella, Parmesan, Swiss	Millet	Pumpkin seeds (pepita),	maltitol (965),
Nashi fruit	Sugar snap peas		Oats	Sesame seeds	isomalt (953)
Nectarines	Alfalfa		Oat bran	Sunflower seeds, Tahini*	Garlic-infused olive oil
Peaches	Bamboo shoots		Polenta		Herbs
Pears	Bean sprouts		Quinoa		Spices
Persimmon	Beans (green)		Rice		Ginger
Plums	Beetroot*		Sweet biscuit*		Small amounts of regular milk as an ingredient
Tamarillo	Bok choy				
Watermelon	Broccoli*	Butter			
Avocado*	Brussels sprouts*	Cream			Maple syrup, Golden syrup
Banana	Butternut pumpkin*	Margarine			
Blueberry	Cabbage (savoy)*	Oat milk			
Canteloupe	Capsicum	Rice milk			
Carambola	Carrot	Lactose free ice cream			
Cherries*	Cauliflower				
	Celery*				

(Continued)

Table 14.2 (Continued)

Fruit and fruit products	Vegetables and vegetable products	Milk products	Grain and starch foods	Legumes, nuts and seeds	Others
Dragon fruit	Chives	Lactose free yoghurt			Sugar (sucrose), glucose, stevia, any other artificial sweeteners not ending in 'ol' (e.g. aspartame)
Dried fruit*	Choy sum	Fromage frais*			
Durian	Cucumber	Yoghurt – cow, sheep, goat*			
Grapefruit	Eggplant	Soft cheeses*			
Grapes	Endive	e.g. cottage*,			
Honeydew melon	Fennel bulb*	ricotta*, quark*,			
Kiwifruit	Green peas*	cream cheese*,			
Lemon	Lettuce	mascarpone*,			
Lime	Olives	crème fraiche*			
Longon*	Parsnip				
Lychee*	Potato				
Mandarin	Pumpkin (Jap)				
Orange	Radish				
Passionfruit	Rocket				
PawPaw	Silverbeet				
Pineapple	Spinach				
Pomegranate*	Spring onion (green part only)				
Prickly Pear	Squash				
Rambutan*	Swede				
Raspberry	Sweet corn*				
Rhubarb	Sweet potato*				
Strawberry	Tomato				
Tangelo	Turnip				
	Zucchini				

*Indicates foods that contain a lesser amount of FODMAPs, these can be eaten, but not in large amounts.

A significant relationship between depression and nutritional status in IBD patients has been reported, manifesting in many ways, including a poor relationship with food and food avoidance. People with IBD often follow an overly restricted diet and may be anxious to attempt to incorporate new foods into their diet. Practitioners should look for 'fear of food' flags, and offer empathetic encouragement to seek professional psychological support if indicated. There are many types of therapies that can be used to manage mental health issues in patients with IBD (see Chapters 19 and 20). A review by Graff *et al.* found that there is significantly poorer adherence to treatment regimens in people with co-existing mental health issues (Graff *et al.* 2009). This is likely to have implications in regards to achieving nutritional management goals in an IBD patient; therefore, psychotherapies may be helpful and sometimes necessary. Impaired psychological health should be a management priority in patients with IBD to optimise quality of life and nutritional status (Addolorato *et al.* 1997).

Current limitations and future considerations

- The efficacy of probiotic supplementation is limited by the present knowledge of strains/species. As research in this area grows, wider benefits of probiotic supplementation may be realised
- Much of the data regarding nutritional status of IBD patients has been generated prior to the common use of biologics and immunotherapies; data trends incorporating the clinical presentation as seen today are needed
- The nutritional status of IBD patients with inactive disease is less well understood
- The effect of omega-3 as a dietary anti-inflammatory agent in IBD remains inconclusive and further studies are warranted
- The role of short-chain fatty acids, produced as a by-product of anaerobic bacterial fermentation of undigested carbohydrates and fibres on colonocytes requires further studies

Practical recommendations

- The dietitian experienced in managing IBD should be considered an essential member of the patient's management team
- There is no special diet for IBD – the patient should work with the dietitian to establish individual diet and nutritional goals for optimum nutritional status
- Monitor weight and nutritional biochemistry regularly, and address any nutritional issues early
- Advice regarding supplementation to account for any drug-nutrient interactions, as appropriate
- Enteral feeding is as effective in inducing remission in children with Crohn's disease as corticosteroids, and therefore a preferable alternative

- In patients with ongoing GI symptoms (IBS-like) with inactive disease, the low FODMAP diet may be of benefit for symptom control
- Impaired psychological wellbeing is common in active and inactive disease. Psychotherapy has the potential to promote and maintain a nutritionally adequate diet

Learning points

- IBD is associated with malnutrition due to inadequate oral intake, malabsorption, enteric losses of nutrients, increased requirements, and/or drug-induced malabsorption
- Nutrition should be a priority for the patient and practitioner
- There is no special diet for IBD – a balanced and varied diet is recommended, as tolerated for all
- Nutritional therapy including enteral nutrition, vitamin/mineral and fat supplements, and a diet low in fermentable oligosaccharides, disaccharide, monosaccharide and polyols (FODMAPs) may be useful in certain conditions
- Psychological strategies can be helpful to optimise nutritional status

References

Addolorato, G, Capristo, E, Stefanini, GF and Gasbarrini, G (1997). Inflammatory bowel disease: a study of the association between anxiety and depression, physical morbidity, and nutritional status. *Scand J Gastroenterol*, vol. 32, no. 10, pp. 1013–21.

Barrett, JS, Gearry, RB, Irving, PM, Muir, JG, Haines, ML and Gibson, PR (2009a). Dietary poorly absorbed short-chain carbohydrates (FODMAPs) increase the volume and fermentable substrate content of ileal output. *Gastroenterology*, vol. 136, no. 5, p. A876.

Barrett, JS, Irving, PM, Shepherd, SJ, Muir, JG and Gibson, PR (2009b). Comparison of the prevalence of fructose and lactose malabsorption across chronic intestinal disorders. *Aliment Pharmacol Ther*, vol. 30, no. 2, pp. 165–74.

Croagh, C, Shepherd, SJ, Berryman, M, Muir, JG and Gibson, PR (2007). Pilot study on the effect of reducing dietary FODMAP intake on bowel function in patients without a colon. *Inflamm Bowel Dis*, vol. 13, no. 12, pp. 1522–8.

Gearry, RB, Irving, PM, Barrett, JS, Nathan, DM, Shepherd, SJ and Gibson, PR (2009). Reduction of dietary poorly absorbed short-chain carbohydrates (FODMAPs) improves abdominal symptoms in patients with inflammatory bowel disease-a pilot study. *J Crohns Colitis*, vol. 3, no. 1, pp. 8–14.

Gibson, PR and Shepherd, SJ (2010). Evidence-based dietary management of functional gastrointestinal symptoms: the FODMAP approach. *J Gastroenterol Hepatol*, vol. 25, no. 2, pp. 252–8.

Graff, LA, Walker, JR and Bernstein, CN (2009). Depression and anxiety in inflammatory bowel disease: a review of comorbidity and management. *Inflamm Bowel Dis*, vol. 15, no. 7, pp. 1105–18.

Graff, LA, Walker, JR, Lix, L, Clara, I, Rawsthorne, P, Rogala, L, Miller, N, Jakul, L, McPhail, C, Ediger, J and Bernstein, CN (2006). The relationship of inflammatory bowel disease type and activity to psychological functioning and quality of life. *Clin Gastroenterol Hepatol*, vol. 4, no. 12, pp. 1491–501.

Haller, D, Antoine, JM, Bengmark, S, Enck, P, Rijkers, GT and Lenoir-Wijnkoop, I (2010). Guidance for substantiating the evidence for beneficial effects of probiotics: probiotics in chronic inflammatory bowel disease and the functional disorder irritable bowel syndrome. *J Nutr*, vol. 140, no. 3, pp. 690S–7S.

Hartman, C, Eliakim, R and Shamir, R (2009). Nutritional status and nutritional therapy in inflammatory bowel diseases. *World J Gastroenterol*, vol. 15, no. 21, pp. 2570–8.

Leung, BM and Kaplan, BJ (2009). Perinatal depression: prevalence, risks, and the nutrition link—a review of the literature. *J Am Diet Assoc*, vol. 109, no. 9, pp. 1566–75.

Levenstein, S, Prantera, C, Luzi, C and D'Ubaldi, A (1985). Low residue or normal diet in Crohn's disease: a prospective controlled study in Italian patients. *Gut*, vol. 26, no. 10, pp. 989–93.

Lucendo, AJ and De Rezende, LC (2009). Importance of nutrition in inflammatory bowel disease. *World J Gastroenterol*, vol. 15, no. 17, pp. 2081–8.

Mikocka-Walus, AA, Turnbull, DA, Andrews, JM, Moulding, NT and Holtmann, GJ (2008). The effect of functional gastrointestinal disorders on psychological comorbidity and quality of life in patients with inflammatory bowel disease. *Aliment Pharmacol Ther*, vol. 28, no. 4, pp. 475–83.

National Collaborating Centre for Acute Care (2006). Nutrition support in adults oral nutrition support, enteral tube feeding and parenteral nutrition. Available online from www.nice.org.uk/nicemedia/pdf/cg032fullguideline.pdf (accessed 1 March 2014).

Ong, DK, Mitchell, SB, Barrett, JS, Shepherd, SJ, Irving, PM, Biesiekierski, JR, Smith, S, Gibson, PR and Muir, JG (2010). Manipulation of dietary short chain carbohydrates alters the pattern of gas production and genesis of symptoms in irritable bowel syndrome. *J Gastroenterol Hepatol*, vol. 25, no. 8, pp. 1366–73.

Roberge, C, Tran, M, Massoud, C, Poiree, B, Duval, N, Damecour, E, Frout, D, Malvy, D, Joly, F, Lebailly, P and Henry-Amar, M (2000). Quality of life and home enteral tube feeding: a French prospective study in patients with head and neck or oesophageal cancer. *Br J Cancer*, vol. 82, no. 2, pp. 263–9.

Shepherd, SJ (2013). *Low FODMAP Recipes*. Sydney: Penguin Books.

Shepherd, SJ, Lomer, MC and Gibson, PR (2013). Short-chain carbohydrates and functional gastrointestinal disorders. *Am J Gastroenterol*, vol. 108, no. 5, pp. 707–17.

Shepherd, SJ, Parker, FC, Muir, JG and Gibson, PR (2008). Dietary triggers of abdominal symptoms in patients with irritable bowel syndrome: randomized placebo-controlled evidence. *Clin Gastroenterol Hepatol*, vol. 6, no. 7, pp. 765–71.

Chapter 15

Fatigue and IBD

Daniel van Langenberg

Introduction

Fatigue is a normal psycho-physiological state or symptom in all humans, although the '*raison d'être*' for fatigue remains obscure. Theoretically, fatigue in humans appears to exist as a protective mechanism, intervening where optimal performance is no longer achievable, and thus, preventing injury or harm to the person from ongoing (over)activity. For instance, in the case of systemic infection, fatigue is a major component of 'sickness behaviour', limiting activity in order to divert resources from 'ergotropic' to 'trophotropic' systems (Romani 2008). However, in chronic diseases like inflammatory bowel disease (IBD), for some reason, there is an increasingly recognised propensity for 'pathological' fatigue to occur, not only purely as a homeostatic function, but rather a pervasive, potentially unrelenting symptom in its own right. The fatigued patient is therefore a major challenge for the clinician, as current research suggests that the aetiopathogenesis of fatigue is a complex web of biological, psychological and behavioural components, of which each must somehow be addressed (van Langenberg and Gibson 2010).

Impact of fatigue on the patient

Patients with IBD frequently report fatigue as one of their most pressing disease-related concerns (Casellas *et al.* 1999). Moreover, the severity of fatigue reported via surveys appears to correlate with poorer quality of life scores and those with severe fatigue are more likely to be underemployed, unemployed or reliant on disability/welfare support (Bernklev *et al.* 2006; van Langenberg and Gibson 2010, 2014). Also, they are more likely to suffer comorbid mood disorders (Graff *et al.* 2013).

Despite recent advancements in IBD therapeutics, often fatigue is resistant to treatment escalation, including to newer anti-tumour necrosis factor (TNF) therapies, implying that fatigue may not purely be an inflammation-related symptom in many patients. This observation, along with an increasing awareness of IBD as a multi-systemic and not merely a bowel disease, and improved acceptance of a biopsychosocial model of care, perhaps explain the recent growing interest in the study of fatigue in IBD literature (van Langenberg and Gibson 2010).

Assessment and prevalence of fatigue

One of the inherent difficulties in fatigue-related research has been the lack of a widely accepted definition of fatigue. Broadly speaking, fatigue in chronic diseases is perhaps most aptly described as a 'persistent, overwhelming sense of tiredness, weakness or exhaustion resulting in a decreased capacity for physical and/or mental work' (Dittner *et al.* 2004), and is typically unrelieved by adequate sleep or rest (Cella *et al.* 1998). Furthermore, an important tenet of fatigue in chronic disease is that it can exist as a unique entity in its own right, not merely a component of psychological comorbidity or 'illness behaviour' as many clinicians and sceptics seem to believe (Craig *et al.* 2006; van der Linden *et al.* 1999).

Recent studies have characterised the prevalence of fatigue in IBD widely between 29 per cent and 86 per cent (Jelsness-Jorgensen *et al.* 2011; Minderhoud *et al.* 2007). The actual number depends on which instrument is used (the Fatigue Impact Scale and Multidimensional Fatigue Inventory being the most commonly used self-report surveys in IBD studies) and the relative proportions of active versus inactive, Crohn's disease versus ulcerative colitis in each case (van Langenberg and Gibson 2010).

Apart from a definition, conceptualising fatigue via a multidimensional construct is also useful, that is, there are objectively measurable and subjective aspects of fatigue that are potentially separable components or indeed parts of a syndrome (Echteld *et al.* 2007). By embracing this concept, one can then 'divide and conquer' fatigue, which is otherwise amorphous. Hence, 'physical fatigue' may be defined subjectively (e.g. by patients) as a feeling of weakness or difficulty completing or initiating a manual task and objectively described by a measurable decrease in performance with a repeated, prolonged physical activity. In contrast, 'cognitive fatigue' may be described as a clouding of thought or difficulty concentrating and objectively represented by a measurable decrease in cognitive performance (e.g. memory) with repeat and/or prolonged testing. Finally, psychosocial or the affective dimension of fatigue may be described by decreased motivation, low mood and/or lack of energy. Thus, it follows that individuals may exhibit these dimensions of fatigue in varying degrees, and theoretically require specific therapeutic approaches for each dimension (van Langenberg and Gibson 2014).

Despite their inherent subjectivity, these self-report surveys appear to correlate reasonably well with objective markers of fatigue. For instance, objective muscle fatigue testing via a dynamometer and cognitive testing via a computerised visuospatial processing test in a cohort of patients with Crohn's disease both significantly correlated with the physical dimension and cognitive dimensions of the FIS respectively (van Langenberg *et al.* 2011, 2014).

Potential causes of fatigue relevant to IBD

Active inflammation

Most studies in this field have similarly demonstrated that the severity and activity of IBD is inexorably linked with fatigue severity in patients, signifying the important role of IBD-related inflammation in fatigue pathogenesis. However, as mentioned, IBD patients with inactive disease still often complain of fatigue. Along with active inflammation, poor sleep quality and psychological stress/co-morbidity appear to be the next two most prevalent, independently associated factors implicated in fatigue genesis. Together these three factors account for approximately 50 per cent of the effect size in fatigue based on regression analyses in multiple studies (Graff *et al.* 2011, 2013; van Langenberg and Gibson 2014).

Sleep disturbance

While concurrent corticosteroid therapy frequently causes insomnia in IBD patients (Fardet *et al.* 2009), many patients without corticosteroids also complain of sleep fragmentation in particular, along with feeling unrefreshed following their nightly slumber. This does not appear to be exclusively due to nocturnal symptoms interrupting sleep, such as abdominal pain or nocturnal diarrhoea. Furthermore, given the importance of sleep to immune reconstitution, poor sleep in turn may be deleterious to disease activity in IBD (Irwin 2002).

Nevertheless, few have studied sleep quality in IBD. Keefer *et al.* (2006) found that subjects reported significantly prolonged sleep latency, increased sleep fragmentation, higher rates of using sedatives and increased day-time fatigue (Keefer *et al.* 2006; Ranjbaran *et al.* 2007). Moreover, given that a similar pro-inflammatory cytokine cascade including TNF and interleukin (IL)-6 is implicated in both fatigue (Inagaki *et al.* 2008; Swain 2000) and sleep disturbances (Kapsimalis *et al.* 2008), as well as in the pathogenesis of Crohn's disease (Strober and Fuss 2011), it is unsurprising that all three conditions commonly coexist, albeit the exact mechanisms of interplay are uncertain.

Psychological comorbidity

Fatigue is depicted as a core symptom of depressive disorders. Undeniably, there is a high correlation between fatigue and psychological comorbidity, but this does not imply causality, or if both are epiphenomena only. For instance, Dryman and Eaton (1991) showed that fatigue predicted the onset of depression over the following 12 months (Dryman and Eaton 1991). Conversely, another study suggested fatigue may exist as either a prodrome or consequence of psychiatric illness (Merikangas *et al.* 1994). Perhaps most definitively, van der Linden *et al.* (1999) measured fatigue and psychological comorbidity over three time-points in 1,177 outpatients, concluding that a 'pure' fatigue state does exist, independently of any psychological disorder. Furthermore, this 'pure' fatigue did not predict subsequent psychological disorder (van der Linden *et al.* 1999). Anecdotally, it appears that fatigue manifests in many patients with no history or current sign of psychological comorbidity.

Other contributors to fatigue

Other potential causes for fatigue in patients with IBD are legion, as shown in Table 15.1. Of note, micronutrient deficiencies arising from malabsorptive effects decreased oral intake and/or inflammatory effects on transport and utilisation are likely underestimated (and easily correctable) factors contributing to fatigue in IBD. For instance, iron deficiency ($\pm$ anaemia) appears important – in one study, iron supplementation improved cognitive functioning in non-anaemic, iron deficient young females (Bruner *et al.* 1996). Another trial showed a 29 per cent improvement in fatigue in females with borderline/low serum ferritin who received oral iron supplementation for 1 month, versus no supplement (Verdon *et al.* 2003). However, a recent study failed to demonstrate an association between iron deficiency and fatigue in a population-based IBD cohort (Goldenberg *et al.* 2013). Other micronutrients such as vitamin D3, magnesium and vitamin B group supplements appear important in particular to alleviating the physical dimension of fatigue (Costantini and Pala 2013; van Langenberg *et al.* 2014).

A biopsychosocial approach to fatigue in the IBD patient

Optimisation of anti-inflammatory therapies in the fatigued IBD patient is a key initial step in management, given fatigue is inextricably linked with inflammation and the activity of intestinal disease. If/once this has been objectively assessed as inactive, one can then explore approaches to other potential contributing factors, as in Figure 15.1, including the removal of fatigue-inducing medications, screening for other fatigue-causing medical comorbidities and modification of lifestyle factors. For example, in significant physical fatigue, institution of a graded exercise programme or regular rest periods/decreased workload may be simple measures to alleviate fatigue and build endurance lost with chronic deconditioning. Moreover, establishment of optimal sleep hygiene practices should be considered. Also, in those with considerable symptom burden despite control of inflammatory activity, institution of a low fermentable oligosaccharides, disaccharide, monosaccharide and polyols (FODMAP) diet may be helpful in alleviating fatigue, as well as reducing irritable bowel syndrome (IBS)-type symptoms, which frequently are cofactors in severely fatigued IBD patients (Jelsness-Jorgensen *et al.* 2012).

Repletion of micronutrients, such as iron, vitamin D3, magnesium and vitamin B group vitamins, should be considered in all IBD patients with ongoing fatigue.

Table 15.1 Potentially important contributors to fatigue in Crohn's disease

Factor (in alphabetical order)	Proposed mechanism/comment
Active inflammatory disease (direct)	Proinflammatory cytokine mediated
Anaemia (± iron deficiency)	
Endocrine causes	i.e. Secondary to corticosteroid
• Hypothyroidism	therapy
• Testosterone deficiency/hypogonadism	
• Adrenocortical insufficiency (primary/secondary)	
• Hypoglycaemia	
• Growth hormone/IGF-1 deficiency	
Infections	
• Viral (e.g. EBV, CMV, hepatitides, HIV, other)	
• Bacterial	
• Other (e.g. parasitic, Lyme disease, Rickettsial)	
Iron deficiency without anaemia	
Medical comorbidities (other)	Including coeliac disease
Medications (IBD therapies or others)	e.g. Azathioprine, methotrexate (transient/reversible)
Miscellaneous (other)	e.g. Abnormal illness behaviour, ME/CFS, fibromyalgia
Neurobiological causes (central fatigue)	Altered neurotransmission (e.g. 5HT, NA)
• Psychological 'stress'	Defective CRH release
Nutrition-related	Malabsorption, inflammation-
• Macronutrient deficiency	related, post-ileojejunal resection
• Micronutrient deficiency	
• Excessive delivery of short-chain carbohydrates to the distal small bowel and colon	
Other or 'cryptogenic'	
Physiological	e.g. Overwork, shift work, care of newborn, jet lag, bereavement, etc.
Psychological comorbidity	IBD-related or unrelated
Sleep quality (poor)	Direct inflammation-mediated
• Caffeine/alcohol/CNS stimulant use	sleep disturbance? (Keefer
• Life stressors/Ppsychological comorbidity	*et al.* 2006)
• IBD- related (e.g. pain, nocturnal diarrhea)	
• Obstructive sleep apnoea/other medical cause	
• Sedentary lifestyle (lack of exercise)	
• Poor sleep behaviour	

IGF-1, insulin-like growth factor-1; EBV, Epstein-Barr virus; CMV, Cytomegalovirus; IBD, inflammatory bowel disease; ME/CFS, myalgic encephalomyelitis/chronic fatigue syndrome; CRH, corticotrophin releasing hormone; CNS, central nervous system. Table adapted with permission from van Langenberg and Gibson (2010).

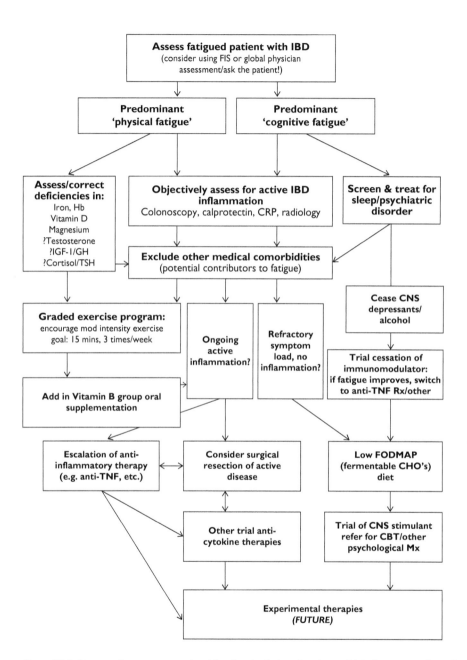

Figure 15.1 Proposed management algorithm for the fatigued patient with inflammatory bowel disease (IBD) using a dimension-based (physical or cognitive fatigue) approach.

Finally, cognitive behavioural therapy (CBT) has been used to alleviate fatigue with considerable success in the chronic fatigue syndrome (CFS) population (Deale *et al.* 1997). Extrapolating to fatigue in IBD, CBT may be a useful tool to affect hypothesised brain plasticity, and thus, help modulate the intertwining pathways of fatigue, sleep and other neurobiological sequelae seen in many patients with IBD. Other techniques with robust evidence for efficacy in the IBS population, such as hypnotherapy, warrant investigation. Finally, engaging patients in adaptive coping strategies and mindfulness-based stress reduction approaches may be other avenues to manage fatigue that have recently been shown to be effective in IBD and IBS regarding other refractory symptoms (e.g. pain), in turn, resulting in improved quality of life outcomes (Graff *et al.* 2009; Knowles *et al.* 2011).

Conclusions

Fatigue as an entity may be aptly described as a paradox. It is a complex syndrome of interconnected features, yet is typically and simply described as a symptom. It is notoriously hard to define yet we all know exactly what it is from personal experience. It exists as a physiological but also pathological condition, and, with relevance to patients with chronic diseases like IBD, it is often debilitating, yet has traditionally been ignored by clinicians and researchers alike. In adopting a biopsychosocial approach to management of IBD, one cannot ignore fatigue, therefore, clinicians must develop a tailored, systematic approach to the fatigued patient even where the evidence for such an approach still lags behind the clinical reality.

Current limitations and future considerations

- There are minimal data available to support an evidence-based approach to the management of fatigue in IBD currently
- Further incisive research is required to delineate the pathogenic pathways driving fatigue in chronic diseases, including IBD
- Prospective trials are required to evaluate the effects of putative therapies for fatigue such as the effect of iron or vitamin D supplementation or the use of certain anti-inflammatory or other targeted therapies

Practical recommendations

- The hallmarks of fatigue management in IBD include the amelioration of active disease, screening for, and treating, psychological comorbidity and lifestyle modification in order to minimise effects of fatigue on daily living
- In most cases, the cause and contributors to fatigue are likely multifactorial and require a multifaceted, trial-and-error approach based on the available evidence

Learning points

- Fatigue is highly prevalent in patients with IBD and often debilitating
- Major contributors to fatigue in IBD include concurrent disease activity, sleep disturbance and psychological comorbidity

References

Bernklev, T, Jahnsen, J, Henriksen, M, Lygren, I, Aadland, E, Sauar, J, Schulz, T, Stray, N, Vatn, M and Moum, B (2006). Relationship between sick leave, unemployment, disability, and health-related quality of life in patients with inflammatory bowel disease. *Inflamm Bowel Dis*, vol. 12, no. 5, pp. 402–12.

Bruner, AB, Joffe, A, Duggan, AK, Casella, JF and Brandt, J (1996). Randomised study of cognitive effects of iron supplementation in non-anaemic iron-deficient adolescent girls. *Lancet*, vol. 348, no. 9033, pp. 992–6.

Casellas, F, Lopez-Vivancos, J, Vergara, M and Malagelada, J (1999). Impact of inflammatory bowel disease on health-related quality of life. *Dig Dis*, vol. 17, no. 4, pp. 208–18.

Cella, D, Peterman, A, Passik, S, Jacobsen, P and Breitbart, W (1998). Progress toward guidelines for the management of fatigue. *Oncology (Williston Park)*, vol. 12, no. 11A, pp. 369–77.

Costantini, A and Pala, MI (2013). Thiamine and fatigue in inflammatory bowel diseases: an open-label pilot study. *J Altern Complement Med*, vol. 19, no. 8, pp. 704–8.

Craig, A, Tran, Y, Wijesuriya, N and Boord, P (2006). A controlled investigation into the psychological determinants of fatigue. *Biol Psychol*, vol. 72, no. 1, pp. 78–87.

Deale, A, Chalder, T, Marks, I and Wessely, S (1997). Cognitive behavior therapy for chronic fatigue syndrome: a randomized controlled trial. *Am J Psychiatry*, vol. 154, no. 3, pp. 408–14.

Dittner, AJ, Wessely, SC and Brown, RG (2004). The assessment of fatigue: a practical guide for clinicians and researchers. *J Psychosom Res*, vol. 56, no. 2, pp. 157–70.

Dryman, A and Eaton, WW (1991). Affective symptoms associated with the onset of major depression in the community: findings from the US National Institute of Mental Health Epidemiologic Catchment Area Program. *Acta psychiatr Scand*, vol. 84, no. 1, pp. 1–5.

Echteld, MA, Passchier, J, Teunissen, S, Claessen, S, de Wit, R and van der Rijt, CC (2007). Multidimensional fatigue and its correlates in hospitalised advanced cancer patients. *Eur J Cancer*, vol. 43, no. 6, pp. 1030–6.

Fardet, L, Blanchon, T, Perdoncini-Roux, A, Kettaneh, A, Tiev, K, Turbelin, C, Dorleans, Y, Cabane, J and Hanslik, T (2009). [Internal medicine physicians' perception of frequency and impact of corticosteroid-induced adverse events]. *Rev Med Interne*, vol. 30, no. 2, pp. 113–8. [In French].

Goldenberg, BA, Graff, LA, Clara, I, Zarychanski, R, Walker, JR, Carr, R, Rogala, L, Miller, N and Bernstein, CN (2013). Is iron deficiency in the absence of anemia associated with fatigue in inflammatory bowel disease? *Am J Gastroenterol*, vol. 108, no. 9, pp. 1392–7.

Graff, LA, Clara, I, Walker, JR, Lix, L, Carr, R, Miller, N, Rogala, L and Bernstein, CN (2013). Changes in fatigue over 2 years are associated with activity of inflammatory bowel disease and psychological factors. *Clin Gastroenterol Hepatol*, vol. 11, no. 9, pp. 1140–6.

Graff, LA, Vincent, N, Walker, JR, Clara, I, Carr, R, Ediger, J, Miller, N, Rogala, L, Rawsthorne, P, Lix, L and Bernstein, CN (2011). A population-based study of fatigue and sleep difficulties in inflammatory bowel disease. *Inflamm Bowel Dis*, vol. 17, no. 9, pp. 1882–9.

Graff, LA, Walker, JR, Clara, I, Lix, L, Miller, N, Rogala, L, Rawsthorne, P and Bernstein, CN (2009). Stress coping, distress, and health perceptions in inflammatory bowel disease and community controls. *Am J Gastroenterol*, vol. 104, no. 12, pp. 2959–69.

Inagaki, M, Isono, M, Okuyama, T, Sugawara, Y, Akechi, T, Akizuki, N, Fujimori, M, Mizuno, M, Shima, Y, Kinoshita, H and Uchitomi, Y (2008). Plasma interleukin-6 and fatigue in terminally ill cancer patients. *J Pain Symptom Manage*, vol. 35, no. 2, pp. 153–61.

Irwin, M (2002). Effects of sleep and sleep loss on immunity and cytokines. *Brain Behav Immun*, vol. 16, no. 5, pp. 503–12.

Jelsness-Jorgensen, LP, Bernklev, T, Henriksen, M, Torp, R and Moum, BA (2011). Chronic fatigue is more prevalent in patients with inflammatory bowel disease than in healthy controls. *Inflamm Bowel Dis*, vol. 17, no. 7, pp. 1564–72.

Jelsness-Jorgensen, LP, Bernklev, T and Moum, B (2012). Fatigue and disease-related worries among inflammatory bowel disease patients in remission; is it a reflection of coexisting IBS-like symptoms? A short report. *J Psychosom Res*, vol. 73, no. 6, pp. 469–72.

Kapsimalis, F, Basta, M, Varouchakis, G, Gourgoulianis, K, Vgontzas, A and Kryger, M (2008). Cytokines and pathological sleep. *Sleep Med*, vol. 9, no. 6, pp. 603–14.

Keefer, L, Stepanski, EJ, Ranjbaran, Z, Benson, LM and Keshavarzian, A (2006). An initial report of sleep disturbance in inactive inflammatory bowel disease. *J Clin Sleep Med*, vol. 2, no. 4, pp. 409–16.

Knowles, SR, Wilson, JL, Connell, WR and Kamm, MA (2011). Preliminary examination of the relations between disease activity, illness perceptions, coping strategies, and psychological morbidity in Crohn's disease guided by the common sense model of illness. *Inflamm Bowel Dis*, vol. 17, no. 12, pp. 2551–7.

Merikangas, KR, Wicki, W and Angst, J (1994). Heterogeneity of depression. Classification of depressive subtypes by longitudinal course. *Br J Psychiatry*, vol. 164, no. 3, pp. 342–8.

Minderhoud, IM, Samsom, M and Oldenburg, B (2007). Crohn's disease, fatigue, and infliximab: is there a role for cytokines in the pathogenesis of fatigue? *World J Gastroenterol*, vol. 13, no. 14, pp. 2089–93.

Ranjbaran, Z, Keefer, L, Farhadi, A, Stepanski, E, Sedghi, S and Keshavarzian, A (2007). Impact of sleep disturbances in inflammatory bowel disease. *J Gastroenterol Hepatol*, vol. 22, no. 11, pp. 1748–53.

Romani, A (2008). The treatment of fatigue. *Neurol Sci*, vol. 29 (Suppl 2), pp. S247–9.

Strober, W and Fuss, IJ (2011). Proinflammatory cytokines in the pathogenesis of inflammatory bowel diseases. *Gastroenterology*, vol. 140, no. 6, pp. 1756–67.

Swain, MG (2000). Fatigue in chronic disease. *Clin Sci (Lond)*, vol. 99, no. 1, pp. 1–8.

van der Linden, G, Chalder, T, Hickie, I, Koschera, A, Sham, P and Wessely, S (1999). Fatigue and psychiatric disorder: different or the same? *Psychol Med*, vol. 29, no. 4, pp. 863–8.

van Langenberg, DR and Gibson, PR (2010). Systematic review: fatigue in inflammatory bowel disease. *Aliment Pharmacol Ther*, vol. 32, no. 2, pp. 131–43.

van Langenberg, DR and Gibson, PR (2014). Factors associated with physical and cognitive fatigue in patients with Crohn's disease: a cross-sectional and longitudinal study. *Inflamm Bowel Dis*, vol. 20, no. 1, pp. 115–25 .

van Langenberg, DR, Della Gatta, P, Warmington, SA, Kidgell, DJ, Gibson, PR and Russell, AP (2014). Objectively measured muscle fatigue in Crohn's disease: correlation with self-reported fatigue and associated factors for clinical application. *J Crohns Colitis*, vol. 8, no. 2, pp. 137–46.

van Langenberg, DR, Yelland, GW, Robinson, SR and Gibson, PR (2011). Crohn's disease and subtle cognitive dysfunction: the unheralded 'dark side' of a chronic systemic disease. *J Gastroenterol Hepatol*, vol. 26, (Suppl. 4), pp. A57–8.

Verdon, F, Burnand, B, Stubi, CL, Bonard, C, Graff, M, Michaud, A, Bischoff, T, de Vevey, M, Studer, JP, Herzig, L, Chapuis, C, Tissot, J, Pecoud, A and Favrat, B (2003). Iron supplementation for unexplained fatigue in non-anaemic women: double blind randomised placebo controlled trial. *BMJ*, vol. 326, no. 7399, p. 1124.

Chapter 16

Cross-cultural aspects of IBD

Ray Boyapati and Christopher Leung

Introduction

Culture is defined as an integrated system of learned patterns of behaviour characteristic to a group of people; consequently, it guides beliefs, thoughts, decisions and actions. Cultural beliefs relating to health and illness have a significant effect on how patients manage disease, including perception of disease and pain, the clinician-patient relationship and attitudes towards therapy. Culture has broader implications on clinician-patient interactions, such as patient attitudes towards issues including the importance of family, personal space, eye contact and body language (Juckett 2005). There are also significant ethnic differences in the relationship between pain, emotional expression and disease (Dimsdale 2000). These factors are particularly relevant in inflammatory bowel disease (IBD) where there is a complex interplay between pain, psychological distress and disease activity.

Clinicians should be mindful of their patients' cultural backgrounds and how this may affect disease phenotype and response to the disease. An ability to adapt clinician-patient interactions based on an understanding of cultural influences in IBD is essential to help optimise quality of life. This 'cultural competence' is becoming increasingly important with increasing travel, immigration and globalisation.

Changing epidemiology in IBD

The incidence and prevalence of IBD has been increasing globally. Historically, epidemiological studies have found far higher rates of IBD in Western countries, such as those in Western Europe and North America compared to non-Western countries (Russel and Stockbrugger 1996). This has led to research questionnaires and treatment trials primarily being performed in Caucasian patients. However, a recent systematic review of the literature found an increasing incidence in developing countries paralleling socioeconomic development (Molodecky *et al.* 2012).

This increase in incidence is not just confined to non-Western countries; it also applies to migrants moving to the West. Migrant populations from South Asia have been found to have an even higher rate of IBD than comparative Caucasian cohorts (Pinsk *et al.* 2007; Probert *et al.* 1992). The country to which patients immigrate is also important. Patients from North West Spain immigrating to a more industrialised country had a higher risk of developing IBD, but this was not apparent for those moving to countries of similar or lower industrialisation (Barreiro-de Acosta *et al.* 2011).

Many hypotheses exist as to why industrialisation may promote the development of IBD. These include changes in diet, smoking, infections, medications, a sedentary lifestyle, stress, hygiene, microbial exposure and pollution (Ng *et al.* 2013). Some of these factors such as hygiene, diet and medication use may alter the microbiota of individuals with possible aetiological consequences.

Differences in IBD phenotype between ethnicities

Even within the same country, research suggests that there are key ethnic differences in the phenotype of IBD. This is highly significant as these differences may play an important role in variable behaviour, response to treatment and mechanisms of coping with disease. Using a large North American cohort ($n = 1,126$), Nguyen *et al.* (2006) found African American, Caucasian and Hispanic populations had significant differences in family and surgical history, disease location and extra-intestinal manifestation of disease. Similarly, a comparison between French-Canadian and Caucasian IBD patients in Canada demonstrated very different phenotypic profiles between the two groups (Bhat *et al.* 2009). French-Canadian Crohn's Disease patients were less likely to have stricturing disease, had a tendency towards fistulising disease and had an increased prevalence of sacroiliitis. A systematic review of the literature examining the differences between Asians, Hispanics and African Americans found a male predominance and lower frequency of pancolitis, perianal disease and extra intestinal manifestations in Asians (Hou *et al.* 2009).

In a study from North West London, Walker *et al.* (2011) found patients with South Asian heritage had a higher frequency of extensive colitis and male predominance but a lower risk of colectomy compared to those with Northern European heritage. Studies in South Asians based in Leicestershire (United Kingdom) and British Columbia (Canada) had similar findings (Pinsk *et al.* 2007; Probert *et al.* 1992). Patients with IBD from China may have a different phenotype with male predominance, later onset and less severe phenotype compared to those from developed countries (Wang *et al.* 2010). These studies provide strong support for phenotypic differences between various ethnicities in IBD.

Cultural factors affecting IBD clinicians

Culture also has an important effect on how clinicians respond to patient illness including diagnostic, therapeutic and communication choices. For clinicians, the inability to communicate in a timely, culturally appropriate manner may lead to patient loss of confidence and poor adherence (Sewitch *et al.* 2003). Language barriers, poor cultural awareness and physician bias are some of the factors that may lead to a breakdown of the clinician-patient relationship in culturally discordant interactions. Evidence suggests that in such interactions, there is decreased rapport building and empathy as well as a reduction in participatory decision-making and provision of information (Ferguson and Candib 2002). Specific IBD-related studies on how cultural barriers may affect the clinician-patient relationship are needed.

Cultural influences on patient knowledge and understanding

The importance of patient knowledge in IBD

An important component of chronic disease management is improving patient knowledge and understanding. Meta-analyses in other chronic diseases have demonstrated improved adherence with education (Devine and Pearcy 1996; Devine and Reifschneider 1995). In IBD, poor adherence to therapies can have a devastating impact on the progression of disease. Non-adherence is common, with estimates ranging from between 40 to 72 per cent (Lopez San Roman *et al.* 2005; Sewitch *et al.* 2003).

Within IBD cohort studies, increased disease-specific knowledge has been positively associated with patient satisfaction and improved adherence (Waters *et al.* 2005), as well as reduced disease-related concerns and psychological distress (Moser *et al.* 1995). Underpinning the benefits of enhancing disease-related knowledge may be changes in individual coping patterns. Supporting this idea, Moradkhani *et al.* (2011) found that increased disease-specific knowledge improved beneficial coping strategies in patients (such as active coping, planning, seeking social and emotional support), and in turn, led to greater medication adherence. Despite this, several studies have found that increasing disease specific knowledge in IBD does not necessarily enhance quality of life (Borgaonkar *et al.* 2002; Bregenzer *et al.* 2005; Moradkhani *et al.* 2011; Smart *et al.* 1986; Verma *et al.* 2001) or reduce anxiety (Selinger *et al.* 2013). Clearly, there is a complex relationship between patient disease-specific knowledge and adherence, psychological status and quality of life. Several factors may be important, including patient pre- and post-diagnosis knowledge of IBD, psychological status and coping patterns. These processes will, in turn, be influenced by cultural factors.

Effect of culture on obtaining and using knowledge

There are differences in disease-specific patient knowledge between ethnicities and how knowledge is obtained and used within a society. Leong *et al.* (2004) identified disparities in knowledge and beliefs between IBD patients in Hong Kong and Australia. Australians tended to have fewer misconceptions and have more knowledge about the disease than Chinese patients. This was an expected finding given the lack of community exposure to IBD in the Chinese population, which is due to the historic rarity of the disease. In contrast, a matched cohort study by Blumenstein *et al.* (2013) comparing knowledge in IBD patients from Germany and Ireland did not demonstrate any major differences in knowledge of the disease. There was, however, a variation in how patients obtained information about their disease between the two groups. German patients were more likely to use the internet and newspapers or magazines, obtaining their information from a wider range of sources compared to Irish patients. The outlined studies demonstrate that individually tailored and culturally appropriate patient education is crucial to promote adherence.

Cultural influences on perception of disease

Cultural characteristics affect the manner in which health and illness is perceived, including the emotional response to illness and the effect it has on daily life. Finlay *et al.* (2006) explored IBD specific knowledge and its impact on daily life in a US sample. Results indicated that Caucasians had a much higher fear of dying from a complication of IBD than African Americans, whilst African Americans were more likely to think that their career choices were limited due to the disease compared to Caucasians. The perceived stigma in the African American cohort led to a lower likelihood of discussing their disease with others or contacting IBD support organisations. Understanding these differences may provide an opportunity for clinicians to better target social and psychological support to different cultural groups.

Stigma is a complex concept in which social and cultural factors lead to the characterisation of a particular attribute as undesirable and the discrediting of individuals with that attribute. It is known that perception of stigma related to IBD is widespread and a significant independent predictor of poorer outcome in terms of quality of life, psychological coping and treatment adherence (Taft *et al.* 2009). Cross-cultural IBD specific studies on differences in stigma perception are lacking but it is clear from studies in other illnesses such as HIV and mental illness that large differences exist between cultures (Rao *et al.* 2008; Richards *et al.* 2014). The clinician must be aware of the difference in the way IBD is stigmatised in various societies and cultures, and how this may impact on an individual's disease, such as delay in diagnosis and coping strategies.

Cultural influences on patient concerns

Culture influences attitudes towards disease and health which may affect the relative importance of issues concerning patients dealing with IBD. An IBD study conducted in eight European countries found marked differences in overall level of concern about the illness (Levenstein *et al.* 2001). For example, Portuguese patients had a much higher overall level of concern (score of 51) compared to

Swedish patients (score of 19). In addition, there were wide differences between countries in degrees of concern relating to energy level, access to quality health care, passing the disease onto others, pain or suffering, feeling 'dirty or smelly' and the uncertain nature of the disease.

A separate study on IBD patient concerns in US, Swedish, Austrian and French ulcerative colitis (UC) populations found that although there were similarities in the rank-order of issues in terms of importance, the scores were generally lower in the Swedish population (Hjortswang *et al.* 1998). In addition, the sickness impact profile (SIP) score was markedly lower in the Swedish UC cohort compared to the American UC cohort. The extent to which these differences relate to culture compared to other factors, such as severity of disease and differences in translation (notwithstanding extensive translation-back-translation), remains to be elucidated.

In contrast, a study by Richardson *et al.* (2001) comparing quality of life in English and Canadian paediatric patients with IBD using the Item Reduction Questionnaire (IRQ) found that issues of concern were similar in both populations, with 43 of the highest ranking concerns corresponding for both populations. However, 21 of the 96 items were still ranked significantly differently, which may be a reflection of cultural differences or in IBD type/severity between the populations.

Cultural differences in coping strategies

According to the biopsychosocial model of chronic disease, coping strategy is one of the major psychological variables that may explain the heterogeneity amongst individuals in their ability to effectively manage illness. Social supports are clearly important to patients with IBD and may affect the ability to cope with psychological stress (Sewitch *et al.* 2001). However, there may be cultural differences in the type of social structure surrounding an individual, how this network responds to illness and the use of social support between cultures. For example, an analysis of the Coping Orientations to Problems Experienced (COPE) inventory, a questionnaire measuring 15 coping strategies, found significant differences in the strategies used in the Italian and US populations (Sica *et al.* 1997). The difference in coping strategies between cultures has not been extensively studied in the IBD population.

Cultural influences in treatment preference

Culture may also affect patient preference and attitude towards treatments in IBD. Although there is a belief that some cultures have a poor acceptance of Western medicine leading to high use of alternative therapies, cohort studies in IBD have found no significant differences between cultures in this regard (Leong *et al.* 2004; Moody *et al.* 1998). These studies did reveal high rates of alternative therapy use in the IBD population across cultures (up to 33 per cent).

Interestingly, there are ethnic differences in the type of alternative therapies used. In the IBD study outlined above (Leong *et al.* 2004), there was a trend towards higher use of Chinese herbs in the Hong Kong cohort. A Californian cross sectional survey showed differences in the type of alternative therapy used between ethnic groups (Hsiao *et al.* 2006). For example, Asian Americans were more likely to use acupuncture and traditional Chinese medicine, whereas Caucasians were more likely to visit an osteopath. The outlined studies indicate that patients with IBD are likely to use alternative therapies that may be, in part, culturally influenced.

Conclusion

The increasing incidence of IBD in non-Western ethnicities means that cultural competence is becoming increasingly important. Adaptations in interactions with patients based on a cross-cultural appreciation of the differences in IBD phenotype, level of knowledge, perception of disease, type and degree of concern, coping strategies and the type of alternative therapies used is mandatory for the successful IBD clinician.

Current limitations and future considerations

- Developing linguistically and culturally appropriate education tools for both patients and clinicians is an emerging challenge
- Clarifying how knowledge of phenotypic differences between ethnicities may be used by clinicians to modify diagnostic and treatment recommendations
- Further research is required into many cross-cultural aspects of IBD including:
  - more reliable epidemiological data in developing countries, especially in Africa and South America
  - differences in stigma perception
  - variations in disease perception, treatment preference and response
  - how cultural barriers may affect the clinician-patient relationship
  - response to medical therapy between ethnicities
  - the differences in coping strategies between cultures in IBD
  - validation of existing research instruments in non-Caucasian populations

Practical recommendations

- There are ethnic variations in IBD phenotype with differences in sex, onset, severity and extraintestinal manifestations
- Understanding differences in perception of illness and coping strategies between cultures will allow a better understanding of patient behaviour and response to illness
- Appreciating that different cultures use different sources of information can enable culturally effective methods of disseminating knowledge

- Providing information in a way that is culturally appropriate for the individual will reduce anxiety and stigma as well as increase rapport. This will enable improved disease-specific knowledge and better adherence
- Alternative medicine is commonly used in IBD and should be considered in all patients regardless of their cultural background. However, differences may exist in the type of alternative therapy used

Learning points

- The incidence of IBD is rising in non-Western cultures and migrants from such cultures who move to industrialised countries
- There are differences in IBD phenotype between ethnicities
- Culture has an important impact on acquisition and use of knowledge; perception of disease, patient concerns, quality of life, coping strategies and treatment choices in IBD
- Further research is required to understand the changing epidemiology in IBD, the effect of ethnicity on existing and future treatments and cross-cultural influences in IBD

References

Barreiro-de Acosta, M, Alvarez Castro, A, Souto, R, Iglesias, M, Lorenzo, A and Dominguez-Munoz, JE (2011). Emigration to western industrialized countries: a risk factor for developing inflammatory bowel disease. *J Crohns Colitis*, vol. 5, no. 6, pp. 566–9.

Bhat, M, Nguyen, GC, Pare, P, Lahaie, R, Deslandres, C, Bernard, EJ, Aumais, G, Jobin, G, Wild, G, Cohen, A, Langelier, D, Brant, S, Dassopoulos, T, McGovern, D, Torres, E, Duerr, R, Regueiro, M, Silverberg, MS, Steinhart, H, Griffiths, AM, Elkadri, A, Cho, J, Proctor, D, Goyette, P, Rioux, J and Bitton, A (2009). Phenotypic and genotypic characteristics of inflammatory bowel disease in French Canadians: comparison with a large North American repository. *Am J Gastroenterol*, vol. 104, no. 9, pp. 2233–40.

Blumenstein, I, McDermott, E, Keegan, D, Byrne, K, Ellison, M, Doherty, G, Schroder, O and Mulcahy, H (2013). Sources of information and factual knowledge in Europeans with inflammatory bowel diseases: a cross-cultural comparison between German and Irish patients. *J Crohns Colitis*, vol. 7, no. 9, pp. e331–6.

Borgaonkar, MR, Townson, G, Donnelly, M and Irvine, EJ (2002). Providing disease-related information worsens health-related quality of life in inflammatory bowel disease. *Inflamm Bowel Dis*, vol. 8, no. 4, pp. 264–9.

Bregenzer, N, Lange, A, Furst, A, Gross, V, Scholmerich, J and Andus, T (2005). Patient education in inflammatory bowel disease does not influence patients knowledge and long-term psychosocial well-being. *Z Gastroenterol*, vol. 43, no. 4, pp. 367–71.

Devine, EC and Pearcy, J (1996). Meta-analysis of the effects of psychoeducational care in adults with chronic obstructive pulmonary disease. *Patient Educ Couns*, vol. 29, no. 2, pp. 167–78.

Devine, EC and Reifschneider, E (1995). A meta-analysis of the effects of psychoeducational care in adults with hypertension. *Nurs Res*, vol. 44, no. 4, pp. 237–45.

Dimsdale, JE (2000). Stalked by the past: the influence of ethnicity on health. *Psychosom Med*, vol. 62, no. 2, pp. 161–70.

Ferguson, WJ and Candib, LM (2002). Culture, language, and the doctor-patient relationship. *Fam Med*, vol. 34, no. 5, pp. 353–61.

Finlay, DG, Basu, D and Sellin, JH (2006). Effect of race and ethnicity on perceptions of inflammatory bowel disease. *Inflamm Bowel Dis*, vol. 12, no. 6, pp. 503–7.

Hjortswang, H, Strom, M and Almer, S (1998). Health-related quality of life in Swedish patients with ulcerative colitis. *Am J Gastroenterol*, vol. 93, no. 11, pp. 2203–11.

Hou, JK, El-Serag, H and Thirumurthi, S (2009). Distribution and manifestations of inflammatory bowel disease in Asians, Hispanics, and African Americans: a systematic review. *Am J Gastroenterol*, vol. 104, no. 8, pp. 2100–9.

Hsiao, AF, Wong, MD, Goldstein, MS, Yu, HJ, Andersen, RM, Brown, ER, Becerra, LM and Wenger, NS (2006). Variation in complementary and alternative medicine (CAM) use across racial/ethnic groups and the development of ethnic-specific measures of CAM use. *J Altern Complement Med*, vol. 12, no. 3, pp. 281–90.

Juckett, G (2005). Cross-cultural medicine. *Am Fam Physician*, vol. 72, no. 11, pp. 2267–74.

Leong, RW, Lawrance, IC, Ching, JY, Cheung, CM, Fung, SS, Ho, JN, Philpott, J, Wallace and AR, Sung, JJ (2004). Knowledge, quality of life, and use of complementary and alternative medicine and therapies in inflammatory bowel disease: a comparison of Chinese and Caucasian patients. *Dig Dis Sci*, vol. 49, no. 10, pp. 1672–6.

Levenstein, S, Li, Z, Almer, S, Barbosa, A, Marquis, P, Moser, G, Sperber, A, Toner, B and Drossman, DA (2001). Cross-cultural variation in disease-related concerns among patients with inflammatory bowel disease. *Am J Gastroenterol*, vol. 96, no. 6, pp. 1822–30.

Lopez San Roman, A, Bermejo, F, Carrera, E, Perez-Abad, M and Boixeda, D (2005). Adherence to treatment in inflammatory bowel disease. *Rev Esp Enferm Dig*, vol. 97, no. 4, pp. 249–57.

Molodecky, NA, Soon, IS, Rabi, DM, Ghali, WA, Ferris, M, Chernoff, G, Benchimol, EI, Panaccione, R, Ghosh, S, Barkema, HW and Kaplan, GG (2012). Increasing incidence and prevalence of the inflammatory bowel diseases with time, based on systematic review. *Gastroenterology*, vol. 142, no. 1, pp. 46–54.e42; quiz e30.

Moody, GA, Eaden, JA, Bhakta, P, Sher, K and Mayberry, JF (1998). The role of complementary medicine in European and Asian patients with inflammatory bowel disease. *Public Health*, vol. 112, no. 4, pp. 269–71.

Moradkhani, A, Kerwin, L, Dudley-Brown, S and Tabibian, JH (2011). Disease-specific knowledge, coping, and adherence in patients with inflammatory bowel disease. *Dig Dis Sci*, vol. 56, no. 10, pp. 2972–7.

Moser, G, Tillinger, W, Sachs, G, Genser, D, Maier-Dobersberger, T, Spiess, K, Wyatt, J, Vogelsang, H, Lochs, H and Gangl, A (1995). Disease-related worries and concerns: a study on out-patients with inflammatory bowel disease. *Eur J Gastroenterol Hepatol*, vol. 7, no. 9, pp. 853–8.

Ng, SC, Bernstein, CN, Vatn, MH, Lakatos, PL, Loftus, EV, Jr., Tysk, C, O'Morain, C, Moum, B, Colombel, JF and Epidemiology and Natural History Task Force of the International Organization of Inflammatory Bowel Disease (IOIBD) (2013). Geographical variability and environmental risk factors in inflammatory bowel disease. *Gut*, vol. 62, no. 4, pp. 630–49.

Nguyen, GC, Torres, EA, Regueiro, M, Bromfield, G, Bitton, A, Stempak, J, Dassopoulos, T, Schumm, P, Gregory, FJ, Griffiths, AM, Hanauer, SB, Hanson, J, Harris, ML, Kane, SV, Orkwis, HK, Lahaie, R, Oliva-Hemker, M, Pare, P, Wild, GE, Rioux, JD, Yang, H,

Duerr, RH, Cho, JH, Steinhart, AH, Brant, SR and Silverberg, MS (2006). Inflammatory bowel disease characteristics among African Americans, Hispanics, and non-Hispanic Whites: characterization of a large North American cohort. *Am J Gastroenterol*, vol. 101, no. 5, pp. 1012–23.

Pinsk, V, Lemberg, DA, Grewal, K, Barker, CC, Schreiber, RA and Jacobson, K (2007). Inflammatory bowel disease in the South Asian pediatric population of British Columbia. *Am J Gastroenterol*, vol. 102, no. 5, pp. 1077–83.

Probert, CS, Jayanthi, V, Pinder, D, Wicks, AC and Mayberry, JF (1992). Epidemiological study of ulcerative proctocolitis in Indian migrants and the indigenous population of Leicestershire. *Gut*, vol. 33, no. 5, pp. 687–93.

Rao, D, Pryor, JB, Gaddist, BW and Mayer, R (2008). Stigma, secrecy, and discrimination: ethnic/racial differences in the concerns of people living with HIV/AIDS. *AIDS Behav*, vol. 12, no. 2, pp. 265–71.

Richards, M, Hori, H, Sartorius, N and Kunugi, H (2014). Cross-cultural comparisons of attitudes toward schizophrenia amongst the general population and physicians: a series of web-based surveys in Japan and the United States. *Psychiatry Res*, vol. 215, no. 2, pp. 300–7.

Richardson, G, Griffiths, AM, Miller, V and Thomas, AG (2001). Quality of life in inflammatory bowel disease: a cross-cultural comparison of English and Canadian children. *J Pediatr Gastroenterol Nutr*, vol. 32, no. 5, pp. 573–8.

Russel, MG and Stockbrugger, RW (1996). Epidemiology of inflammatory bowel disease: an update. *Scand J Gastroenterol*, vol. 31, no. 5, pp. 417–27.

Selinger, CP, Lal, S, Eaden, J, Jones, DB, Katelaris, P, Chapman, G, McDonald, C, Leong, RW and McLaughlin, J (2013). Better disease specific patient knowledge is associated with greater anxiety in inflammatory bowel disease. *J Crohns Colitis*, vol. 7, no. 6, pp. e214–8.

Sewitch, MJ, Abrahamowicz, M, Barkun, A, Bitton, A, Wild, GE, Cohen, A and Dobkin, PL (2003). Patient nonadherence to medication in inflammatory bowel disease. *Am J Gastroenterol*, vol. 98, no. 7, pp. 1535–44.

Sewitch, MJ, Abrahamowicz, M, Bitton, A, Daly, D, Wild, GE, Cohen, A, Katz, S, Szego, PL and Dobkin, PL (2001). Psychological distress, social support, and disease activity in patients with inflammatory bowel disease. *Am J Gastroenterol*, vol. 96, no. 5, pp. 1470–9.

Sica, C, Novara, C, Dorz, S and Sanavio, E (1997). Coping strategies: evidence for cross-cultural differences? A preliminary study with the Italian version of coping orientations to problems experienced (COPE). *Pers Individ Dif*, vol. 23, no. 6, pp. 1025–9.

Smart, H, Mayberry, J, Calcraft, B, Morris, JS and Rhodes, J (1986). Effect of information booklet on patients' anxiety levels and consultation rates in Crohn's disease. *Public Health*, vol. 100, no. 3, pp. 184–6.

Taft, TH, Keefer, L, Leonhard, C and Nealon-Woods, M (2009). Impact of perceived stigma on inflammatory bowel disease patient outcomes. *Inflamm Bowel Dis*, vol. 15, no. 8, pp. 1224–32.

Verma, S, Tsai, HH and Giaffer, MH (2001). Does better disease-related education improve quality of life? A survey of IBD patients. *Dig Dis Sci*, vol. 46, no. 4, pp. 865–9.

Walker, DG, Williams, HR, Kane, SP, Mawdsley, JE, Arnold, J, McNeil, I, Thomas, HJ, Teare, JP, Hart, AL, Pitcher, MC, Walters, JR, Marshall, SE and Orchard, TR (2011). Differences in inflammatory bowel disease phenotype between South Asians and Northern Europeans living in North West London, UK. *Am J Gastroenterol*, vol. 106, no. 7, pp. 1281–9.

Wang, YF, Ouyang, Q and Hu, RW (2010). Progression of inflammatory bowel disease in China. *J Dig Dis*, vol. 11, no. 2, pp. 76–82.

Waters, BM, Jensen, L and Fedorak, RN (2005). Effects of formal education for patients with inflammatory bowel disease: a randomized controlled trial. *Can J Gastroenterol*, vol. 19, no. 4, pp. 235–44.

Chapter 17

Psychological assessment and the use of questionnaires in IBD cohorts

Simon R. Knowles

Introduction

Underpinning any successful psychological intervention involves a comprehensive assessment, diagnosis, and formulation. Groth-Marnat (2003) identifies that the early forms of the psychological assessment were primarily based on medical formats. However, over time the modern day methods of psychological assessment have appeared and can involve multiple theoretical approaches, including psychoanalytic, humanistic, behavioral, cognitive, and cognitive-behavioral. While the majority of clinicians use a semi-structured approach (i.e. having a standard set of basic questions and then allowing open ended, and follow-up questions, into particular areas of clinical focus), the development of diagnostic criteria [e.g. Diagnostic and Statistical Manual (American Psychiatric Association, American Psychiatric Association, DSM-5 Task Force 2013)] or the International Statistical Classification of Diseases and Related Health Problems (National Centre for Classification in Health 2010) and the need for standardized methods for research has led to the development of structural diagnostic approaches, such as the Mini-International Neuropsychiatric Interview (M.I.N.I.; Sheehan *et al.* 1998) and Structured Clinical Interview for DSM (SCID; First and Spitzer 2002). This Chapter will briefly review the key features of a psychological assessment, with an emphasis on inflammatory bowel disease (IBD)-specific questions. The Chapter will then identify currently available questionnaires that can be utilized in an IBD cohort to assess multiple psychosocial domains (e.g. anxiety, depression, stress, disease activity, illness perceptions, and quality of life).

Assessment, formulation and diagnosis of psychopathology in IBD cohorts

Patient trust and engagement are key components of any psychological assessment. Without them, any formulation and working diagnosis is at risk of bias and being invalid. At an assessment, both the clinician and patient are assessing each other out in terms of skill, knowledge, and compatibility. A common reason for failure in psychological therapy is a lack of trust and engagement by patients. While therapeutic failure can be due to interpersonal factors (e.g. personality, past history or problematic relationships – including therapeutic), it can also be due to the lack of empathy or knowledge about IBD and/or its impact on the patient's life shown by the clinician. Given this, clinicians should ensure that they have a good working knowledge of IBD, including its etiology, epidemiology, current diagnostic and treatment methods, the role of the brain-gut-axis, and the psychological/psychosocial consequences of IBD prior to undertaking an assessment of a patient with IBD.

A standard psychological assessment should include a comprehensive history and mental state examination (Castle and Bassett 2013). See Table 17.1 for a summary of the components involved in a standard psychological assessment. For a more detailed overview of psychological assessment procedures, see Castle and Bassett (2013) and Toy and Klamen (2012). After an assessment, the clinician should work to develop a formulation. This formulation should represent the cumulative, interrelated, and concise summary of the key features of the patient's underlying concerns and symptoms. One of the most efficient ways to explore and construct a formulation is using a matrix (see Table 17.2). Once a formulation has been completed, the clinician can then develop a working diagnosis based upon standard diagnostic nomenclature, such as the Diagnostic and Statistical Manual (DSM-5; American Psychiatric Association, American Psychiatric Association, DSM-5 Task Force 2013) or the International Statistical Classification of Diseases and Related Health Problems (ICD-10; National Centre for Classification in Health 2010). This formulation and diagnosis should then be used to shape the type and format of psychotherapy.

Basic information

Basic information includes full name, address, contact number/s, date of birth, gender, marital status, occupation, and emergency person contact details. Circumstances of the interview (e.g. when and where assessment conducted), reason for the referral, and sources of information (e.g. interview, referral letter).

Primary and secondary concern/s

The patient's primary and secondary concerns should be identified. This should include details relating to its history, frequency, intensity, duration, and how it impacts upon the patient across their life domains (e.g. family, friends, education, work, sexual, and hobbies/interests). Identification of internal and external factors that either attenuate or exacerbate patient concerns.

Medications

Current medications (including complementary, over the counter and prescribed) being taken, including dosage and duration of use. Details on drug sensitivities and allergies should also be recorded.

Table 17.1 Key components of a psychological assessment

Basic information:

Includes full name, address, contact number/s, date of birth, gender, marital status, occupation, and emergency person contact details. Circumstances of the interview (e.g. when and where assessment conducted), reason for the referral, and sources of information (e.g. interview, referral letter).

Primary and secondary concern/s:

Patient's primary and secondary concerns should be identified. This should also include details relating to its history, frequency, intensity, duration, and how it impacts upon the patient across their life domains (e.g. family, friends, education, work, sexual, and hobbies/interests). Identification of internal and external factors that either attenuate or exacerbate patient concerns.

Medications:

Current medications (including complementary, over the counter and prescribed) being taken, including dosage and duration of use. Details on drug sensitivities and allergies should also be recorded.

Psychiatric history:

Current or past diagnoses, admissions and treatments. Details relating to when, where, duration and format of therapy, name/location of health professional/s involved, and history of pharmaceutical therapy.

Medical history:

Current and past medical illnesses including date of diagnosis, symptoms, frequency, intensity, duration, treatment/s, and current status.

Drug and alcohol history:

Substance use, history of substance abuse and dependency

Forensic history:

Current or past criminal charges, convictions, sentences or court orders.

Social history and lifestyle:

Social support structures, current finances and/or housing issues, cultural and religious background/beliefs, and hobbies/interests.

Family history:

Family genogram, details relating to family functioning, and family physical and psychiatric health history.

Personal history:

Psychosocial and educational development e.g. any birth complications, difficulties relating to motor, verbal and social milestones, past traumas or experiences of significant stressors, experiences/difficulties relating to schooling (e.g. experiences of bullying, non-attendance, academic abilities), highest level of education, employment history and experiences, relationship and psychosexual development experiences, and perceived personal strengths/ weaknesses.

Pre-morbid personality:

Personality traits, predominant coping patterns, ability to manage conflict and anger.

Psychological assessment in IBD cohorts 153

Table 17.1 (Continued)

Mental status:

Appearance and behavior (e.g. neat and tidy, well-groomed), mood and affect (e.g. range, appropriateness, blunted), speech (tone, quality, volume), thought stream (rate, form and amount), thought process and content (e.g. logical, coherent, delusions, tangential), perceptions (e.g. hallucinations, illusions), cognition (e.g. capacity for abstract thought, intelligence), and insight (e.g. patient has an understanding of their symptoms and consequences of their actions). A mini-mental state examination (Folstein *et al.* 1975) may also be of value if there are concerns about patients experiencing cognitive difficulties, especially involving psychiatric conditions including delirium or dementia.

Table 17.2 Standard formulation matrix (Adapted from Castle and Bassett 2013)

		Biopsychosocial factors		
		Biological	Psychological	Social
The 4 Ps of formulation	Predisposing factors			
	Precipitating factors			
	Perpetuating factors			
	Protective factors			

Psychiatric history

Current or past diagnoses, admissions and treatments. Details relating to when, where, duration and format of therapy, name/location of health professional/s involved, and history of pharmaceutical therapy.

Medical history

Current and past medical illnesses including date of diagnosis, symptoms, frequency, intensity, duration, treatment/s, and current status.

Drug and alcohol history

Substance use, history of substance abuse and dependency.

Forensic history

Current or past criminal charges, convictions, sentences or court orders.

Social history and lifestyle

Social support structures, current finances and/or housing issues, cultural and religious background/beliefs, and hobbies/interests.

Family history

Family genogram, details relating to family functioning, and family physical and psychiatric health history.

Personal history

Psychosocial and educational development, for example, any birth complications, difficulties relating to motor, verbal and social milestones, past traumas or experiences of significant stressors, experiences/difficulties relating to schooling (e.g. experiences of bullying, non-attendance, academic abilities), highest level of education, employment history and experiences, relationship and psychosexual development experiences, and perceived personal strengths/weaknesses.

Pre-morbid personality

Personality traits, predominant coping patterns, ability to manage conflict and anger.

Mental status

Appearance and behavior (e.g. neat and tidy, well groomed), mood and affect (e.g. range, appropriateness, blunted), speech (tone, quality, volume), thought stream (rate, form and amount), thought process and content (e.g. logical, coherent, delusions, tangential), perceptions (e.g. hallucinations, illusions), cognition (e.g. capacity for abstract thought, intelligence), and insight (e.g. patient has an understanding of their symptoms and consequences of their actions). A mini-mental state examination (Folstein *et al.* 1975) may also be of value if there are concerns about patients experiencing cognitive difficulties, especially involving psychiatric conditions, including delirium or dementia.

IBD-specific patient questions to consider

- What are the symptoms of IBD that you experience? (incl. frequency, intensity, duration)
- What are the primary concerns or worries you have in relation to IBD?
- Do you feel you have enough information and support to help manage your symptoms?
- How much have you told your family/partner/friends/co-workers about your IBD?

- How do your family/partner/friends/co-workers communicate with you (or react) when you talk about having IBD and/or experience flare-ups and/or associated difficulties?
- Are there ways you have found help you manage the physical impact of IBD on your life? If so, what are they?
- Are there ways you have found help you manage the psychological impact of IBD on your life? If so, what are they?
- Do you use, or have you thought about, getting in contact with your local IBD organization/association, support-groups?
- To you, what defines when your illness is well-managed and/or in a non-active phase?
- What do you believe helps get your IBD under control and/or in remission?
- How do you manage when your IBD is active, does this differ when your IBD is not-active?
- What are the warning signs in relation to your IBD and/or psychological symptoms that suggest you need to get help? Has this happened before, and if so what did you do?
- Do you have any questions about IBD?

Self-report questionnaires

There are numerous questionnaires available, far beyond the scope of this chapter to identify and review. However, a summary of questionnaires used to assess patient psychosocial domains (e.g. disease activity, anxiety, depression, stress, illness perceptions, and quality of life) is provided in Table 17.3. The selection of questionnaires should be based upon their requirements, these may include whether the questionnaires are clinician or patient completed, research and/or patient-focused, questionnaire length and time-to complete limitations, and singular versus multi-component assessment. Copyright, permission, and cost-to-use issues also need to be considered. Several books are available that identify and review developed questionnaires (including their psychometric properties), these include health status measures (McDowell 2006) and quality of life (Bowling 2005). In terms of assessing coping, several recent papers may be of value (Kato 2013; Steed 1998).

Conclusions

A comprehensive psychological assessment is essential to attaining a valid formulation and working hypothesis of a patient's psychological symptoms. To do this, clinicians need to have a good working knowledge of IBD, including its etiology, epidemiology, and current diagnostic and treatment methods. Clinicians should also explore specific IBD related patient concerns and perceptions, including what active versus non-active disease and well-controlled disease means to them. There are numerous standardized questionnaires available to assess wellbeing

Table 17.3 Summary of questionnaires that can be utilised in inflammatory bowel disease (IBD) cohorts to assess multiple psychosocial domains (e.g. anxiety, depression, stress, disease activity, illness perceptions, and quality of life)

Area of assessment/questionnaire	Advantages	Disadvantages
Disease activity		
The Manitoba Index (Clara *et al.* 2009)	Single item measure of disease activity for CD and UC, developed and validated using a large IBD cohort; strongly correlated with the Harvey-Bradshaw Index, Powell-Tuck Index, and IBDQ, patient-completed	Single item measure, may be biased when patient also has comorbid IBS
Crohn's Disease Activity Index (CDAI) (Best *et al.* 1976)	Gold standard measure of CD activity, highly published	Requires biological data and completion by medical expert
Ulcerative Colitis Disease Activity Index (UCDAI) (Sutherland *et al.* 1987)	Highly published measure of UC disease activity	Requires biological data and completion by medical expert
Harvey Bradshaw Index (HBI) (Harvey & Bradshaw 1980)	Highly published measure of UC disease activity	Requires completion by medical expert
Lichtiger Scale (Lichtiger *et al.* 1994)	Less published measure of UC disease activity	Requires completion by medical expert
Bowel Symptom Severity Scale (BSSS) (Boyce *et al.* 2000)	Patient-completed, assesses frequency, level of distress and interference of bowel symptoms	Developed and validated for Irritable Bowel Syndrome cohorts, few or no IBD-cohort data published
Powel Tuck Index (Powell-Tuck *et al.* 1978)	Highly published measure of UC disease activity	Requires completion by medical expert
General psychological wellbeing		
K10 or K6 (Kessler *et al.* 2002)	Strong psychometric properties, population data, highly published, patient-completed	Few or no IBD-cohort data published
General Health Questionnaire (GHQ) (28-item), (12-item) (Goldberg 1972)	Strong psychometric properties, population data, highly published, patient-completed	Few or no IBD-cohort data published

Table 17.3 (Continued)

Area of assessment/questionnaire	Advantages	Disadvantages
Anxiety, depression, stress		
Beck Depression Inventory (BDI-II) (1996 revision) (Beck *et al.* 1996)	Strong psychometric properties, population data, highly published, patient-completed	
Beck Anxiety Inventory (BAI) (Beck and Steer 1993)	Strong psychometric properties, population data, highly published, patient-completed	
Hospital Anxiety and Depression Scale (HADS) (Zigmond and Snaith 1983)	Strong psychometric properties, population data, highly published, patient-completed	
Depression, Anxiety and Stress Scale (DASS) (Lovibond and Lovibond 1995)	Strong psychometric properties, highly published, patient-completed	Few or no IBD-cohort data published
Perceived Stress Scale (PSS) (Cohen, Kamarck and Mermelstein 1983)	Strong psychometric properties, highly published, patient-completed	Few or no IBD-cohort data published
State-Trait Anxiety Inventory (STAI) (Spielberger *et al.* 1983)	Strong psychometric properties, highly published, assesses both state and trait levels of anxiety, patient-completed	
Illness perceptions		
Illness Perception Questionnaire (IPQ) (Weinman *et al.* 1996)	Strong psychometric properties, highly published, patient-completed	Not IBD-specific, few or no IBD-cohort data published, no normed data
Illness Perception Questionnaire-Revised (IPQ-R) (Moss-Morris *et al.* 2002)	Strong psychometric properties, highly published, patient-completed	Not IBD-specific, few or no IBD-cohort data published, no normed data
Brief Illness Perception Questionnaire (Brief-IPQ) (Broadbent *et al.* 2006)	Strong psychometric properties, highly published, patient-completed	Not IBD-specific, few or no IBD-cohort data published, no normed data
Coping		
Brief COPE (COPE) (Carver *et al.* 1989)	Strong psychometric properties, highly published, patient-completed	
Ways of Coping Questionnaire (WOCQ) (Folkman and Lazarus 1985)	Strong psychometric properties, highly published, patient-completed	

(Continued)

Table 17.3 (Continued)

Area of assessment/questionnaire	Advantages	Disadvantages
Coping strategies Inventory (CSI) (Moos 1988)	Strong psychometric properties, patient-completed	Few or no IBD-cohort data published
Coping Inventory for Stressful Situations (CISS) (Endler and Parker 1990)	Strong psychometric properties, patient-completed	Few or no IBD-cohort data published
Quality of life		
Inflammatory Bowel Disease Questionnaire (IBDQ) 36-item (Guyatt *et al.* 1989), 9-item (Casellas *et al.* 2004)	Strong psychometric properties, highly published, patient-completed	Measures bowel symptoms and will cross-correlate with disease-specific measures
Short Inflammatory Bowel Disease Questionnaire (SIBDQ) (Irvine *et al.* 1996)	Strong psychometric properties, highly published, patient-completed, shorter than the IBDQ	Measures bowel symptoms and will cross-correlate with disease-specific measures
Inflammatory Bowel Disease Patient Concerns (RFIPC) (Drossman *et al.* 1991)	Strong psychometric properties, well published, patient-completed, focus on patient concerns	
World Health Organization Quality of Life (WHOQoL) 100-item (Power *et al.* 1999), WhoQoL BREF 26-item (Skevington *et al.* 2004), WHOQoL 8-item (Schmidt, Muhlan and Power 2006)	Strong psychometric properties, highly published, patient-completed, normed-data published	
Medical Outcomes Study Short-Form: SF-36 (36-item) (Ware *et al.* 2007), SF-12 (12-item) (Ware *et al.* 2002)	Strong psychometric properties, highly published, patient-completed, normed-data published	Measure of health status

Table 17.3 (Continued)

Area of assessment/questionnaire	Advantages	Disadvantages
Structures psychological assessments		
Mini-International Neuropsychiatric Interview (M.I.N.I.) SCID-5-RV (Sheehan *et al.* 1998)	Strong psychometric properties, highly published	Few or no IBD-cohort data published
Structured Clinical Interview for DSM-IV-TR Axis I Disorders, Patient Edition. (SCID-I/P) (First & Spitzer 2002).	Strong psychometric properties, highly published	Few or no IBD-cohort data published

CD, Crohn's disease; UC, ulcerative colitis; IBS, irritable bowel syndrome.

(e.g. IBD symptoms and status, anxiety, depression, stress, illness perceptions, and quality of life) that can be used at the initial assessment and throughout therapy to help assess patient psychological status, progress, and direction of therapy.

Current limitations and future considerations

- Many psychologists and allied health professional work without having a good understanding of IBD and its symptoms, course, and diagnostic and treatment options
- Often psychological therapies do not involve the integration of self-report questionnaires in therapy to help assess patient status, and guide the therapeutic process
- There is a lack of consistency in the use of self-report questionnaires in research that limits comparisons across research studies, cultures, and time

Practical recommendations

- A working knowledge of IBD and its impact on patient life domains is essential when working with patients who live with this condition
- Psychological assessments involving IBD patients should not only explore and evaluate patient disease activity and mental health, but also the influence of IBD on the patient's domains of life, including family, friends, education, work, sexual, and hobbies/interests
- A comprehensive psychological assessment should be based upon the integration of multiple information sources, including interview, self-report questionnaires, and other records where possible (e.g. case notes, referral letters)
- In addition to the psychological assessment, ongoing review of patient progress in terms of perceptions and symptoms should be assessed regularly by both interview and self-report questionnaires
- Responses from self-report questionnaires should be used, and integrated into, therapy sessions to promote patient-oriented ownership of therapy and progress. Responses from self-report questionnaires should also be used to reassess both the formulation and working diagnosis

Learning points

- Underpinning any successful psychological intervention involves a comprehensive assessment, diagnosis, and formulation
- Utilization of interview, questionnaire, and other information sources (e.g. case notes, referral letters) are often required to develop a comprehensive and valid assessment
- IBD-specific patient issues should be explored, these include IBD symptoms, impact of IBD on mental health, and the impact of IBD on patient life-domains (e.g. family, friends, education, work, sexual, hobbies/interests)

- Numerous self-report questionnaires assessing multiple psychosocial domains (e.g. anxiety, depression, stress, disease activity, illness perceptions, and quality of life) are readily available and should be considered for integration into the initial assessment and ongoing review of patient progress

References

American Psychiatric Association, American Psychiatric Association and DSM-5 Task Force (2013). *Diagnostic and statistical manual of mental disorders: DSM-5*, 5th edn. Washington, DC: American Psychiatric Association.

Beck, AT and Steer, RA (1993). *Beck Anxiety Inventory Manual*. San Antonio: Psychological Corporation.

Beck, AT, Steer, RA and Brown, GK (1996). *Manual for the Beck Depression Inventory-II*. San Antonio: Psychological Corporation.

Best, WR, Becktel, JM, Singleton, JW and Kern, F, Jr. (1976). Development of a Crohn's disease activity index. National Cooperative Crohn's Disease Study. *Gastroenterology*, vol. 70, no. 3, pp. 439–44.

Bowling, A (2005). *Measuring health: a review of quality of life measurement scales*, 3rd edn. Maidenhead: Open University Press.

Boyce, P, Gilchrist, J, Talley, NJ and Rose, D (2000). Cognitive-behaviour therapy as a treatment for irritable bowel syndrome: a pilot study. *Aust N Z J Psychiatry*, vol. 34, no. 2, pp. 300–9.

Broadbent, E, Petrie, KJ, Main, J and Weinman, J (2006). The brief illness perception questionnaire. *J Psychosom Res*, vol. 60, no. 6, pp. 631–7.

Carver, CS, Scheier, MF and Weintraub, JK (1989). Assessing coping strategies: a theoretically based approach. *J Pers Soc Psychol*, vol. 56, no. 2, pp. 267–83.

Casellas, F, Alcala, MJ, Prieto, L, Miro, JR and Malagelada, JR (2004). Assessment of the influence of disease activity on the quality of life of patients with inflammatory bowel disease using a short questionnaire. *Am J Gastroenterol*, vol. 99, no. 3, pp. 457–61.

Castle, D and Bassett, D (2013). *A primer of clinical psychiatry*, 2nd edn. Marrickville: Churchill Livingstone.

Clara, I, Lix, LM, Walker, JR, Graff, LA, Miller, N, Rogala, L, Rawsthorne, P and Bernstein, CN (2009). The Manitoba IBD Index: evidence for a new and simple indicator of IBD activity. *Am J Gastroenterol*, vol. 104, no. 7, pp. 1754–63.

Cohen, S, Kamarck, T and Mermelstein, R (1983). A global measure of perceived stress. *J Health Soc Behav*, vol. 24, no. 4, pp. 385–96.

Drossman, DA, Leserman, J, Li, ZM, Mitchell, CM, Zagami, EA and Patrick, DL (1991). The rating form of IBD patient concerns: a new measure of health status. *Psychosom Med*, vol. 53, no. 6, pp. 701–12.

Endler, NS and Parker, JDA (1990). *Coping inventory for stressful situations*. Toronto: Multi-Health Systems.

First, MB and Spitzer, RL (2002). *Structured Clinical Interview for DSM-IV-TR Axis I Disorders, Research Version, Patient Edition. (SCID-I/P)*. New York: Biometrics Research, New York State Psychiatric Institute.

Folkman, S and Lazarus, RS (1985). If it changes it must be a process: study of emotion and coping during three stages of a college examination. *J Pers Soc Psychol*, vol. 48, no. 1, pp. 150–70.

Folstein, MF, Folstein, SE and McHugh, PR (1975). "'Mini-mental state". A practical method for grading the cognitive state of patients for the clinician. *J Psychiatr Res*, vol. 12, no. 3, pp. 189–98.

Goldberg, DP (1972). *The detection of psychiatric illness by questionnaire*. London: Oxford University Press.

Groth-Marnat, G (2003). *Handbook of psychological assessment*, 4th edn. Hoboken: John Wiley & Sons.

Guyatt, G, Mitchell, A, Irvine, EJ, Singer, J, Williams, N, Goodacre, R and Tompkins, C (1989). A new measure of health status for clinical trials in inflammatory bowel disease. *Gastroenterology*, vol. 96, no. 3, pp. 804–10.

Harvey, RF and Bradshaw, JM (1980). A simple index of Crohn's-disease activity. *Lancet*, vol. 1, no. 8167, p. 514.

Irvine, EJ, Zhou, Q and Thompson, AK (1996). The Short Inflammatory Bowel Disease Questionnaire: a quality of life instrument for community physicians managing inflammatory bowel disease. CCRPT Investigators. Canadian Crohn's Relapse Prevention Trial. *Am J Gastroenterol*, vol. 91, no. 8, pp. 1571–8.

Kato, T (2013). Frequently used coping scales: a meta-analysis. *Stress Health*, doi: 10.1002/smi.2557.

Kessler, RC, Andrews, G, Colpe, LJ, Hiripi, E, Mroczek, DK, Normand, SL, Walters, EE and Zaslavsky, AM (2002). Short screening scales to monitor population prevalences and trends in non-specific psychological distress. *Psychol Med*, vol. 32, no. 6, pp. 959–76.

Lichtiger, S, Present, DH, Kornbluth, A, Gelernt, I, Bauer, J, Galler, G, Michelassi, F and Hanauer, S (1994). Cyclosporine in severe ulcerative colitis refractory to steroid therapy. *N Engl J Med*, vol. 330, no. 26, pp. 1841–5.

Lovibond, SH and Lovibond, PF (1995). *Manual for the depression anxiety stress scales*, 2nd edn. Sydney: Psychology Foundation.

McDowell, I (2006). *Measuring health a guide to rating scales and questionnaires*, 3rd edn. New York, Oxford: Oxford University Press.

Moos, LH (1988). *The coping response inventory manual*. Palo Alto: Social Ecology Laboratory, Stanford University and Department of Veterans Affairs Medical Centers.

Moss-Morris, R, Weinman, J, Petrie, KJ, Horne, R, Cameron, LD and Buick, D (2002). The Revised Illness Perception Questionnaire (IPQ-R). *Psychol Health*, vol. 17, no. 1, pp. 1–16.

National Centre for Classification in Health (Australia) (2010). *The International statistical classification of diseases and related health problems, tenth revision, Australian modification (ICD-10-AM)*, 7th edn, 5 vols. Lidcombe: National Centre for Classification in Health.

Powell-Tuck, J, Bown, RL and Lennard-Jones, JE (1978). A comparison of oral prednisolone given as single or multiple daily doses for active proctocolitis. *Scand J Gastroenterol*, vol. 13, no. 7, pp. 833–7.

Power, M, Harper, A and Bullinger, M (1999). The World Health Organization WHOQOL-100: tests of the universality of quality of life in 15 different cultural groups worldwide. *Health Psychol*, vol. 18, no. 5, pp. 495–505.

Schmidt, S, Muhlan, H and Power, M (2006). The EUROHIS-QOL 8-item index: psychometric results of a cross-cultural field study. *Eur J Public Health*, vol. 16, no. 4, pp. 420–8.

Sheehan, DV, Lecrubier, Y, Sheehan, KH, Amorim, P, Janavs, J, Weiller, E, Hergueta, T, Baker, R and Dunbar, GC (1998). The Mini-International Neuropsychiatric Interview

(M.I.N.I.): the development and validation of a structured diagnostic psychiatric interview for DSM-IV and ICD-10. *J Clin Psychiatry*, vol. 59, (Suppl 20), pp. 22–33; quiz 4–57.

Skevington, SM, Lotfy, M, O'Connell, KA and WHOQOL Group (2004). The World Health Organization's WHOQOL-BREF quality of life assessment: psychometric properties and results of the international field trial. A report from the WHOQOL group. *Qual Life Res*, vol. 13, no. 2, pp. 299–310.

Spielberger, CD, Gorssuch, RL, Lushene, PR, Vagg, PR and Jacobs, GA (1983). *Manual for the State-Trait Anxiety Inventory.* Palo Alto: Consulting Psychologists Press, Inc.

Steed, LG (1998). A crituque of coping scales. *Aust Psychol*, vol. 33, no. 3, pp. 193–202.

Sutherland, LR, Martin, F, Greer, S, Robinson, M, Greenberger, N, Saibil, F, Martin, T, Sparr, J, Prokipchuk, E and Borgen, L (1987). 5-Aminosalicylic acid enema in the treatment of distal ulcerative colitis, proctosigmoiditis, and proctitis. *Gastroenterology*, vol. 92, no. 6, pp. 1894–8.

Toy, EC and Klamen, DL (2012). *Case files. Psychiatry.* New York: McGraw-Hill Health Professions Div.

Ware, JE, Kosinski, M, Bjorner, JB, Turner-Bowker, DM, Gandek, B and Maruish, ME (2007). *User's manual for the SF-36v2TM health survey*, 2nd edn. Lincoln: QualityMetric Inc.

Ware, JE, Kosinski, M, Turner-Bowker, DM and Gandek, B (2002). *How to score version 2 of the SF-12v2® health survey.* Lincoln: QualityMetric Inc.

Weinman, J, Petrie, KJ, Moss-Morris, R and Horne, R (1996). The illness perception questionnaire: A new method for assessing the cognitive representation of illness. *Psychol Health*, vol. 11, no. 3, pp. 431–45.

Zigmond, AS and Snaith, RP (1983). The hospital anxiety and depression scale. *Acta Psychiatr Scand*, vol. 67, no. 6, pp. 361–70.

Chapter 18

IBD, psychosocial functioning and the role of nurses

Julie Duncan

Introduction

Although inflammatory bowel disease (IBD) is undoubtedly organic, the influence of psychological factors, such as stress, anxiety or depression, upon disease activity and health-related quality of life (HRQOL) is increasingly considered important. Modern IBD services are multi-disciplinary and specialist nurses are now seen as core to a good IBD team with greater responsibilities for the direct care and management of IBD patients. They are often the first point of contact to the patient; therefore, they are well placed to play an important role in the assessment or management of psychosocial issues associated with IBD. This Chapter will provide a nursing view on management of psychological problems in IBD and explore the role of the specialist nurse within the multidisciplinary team.

Impact of IBD symptoms on daily life

Symptoms of IBD including fatigue, pain, bowel frequency, urgency or faecal incontinence (FI), may impact on personal and family relationships, social functioning, employment, body image and lead to social isolation (Chelvanayagam and Emmanuel 2011; Dibley and Norton 2013; Sajadinejad *et al.* 2012). A European-wide survey of 5,000 people with IBD reported that 49 per cent feel IBD symptoms have a significant effect on their life. More than half surveyed felt they had not met their educational or work potential; many reported being unable to work full-time, or at all, and 61 per cent worried about taking time off work due to IBD (Wilson *et al.* 2011). Clearly, work absences and unfulfilled potential may have financial and career consequences to individuals personally, along with a national impact, such as the need for social benefits or disability allowances.

A meta-synthesis of qualitative studies exploring living with IBD identified FI and, importantly, fear of incontinence as having disabling effects on people's lives. Social stigma and embarrassment related to FI may also lead to social avoidance behaviours and, thus, social isolation (Kemp *et al.* 2012). The impact FI has on people with IBD is important, particularly in light of recent nurse-led studies that show that two thirds of IBD patients have experienced these deleterious symptoms (Duncan *et al.* 2013; Norton *et al.* 2013).

Fatigue has been identified as a symptom of core concern to people with IBD (Wilson *et al.* 2011), both in terms of physical and psychological effects (Czuber-Dochan *et al.* 2013; de Rooy *et al.* 2001) and its impact on working abilities (Wilson *et al.* 2011). It may relate to a complex interplay of physical, psychological and pharmacological factors (Czuber-Dochan *et al.* 2013; Lee *et al.* 2009; O'Connor *et al.* 2013) (see Chapter 15) and is often a topic of discussion raised by patients in IBD nurse-led clinics.

Pain is commonly cited as an important contributor to poor HRQOL (Janke *et al.* 2005; O'Connor *et al.* 2013; Wilson *et al.* 2011). Pain may be abdominal but can also relate to extra-gastrointestinal manifestations, such as arthralgia, erythema nodosum or iritis. It is important to remember abdominal pain may not reflect IBD activity such as inflammation or obstruction, and many people have overlapping symptoms contributable to functional gastrointestinal disorders such as irritable bowel syndrome (Docherty *et al.* 2011).

Physical changes related to IBD or its management may have negative effects on body image. Many symptoms of IBD may not be apparent but others, such as significant weight loss, abdominal fistulae, perianal disease, central line insertion or stoma formation are potentially more visible. Perianal disease with associated anatomical changes, presence of a seton suture or leakage can be embarrassing and, anecdotally, may affect intimacy, relationships or the ability to work to full potential. The majority of studies evaluating adaption to stoma formation are not IBD-specific; however, there is evidence that people who have undergone stoma forming surgery may experience emotions akin to loss or grief associated with body changes, potential or actual changes to fertility, relationships, life roles or working (Junkin and Beitz 2005). Nevertheless, other studies suggest patients can, and do, adapt to life with colostomy (Norton *et al.* 2005). Body image is much more complex than physical changes which are obvious to self and others, but represents the way one feels about their body. Changes (seen and unseen) may influence self-concept, self-esteem and self-worth. This may include a new diagnosis of IBD and the resulting invasive investigations, treatments or side effects of these (Burch 2008).

All these physical manifestations of IBD clearly have potential to impact upon HRQOL, coping strategies and influence mood disorders. Therefore, the nurse caring for people with IBD should consider these factors during their encounters.

Psychological influences on IBD

The aim of IBD management is to have the patient at the centre of decision-making, working with the multi-disciplinary team. However, this also implies a willing and able partnership. Therefore, the clinical team should be aware of psychological factors that may influence adherence, coping and adjustment to chronic disease, perceptions of disease severity or pain or affect health-care utilisation. As has been seen in Chapters 2 and 3, psychological stress (Maunder and Levenstein 2008), anxiety and depression (Kovacs and Kovacs 2007; Lerebours *et al.* 2007; Walker *et al.* 1995; Walker *et al.* 2008; Wells *et al.* 1988), and even personality traits, such as neuroticism, perfectionism, hostility or dependency are all important in terms of illness behaviour, perception and adjustment to diagnosis. These may impact on HRQOL and the ability to cope (Boye *et al.* 2008). Mood disorders may also present as adverse effects of IBD therapy, such as corticosteroids. Depression may influence adherence to IBD treatments, and thus, impact on disease course and outcome. Nurses should, therefore, consider depression as a possible influence whilst supporting patients to adhere and engage with pre-scribed regimens.

Psychological interventions in the management of IBD

As will be shown in Chapters 19 and 20, there are limiting methodological factors in studies which have investigated psychological interventions in IBD, and all have been used as supplementary rather than exclusive treatments. Although the evidence for benefit is limited (Timmer *et al.* 2011), psychological interventions remain an appropriate adjunct to IBD therapy. The UK IBD Standards (IBD Standards Group 2013) acknowledge the necessity of having a psychologist or psychotherapist within the wider IBD team, but the accessibility of these services is still variable and may pose a challenge to many clinical teams.

We have acknowledged that powerful psychological factors influence patients' response to illness and its treatment. However, the clinician is not without their own psychological influences and this may contribute to their own responses and decision-making. Most clinicians working within gastroenterology will not be trained in psychiatry or psychotherapy and may be naïve to psychotherapeutic dynamics. From personal experience, the ability to work closely with a dedicated psychotherapist within a gastrointestinal service allows exploration of these dynamics (both patient-specific and clinician-specific), and helps the clinician identify psychological barriers to treatment whilst increasing confidence to acknowledge these directly to the patient (Stern 2003).

Role of the specialist nurse in IBD

IBD clinical nurse specialists were first established in the UK during the mid-1990s to improve quality of care, education and support for people with IBD. The role has proliferated in recent years, not only in the UK but throughout Europe and beyond, and has become core to service standards (IBD Standards Group 2013). As well as advanced practice roles such as case management and prescribing, the IBD clinical nurse specialists (CNS) provides education, practical and emotional support, an accessible point of contact, a supportive link between patients and other members of the MDT, co-ordination of the patients' journey and are the key drivers to service development (Belling *et al.* 2009; IBD Standards Group 2013; O'Connor *et al.* 2013).

Provision of support may be in the form of time to listen whilst in clinic, or during contact on the advice line. Advice lines are often set up as a point of contact and to provide rapid access to IBD specialists, which can be reassuring to patients. As the majority of patients worry about taking time off work to attend appointments or investigations, offering alternative ways of follow-up, such as virtual or telephone clinics within IBD service provision can be a useful way to support patients in their long-term condition and may enhance a therapeutic relationship. It has been reported that up to 63 per cent find benefit from joining an IBD patient organisation and approximately 40 per cent feel more positive meeting others with IBD (Wilson *et al.* 2011). Therefore, providing information about local and national patient support groups or organisations is a useful nursing intervention and a source of further support.

As demonstrated in Chapter 13, treatments for IBD can be associated with significant, potentially serious, side effects. CNSs can act as a resource, using expert knowledge to increase understanding or awareness of treatments' benefits and risks, supporting the decision-making process and informed choice (Greveson and Woodward 2013). Similarly, developing a therapeutic relationship and encouraging active engagement in treatment may support adherence to therapy and monitoring and, ultimately, improve symptoms and HRQOL.

Supporting people to take responsibility for the management of chronic diseases has been a key priority for the UK's Department of Health, empowering people to actively self-manage where possible but providing access to specialist advice and individualised care when needed (Department of Health 2001). Educational and self-management programmes are an area of intervention IBD CNSs have had active involvement. Whereas, these may not immediately be apparent as being psychological therapies, they have been included as such in the Cochrane report reviewing psychological interventions in IBD because of the skills used to deliver the interventions (Timmer *et al.* 2011). As opposed to health education which is the provision of information, self-management programmes are interventions that support behaviour change and the ability to manage symptoms, treatments, chronic disease adaptation and lifestyle adjustment. Healthcare professionals delivering such programmes often use a combination of education and psychological interventions, such as cognitive behavioural therapy, stress management or relaxation techniques aiming to improve coping skills, problem solving, personal planning or goal setting as well as information-giving (Barlow *et al.* 2010). Although the heterogeneity of studies investigating self-management programmes is such that the evidence is not robust, there is some indication these may improve psychological wellbeing, disease-related knowledge and are possibly associated with less hospital visits and quicker treatment of relapse (Kennedy *et al.* 2010; Robinson *et al.* 2001). Education alone has not been shown to achieve these outcomes; indeed there is evidence that structured education, whilst improving knowledge, does not improve HRQOL

(Jaghult *et al.* 2007; Oxelmark *et al.* 2007; Verma *et al.* 2001; Waters *et al.* 2005). Despite the paucity of robust evidence, it could be argued that supported self-management should form part of an integrated biopsychosocial approach to the management of IBD along with medical, dietary, psychological or surgical treatments. It should be noted, however, that not all people with IBD want, or are able to, participate in active self-management and this needs to be considered when offering such programmes.

Conclusion

Psychological influences both upon and as a result of IBD are complex, multi-factorial and an essential aspect of disease assessment and management. Nurses should have an awareness of the psychological processes that can affect their patient's journey, and can provide an important link to the multidisciplinary team and to psychological services. The nurses' place within the IBD team is such that they can provide an important role in the assessment, support and onward referral of patients requiring psychological intervention.

Current limitations and future considerations

- IBD patient access to psychological therapies can be inconsistent
- There is a clear need for psychological services to be offered as part of IBD service provision for those who require it
- The impact on outcomes and quality of care by the IBD specialist nurse is yet to be fully established and should be addressed in research

Practical recommendations

- Educational and self-management programmes, which can be provided by specialist nurses, may be useful tools in the holistic management of people with IBD
- Building therapeutic relationships may help identify barriers to treatment adherence, and circumvent these

Learning points

- Mental disorders are prevalent amongst those with chronic disease and can impact on health related quality of life, adjustment to diagnosis and be a barrier to treatment adherence
- Specialist nurses in IBD are well-placed to identify psychological issues and provide a link to psychological services and the multidisciplinary team
- Education and self-management programmes can be utilised to support behaviour change and engage people with IBD to have greater control over their disease

References

Barlow, C, Cooke, D, Mulligan, K, Beck, E and Newman, S (2010). A critical review of self-management and educational interventions in inflammatory bowel disease. *Gastroenterol Nurs*, vol. 33, no. 1, pp. 11–8.

Belling, R, McLaren, S and Woods, L (2009). Specialist nursing interventions for inflammatory bowel disease. *Cochrane Database Syst Rev*, no. 4, p. CD006597.

Boye, B, Jahnsen, J, Mokleby, K, Leganger, S, Jantschek, G, Jantschek, I, Kunzendorf, S, Benninghoven, D, Wilhelmsen, I, Sharpe, M, Blomhoff, S, Malt, UF and Lundin, KE (2008). The INSPIRE study: are different personality traits related to disease-specific quality of life (IBDQ) in distressed patients with ulcerative colitis and Crohn's disease? *Inflamm Bowel Dis*, vol. 14, no. 5, pp. 680–6.

Burch, J (2008). Other stoma issues. In: Burch, J (ed). *Stoma Care*. Chichester: Wiley-Blackwell.

Chelvanayagam, S and Emmanuel, A (2011). Psychosocial aspects of inflammatory bowel disease. In: Whayman, K, Duncan, J and O'Connor, M (eds). *Inflammatory Bowel Disease Nursing*. London: Quay Books.

Czuber-Dochan, W, Ream, E and Norton, C (2013). Review article: description and management of fatigue in inflammatory bowel disease. *Aliment Pharmacol Ther*, vol. 37, no. 5, pp. 505–16.

de Rooy, EC, Toner, BB, Maunder, RG, Greenberg, GR, Baron, D, Steinhart, AH, McLeod, R and Cohen, Z (2001). Concerns of patients with inflammatory bowel disease: results from a clinical population. *Am J Gastroenterol*, vol. 96, no. 6, pp. 1816–21.

Department of Health (2001). *The expert patient: a new approach to chronic disease management for the 21st century*. London: Department of Health.

Dibley, L and Norton, C (2013). Experiences of fecal incontinence in people with inflammatory bowel disease: self-reported experiences among a community sample. *Inflamm Bowel Dis*, vol. 19, no. 7, pp. 1450-62.

Docherty, MJ, Jones, RC, 3rd and Wallace, MS (2011). Managing pain in inflammatory bowel disease. *Gastroenterol Hepatol (N Y)*, vol. 7, no. 9, pp. 592–601.

Duncan, J, Sebepos-Rogers, G, Poole-Wilson, O, To, C, Canavan, JB, Kariyawasam, V, Ward, M, Goel, R, Patel, K, Stanton, A, Sastrillo, M, Anderson, S, Taylor, K, Sanderson, J and Irving, P (2013). Prevalence of faecal incontinence in adults with inflammatory bowel disease. *Gut*, vol. 62, (Suppl 1), pp. A162–3.

Greveson, K and Woodward, S (2013). Exploring the role of the inflammatory bowel disease nurse specialist. *Br J Nurs*, vol. 22, no. 16, pp. 952–4, 956–8.

IBD Standards Group (2013). Quality Care Service Standards for the Healthcare of People who have inflammatory bowel disease (IBD) 2013 Update. Available online from www.ibdstandards.org.uk/uploaded_files/IBDstandards.pdf (accessed 11 March 2014).

Jaghult, S, Larson, J, Wredling, R and Kapraali, M (2007). A multiprofessional education programme for patients with inflammatory bowel disease: a randomized controlled trial. *Scand J Gastroenterol*, vol. 42, no. 12, pp. 1452–9.

Janke, KH, Klump, B, Gregor, M, Meisner, C and Haeuser, W (2005). Determinants of life satisfaction in inflammatory bowel disease. *Inflamm Bowel Dis*, vol. 11, no. 3, pp. 272–86.

Junkin, J and Beitz, JM (2005). Sexuality and the person with a stoma: implications for comprehensive WOC nursing practice. *J Wound Ostomy Continence Nurs*, vol. 32, no. 2, pp. 121–8; quiz 9–30.

Kemp, K, Griffiths, J and Lovell, K (2012). Understanding the health and social care needs of people living with IBD: a meta-synthesis of the evidence. *World J Gastroenterol*, vol. 18, no. 43, pp. 6240–9.

Kennedy, A, Nelson, E, Reeves, D, Richardson, G, Roberts, C, Robinson, A, Rogers, A, Sculpher, M and Thompson, D (2010). A randomised controlled trial to assess the impact of a package comprising a patient-orientated, evidence-based self-help guidebook and patient-centered consultations on disease management and satisfaction in inflammatory bowel disease. *Health Technol Assess*, vol. 7, no. 28, pp. 1–132.

Kovacs, Z and Kovacs, F (2007). Depressive and anxiety symptoms, dysfunctional attitudes and social aspects in irritable bowel syndrome and inflammatory bowel disease. *Int J Psychiatry Med*, vol. 37, no. 3, pp. 245–55.

Lee, TW, Iser, JH, Sparrow, MP, Newnham, ED, Headon, BJ and Gibson, PR (2009). Thiopurines, a previously unrecognised cause for fatigue in patients with inflammatory bowel disease. *J Crohns Colitis*, vol. 3, no. 3, pp. 196–9.

Lerebours, E, Gower-Rousseau, C, Merle, V, Brazier, F, Debeugny, S, Marti, R, Salomez, JL, Hellot, MF, Dupas, JL, Colombel, JF, Cortot, A and Benichou, J (2007). Stressful life events as a risk factor for inflammatory bowel disease onset: a population-based case-control study. *Am J Gastroenterol*, vol. 102, no. 1, pp. 122–31.

Maunder, RG and Levenstein, S (2008). The role of stress in the development and clinical course of inflammatory bowel disease: epidemiological evidence. *Curr Mol Med*, vol. 8, no. 4, pp. 247–52.

Norton, C, Burch, J and Kamm, MA (2005). Patients' views of a colostomy for fecal incontinence. *Dis Colon Rectum*, vol. 48, no. 5, pp. 1062–9.

Norton, C, Dibley, LB and Bassett, P (2013). Faecal incontinence in inflammatory bowel disease: associations and effect on quality of life. *J Crohns Colitis*, vol. 7, no. 8, pp. e302–11.

O'Connor, M, Bager, P, Duncan, J, Gaarenstroom, J, Younge, L, Detre, P, Bredin, F, Dibley, L, Dignass, A, Gallego Barrero, M, Greveson, K, Hamzawi, M, Ipenburg, N, Keegan, D, Martinato, M, Murciano Gonzalo, F, Pino Donnay, S, Price, T, Ramirez Morros, A, Verwey, M, White, L and van de Woude, CJ (2013). N-ECCO consensus statements on the European nursing roles in caring for patients with Crohn's disease or ulcerative colitis. *J Crohns Colitis*, vol. 7, no. 9, pp. 744–64.

Oxelmark, L, Magnusson, A, Lofberg, R and Hilleras, P (2007). Group-based intervention program in inflammatory bowel disease patients: effects on quality of life. *Inflamm Bowel Dis*, vol. 13, no. 2, pp. 182–90.

Robinson, A, Thompson, DG, Wilkin, D, Roberts, C and Northwest Gastrointestinal Research Group (2001). Guided self-management and patient-directed follow-up of ulcerative colitis: a randomised trial. *Lancet*, vol. 358, no. 9286, pp. 976–81.

Sajadinejad, MS, Asgari, K, Molavi, H, Kalantari, M and Adibi, P (2012). Psychological issues in inflammatory bowel disease: an overview. *Gastroenterol Res Pract*, vol. 2012, p. 106502.

Stern, JM (2003). Psychiatry, psychotherapy and gastroenterology – bringing it all together. *Aliment Pharmacol Ther*, vol. 17, no. 2, pp. 175–84.

Timmer, A, Preiss, JC, Motschall, E, Rucker, G, Jantschek, G and Moser, G (2011). Psychological interventions for treatment of inflammatory bowel disease. *Cochrane Database Syst Rev*, no. 2, p. CD006913.

Verma, S, Tsai, HH and Giaffer, MH (2001). Does better disease-related education improve quality of life? A survey of IBD patients. *Dig Dis Sci*, vol. 46, no. 4, pp. 865–9.

Walker, EA, Gelfand, AN, Gelfand, MD and Katon, WJ (1995). Psychiatric diagnoses, sexual and physical victimization, and disability in patients with irritable bowel syndrome or inflammatory bowel disease. *Psychol Med*, vol. 25, no. 6, pp. 1259–67.

Walker, JR, Ediger, JP, Graff, LA, Greenfeld, JM, Clara, I, Lix, L, Rawsthorne, P, Miller, N, Rogala, L, McPhail, CM and Bernstein, CN (2008). The Manitoba IBD cohort study: a population-based study of the prevalence of lifetime and 12-month anxiety and mood disorders. *Am J Gastroenterol*, vol. 103, no. 8, pp. 1989–97.

Waters, BM, Jensen, L and Fedorak, RN (2005). Effects of formal education for patients with inflammatory bowel disease: a randomized controlled trial. *Can J Gastroenterol*, vol. 19, no. 4, pp. 235–44.

Wells, KB, Golding, JM and Burnam, MA (1988). Psychiatric disorder in a sample of the general population with and without chronic medical conditions. *Am J Psychiatry*, vol. 145, no. 8, pp. 976–81.

Wilson, BS, Lonnfors, S, Vermeire, S, Greco, M, Hommes, DW, Bell, C and Avedano, L (2011). The true impact of ibd: a european crohn's and ulcerative colitis patient life. Available online from http://efcca-solutions.net/media/jointhefight/ImpactReport. pdf (accessed 20 December 2013).

Chapter 19

Psychological treatment outcomes in IBD, methodological issues, and future directions

Lesley A. Graff

Psychological interventions

Psychotherapy, very broadly, is an intervention approach that uses a range of techniques, in the context of a relationship between the therapist and patient, in order to facilitate changes. These changes encompass improved health and mental health, and enhanced positive functioning (Prochaska and Norcross 2013). Psychological treatment describes those interventions applied in a healthcare context (Barlow 2006). There is a large body of evidence supporting the efficacy and clinical utility of psychological treatments (Roth and Fonagy 2005), with many of these therapies established as first-line interventions for common mental health problems (e.g., panic disorder, depression). In recent decades, these treatments have had wider application to chronic health conditions, such as heart disease and back pain, with positive outcomes on clinical indices (Hoffman *et al.* 2007). Psychophysiological research has identified changes in autonomic nervous system functioning (Bonaz and Bernstein 2013) and brain blood flow (Karlsson 2011) as potential biological mechanisms for symptom improvements with these "talk therapies". While psychological interventions are well-established as efficacious in the functional gastrointestinal disorders (Ford *et al.* 2009), their clinical utility in inflammatory bowel disease (IBD) is less clear (Timmer *et al.* 2011).

Psychological treatments in IBD

Psychological processes are evident in inflammatory bowel diseases (IBD). Studies have found higher rates of comorbid anxiety and depression (Graff *et al.* 2009), and suggest a causal relationship for stress in gastrointestinal (GI) tract disturbances and inflammation (Santos *et al.* 2008). Prospective studies suggest that stress and mood disorders can adversely affect disease course in IBD, including more frequent disease flares and shorter time to relapse (Bernstein *et al.* 2010; Mittermaier *et al.* 2004). In addition, those with IBD can be at risk for body image concerns, lower self-esteem, and poorer quality of life compared to healthy individuals (Mikocka-Walus and Graff 2014). IBD patients were found

Psychological treatment outcomes in IBD 173

to be receptive to psychological support in order to facilitate their coping and disease management (Miehsler *et al.* 2008). All of these factors suggest a role for psychological interventions in IBD.

Several different types of psychological interventions have been assessed with IBD patients. They were broadly categorized in a recent systematic review as psychoeducation, stress management, psychodynamic therapy, cognitive behavioral therapy (CBT), and hypnosis (Knowles *et al.* 2013). Psychoeducation refers to disease-specific information for patients aimed at enhancing knowledge and understanding of the disease and patient role. However, it has been argued that the education component as a stand-alone intervention does not constitute psychological therapy (Knowles *et al.* 2013; McCombie *et al.* 2013). Stress management involves a focus on ways to develop or enhance relaxation and stress reduction (e.g., biofeedback, diaphragmatic breathing, problem solving). Psychodynamic therapy aims to address problematic ways of relating to others (e.g., insecure attachment), using therapeutic tools like interpretation, free association and empathic validation. CBT aims to modify maladaptive thoughts (cognitions) and behavior, focusing on the relationship among thoughts, emotions, and behaviors. CBT incorporates interventions such as cognitive reframing, systematic desensitization, behavioral activation, and goal setting. Hypnotherapy uses hypnotic induction and suggestion to facilitate relaxation and positive functioning.

There have been five systematic reviews of psychological treatment for IBD patients since 2006, collectively evaluating studies of adults and the few for adolescents (Goodhand *et al.* 2009; Knowles *et al.* 2013; McCombie *et al.* 2013; Timmer *et al.* 2011; von Wietersheim and Kessler 2006). The number of reviews might imply a plethora of treatment studies in this area. However, the maximum number of studies evaluated in any review was 21, and they generally encompassed four to five different types of treatment, reflecting that only a handful of studies are available for each of the psychological treatment approaches.

The von Wietersheim and Kessler (2006) review evaluated 14 studies, including both psychoeducational and therapy interventions. They determined there was sufficient evidence that the interventions reduced psychological distress, but there was no clear benefit for disease course. Goodhand *et al.* (2009) evaluated 17 studies, clustering them by type: psychodynamic, cognitive behavioral, support/education, and hypnotherapy. They concluded that IBD patients benefitted from CBT in particular, on outcomes of mood disorder and quality of life, when the treatment was targeted at psychological symptoms, whereas the psychodynamic and education approaches had little effect. Regardless of the intervention type, there was little impact on clinical disease. However, they noted most studies included patients in remission or a mixed sample of active/inactive IBD, making it more difficult to detect a positive effect. Hypnotherapy was viewed as a promising new approach for IBD symptoms, based on a few, small, uncontrolled studies.

A Cochrane review (Timmer *et al.* 2011) assessed 21 controlled studies, 19 of which were included in a meta-analysis to evaluate psychological intervention outcomes. For the meta-analysis, three types of psychotherapy (psychodynamic, CBT, and stress management) were pooled, as were the educational intervention studies ($n = 10$). They concluded that psychological intervention was essentially ineffective for outcomes of distress, disease activity, or quality of life, with the exception of treatment for adolescents improving mood. While the review was carefully done following a rigorous process, two fundamental issues raised questions about the conclusions. The pooling of therapy types, each of which have differing efficacy for psychological outcomes in other clinical settings, may have diluted or weakened any positive effect in the meta-analysis. In fact, the conclusion that psychological therapy was beneficial for adolescents may have had less to do with the age of the participants and more to do with the point that the only studies evaluated for this age group were both CBT-based; CBT is a well-established treatment for depression. Second, half of the included studies provided an educational intervention, which as noted earlier, does not incorporate the more complex features of a psychological therapy. As such, it does not seem appropriate to conclude that psychological treatment is ineffective based on those studies.

Two recent systematic reviews addressed shortcomings of the prior reviews, albeit with somewhat different approaches (Knowles *et al.* 2013; McCombie *et al.* 2013). Both include well-detailed summary tables of the studies that were reviewed, for further reference. McCombie and colleagues (2013) reassessed all the Cochrane review papers, ultimately evaluating 18 controlled studies of psychological treatment, including eight used in the Cochrane review, three that group had excluded, and seven published since. Psychoeducational studies were excluded. They examined a variety of outcomes (e.g., anxiety, depression, quality of life, GI symptoms, disease relapse, hospitalization). However, similar to Timmer *et al.* (2011), they synthesized findings across the various types of psychological treatment. For almost every outcome, they concluded the findings were mixed, with the exception of agreement of positive outcomes for pain (two studies) and fatigue (two studies). Closer examination of the *types* of psychological treatment associated with positive effects for the various outcomes suggested that CBT and its variants were most commonly contributing to positive outcomes, and counselling and psychodynamic therapy more typically had negative results.

The Knowles *et al.* (2013) review excluded psychoeducational studies, and included both controlled and uncontrolled studies of the main types of psychological treatment used for adults with IBD (i.e., stress management, CBT, psychodynamic therapy, hypnotherapy). A priori definitions of these treatments were used to carefully categorize each study after reviewing the description of the intervention, resulting in inclusion of 16 research reports. They reviewed psychological and disease outcomes, comparing within these clinically logical groupings of treatment type, rather than collapsing across them. Stress management studies ($n = 5$) had mixed outcomes, with one reporting improved anxiety, and two reporting reduction in clinical disease indices post-treatment. The CBT interventions ($n = 5$) more consistently resulted in improved psychological distress, with modest but unsustained changes in gastrointestinal symptoms. Two of the four psychodynamic studies found reductions in psychological distress, and one reported decreased healthcare utilization. Hypnosis had a small but positive effect on gut and immune functioning. There was only limited evidence of improved quality of life for any of the treatments.

Overall, there are a number of common themes through these reviews. Despite the differences in evaluation approaches, there is a convergence of support for positive effect of psychological treatments on psychological conditions such as anxiety or depression. This is not to suggest that therapy will benefit all IBD patients, but it may be of particular value for those with co-occurring psychological distress. In a recent study, 43 percent of IBD patients ($n = 231$) reported anxiety or depressive symptoms above clinical threshold, but only 18 percent and 21 percent, respectively, obtained psychological or pharmacological intervention (Bennebroek Evertsz *et al.* 2012). Given the contribution of depression to worsening disease (Mittermaier *et al.* 2004), psychological interventions may also provide indirect clinical benefit for IBD, although that has not yet been established.

With regard to clinical disease outcomes, there is not consistent evidence of improved GI symptoms, and there has been virtually no measurement of impact on inflammatory processes. Nevertheless, findings suggest potential for psychological treatments to improve clinical outcomes, and are especially promising for aspects such as pain, fatigue, and medication adherence.

In order to optimally determine benefit, it is important to consider not just the overall intervention approach of "therapy", but to examine the outcomes related to specific types of psychological treatment, as is done in other clinical research. That is, biologics, antidepressants, or antibiotics are not studied as "medications", but are evaluated separately. Examining the types of therapies indicated consistent positive outcomes for CBT, generally negative outcomes for psychodynamic therapy, and a potential for direct disease impact with hypnotherapy. Chapter 20 provides a more in-depth discussion of CBT and hypnosis, and their application in IBD.

Methodological issues in IBD treatment studies

An overarching theme raised in all the systematic reviews is the low methodological quality of many of the studies, which hampers definitive conclusions and may well be underestimating treatment effect. For example, it is not surprising there are few positive effects of psychological treatment on disease outcomes when studies have rarely included patients with active disease. Instead, most participants had mild or quiescent IBD at baseline, contributing to floor effects on outcome measures. Similarly, the majority of studies did not screen for psychological status, and many simply measured mood or anxiety symptoms without clinical assessment of diagnostic status (e.g., depression).

Most studies were underpowered to detect change in disease activity and other clinical outcomes. Only a minority had more than 50 participants, despite two trial arms and multiple outcome measures. There is also some question of whether all the relevant outcomes are being assessed. McCombie *et al.* (2013) argued that these interventions can reduce illness costs (e.g., days in hospital; missed work-days), as demonstrated in the only two studies that evaluated cost effectiveness. However, healthcare utilization or disability is rarely measured.

Other issues relate to the description and delivery of the treatment approaches. The treatments were not always clearly described, making them difficult to categorize or replicate. One systematic review (Knowles *et al.* 2013) illustrated the potential for confusion, showing a treatment study that was categorized three different ways (e.g., stress management, psychoeducation, CBT), depending on the review. There has been little information in the studies about consistency of delivery (e.g., fidelity checks), expertise of delivery (e.g., therapist training/ experience), or patient uptake (e.g., treatment engagement measures). This is especially relevant as one unique aspect of psychological treatment is the challenge in delivering standardized therapy. Unlike medication, which is factory-prepared, therapy is a dynamic process that involves techniques and tools delivered in the context of a relationship; the patient, therapist and what occurs in the interaction all contribute to change mechanisms and outcomes (Barber 2009). Content can be manualized, but processes such as therapeutic alliance (i.e., patient-therapist connection and trust) also need to be assessed and accounted for, yet they rarely have been evaluated in the IBD context. Finally, it is acknowledged that blinding participants to a treatment or control condition is not practical for psychological interventions, however, only about a third of the treatment studies reported some other type of blinding (e.g., independent assessors).

Addressing methodological challenges

Many of the study weaknesses identified in the systematic reviews are not unique to psychological intervention in IBD, but reflect challenges inherent in clinical and/or psychological treatment research. Several fundamental improvements can strengthen future randomized controlled trials (RCTs) in this area. They encompass aspects such as power, measurement, and follow-up, summarized in Table 19.1 (Section A). The appropriate control condition needs particular consideration. It is of central significance in RCTs, as results are as strongly influenced by the control condition selection as they are by the nature of the intervention (Mohr *et al.* 2009). In psychological treatment trials, control conditions commonly used are no-treatment (e.g., waitlist), treatment outside the study [e.g., treatment-as-usual (TAU)] and study-defined treatment (e.g., attention condition, active treatment components). TAU is seen as a reasonable control condition in IBD studies, as the majority of IBD patients will only have exposure to medical, not psychological treatment, and psychological treatment is not intended to replace usual medical approaches.

Table 19.1 Recommendations to improve psychological treatment trials in IBD

A. Core improvements	
Adequate power	Consider a priori power calculations and multi-site recruitment to obtain a sufficient sample
Breadth of inclusion criteria and participant screening	Ensure an appropriate range of disease activity and elevated psychological distress (e.g. subclinical to clinical psychopathology) to minimize floor effects for primary outcomes
Expanded disease activity assessment	Include both clinical indices and practical noninvasive disease biomarkers (e.g. fecal calprotectin)
Validated measures that are sensitive to change	Use for primary outcomes (e.g. psychological, clinical disease), secondary outcomes (e.g. quality of life, disability, health care utilization) and for theorized change mechanisms (Doss 2004), the latter involving, for example, maladaptive thoughts targeted in CBT, stress levels or heart rate variability targeted in stress management
Clearly described treatment protocols	Identify the type of treatment, with sufficient detail of the components to facilitate comparison and replication
Appropriate control condition	Consider TAU as a practical control condition; TAU has been argued to be an acceptable comparison if the TAU is representative of what patients usually have access to (Mohr *et al.* 2009); TAU has been commonly, not universally used in IBD studies
High quality treatment delivery	Ensure sufficient training and/or use of expert therapists, evaluation of delivery to ensure fidelity to the treatment protocol, and evaluation of therapy processes such as therapeutic alliance
Blinding where feasible	Apply blinding to assessors and statisticians, recognizing blinding is unrealistic to achieve for patients and treatment providers in psychological treatment trials
Sufficient follow-up	Track outcomes for a year or longer, particularly when measuring disease outcomes, given the natural history of IBD and disease relapse frequency; many but not all IBD treatment studies tracked outcomes for 12 months
B. Novel considerations	
Patient stratification by relevant chronic disease factors	Categorize by longitudinal disease history (e.g. early post-diagnosis; fluctuating active/inactive), and consider refractory or positive response to other treatments
Patient readiness and treatment engagement	Assess readiness for change and engagement in treatment, as these can account for significant variance in outcomes (Shean 2012)

(*Continued*)

Table 19.1 (Continued)

Patient-focused dosing	Adjust dose or treatment modules within a pre-set range, depending on patient response, to more closely align with clinical practice
Mixed methods design	Implement mixed methods within the same study, supplementing an RCT design with *qualitative review* of the treatment, and *systematic case studies* of patients with contrasting outcomes, to provide a more powerful understanding of quantitative outcomes, which can then hasten translation to effectiveness (Dattilio *et al.* 2010)
Responder/nonresponder comparisons	Utilize qualitative evaluation of treatment responders and nonresponders or dropouts, to guide further development of treatment components (Barlow *et al.* 2013, Fava *et al.* 2013)
Multilevel statistical modelling	Incorporate more complex statistical analyses given the complexity of the factors to assess and control for; multilevel statistical modelling has been advocated for psychological treatment research generally (Fava *et al.* 2013), and with IBD samples (Knowles *et al.* 2013)

TAU, treatment-as-usual; IBD, inflammatory bowel disease.

Table 19.1, Section B summarizes recommendations that focus on enhancing clinic-ready knowledge, to facilitate the transition from efficacy to effectiveness, highlighting the following:

- Well-defined patient groups are essential to the interpretation and application of study findings (Barlow *et al.* 2013). Patients with chronic disease can be quite heterogeneous, even after accounting for current disease status and psychopathology. Stratification related to disease history has been encouraged in chronic disease treatment trials to better define relevant clinical characteristics (Fava *et al.* 2013).
- Patients have a significant role in psychological treatments as they are not simply passive recipients. However, aspects such as readiness for change have rarely been assessed in IBD studies.
- Designs that adjust dose or type of treatment depending on patient response have been used in pharmacological studies to better approximate clinic application (Fava *et al.* 2013). This adaptive design approach has also been implemented in some psychological therapy studies to improve external validity, with good success (Barlow *et al.* 2013).
- RCTs are seen as the gold standard for clinical treatment research. However, there has been argument that this design has disadvantages in the context of chronic disease studies (Dattilio *et al.* 2010; Fava *et al.* 2013). RCTs were originally used in medicine to investigate treatment outcomes in acute disease, and lean heavily on the assumption of the average untreated patient (Fava *et al.* 2013); patients with chronic disease typically have had treatment exposure prior to the current investigation. A related criticism is that RCT design optimizes internal validity but can undermine external validity, and as such does not adjust for practical needs when translating to the clinic (Hayes *et al.* 2013). Recently, mixed method designs, optimally within the same treatment study, have been encouraged to enhance RCTs (Dattilio *et al.* 2010).

Going forward, researchers should be strategic in their selection of treatment type. Treatment trials are costly; consider a specific treatment's evidence base in other applications (e.g., mental health, chronic disease), as well as current promising findings in the IBD literature. Feasibility of intervention delivery in the healthcare system should also be considered. Arguably it would be impractical to develop costly high intensity therapies (e.g., >20 hours) if shorter-term therapies can be established as effective, especially in the current climate of healthcare cost containment.

Conclusions

Psychological treatments can be beneficial for IBD patients. These interventions may have differing effects on psychological and disease outcomes, depending on the treatment type. There is the potential for direct improvement of GI symptoms, disease course, and cost-offset, but this has not yet been clearly established.

Current limitations and future considerations

- Many psychological treatment studies for IBD patients are of low methodological quality, which may underestimate treatment benefit
- There has been little attention to psychological interventions for children and adolescents with IBD
- Future studies need to incorporate changes that address current quality issues related to sample size, patient selection, treatment delivery, and disease activity measurement

Practical recommendations

- Given the role of stress in IBD disease course, and the higher rate of comorbid depression, psychological care is relevant for individuals with IBD
- Psychological treatment, especially CBT and possibly hypnosis, can be beneficial for IBD patients and should be considered
- Psychological treatment may be indicated particularly for IBD patients with distress or clinical comorbidity; these individuals are often undertreated
- Treatment studies, strategically focusing on interventions that can be practically delivered in the health care system, would optimally include a mixed methods design, incorporating recommendations from the general therapy literature related to the therapist and to treatment delivery

Learning points

- Psychological treatments have been established as effective with various mental health and medical conditions
- Common treatment types include psychodynamic, cognitive behavioral, and hypnosis
- Psychological interventions for IBD patients, most typically CBT, have often reduced psychological symptoms, but have less commonly shown benefit for GI symptoms
- Treatment effectiveness may be underestimated due to method quality issues such as inadequate power, and restricted range in patient selection (e.g., mild or inactive disease)

References

Barber, JP (2009). Toward a working through of some core conflicts in psychotherapy research. *Psychother Res*, vol. 19, no. 1, pp. 1–12.
Barlow, DH (2006). Psychotherapy and psychological treatments: the future. *Clin Psychol-Sci Pr*, vol. 13, pp. 216–20.

Barlow, DH, Boswell, JF and Thompson-Hollands, J (2013). Eysenck, Strupp, and 50 years of psychotherapy research: a personal perspective. *Psychotherapy (Chic)*, vol. 50, no. 1, pp. 77–87.

Bennebroek Evertsz, F, Thijssens, NA, Stokkers, PC, Grootenhuis, MA, Bockting, CL, Nieuwkerk, PT and Sprangers, MA (2012). Do inflammatory bowel disease patients with anxiety and depressive symptoms receive the care they need? *J Crohns Colitis*, vol. 6, no. 1, pp. 68–76.

Bernstein, CN, Singh, S, Graff, LA, Walker, JR, Miller, N and Cheang, M (2010). A prospective population-based study of triggers of symptomatic flares in IBD. *Am J Gastroenterol*, vol. 105, no. 9, pp. 1994–2002.

Bonaz, BL and Bernstein, CN (2013). Brain-gut interactions in inflammatory bowel disease. *Gastroenterology*, vol. 144, no. 1, pp. 36–49.

Dattilio, FM, Edwards, DJ and Fishman, DB (2010). Case studies within a mixed methods paradigm: toward a resolution of the alienation between researcher and practitioner in psychotherapy research. *Psychotherapy (Chic)*, vol. 47, no. 4, pp. 427–41.

Doss, B (2004). Changing the way we study change in psychotherapy. *Clinical Psychology: Science and Practice*, vol. 11, pp. 368–86.

Fava, GA, Tomba, E and Tossani, E (2013). Innovative trends in the design of therapeutic trials in psychopharmacology and psychotherapy. *Prog Neuropsychopharmacol Biol Psychiatry*, vol. 40, pp. 306–11.

Ford, AC, Talley, NJ, Schoenfeld, PS, Quigley, EM and Moayyedi, P (2009). Efficacy of antidepressants and psychological therapies in irritable bowel syndrome: systematic review and meta-analysis. *Gut*, vol. 58, no. 3, pp. 367–78.

Goodhand, JR, Wahed, M and Rampton, DS (2009). Management of stress in inflammatory bowel disease: a therapeutic option? *Expert Rev Gastroenterol Hepatol*, vol. 3, no. 6, pp. 661–79.

Graff, LA, Walker, JR and Bernstein, CN (2009). Depression and anxiety in inflammatory bowel disease: a review of comorbidity and management. *Inflamm Bowel Dis*, vol. 15, no. 7, pp. 1105–18.

Hayes, SC, Long, DM, Levin, ME and Follette, WC (2013). Treatment development: can we find a better way? *Clin Psychol Rev*, vol. 33, no. 7, pp. 870–82.

Hoffman, BM, Papas, RK, Chatkoff, DK and Kerns, RD (2007). Meta-analysis of psychological interventions for chronic low back pain. *Health Psychol*, vol. 26, no. 1, pp. 1–9.

Karlsson, H (2011). How psychotherapy changes the brain. Psychiatric Times. Available online at www.psychiatrictimes.com/psychotherapy/how-psychotherapy-changes-brain%3E (accessed 30 December 2013).

Knowles, SR, Monshat, K and Castle, DJ (2013). The efficacy and methodological challenges of psychotherapy for adults with inflammatory bowel disease: a review. *Inflamm Bowel Dis*, vol. 19, no. 12, pp. 2704–15.

McCombie, AM, Mulder, RT and Gearry, RB (2013). Psychotherapy for inflammatory bowel disease: a review and update. *J Crohns Colitis*, vol. 7, no. 12, pp. 935–49.

Miehsler, W, Weichselberger, M, Offerlbauer-Ernst, A, Dejaco, C, Reinisch, W, Vogelsang, H, Machold, K, Stamm, T, Gangl, A and Moser, G (2008). Which patients with IBD need psychological interventions? A controlled study. *Inflamm Bowel Dis*, vol. 14, no. 9, pp. 1273–80.

Mikocka-Walus, A and Graff, LA (2014). Psychological considerations in gastrointestinal disorders. In: Vogele, C (ed.). *International Encyclopedia of Social and Behavioral Sciences*, 2nd edn. London: Elsevier.

Mittermaier, C, Dejaco, C, Waldhoer, T, Oefferlbauer-Ernst, A, Miehsler, W, Beier, M, Tillinger, W, Gangl, A and Moser, G (2004). Impact of depressive mood on relapse in patients with inflammatory bowel disease: a prospective 18-month follow-up study. *Psychosom Med*, vol. 66, no. 1, pp. 79–84.

Mohr, DC, Spring, B, Freedland, KE, Beckner, V, Arean, P, Hollon, SD, Ockene, J and Kaplan, R (2009). The selection and design of control conditions for randomized controlled trials of psychological interventions. *Psychother Psychosom*, vol. 78, no. 5, pp. 275–84.

Prochaska, JO and Norcross, JC (2013). *Systems of psychotherapy: a transtheoretical analysis*, 8th edn. Belmont: Brooks/Cole Publishing Company.

Roth, A and Fonagy, P (2005). *What works for whom? A critical review of psychotherapy research*, 2nd edn. New York: Guilford Press.

Santos, J, Alonso, C, Vicario, M, Ramos, L, Lobo, B and Malagelada, JR (2008). Neuropharmacology of stress-induced mucosal inflammation: implications for inflammatory bowel disease and irritable bowel syndrome. *Curr Mol Med*, vol. 8, no. 4, pp. 258–73.

Shean, GD (2012). Some limitations on the external validity of psychotherapy efficacy studies and suggestions for future research. *Am J Psychother*, vol. 66, pp. 227–42.

Timmer, A, Preiss, JC, Motschall, E, Rucker, G, Jantschek, G and Moser, G (2011). Psychological interventions for treatment of inflammatory bowel disease. *Cochrane Database Syst Rev*, no. 2, p. CD006913.

von Wietersheim, J and Kessler, H (2006). Psychotherapy with chronic inflammatory bowel disease patients: a review. *Inflamm Bowel Dis*, vol. 12, no. 12, pp. 1175–84.

Chapter 20

Cognitive behaviour therapy and hypnotherapy for IBD

Laurie Keefer

Introduction

Psychological interventions have been historically applied with modest benefit to subsets of inflammatory bowel disease (IBD) patients, including those reporting high anxiety or multiple disease concerns, however, widespread application has not been supported (Timmer *et al.* 2011; von Wietersheim and Kessler 2006). A review of 18 trials of psychotherapy for IBD demonstrated that psychological interventions may actually show promise with respect to reducing pain, fatigue, relapse rate and hospitalisation and improving medication adherence (McCombie *et al.* 2013). This notion is supported by the work of Knowles and colleagues, who point out that if psychotherapies are grouped according to their theoretical approach and skills-based interventions, such as cognitive behavioural therapy (CBT), they tend to have slightly better impact on IBD (Knowles *et al.* 2013).

Patient heterogeneity, both psychologically and physiologically, have made study of psychological interventions for IBD difficult. Patients vary by disease type [Crohn's disease (CD), colitis, indeterminate], location [small bowel/colon/ upper gastrointestinal (GI)/rectum], disease behaviour (structuring/fistulising) and presence of extra intestinal manifestations, among other things. Disease parameters, psychological wellbeing and quality of life are directly affected by where a patient fits in terms of flare versus remission (Pihl-Lesnovska *et al.* 2010), their current treatment regimen (e.g. corticosteroid use) (Malik *et al.* 2013) and their access to quality care (van der Eijk *et al.* 2004). Compounded by sociodemographic (age, gender, rural versus urban, education, income) and heterogeneity imposed by individual psychological characteristics including presence of psychological distress, coping ability, disease knowledge, social support and other parameters, individual self-management and psychological treatment needs are similarly diverse. Methodological limitations including small sample sizes and inconsistent inclusion/exclusion criteria, coupled with substantial heterogeneity in patient physiological and psychological profiles have limited firm conclusions regarding the benefit of specific psychological therapies, including CBT and hypnotherapy. The reader should keep these in mind as we discuss these interventions in detail below.

Why cognitive-behaviour therapy is well suited for IBD

CBT is a class of therapies that rests on the assumption that patients maintain self-defeating beliefs, inadequate coping and poor self-management skills, which have a direct effect on mood, anxiety, quality of life, or in the case of IBD, symptom management. CBT techniques, which rely heavily on social-cognitive theory, can be respondent and/or operant in nature. Respondent techniques are based on principles of classical conditioning and target physiological responses (e.g. arousal and immune function) to aversive stimuli (e.g. stress). Progressive muscle relaxation, guided imagery, breathing retraining and hypnotherapy are all examples of respondent-based interventions. Operant techniques are based on principles of instrumental conditioning. These techniques work to diminish the cognitive-affective and environmental contingencies that maintain negative health behaviours and instead promote and reinforce acquisition and implementation of healthy behaviours. Operant-based interventions foster change through the direct manipulation of personal consequences through cognitive restructuring, worry control, enhancing motivation, problem solving, and improving perception of self and disease.

At the heart of most theories of behaviour change is self-efficacy (SE), a dynamic and salient feature of social-cognitive theory. SE is determined by the degree of success or mastery an individual believes s/he has with a specific task or goal. SE is strongly influenced by one's ability to self-regulate any physical or emotional discomfort associated with a behaviour change, and persist with goals for a long period of time, even if one encounters obstacles. SE is also strongly influenced by whether one receives reinforcement from key people (e.g. spouse, physician). Behavioural interventions promoting SE have been linked to healthy disease outcomes in cancer (Hoffman *et al.* 2009), multiple sclerosis (Airlie *et al.* 2001), heart disease (Sarkar *et al.* 2009) and diabetes (Bernal *et al.* 2000), and also to long-lasting health behaviour change (McAuley *et al.* 1993). Our experience with the development of behavioural interventions for GI diseases suggests that SE can be acquired and may be one of the most important predictors of successful adaptation to disease-related demands (Keefer *et al.* 2011; Kiebles *et al.* 2010).

Finally, CBT is already a well-established intervention for irritable bowel syndrome (IBS) because it directly targets brain-gut dysregulation as well as some of the cognitive-affective processes that drive GI symptoms, including catastrophizing and visceral anxiety (Labus *et al.* 2007). Overlap between IBD and IBS is about 40 per cent (Halpin and Ford 2012) but the prevalence of catastrophizing and visceral anxiety among IBD patients is less well-known.

The evidence for CBT in IBD

CBT for IBD has been applied broadly in two forms: stress management training, given the potential impact of stress on disease state (Aberra and Lewis 2013; Triantafillidis *et al.* 2013) and self-management skills training.

Stress management for IBD

Stress management training (SMT) is a form of CBT in which patients are taught how to identify stress and the contexts in which it occurs and to generate relaxation skills to reduce the body's physiological and emotional response to stress. In one of the first randomised controlled trials (RCTs) of SMT for IBD, 80 patients with CD were randomised either to a six-session SMT class including autogenic training, time management and assertiveness or to a control. There was a modest decline in disease activity and IBD stress scores, which was not the case in the control condition – these findings are similar to others' (Garcia-Vega and Fernandez-Rodriguez 2004). In the recent INSPIRE study (Boye *et al.* 2011), 58 ulcerative colitis (UC) and 56 CD with high stress and active disease were randomised to treatment as usual (TAU) or SMT, which included three group sessions focused on psychoeducation, problem-solving and relaxation and six to nine individual sessions of CBT focused on applying coping strategies and SMT principles to patient-identified stressors. Participants were followed over a year. There were no changes in relapse or disease activity, but some improvement in IBDQ among the UC patients was noted.

To summarize, SMT may demonstrate improvement in psychological factors including perceived stress and quality of life, but may not be the most effective version of CBT for IBD. An alternative approach to CBT for IBD is one that targets a specific self-management skill and/or addresses a single symptom.

Self-management skills for IBD

In the 'Project Management for CD' study (Keefer *et al.* 2012), CBT focused on a single health behaviour that undermined the efficacy of the patient's treatment for his/her CD (e.g. smoking, medication adherence). CBT was provided individually over six weekly sessions to 16 adults with quiescent CD and mirrored project management methodology. This included viewing CD as a project that could be managed, allocating personal resources to disease management (e.g. assertiveness around saying no, choosing which aspects of their life they valued most, etc.), self-monitoring of progress, removing barriers, consulting with experts (nutritionist, personal trainer, smoking cessation support group) and risk management. Another 12 adults with quiescent CD underwent TAU. While sample size was small and results were preliminary, project management outperformed TAU in each target domain – IBDQ total score, IBDQ bowel and systemic subscales, IBD self-efficacy and perceived stress.

In another study focused on fatigue in IBD (Vogelaar *et al.* 2011), 29 patients with quiescent CD and high fatigue scores were randomised to solution focused therapy (SFT), problem solving therapy positive control group or treatment as usual. SFT was administered in the form of five sessions over 12 weeks and offered a wide range of CBT skills focused on helping a patient make a behaviour change around fatigue. SFT improved fatigue ratings in greater than 85 per cent of patients and was superior to the control groups. SFT was superior to both problem solving therapy (SMT) and TAU.

Data is mounting around the notion that behavioural interventions that target self-management skills rather than psychological distress or stress could be critical to IBD management. However, data around gut-directed hypnotherapy is also mounting, probably for its more obvious impact on the underlying disease process.

Gut-directed hypnotherapy and IBD

Hypnotherapy (HYP) has garnered empirical support in cancer (Jensen *et al.* 2012), rheumatoid arthritis (Horton-Hausknecht *et al.* 2000) and chronic pain (Jensen 2009), and may work through both immune and inflammatory pathways (Kiecolt-Glaser *et al.* 2001; Miller and Cohen 2001; Wood *et al.* 2003). HYP decreases length of hospitalisation, need for pain medication and fosters faster wound healing (Ginandes *et al.* 2003). Gut-directed HYP, which means that posthypnotic suggestions are aimed around gastrointestinal health and function, is a well-established intervention for functional bowel conditions with documented effects on motility, pain, visceral sensitivity and rectal pain thresholds (Palsson 2010). Gut-directed HYP has been successfully applied to IBD, initially reported in the form of case series (Emami *et al.* 2009; Keefer and Keshavarzian 2007; Miller and Whorwell 2008) and more recently in two RCTs, both in UC. In one exciting study, 25 patients with active UC underwent sigmoidoscopy with rectal biopsy and randomization to either: one 50-minute session of gut-directed HYP, which included suggestions around relief from inflammation, pain, bleeding and diarrhoea, in addition to stress reduction, or to a control group in which they listened to relaxing music of their choice. HYP was associated with reductions in mucosal release of substance P, histamine and interleukin (IL)-13 and serum levels of IL-6 (Mawdsley *et al.* 2008).

In the ulcerative colitis relapse prevention trial, seven sessions of gut-directed HYP versus time/attention-control condition among quiescent UC patients yielded similar results (Keefer *et al.* 2013). In this study, 50 patients with a relapse rate of 1.3 times per year were followed over a 1-year period to determine the impact of seven sessions of HYP on relapse rate. HYP was shown to be superior to the active control group, prolonging remission by a conservative estimate of 2.5 months, with a substantial difference between HYP (68 per cent) and TAC (40 per cent) in terms of proportion that still in remission at 1 year.

Gut-directed HYP is showing promise in addressing disease activity, and relapse in UC, and may be a useful adjunct to standard care. Again, as a respondent-based intervention, gut-directed HYP might be useful as part of a broader CBT program, although this has not previously been tested. Another limitation of these results is that HYP has yet to be rigorously tested in CD.

Conclusions

Psychological therapies have not been routinely recommended for patients with IBD. However, when considered according to class of therapies, CBT and HYP garner the most support. The success of these two interventions in particular is likely because both therapies target self-efficacy and place a premium on the development of effective disease self-management skills. The existing evidence suggests that CBT is most effective when applied to a single behaviour or symptom, with less support around SMT. Gut-directed HYP also shows substantial promise in both active and quiescent UC and could possibly operate through immuno-inflammatory mechanisms IBD.

Current limitations and future considerations

- Patients with IBD vary by disease type, location, and behaviour, as well as the presence of extraintestinal manifestations, surgical history, disease severity and frequency of flare. Data demonstrates substantial differences in disease outcome, psychological wellbeing and quality of life based on these parameters (Malik *et al.* 2013; Pihl-Lesnovska *et al.* 2010; Rochelle and Fidler 2013; van der Eijk *et al.* 2004). Coupled with sociodemographic and psychological heterogeneity, psychological treatment needs are diverse and are therefore difficult to study
- Behavioural interventional research for IBD requires large samples of patients to account for heterogeneity and diverse needs – given the time-consuming nature of psychological treatment, this is often not feasible
- There is a paucity of user-friendly, psychometrically stable outcomes measures that apply to capturing outcome in psychological therapy trials for IBD (Chapter 17). While there are excellent measures for depression, anxiety and other psychological states and traits, there are few measures that examine self-management outcomes (adherence, self-efficacy, health knowledge, etc.). There are few reliable biomarkers for IBD, making it difficult to correlate clinical symptoms with disease activity (Bressenot *et al.* 2013)
- There is limited information on the use of CBT or HYP through internet-based protocols. However, given the lack of qualified providers and the time and financial barriers associated with in-person behavioural therapy programs, this is an important area of inquiry

Practical recommendations

- CBT framed around a specific health behaviour or symptom rather than stress as a whole seems to garner more benefit on disease outcomes
- If considering gut-directed HYP, ensure buy-in by directing patients to recent research showing the impact of gut-directed HYP on inflammatory biomarkers and relapse rates

Learning points

- Successful psychological interventions for the full range of IBD patients tend to be skills-based. Mounting evidence supports two forms of psychotherapy for IBD – CBT and gut-directed hypnotherapy

- CBT is most likely to affect IBD outcomes when it is applied to the development of self-management skills. Stress management can be helpful, but yields less conclusive findings in the disease outcome realm
- Gut-directed hypnotherapy, tested in active and quiescent UC, has effects on inflammatory markers and relapse rates. Less is known about its impact on CD

References

Aberra, FN and Lewis, JD (2013). As in the chicken or the egg: stress or inflammatory bowel disease? *Clin Gastroenterol Hepatol*, vol. 11, no. 1, pp. 63–4.

Airlie, J, Baker, GA, Smith, SJ and Young, CA (2001). Measuring the impact of multiple sclerosis on psychosocial functioning: the development of a new self-efficacy scale. *Clin Rehabil*, vol. 15, no. 3, pp. 259–65.

Bernal, H, Woolley, S, Schensul, JJ and Dickinson, JK (2000). Correlates of self-efficacy in diabetes self-care among Hispanic adults with diabetes. *Diabetes Educ*, vol. 26, no. 4, pp. 673–80.

Boye, B, Lundin, KE, Jantschek, G, Leganger, S, Mokleby, K, Tangen, T, Jantschek, I, Pripp, AH, Wojniusz, S, Dahlstroem, A, Rivenes, AC, Benninghoven, D, Hausken, T, Roseth, A, Kunzendorf, S, Wilhelmsen, I, Sharpe, M, Blomhoff, S, Malt, UF and Jahnsen, J (2011). INSPIRE study: does stress management improve the course of inflammatory bowel disease and disease-specific quality of life in distressed patients with ulcerative colitis or Crohn's disease? A randomized controlled trial. *Inflamm Bowel Dis*, vol. 17, no. 9, pp. 1863–73.

Bressenot, A, Geboes, K, Vignaud, JM, Gueant, JL and Peyrin-Biroulet, L (2013). Microscopic features for initial diagnosis and disease activity evaluation in inflammatory bowel disease. *Inflamm Bowel Dis*, vol. 19, no. 8, pp. 1745–52.

Emami, MH, Gholamrezaei, A and Daneshgar, H (2009). Hypnotherapy as an adjuvant for the management of inflammatory bowel disease: a case report. *Am J Clin Hypn*, vol. 51, no. 3, pp. 255–62.

Garcia-Vega, E and Fernandez-Rodriguez, C (2004). A stress management programme for Crohn's disease. *Behav Res Ther*, vol. 42, no. 4, pp. 367–83.

Ginandes, C, Brooks, P, Sando, W, Jones, C and Aker, J (2003). Can medical hypnosis accelerate post-surgical wound healing? Results of a clinical trial. *Am J Clin Hypn*, vol. 45, no. 4, pp. 333–51.

Halpin, SJ and Ford, AC (2012). Prevalence of symptoms meeting criteria for irritable bowel syndrome in inflammatory bowel disease: systematic review and meta-analysis. *Am J Gastroenterol*, vol. 107, no. 10, pp. 1474–82.

Hoffman, AJ, von Eye, A, Gift, AG, Given, BA, Given, CW and Rothert, M (2009). Testing a theoretical model of perceived self-efficacy for cancer-related fatigue self-management and optimal physical functional status. *Nurs Res*, vol. 58, no. 1, pp. 32–41.

Horton-Hausknecht, JR, Mitzdorf, U and Melchart, D (2000). The effect of hypnosis therapy on the symptoms and disease activity in rheumatoid arthritis. *Psychol Health*, vol. 14, no. 6, pp. 1089–104.

Jensen, MP (2009). Hypnosis for chronic pain management: a new hope. *Pain*, vol. 146, no. 3, pp. 235–7.

Jensen, MP, Gralow, JR, Braden, A, Gertz, KJ, Fann, JR and Syrjala, KL (2012). Hypnosis for symptom management in women with breast cancer: a pilot study. *Int J Clin Exp Hypn*, vol. 60, no. 2, pp. 135–59.

Keefer, L and Keshavarzian, A (2007). Feasibility and acceptability of gut-directed hypnosis on inflammatory bowel disease: a brief communication. *Int J Clin Exp Hypn*, vol. 55, no. 4, pp. 457–66.

Keefer, L, Doerfler, B and Artz, C (2012). Optimizing management of Crohn's disease within a project management framework: results of a pilot study. *Inflamm Bowel Dis*, vol. 18, no. 2, pp. 254–60.

Keefer, L, Kiebles, JL and Taft, TH (2011). The role of self-efficacy in inflammatory bowel disease management: preliminary validation of a disease-specific measure. *Inflamm Bowel Dis*, vol. 17, no. 2, pp. 614–20.

Keefer, L, Taft, TH, Kiebles, JL, Martinovich, Z, Barrett, TA and Palsson, OS (2013). Gut-directed hypnotherapy significantly augments clinical remission in quiescent ulcerative colitis. *Aliment Pharmacol Ther*, vol. 38, no. 7, pp. 761–71.

Kiebles, JL, Doerfler, B and Keefer, L (2010). Preliminary evidence supporting a framework of psychological adjustment to inflammatory bowel disease. *Inflamm Bowel Dis*, vol. 16, no. 10, pp. 1685–95.

Kiecolt-Glaser, JK, Marucha, PT, Atkinson, C and Glaser, R (2001). Hypnosis as a modulator of cellular immune dysregulation during acute stress. *J Consult Clin Psychol*, vol. 69, no. 4, pp. 674–82.

Knowles, SR, Monshat, K and Castle, DJ (2013). The efficacy and methodological challenges of psychotherapy for adults with inflammatory bowel disease: a review. *Inflamm Bowel Dis*, vol. 19, no. 12, pp. 2704–15.

Labus, JS, Mayer, EA, Chang, L, Bolus, R and Naliboff, BD (2007). The central role of gastrointestinal-specific anxiety in irritable bowel syndrome: further validation of the visceral sensitivity index. *Psychosom Med*, vol. 69, no. 1, pp. 89–98.

McAuley, E, Lox, C and Duncan, TE (1993). Long-term maintenance of exercise, self-efficacy, and physiological change in older adults. *J Gerontol*, vol. 48, no. 4, pp. P218–24.

McCombie, AM, Mulder, RT and Gearry, RB (2013). Psychotherapy for inflammatory bowel disease: a review and update. *J Crohns Colitis*, vol. 7, no. 12, pp. 935–49.

Malik, BA, Gibbons, K, Spady, D, Lees, G, Otley, A and Huynh, HQ (2013). Health-related quality of life in pediatric ulcerative colitis patients on conventional medical treatment compared to those after restorative proctocolectomy. *Int J Colorectal Dis*, vol. 28, no. 3, pp. 325–33.

Mawdsley, JE, Jenkins, DG, Macey, MG, Langmead, L and Rampton, DS (2008). The effect of hypnosis on systemic and rectal mucosal measures of inflammation in ulcerative colitis. *Am J Gastroenterol*, vol. 103, no. 6, pp. 1460–9.

Miller, GE and Cohen, S (2001). Psychological interventions and the immune system: a meta-analytic review and critique. *Health Psychol*, vol. 20, no. 1, pp. 47–63.

Miller, V and Whorwell, PJ (2008). Treatment of inflammatory bowel disease: a role for hypnotherapy? *Int J Clin Exp Hypn*, vol. 56, no. 3, pp. 306–17.

Palsson, OS (2010). Hypnosis treatment for gut problems. *Eur Gastroenterol Hepatol Rev*, vol. 6, no. 1, pp. 42–6.

Pihl-Lesnovska, K, Hjortswang, H, Ek, AC and Frisman, GH (2010). Patients' perspective of factors influencing quality of life while living with Crohn disease. *Gastroenterol Nurs*, vol. 33, no. 1, pp. 37–44; quiz 5–6.

Rochelle, TL and Fidler, H (2013). The importance of illness perceptions, quality of life and psychological status in patients with ulcerative colitis and Crohn's disease. *J Health Psychol*, vol. 18, no. 7, pp. 972–83.

Sarkar, U, Ali, S and Whooley, MA (2009). Self-efficacy as a marker of cardiac function and predictor of heart failure hospitalization and mortality in patients with stable coronary heart disease: findings from the Heart and Soul Study. *Health Psychol*, vol. 28, no. 2, pp. 166–73.

Timmer, A, Preiss, JC, Motschall, E, Rucker, G, Jantschek, G and Moser, G (2011). Psychological interventions for treatment of inflammatory bowel disease. *Cochrane Database Syst Rev*, no. 2, p. CD006913.

Triantafillidis, JK, Merikas, E and Gikas, A (2013). Psychological factors and stress in inflammatory bowel disease. *Expert Rev Gastroenterol Hepatol*, vol. 7, no. 3, pp. 225–38.

van der Eijk, I, Vlachonikolis, IG, Munkholm, P, Nijman, J, Bernklev, T, Politi, P, Odes, S, Tsianos, EV, Stockbrugger, RW, Russel, MG and EC-IBD Study Group (2004). The role of quality of care in health-related quality of life in patients with IBD. *Inflamm Bowel Dis*, vol. 10, no. 4, pp. 392–8.

Vogelaar, L, Van't Spijker, A, Vogelaar, T, van Busschbach, JJ, Visser, MS, Kuipers, EJ and van der Woude, CJ (2011). Solution focused therapy: a promising new tool in the management of fatigue in Crohn's disease patients psychological interventions for the management of fatigue in Crohn's disease. *J Crohns Colitis*, vol. 5, no. 6, pp. 585–91.

von Wietersheim, J and Kessler, H (2006). Psychotherapy with chronic inflammatory bowel disease patients: a review. *Inflamm Bowel Dis*, vol. 12, no. 12, pp. 1175–84.

Wood, GJ, Bughi, S, Morrison, J, Tanavoli, S, Tanavoli, S and Zadeh, HH (2003). Hypnosis, differential expression of cytokines by T-cell subsets, and the hypothalamo-pituitary-adrenal axis. *Am J Clin Hypn*, vol. 45, no. 3, pp. 179–96.

Chapter 21

Antidepressants and IBD

Antonina A. Mikocka-Walus

Introduction

Antidepressants – including tricyclic antidepressants (TCAs), selective serotonin reuptake inhibitors (SSRIs), serotonin-norepinephrine reuptake inhibitors (SNRIs), monoamine oxidase inhibitors (MAOIs) and other atypical drugs, such as bupropion, mirtazapine, nefazodone and trazodone – are nowadays becoming the first line treatment for depression and/or anxiety. The reasons for their widespread use include their accessibility, a relatively small cost and increasingly improved safety profiles. The result of this treatment, if effective, is apparent after only few weeks, which contrasts with a much longer waiting time in the case of psychotherapy.

Although antidepressants have been widely researched there has been ongoing controversy regarding their efficacy (Kirsch 2010), particularly in mild to moderate depression, but also because in general their use is suspected to be associated with a particularly large placebo effect. The controversy however has not significantly influenced their prescribing, with millions of people worldwide taking antidepressants. In particular, 11 per cent of Americans aged 12 years and older and 10 per cent of middle-aged Europeans take antidepressant medication (Blanchflower and Oswald 2012; Pratt *et al.* 2011). In the US, antidepressants have been reported as the most commonly prescribed therapeutic class in the recent report by the IMS Institute for Healthcare Informatics (2012).

Antidepressants, chronic disease and gastrointestinal symptoms

Antidepressants have been widely studied in the context of chronic disease, with reportedly good effects not only on quality of life (QOL) and psychological parameters but also on somatic symptoms. A recent Cochrane systematic review including 51 studies ($n = 3603$) demonstrated that antidepressants are superior to placebo in treating depression in the physically ill (Rayner *et al.* 2010). In addition, studies with healthy volunteers have demonstrated that antidepressants can improve immunoregulatory activity (Szuster-Ciesielska *et al.* 2003), lead to a reduction in the need for steroids in asthma sufferers (Brown *et al.* 2005) and to further possible improvements in overall immune functions (Krommydas *et al.* 2005), which may make them particularly suitable for use in inflammatory conditions.

In the context of gastroenterology, antidepressants have been commonly used to treat functional gastrointestinal disorders (FGiDs), such as irritable bowel syndrome (IBS). A meta-analysis (Ford *et al.* 2009) has shown that the relative risk of IBS symptoms persisting with antidepressants versus placebo was 0.66 [95 per cent confidence interval (CI), 0.57 to 0.78], with similar treatment effects for both TCAs and SSRIs.

A subsequent Cochrane systematic review (Ruepert *et al.* 2011) showed that antidepressants are more effective than placebo for improvement of abdominal pain [54 per cent versus 37 per cent; 8 studies; 517 patients; relative risk (RR) 1.49; 95 per cent CI 1.05 to 2.12; $p = 0.03$; numbers needed to treat (NNT) = 5], global assessment (59 per cent versus 39 per cent of placebo; 11 studies; 750 patients; RR 1.57; 95 per cent CI 1.23 to 2.00; $p < 0.001$; NNT = 4) and symptom score (53 per cent versus 26 per cent of placebo; 3 studies; 159 patients; RR 1.99; 95 per cent CI 1.32 to 2.99; $p = 0.001$; NNT = 4), with a subgroup analysis indicating that the SSRIs particularly improve global assessment while the TCAs help abdominal pain and bowel symptoms.

The evidence of the effectiveness of antidepressants in inflammatory bowel disease (IBD) has only emerged in the recent years and the scientific inquiry has not been as thorough as in the case of FGiDs. The reason for it may be the lack of awareness of the impact mental disorders have on the symptoms and activity of IBD, which has been gaining popularity only in the last 10 years, with studies demonstrating the role of stress (Bernstein *et al.* 2010), depression (Mittermaier *et al.* 2004) or documented psychiatric history (van Langenberg *et al.* 2010) in predicting disease activity and hospitalisations but also compliance with treatment (Shale and Riley 2003).

Another reason may be a false notion that mental disorders are not highly prevalent in IBD – the 12-month prevalence is approximately 15 per cent, which amounts to triple of the rate in the general population (Fuller-Thomson and Sulman 2006) and the life-time prevalence is 27 per cent versus 12 per cent in the community (Walker *et al.* 2008). Another misconception may be that antidepressants are to be prescribed just to treat mental health symptoms while there is in fact good evidence on their efficacy in managing bowel symptoms (Ford *et al.* 2009). Regardless, antidepressant treatment in IBD is starting to receive more attention from researchers worldwide, and thus, this Chapter provides an overview of the current studies on the use of antidepressants in IBD and the impact of this treatment on mental health and disease activity parameters.

How frequently are antidepressants used in IBD?

In the largest study to date, a controlled Finnish study (Haapamaki *et al.* 2013), with 2,831 adult IBD patients and 5,662 general population controls matched for age, gender and hospital district, recruited from a national social insurance institution register and the Finnish Crohn's and Colitis Association, 21.5 per cent of IBD patients versus 16 per cent of controls were reported to have used antidepressants ($p < 0.001$). Use of antidepressants [odds ratio (OR): 1.44, 95 per cent CI: 1.28–1.61] was significantly more common in IBD than in controls. In addition, patients in remission used antidepressants ($p = 0.015$, OR: 0.78, 95 per cent CI: 0.64–0.95) significantly less frequently than did those with active disease.

In the Canadian study reporting on results from two nationally representative surveys, one with 1,438 IBD respondents and the other with 3,076 respondents (Fuller-Thomson and Sulman 2006), the rate of antidepressant use in the past month was found to be 13.7 per cent and 10.1 per cent, respectively. In both surveys, there was a significant difference in the rate of antidepressants used between those patients who were depressed and those without depression (9.2 per cent vs. 40.2 per cent and 7.2 per cent vs. 26.2 per cent, respectively, $p < 0.001$), though interestingly a significant number of people without depression were taking antidepressants.

In a smaller retrospective Australian study with a tertiary clinic population ($n = 287$), a life-time use of antidepressants was noted to be just below 30 per cent, indicating their higher prevalence in patients with more serious disease presentation (Mikocka-Walus, A $et\ al.$ 2012).

Antidepressants for depression and IBD activity

Two systematic reviews have been conducted on the role of antidepressants in IBD (Mikocka-Walus $et\ al.$ 2006, 2009). In the first review, 12 human studies were identified, all non-randomised (Mikocka-Walus $et\ al.$ 2006). In ten papers, paroxetine, bupropion and phenelzine were suggested to be effective for treating both psychological and somatic symptoms in patients suffering from IBD. Amitriptyline was found ineffective for treating somatic symptoms of IBD. Mirtazapine was not recommended for IBD patients. Although the reviewed papers pointed towards a beneficial effect of treatment with antidepressants in patients with IBD, due to the lack of reliable data, the review concluded that it was not possible to judge the efficacy of antidepressants in IBD.

In the second review, a positive effect of antidepressants (i.e. desipramine and fluoxetine) on inflammation in animal models of gastrointestinal inflammation was identified in three randomised controlled trials (Mikocka-Walus $et\ al.$ 2009). In the trial by Varghese (Varghese $et\ al.$ 2006), desipramine resulted in less severe colitis than placebo. In particular, in mice receiving desipramine, reduced microscopic damage was observed (1.4 ± 0.16 vs. 2.17 ± 0.31, $p < 0.05$), a trend towards reduction in macroscopic damage was also seen (3.0 ± 0.29 vs. 3.94 ± 0.44, $p = 0.07$) as well as reduced attenuation of colonic MPO (myeloperoxidase) activity (0.6 ± 0.1 vs. 3.04 ± 0.95, $p < 0.05$). In the study by Ghia $et\ al.$ (2008), desipramine improved values for the histological score from 2.7 ± 0.25 to 1.12 ± 0.21 ($p < 0.05$), CRP levels decreased from 34.1 ± 0.7 to 25.1 ± 2.3ng/ml ($p < 0.05$)

and cytokine fold increases were 0.31 ± 0.22 ($p < 0.05$), 0.5 ± 0.33 ($p < 0.05$) and 1.02 ± 0.2 ($p < 0.05$) for IL-1β, IL-6, and TNF-α, respectively, compared with controls. Similar trends were observed by Guemei *et al.* (2008), for example, serum Il-1β concentrations were significantly lower in rats receiving 10mg fluoxetine (275.03 ± 15.05), 20mg fluoxetine (371.36 ± 7.44), 20mg desipramine (422.12 ± 5.17) or 10mg desipramine (493.23 ± 1.83) compared to controls (577.13 ± 5.85) (all $p < 0.001$). Similarly, reductions in serum TNFα were observed in rats receiving 20mg desipramine (3.73 ± 0.17), 10mg desipramine (6.63 ± 0.16), 20mg fluoxetine (7.71 ± 0.18) or 10mg fluoxetine (7.71 ± 0.18) compared to controls (13.92 ± 0.28) (all $p < 0.001$).

A recent small ($n = 29$) retrospective case-matched study from a UK group has demonstrated the role of antidepressants in managing disease activity in humans (Goodhand *et al.* 2012). In particular, IBD patients had fewer relapses and courses of steroids in the year after starting an antidepressant than in the year before {1 [0–4] [median (range)] vs. 0 [0–4], $p = 0.002$; 1 [0–3] vs. 0 [0–4], $p < 0.001$, respectively}, while the controls showed no changes between years 1 and 2 in relapses [1 (0–4) vs. 1 (0–3), respectively] or courses of steroids [1 (0–2) vs. 0 (0–3)].

In the retrospective uncontrolled case-note audit with current and past antidepressant users ($n = 287$) (Mikocka-Walus, A *et al.* 2012), it was shown that while taking antidepressants, the majority of patients had inactive disease. In particular, 15 (29.4 per cent) of 51 patients currently taking antidepressants had inactive disease but presented with functional bowel disorders. Another 11 (21.5 per cent) patients had full remission with no disease activity. Two (3.9 per cent) patients had active disease. In the remaining 23 (45 per cent) patients, no data were recorded suggesting that the disease was quiescent. In the 71 past antidepressant users, 19 (26.7 per cent) had inactive disease but presented with functional symptoms, 12 (16.9 per cent) patients had active disease and nine (12.6 per cent) had inactive disease.

In a cross-sectional exploratory online survey with the members of the Crohn's and Colitis of Australia who used antidepressants, of current antidepressants users ($n = 65$), 87 per cent reported that antidepressants improved their psychological wellbeing (Mikocka-Walus and Andrews 2014). The majority of respondent-vbserved no change in IBD activity while on antidepressants, however, 16 (25 per cent) believed antidepressants improved their IBD. However, the number of people reporting very well controlled and only mildly active IBD increased during antidepressant therapy from 46 per cent at therapy initiation to 66 per cent when ceasing them ($n = 28$ and $n = 43$, respectively, $p = 0.016$). Nearly 58 per cent of respondents reported antidepressant-related side effects, including weight gain, lethargy or drowsiness, decreased libido, dry mouth and insomnia, however, no major adverse events. Most (84 per cent) respondents would recommend antidepressants to other people living with IBD and 81 per cent reported willingness to participate in clinical trials with antidepressants. Similar observations were made in past antidepressant users.

In a small qualitative study, 15 IBD sufferers currently on antidepressants were interviewed in relation to their attitudes towards antidepressants, and all reported a positive response to antidepressants mostly with respect to improved mental health. One third of patients felt that antidepressants had specifically improved their IBD course. Nine patients (60.0 per cent) had a generally positive attitude towards antidepressants, four patients (26.7 per cent) were ambivalent, and two patients (13.3 per cent) held a negative view towards antidepressants, while 12 patients (80.0 per cent) stated that they would be willing to participate in clinical trials with antidepressants (Mikocka-Walus, AA *et al.* 2012).

Doctors' attitudes towards the treatment with antidepressants have been examined in one study with a small ($n = 18$) but representative sample of gastroenterologists (Mikocka-Walus *et al.* 2007). Of the interviewed doctors, 78 per cent reported treating IBD patients with antidepressants for pain, depression and/or anxiety and insomnia. Antidepressants were found to be useful in improving psychosocial wellbeing, quality of life, and self-management of the disease by patients.

Conclusions

Antidepressants are frequently used in IBD. However, there are currently no randomised controlled trials that have examined their effectiveness in treating depression, bowel symptoms or inflammation in IBD, therefore, such studies are warranted. The existing evidence coming from retrospective and cross-sectional studies suggests their possible role in delaying flares and better management of bowel symptoms, with improved psychological functioning. Antidepressants seem to be well tolerated and accepted by IBD patients.

Current limitations and future considerations

- There are no randomised controlled trials on antidepressants in IBD available
- Current evidence does not demonstrate which types of antidepressants may be more effective in IBD than others and what doses should be used, although animal trials point to the use of small doses of desipramine and fluoxetine as agents with some anti-inflammatory properties
- It is unclear whether antidepressants are equally helpful in clinical versus sub-clinical depression in IBD as is whether they may be more helpful to IBD sufferers who report functional symptoms while in remission
- The interactions of antidepressants with standard drug treatment in IBD are also unknown and should be investigated as should their role in addressing mood changes resulting from the use of steroids
- Future clinical trials with antidepressants should evaluate their impact on symptoms but also on inflammatory parameters to verify the animal data observations
- Mechanisms of antidepressants action in IBD should be tested including their impact on inflammation, mood and bowel symptoms

Practical recommendations

- Antidepressants are commonly used in patients with IBD, with no serious adverse effects reported
- No current guidelines on the treatment of IBD patients with antidepressants exist and thus clinicians should consult general guidelines on treating depression in the medically ill (NICE 2009) and guidelines on treating functional symptoms in patients with FGiDs (NICE 2008)
- In spite of the encouraging data coming from existing retrospective and cross-sectional studies, there is currently no high quality evidence available on the role of antidepressants in managing inflammation and IBD symptoms, and thus, antidepressants should not be used as a replacement of or routine adjunct to the standard treatment until clinical trials establish their efficacy in IBD

Learning points

- Antidepressants are becoming the first line treatment for depression and/or anxiety
- There is good evidence for their efficacy in functional gut disorders with respect to global functioning but also pain and bowel symptoms
- There is a dearth of high quality evidence for efficacy of antidepressants in IBD, however, preliminary observations suggest their possible role in improving mental health and disease course
- Randomised controlled trials on the role of antidepressants to manage both psychological and physical symptoms of IBD are warranted

References

Bernstein, CN, Singh, S, Graff, LA, Walker, JR, Miller, N and Cheang, M (2010). A prospective population-based study of triggers of symptomatic flares in IBD. *Am J Gastroenterol*, vol. 105, no. 9, pp. 1994–2002.

Blanchflower, DG and Oswald, AJ (2012). *Antidepressants and age in 27 European countries: evidence of a u-shape in human well-being through life*. Coventry: University of Warwick. Available online from www2.warwick.ac.uk/fac/soc/economics/staff/academic/oswald/ (accessed 31 May 2014).

Brown, ES, Vigil, L, Khan, DA, Liggin, JD, Carmody, TJ and Rush, AJ (2005). A randomized trial of citalopram versus placebo in outpatients with asthma and major depressive disorder: a proof of concept study. *Biol Psychiatry*, vol. 58, no. 11, pp. 865–70.

Ford, AC, Talley, NJ, Schoenfeld, PS, Quigley, EM and Moayyedi, P (2009). Efficacy of antidepressants and psychological therapies in irritable bowel syndrome: systematic review and meta-analysis. *Gut*, vol. 58, no. 3, pp. 367–78.

Fuller-Thomson, E and Sulman, J (2006). Depression and inflammatory bowel disease: findings from two nationally representative Canadian surveys. *Inflamm Bowel Dis*, vol. 12, no. 8, pp. 697–707.

Ghia, JE, Blennerhassett, P and Collins, SM (2008). Impaired parasympathetic function increases susceptibility to inflammatory bowel disease in a mouse model of depression. *J Clin Invest*, vol. 118, no. 6, pp. 2209–18.

Goodhand, JR, Greig, FI, Koodun, Y, McDermott, A, Wahed, M, Langmead, L and Rampton, DS (2012). Do antidepressants influence the disease course in inflammatory bowel disease? A retrospective case-matched observational study. *Inflamm Bowel Dis*, vol. 18, no. 7, pp. 1232–9.

Guemei, AA, El Din, NM, Baraka, AM and El Said Darwish, I (2008). Do desipramine [10,11-dihydro-5-[3-(methylamino) propyl]-5H-dibenz[b,f]azepine monohydrochloride] and fluoxetine [N-methyl-3-phenyl-3-[4-(trifluoromethyl)phenoxy]-propan-1-amine] ameliorate the extent of colonic damage induced by acetic acid in rats? *J Pharmacol Exp Ther*, vol. 327, no. 3, pp. 846–50.

Haapamaki, J, Tanskanen, A, Roine, RP, Blom, M, Turunen, U, Mantyla, J, Farkkila, MA and Arkkila, PE (2013). Medication use among inflammatory bowel disease patients: excessive consumption of antidepressants and analgesics. *Scand J Gastroenterol*, vol. 48, no. 1, pp. 42–50.

IMS Institute for Healthcare Informatics (2012). *The use of medicines in the United States: review of 2011.* Parsippany: IMS Institute for Healthcare Informatics.

Kirsch, I (2010). *The emperor's new drugs: exploding the antidepressant myth.* New York: Basic Books.

Krommydas, G, Gourgoulianis, KI, Karamitsos, K, Krapis, K, Kotrotsiou, E and Molyvdas, PA (2005). Therapeutic value of antidepressants in asthma. *Med Hypotheses*, vol. 64, no. 5, pp. 938–40.

Mikocka-Walus, A and Andrews, JM (2014). Attitudes towards antidepressants among people living with inflammatory bowel disease: an online Australia-wide survey. *J Crohns Colitis*, vol. 8, no. 4, pp. 296–303.

Mikocka-Walus, A, Clarke, D and Gibson, P (2009). Can antidepressants influence the course of inflammatory bowel disease (IBD)? The current state of research. *Eur Gastroenterol Hepatol Rev*, vol. 5, no. 1, pp. 48–53.

Mikocka-Walus, A, Gordon, AL, Stewart, BJ and Andrews, JM (2012). The role of antidepressants in the management of inflammatory bowel disease (IBD): a short report on a clinical case-note audit. *J Psychosom Res*, vol. 72, no. 2, pp. 165–7.

Mikocka-Walus, A, Turnbull, DA, Moulding, NT, Wilson, IG, Andrews, JM and Holtmann, GJ (2006). Antidepressants and inflammatory bowel disease: a systematic review. *Clin Pract Epidemiol Ment Health*, vol. 2, p. 24.

Mikocka-Walus, A, Turnbull, DA, Moulding, NT, Wilson, IG, Andrews, JM and Holtmann, GJ (2007). "It doesn't do any harm, but patients feel better": a qualitative exploratory study on gastroenterologists' perspectives on the role of antidepressants in inflammatory bowel disease. *BMC Gastroenterol*, vol. 7, p. 38.

Mikocka-Walus, AA, Turnbull, D, Holtmann, G and Andrews, JM (2012). An integrated model of care for inflammatory bowel disease sufferers in Australia: development and the effects of its implementation', *Inflamm Bowel Dis*, vol. 18, no. 8, pp. 1573–81.

Mittermaier, C, Dejaco, C, Waldhoer, T, Oefferlbauer-Ernst, A, Miehsler, W, Beier, M, Tillinger, W, Gangl, A and Moser, G (2004). Impact of depressive mood on relapse in patients with inflammatory bowel disease: a prospective 18-month follow-up study. *Psychosom Med*, vol. 66, no. 1, pp. 79–84.

NICE (2009). *Depression in adults with a chronic physical health problem: treatment and management.* NICE clinical guideline 91. London: National Institute for Health and Clinical Excellence.

NICE (2008). *Irritable bowel syndrome in adults: diagnosis and management of irritable bowel syndrome in primary care.* NICE clinical guideline 61. London: National Institute for Health and Clinical Excellence.

Pratt, L, Brody, DJ and Gu, Q (2011). Antidepressant use in persons aged 12 and over: United States, 2005–2008. *NCHS Data Brief*, no. 76, pp. 1–8.

Rayner, L, Price, A, Evans, A, Valsraj, K, Higginson, IJ and Hotopf, M (2010). Antidepressants for depression in physically ill people. *Cochrane Database Syst Rev*, no. 3, p. CD007503.

Ruepert, L, Quartero, AO, de Wit, NJ, van der Heijden, GJ, Rubin, G and Muris, JW (2011). Bulking agents, antispasmodics and antidepressants for the treatment of irritable bowel syndrome. *Cochrane Database Syst Rev*, no. 8, p. CD003460.

Shale, MJ and Riley, SA (2003). Studies of compliance with delayed-release mesalazine therapy in patients with inflammatory bowel disease. *Aliment Pharmacol Ther*, vol. 18, no. 2, pp. 191–8.

Szuster-Ciesielska, A, Tustanowska-Stachura, A, Slotwinska, M, Marmurowska-Michalowska, H and Kandefer-Szerszen, M (2003). In vitro immunoregulatory effects of antidepressants in healthy volunteers. *Pol J Pharmacol*, vol. 55, no. 3, pp. 353–62.

van Langenberg, DR, Lange, K, Hetzel, DJ, Holtmann, GJ and Andrews, JM (2010). Adverse clinical phenotype in inflammatory bowel disease: a cross sectional study identifying factors potentially amenable to change. *J Gastroenterol Hepatol*, vol. 25, no. 7, pp. 1250–8.

Varghese, AK, Verdu, EF, Bercik, P, Khan, WI, Blennerhassett, PA, Szechtman, H and Collins, SM (2006). Antidepressants attenuate increased susceptibility to colitis in a murine model of depression. *Gastroenterology*, vol. 130, no. 6, pp. 1743–53.

Walker, JR, Ediger, JP, Graff, LA, Greenfeld, JM, Clara, I, Lix, L, Rawsthorne, P, Miller, N, Rogala, L, McPhail, CM and Bernstein, CN (2008). The Manitoba IBD cohort study: a population-based study of the prevalence of lifetime and 12-month anxiety and mood disorders. *Am J Gastroenterol*, vol. 103, no. 8, pp. 1989–97.

Chapter 22

Complementary and alternative medicine in IBD

Randi Opheim and Bjørn Moum

Introduction

The World Health Organization (WHO) defines complementary and alternative medicine (CAM) as a 'broad set of health care practices that are not part of that country's own tradition and are not integrated into the dominant health care system' (WHO 2000). CAM includes a wide range of therapies, products and practices, such as (i) visits to alternative health care practitioners, for example, acupuncturist, homeopath, and healer; (ii) use of herbal medicine and dietary supplements; and (iii) self-help practices, for example, meditation, yoga, prayer and relaxation techniques. Traditional health care systems, for example, traditional Chinese medicine, Indian Ayurveda, homeopathy and naturopathy combine several of these therapies in their treatment regimens. CAM is heterogeneous, and this is exemplified by the national legal status and regulation of alternative health care providers and the terminology used. In most countries, CAM is not covered by national insurance systems, and users pay almost all CAM-related costs out of their own pocket (Thomas *et al.* 2001). Although the efficacy of CAM is a controversial issue that generates considerable professional and public debate a high proportion of the general population and the chronically ill turn to CAM (Harris *et al.* 2012).

CAM use among IBD patients

Population-based and selected cohort studies have shown that CAM use is common among inflammatory bowel disease (IBD) patients (Fernandez *et al.* 2012; Koning *et al.* 2013; Lakatos *et al.* 2010; Opheim *et al.* 2012b; Rawsthorne *et al.* 2012; Weizman *et al.* 2012). A review of Hilsden *et al.*, in 2011, showed that past or current CAM use varied from 21 percent to 60 percent among IBD patients from North America and Europe. Whether CAM is utilised to help with IBD has been reported in some studies, but not in others. The type and rate of use of individual modalities vary across countries and geographical areas. As an example, homeopathy and acupuncture were more frequently reported by the European IBD patients compared to North American IBD patients (Abitbol *et al.* 2014;

Hilsden *et al.* 2011; Opheim *et al.* 2012a, 2012b). A Norwegian study has found that IBD patients attending outpatient clinics at hospitals most frequently used acupuncture, which was comparable to the use in the general population of Norway (Opheim *et al.* 2012a). A systematic review of Harris *et al.* (2012) showed that CAM was frequently used by general populations in a number of countries. The 12-month prevalence of all types of CAM in the reviewed studies ranged from 9.8 to 76 percent. The wide variation was due to how CAM was defined and the high variability of CAM modalities investigated (Harris *et al.* 2012). In this regard, patients appear to use CAM that is available and common in their culture, suggesting that a uniform profile of CAM use worldwide is unlikely.

Factors associated with CAM use

In the general population, studies have persistently shown that CAM users are more likely to be women, better educated, middle-aged, and that they report poorer health status than non-users (Harris *et al.* 2012). Among IBD patients, population-based studies have found female gender, younger age, and higher education level to be independently associated with CAM use (Koning *et al.* 2013; Opheim *et al.* 2012b; Rawsthorne *et al.* 2012). However, similar results have not consistently been found in hospital-based studies (Hilsden *et al.* 2011). Several disease-related factors have been found to be independently associated with CAM use, such as disease duration and hospitalization rates (Hilsden *et al.* 1998), disease activity (Li *et al.* 2005), extra-intestinal complications (Fernandez *et al.* 2012), experience of adverse effects in response to conventional IBD medications (Opheim *et al.* 2012a; Weizman *et al.* 2012), use of corticosteroid and azathioprine (Lakatos *et al.* 2010; Langhorst *et al.* 2005) and comorbid conditions (Ganguli *et al.* 2004; Opheim *et al.* 2012a; Sirois 2008). Thus, factors associated with CAM use among IBD patients seem to be dependent of the sample being studied (e.g., population-based versus hospital based) (Hilsden *et al.* 2011).

Patient reported reasons for CAM use and perceived benefit

Several studies have examined IBD patients' reasons for and beliefs about CAM. Concerns about ineffectiveness of conventional medical therapy (Bertomoro *et al.* 2010; Hilsden *et al.* 1999; Lakatos *et al.* 2010; Langhorst *et al.* 2007; Li *et al.* 2005; Rawsthorne *et al.* 1999; Weizman *et al.* 2012) and CAM use as a contribution to personal control of the disease and health in general (Bensoussan *et al.* 2006; Ganguli *et al.* 2004; Hilsden *et al.* 2003; Langhorst *et al.* 2007; Sirois 2008) have been reported frequently. A large cross-sectional study of members of the Crohn's and colitis organization in Canada ($n = 2,828$) found that reasons for *not* using CAM were that conventional medical treatment was successful in treating their disease and believing there was a lack of evidence for the efficacy of CAM (Li *et al.* 2005). A multicentre study including 289 IBD

Complementary and alternative medicine 201

patients found that those who experienced conventional medical treatment to be satisfactory were less likely to use CAM (Rawsthorne *et al.* 1999). However, in a prospective longitudinal study including 309 IBD patients, only 18 percent of the CAM users reported their use of CAM for IBD related reasons (Rawsthorne *et al.* 2012).

IBD patients using CAM do so because they anticipate certain outcomes or benefits. In general, it may seem that the belief in the benefit of CAM may be the motivation to use CAM (Hilsden *et al.* 2011; Sirois 2008). In the national survey in Canada including 2,828 IBD patients, the most commonly reported benefits were improved wellbeing and energy level, an improved control over their disease, and relief of IBD symptoms (Hilsden *et al.* 2003). In a study of 101 British IBD patients, 53 percent (15/28) of the CAM users stated that they benefited 'quite well or very well' by their CAM use (Langmead *et al.* 2002). In a population-based study of 517 Norwegian IBD patients, 36 percent (56/157) of the CAM users were 'mostly satisfied' or 'very satisfied' with the treatment (Opheim *et al.* 2012b).

Factors influencing the patients' decision to use CAM were explored in a small qualitative study of 14 IBD patients (Scott *et al.* 2003). The study revealed that the decision to use CAM was based upon an understanding of the interrelationship between biological, psychological, and social factors. Their symptoms, their health beliefs and perceived sources of social support, all contributed to their individual experience of illness. The participants generally started to use CAM when medical treatment failed to control their symptoms or to avoid side effects from conventional medical treatment. They reportedly felt that their health was a personal responsibility and they were concerned with a healthy life style including drinking and smoking habits and exercise. The participants also expressed a wish to be included in treatment decisions and in collaboration with health care providers to develop strategies to meet their individual needs (Scott *et al.* 2003).

Association between CAM use and HRQoL

Although it is generally assumed that CAM may have beneficial influence on wellbeing and quality of life, only a few observational studies in IBD populations have investigated this association. In a prospective longitudinal study of 309 IBD patients, the relationship between CAM use and psychological factors including HRQoL was measured at four time points over a 4.5 year period (Rawsthorne *et al.* 2012). No differences between CAM users and non-users were found with regard to perceived stress and personality characteristics including neuroticism, openness, extraversion, agreeableness, conscientiousness, health anxiety, mastery, or IBD specific HRQoL.

A study that assessed provider based CAM use in three chronic illness groups including 110 IBD patients, found that respondents with higher perceived control over health [odds ratio (OR) 1.47, 95 per cent confidence interval (CI): 1.15

to 1.89, $p = 0.002$] and higher reward motivation (OR 1.56, 95 per cent CI: 1.01 to 2.39, $p = 0.044$) were more likely to use CAM (Sirois 2008). The odds of using CAM were lower for individuals who believed that health was a matter of chance (OR 0.81, 95 per cent CI: 0.65 to 0.99, $p = 0.043$), for those reporting more stress (OR 0.89, 95 per cent CI: 0.79 to 1.00, $p = 0.054$), and for those who were coping effectively with the emotional aspects of their illness (OR 0.65, 95 per cent CI: 0.53 to 0.79, $p < 0.001$). In this study however, the IBD patients' responses were not analysed separately from other participants.

In the majority of studies assessing the relationship between CAM use and HRQoL disease specific HRQoL questionnaires have been used. A study of 101 IBD patients from out-patient clinics in the United Kingdom found an independent association between CAM use and reduced emotional function, measured by IBDQ (OR = 0.57, 95 per cent CI 0.35 to 0.9, $p = 0.01$) (Langmead *et al.* 2002). A cross-sectional study of 99 IBD patients from Canada reported comparable rates of IBDQ scores between CAM users and non-users (Ganguli *et al.* 2004). A study of 380 Canadian IBD patients from out-patient clinics found no difference between CAM users and non-users in disease-specific HRQoL scores determined by the Short Form IBD Questionnaire (SIBDQ) (Weizman *et al.* 2012). An internet survey of 767 IBD patients from France found that the rates of good HRQoL (defined by a SIBDQ score >50) were higher among CAM users compared to non-users (OR = 1.57, $p = 0.06$) (Abitbol *et al.* 2014).

Studies assessing fatigue in IBD have found that it is a common experience, even when the disease is quiescent (Czuber-Dochan *et al.* 2013). The relationship between fatigue (measured with the Fatigue Severity Scale) and CAM use was assessed among 428 Norwegian IBD patients attending outpatient clinics and a significant association between fatigue and CAM use was observed in the ulcerative colitis group (OR 2.20, 95 per cent CI: 1.09 to 4.44, $p = 0.03$). This relationship was not observed among Crohn's disease patients (Opheim *et al.* 2014).

Evaluating effectiveness of CAM

Although CAM use has been widely investigated, there has been an ongoing controversy regarding its efficacy. Despite promising results from some studies, systematic reviews assessing the efficacy of CAM, such as acupuncture and herbal medicine, in IBD have shown that there is no robust evidence for their efficacy on generally accepted outcomes such as disease activity scores (Ji *et al.* 2013; Ng *et al.* 2013; Schneider *et al.* 2007). However, the majority of CAM approaches have focused on holistic care, with an emphasis on health as a product of biological, psychological, social, and spiritual dimensions (Wiles and Rosenberg 2001). Important therapeutic elements are improving health and wellbeing and individual resources and efforts are often emphasised. The quality of the interaction and the communication between the patients and the therapist is also an important therapeutic focus. Hence, the patient's perspective is crucial in understanding the process and outcomes of CAM interventions (Durber and Otley 2005; Hilsden and Verhoef 1998; Hilsden *et al.* 2011). It is argued that in addition to objective outcome parameters of pathology, symptoms and other biological indicators, the individualised treatment benefits such as the subjective experience of health related changes, in general, and how participants experience the intervention should be included as outcome measures in randomised controlled trials assessing the efficacy of CAM therapies (Verhoef *et al.* 2005).

Conclusion

CAM use is common among IBD patients. There is a gap between the frequency of CAM use and the evidence-based efficacy of CAM. Reasons for CAM use are related to disease specific concerns, as well as a wish to take personal control over disease and health in general. IBD patients seem to use CAM because it allows them to take an active role in managing health and disease. Observational studies assessing the relationship between general wellbeing, quality of life and CAM use have shown inconclusive results.

Current limitations and future considerations

- A lack of a uniform and generally accepted definition of CAM makes it difficult to determine absolute usage rates
- Scientific evidence for CAM's efficacy and safety has not been adequately determined and the majority of studies have produced inconsistent results
- Observational studies assessing the relationship between general wellbeing, quality of life and CAM use are few and the results inconclusive
- A consensus regarding the CAM definition is needed to facilitate direct comparison of CAM use between populations, regions or countries
- Further research is needed to explore whether CAM services, products and practices are useful to improve self-care and HRQoL
- Health related outcomes such as HRQoL, wellbeing, self-efficacy and fatigue should be included in RCTs evaluating the efficacy of CAM therapies
- Prospective longitudinal studies in IBD populations are warranted to provide further knowledge on the variability and stability of CAM use over time

Practical recommendations

- Ask the patients about CAM use
- Clinicians need to make an effort to understand why their patients use CAM and what are the benefits experienced, and also consider any adverse interactions with the prescribed medical treatment
- Incorporation of CAM-related courses in educating nurses and medical students will enhance the ability of these health care professionals to evaluate CAM and to better advice their patients

Learning points

- Use of CAM is common among IBD patients
- There is a gap between the frequency of CAM use and the evidence-based efficacy of CAM
- Reasons for CAM use are related to disease specific concerns as well as a wish to take personal control over disease and health in general
- Observational studies investigating associations between HRQoL, general wellbeing and CAM use have shown inconclusive results
- Further research is needed to explore whether CAM services, products, and practices may be useful to improve self-care and HRQoL

References

Abitbol, V, Lahmek, P, Buisson, A, Olympie, A, Poupardin, C, Chaussade, S, Lesgourgues, B and Nahon, S (2014). Impact of complementary and alternative medicine on the quality of life in inflammatory bowel disease: results from a French national survey. *Eur J Gastroenterol Hepatol*, vol. 26, no. 3, pp. 288–94.

Bensoussan, M, Jovenin, N, Garcia, B, Vandromme, L, Jolly, D, Bouche, O, Thiefin, G and Cadiot, G (2006). Complementary and alternative medicine use by patients with inflammatory bowel disease: results from a postal survey. *Gastroen Clin Biol*, vol. 30, no. 1, pp. 14–23.

Bertomoro, P, Renna, S, Cottone, M, Riegler, G, Bossa, F, Giglio, L, Pastorelli, L, Papi, C, Castiglione, F, Angelucci, E, Pica, R, Di Paolo, MC and D'Inca, R (2010). Regional variations in the use of complementary and alternative medicines (CAM) for inflammatory bowel disease patients in Italy: an IG-IBD study. *J Crohns Colitis.*, vol. 4, no. 3, pp. 291–300.

Czuber-Dochan, W, Ream, E and Norton, C (2013). Review article: description and management of fatigue in inflammatory bowel disease. *Aliment Pharmacol Ther*, vol. 37, no. 5, pp. 505–16.

Durber, J and Otley, A (2005). Complementary and alternative medicine in inflammatory bowel disease: keeping an open mind. *Expert Rev Clin Immunol*, vol. 1, no. 2, pp. 277–92.

Fernandez, A, Barreiro-de Acosta, M, Vallejo, N, Iglesias, M, Carmona, A, Gonzalez-Portela, C, Lorenzo, A and Dominguez-Munoz, JE (2012). Complementary and alternative medicine in inflammatory bowel disease patients: frequency and risk factors. *Dig Liver Dis*, vol. 44, no. 11, pp. 904–8.

Ganguli, SC, Cawdron, R and Irvine, EJ (2004). Alternative medicine use by Canadian ambulatory gastroenterology patients: secular trend or epidemic? *Am J Gastroenterol*, vol. 99, no. 2, pp. 319–26.

Harris, PE, Cooper, KL, Relton, C and Thomas, KJ (2012). Prevalence of complementary and alternative medicine (CAM) use by the general population: a systematic review and update. *Int J Clin Pract*, vol. 66, no. 10, pp. 924–39.

Hilsden, RJ, Meddings, JB and Verhoef, MJ (1999). Complementary and alternative medicine use by patients with inflammatory bowel disease: an internet survey. *Can J Gastroenterol*, vol. 13, no. 4, pp. 327–32.

Hilsden, RJ, Scott, CM and Verhoef, MJ (1998). Complementary medicine use by patients with inflammatory bowel disease. *Am J Gastroenterol*, vol. 93, no. 5, pp. 697–701.

Hilsden, RJ and Verhoef, MJ (1998). Complementary and alternative medicine: evaluating its effectiveness in inflammatory bowel disease. *Inflamm Bowel Dis*, vol. 4, no. 4, pp. 318–23.

Hilsden, RJ, Verhoef, MJ, Best, A and Pocobelli, G (2003). Complementary and alternative medicine use by Canadian patients with inflammatory bowel disease: results from a national survey. *Am J Gastroenterol*, vol. 98, no. 7, pp. 1563–8.

Hilsden, RJ, Verhoef, MJ, Rasmussen, H, Porcino, A and Debruyn, JC (2011). Use of complementary and alternative medicine by patients with inflammatory bowel disease. *Inflamm Bowel Dis*, vol. 17, no. 2, pp. 655–62.

Ji, J, Lu, Y, Liu, H, Feng, H, Zhang, F, Wu, L, Cui, Y and Wu, H (2013). Acupuncture and moxibustion for inflammatory bowel diseases: a systematic review and meta-analysis of randomized controlled trials. *Evid Based Complement Alternat Med*, vol. 2013, p. 158352.

Koning, M, Ailabouni, R, Gearry, RB, Frampton, CM and Barclay, ML (2013). Use and predictors of oral complementary and alternative medicine by patients with inflammatory bowel disease: a population-based, case-control study. *Inflamm Bowel Dis*, vol. 19, no. 4, pp. 767–78.

Lakatos, PL, Czegledi, Z, David, G, Kispal, Z, Kiss, LS, Palatka, K, Kristof, T, Nagy, F, Salamon, A, Demeter, P, Miheller, P, Szamosi, T, Banai, J, Papp, M, Bene, L, Kovacs, A, Racz, I and Lakatos, L (2010). Association of adherence to therapy and complementary and alternative medicine use with demographic factors and disease phenotype in patients with inflammatory bowel disease. *J Crohns Colitis*, vol. 4, no. 3, pp. 283–90.

Langhorst, J, Anthonisen, IB, Steder-Neukamm, U, Ludtke, R, Spahn, G, Michalsen, A and Dobos, GJ (2005). Amount of systemic steroid medication is a strong predictor for the use of complementary and alternative medicine in patients with inflammatory bowel disease: results from a German national survey. *Inflamm Bowel Dis*, vol. 11, no. 3, pp. 287–95.

Langhorst, J, Anthonisen, IB, Steder-Neukamm, U, Luedtke, R, Spahn, G, Michalsen, A and Dobos, GJ (2007). Patterns of complementary and alternative medicine (CAM) use in patients with inflammatory bowel disease: perceived stress is a potential indicator for CAM use. *Complement Ther Med*, vol. 15, no. 1, pp. 30–7.

Langmead, L, Chitnis, M and Rampton, DS (2002). Use of complementary therapies by patients with IBD may indicate psychosocial distress. *Inflamm Bowel Dis*, vol. 8, no. 3, pp. 174–9.

Li, FX, Verhoef, MJ, Best, A, Otley, A and Hilsden, RJ (2005). Why patients with inflammatory bowel disease use or do not use complementary and alternative medicine: a Canadian national survey. *Can J Gastroenterol*, vol. 19, no. 9, pp. 567–73.

Ng, SC, Lam, YT, Tsoi, KK, Chan, FK, Sung, JJ and Wu, JC (2013). Systematic review: the efficacy of herbal therapy in inflammatory bowel disease. *Aliment Pharmacol Ther*, vol. 38, no. 8, pp. 854–63.

Opheim, R, Bernklev, T, Fagermoen, MS, Cvancarova, M and Moum, B (2012a). Use of complementary and alternative medicine in patients with inflammatory bowel disease: results of a cross-sectional study in Norway. *Scand J Gastroenterol*, vol. 47, no. 12, pp. 1436–47.

Opheim, R, Fagermoen, MS, Bernklev, T, Jelsness-Jorgensen, LP and Moum, B (2014). Fatigue interference with daily living among patients with inflammatory bowel disease. *Qual Life Res*, vol. 23, no. 2, pp. 707–17.

Opheim, R, Hoivik, ML, Solberg, IC and Moum, B (2012b). Complementary and alternative medicine in patients with inflammatory bowel disease: the results of a population-based inception cohort study (IBSEN). *J Crohns Colitis*, vol. 6, no. 3, pp. 345–53.

Rawsthorne, P, Clara, I, Graff, LA, Bernstein, KI, Carr, R, Walker, JR, Ediger, J, Rogala, L, Miller, N and Bernstein, CN (2012). The Manitoba Inflammatory Bowel Disease Cohort Study: a prospective longitudinal evaluation of the use of complementary and alternative medicine services and products. *Gut*, vol. 61, no. 4, pp. 521–7.

Rawsthorne, P, Shanahan, F, Cronin, NC, Anton, PA, Lofberg, R, Bohman, L and Bernstein, CN (1999). An international survey of the use and attitudes regarding alternative medicine by patients with inflammatory bowel disease. *Am J Gastroenterol*, vol. 94, no. 5, pp. 1298–303.

Schneider, A, Streitberger, K and Joos, S (2007). Acupuncture treatment in gastrointestinal diseases: a systematic review. *World J Gastroenterol*, vol. 13, no. 25, pp. 3417–24.

Scott, CM, Verhoef, MJ and Hilsden, RJ (2003). Inflammatory bowel disease patients' decisions to use complementary therapies: links to existing models of care. *Complement Ther Med*, vol. 11, no. 1, pp. 22–7.

Sirois, FM (2008). Provider-based complementary and alternative medicine use among three chronic illness groups: associations with psychosocial factors and concurrent use of conventional health-care services. *Complement Ther Med*, vol. 16, no. 2, pp. 73–80.

Thomas, KJ, Nicholl, JP and Coleman, P (2001). Use and expenditure on complementary medicine in England: a population based survey. *Complement Ther Med*, vol. 9, no. 1, pp. 2–11.

Verhoef, MJ, Lewith, G, Ritenbaugh, C, Boon, H, Fleishman, S and Leis, A (2005). Complementary and alternative medicine whole systems research: beyond identification of inadequacies of the RCT. *Complement Ther Med*, vol. 13, no. 3, pp. 206–12.

Weizman, AV, Ahn, E, Thanabalan, R, Leung, W, Croitoru, K, Silverberg, MS, Steinhart, AH and Nguyen, GC (2012). Characterisation of complementary and alternative medicine use and its impact on medication adherence in inflammatory bowel disease. *Aliment Pharmacol Ther*, vol. 35, no. 3, pp. 342–9.

WHO (2000). Traditional and complementary medicine: definitions. Available online from www.who.int/medicines/areas/traditional/definitions/en/ (accessed 1 January 2014).

Wiles, J and Rosenberg, MW (2001). 'Gentle caring experience': seeking alternative health care in Canada. *Health Place*, vol. 7, no. 3, pp. 209–24.

Chapter 23

Future directions in IBD
eHealth

Simon R. Knowles

Introduction

Since the mid-1990s, the Internet has revolutionised the way in which people communicate and interact with others. Within the field of medicine, the Internet has provided clinicians with another tool to facilitate communication and promote health behaviours, from an individual level (e.g. patients asked to provide regular updates regarding their current medication/symptoms via a website, email or mobile application) or at a population level (e.g. providing the public with psychoeducation around healthy eating, recommendations and 'how to' guides for cancer surveillance via websites). Although there is much debate as to how eHealth is defined, it can be generally referred to as 'health services and information delivered or enhanced through the Internet and related technologies' (Eysenbach 2001). Examples of eHealth technology include the use of websites (e.g. www.CCFA.org, www.facebook.com), online databases (e.g. www.pubmed.gov), emails, discussion boards, blogs, microblogging (e.g. Twitter), or voice over Internet (e.g. Skype).

Several studies involving gastroenterological cohorts have demonstrated the reliance on the Internet by patients to attain information about their condition (Cima *et al.* 2007), seeking the support from fellow sufferers (Malik and Coulson 2011). The studied cohorts also readily identify the importance and acceptance of eHealth technology for their ongoing disease management (Castro *et al.* 2006; Cross *et al.* 2006). Given these findings, and the fact that there will continue to be increased healthcare demands on finite resources for inflammatory bowel disease (IBD) patients and clinicians, the development and reliance on eHealth technology is undeniable.

eHealth technology brings with it multiple possible advantages for patients with IBD; these include access to information and support 24 hours/365 days a year, access irrespective of location (rural versus metropolitan areas). Individuals can also feel free to express concerns or ask questions often in an anonymous way at time suitable to them without the perceived stigma or taboo associated with talking about bowel symptoms. Patients also readily identify that eHealth technology promotes treatment adherence and empowerment in relation to decision making associated with their condition. Disadvantages of eHealth for patients with IBD are that, while information is plentiful, its quality is too often questionable. Further, the information or advice provided, may not account for individual differences (e.g. with IBD course or symptoms) and be a source of distress rather than comfort and assurance or support.

For clinicians, eHealth offers the opportunity to attain ongoing and up-to-date disease monitoring, provide additional support services that do not necessarily impact upon already stretched and limited healthcare services, and provide another communication tool with which to liaise with their patients. However, eHealth technology can be difficult and costly to develop, and not necessarily provide the one-on-one relationship that is needed for optimal care.

This Chapter will briefly review evidence for the Internet as a primary source of information in IBD cohorts, the role of social media and mobile applications for IBD patients, evidence for the efficacy of eHealth disease management in IBD cohorts and evidence for the efficacy of eHealth psychological distress management in IBD cohorts.

The Internet as a primary source of information in IBD cohorts

Based on a sample of 169 patients with IBD, Cima and colleagues (Cima *et al.* 2007) found that 88 per cent of patients had access to the Internet (either via home or at work) and that using the Internet as the primary source of information about their condition was second only to attaining information from their gastroenterologist (54.4 per cent versus 59.2 per cent). Further evidence for the acceptance of the internet by IBD patients was reported in a letter to the Editor of the *IBD Journal* by Molnar and colleagues (Molnar *et al.* 2010). They explored the use of the 'ask the doctor' forum on a popular Hungarian IBD website (www. crohn-colitic.hu) over a 3-year period. The results indicated that over 1,204 questions were asked, with 58 per cent being related to IBD (details of 42 per cent of non-IBD related questions were not reported by the authors). Questions specific to IBD included asking for a diagnosis regarding symptoms (17 per cent), treatment advice (27.8 per cent), dietary advice (7.9 per cent), and advice about side effects associated with medications (6.9 per cent). In another study investigating Internet use, Panes and colleagues (Panes *et al.* 2002) found that in a sample of 172 Spanish IBD patients, 84 per cent identified interest in having access to a IBD-specific support website overseen by their gastroenterologist, and that 65 per cent would be prepared to pay for this additional service.

In a recent publication, Fortinsky *et al.* (2012) reviewed the results and quality of IBD-related internet searches. They found that when looking for 'inflammatory bowel disease' OR 'Crohn' OR 'ulcerative colitis', the results by the top three search engines were: Google (IBDCrohns.About.com, Familydoctor.org and Wikipedia.org), Yahoo (Wikipedia.org, About.com and WebMD.com), Bing (Wikipedia.org, About.com and Ihateibd.com). As for the quality, the authors identify that many sites found tended to provided generalised information, and did not (or could not) necessarily take into account individual patient-specific medical needs or patient levels of medical knowledge. Consequently, the authors concluded that the information cited on websites might cause misinformation. Based on their review of IBD-specific websites, Fortinsky *et al.* (2012) provide a list of recommended Internet resources, these include: CCFA.org (Crohn's and Colitis Foundation of America), CCFC.ca (Crohn's and Colitis Foundation of Canada), crohnsandcolitis.com.au (Crohn's and Colitis Australia), NASPGHAN. org (North American Society for Pediatric Gastroenterology, Hepatology and Nutrition), MyIBD.org (Foundation for Clinical Research in IBD) and the Mayo Clinic (MayoClinic.org/ibd/). For other reviews exploring the quality of IBD information on the Internet, see Bernard *et al.* (2007) and Langille *et al.* (2004).

To help clinicians provide appropriate advise to patients about where to seek information via the Internet, Fortinsky and colleagues (Fortinsky *et al.* 2012) suggest structured approach that involves the four 'Ds': (i) *Determine* what information the patient wants to attain from the internet (e.g. disease information, medication side effects); (ii) *Direct* patients toward trustworthy sites (e.g. CCFA. org, CCFC.ca, crohnsandcolitis.com.au); (iii) *Discuss* the information patients attain via the internet; and (iv) *Don't dismiss* the perceived importance patients place on information taken from the Internet. See Fortinsky *et al.* (2012), Table 4, for a more detailed review of the suggested structured approach to guiding patients' Internet utilisation.

The role of social media and mobile applications for IBD patients

Social media (e.g. YouTube, Facebook, Twitter) are also a popular means of attaining information about their disease by patients with IBD. As identified by Fortinsky *et al.* (2012), the Crohn's and Colitis Foundation of America and Mayo Clinic have YouTube channels for individuals to obtain information about IBD. Patients themselves continue to utilise social media such as Youtube.com to post videos, Facebook to setup IBD groups/discussion forums and Twitter to identity their everyday feelings and thoughts about IBD. Through these media, patients may develop a sense of normality and comfort because they may attract like-minded individuals. Again, these social media may also facilitate misinformation about IBD and its treatment and cause distress.

With the development of the smartphones and tablets individuals are now readily downloading mobile applications (also known by the term 'apps') to use on their device/s. The significant growth in the use of these applications is in part due to the uptake of mobile devices, and the relatively low cost of purchasing apps, with some even being free to download and use. Numerous applications are readily available to track and monitor IBD symptoms (e.g. MyIBD, MyGITrack, CrohnsTracker) and/or provide psychoeducation about IBD as well (e.g. MyIBD). Despite the proliferation and possible benefits of such applications, these applications do not necessary provide valid measures of disease activity, nor have been necessarily developed by individuals with specific knowledge or qualifications in the area. To date, no scientific evaluation has been undertaken testing the validity or reliability of IBD-specific applications. The reader is recommended to see several systematic reviews exploring the efficacy of mobile applications, these include chronic illness management (de Jongh *et al.* 2012), mental health (Donker *et al.* 2013) and preventative health care (Vodopivec-Jamsek *et al.* 2012).

Evidence for the efficacy of eHealth disease management in IBD cohorts

To date, only a few studies have explored the possible benefits of utilising eHealth involving IBD cohorts. The focus of these eHealth interventions have been on enhancing patient disease-specific knowledge, and/or disease monitoring and medication adherence.

In a large Danish and Irish trial ($n = 333$), Elkjaer *et al.* (2010b) evaluated the efficacy of an online monitoring of ulcerative colitis activity and 5-ASA use in patients versus a historical control group or control group receiving treatment as usual. After an initial 3-hour face-to-face disease-specific and website-focused psychoeducation presentation, patients in the experimental condition were asked to logon to www.constant-care.dk once a week (or daily if in an active disease phase), complete a disease activity score, and follow any recommendations regarding medication dosage changes suggested to them (e.g. 4g daily of 5-ASA for a maximum of 28 days). Patients had the ability to text or email web-program's 'contact doctor' for further follow-up or other questions. Results indicated that 88 per cent of the patients in the experimental group preferred using www.constant-care.dk to help assess and manage their disease when compared to treatment as usual, and that it was associated with improved adherence rates for 5-ASA treatment and quality of life (QoL) and a reduction in the need for acute and routine outpatient visits. Based on these findings, Elkjaer *et al.* (2010b) concluded that www.constant-care.dk provided a safe and cost-effective disease management. Other studies involving www.constant-care.dk, including its development, can be found elsewhere (Elkjaer 2012; Elkjaer *et al.* 2010a).

In a more recent study, Pedersen *et al.* (2012) evaluated a modified version of the constant-care website (www.cd.constant-care.dk) to assess its effectiveness in infliximab (IFX) maintenance therapy for patients with Crohn's disease. Based on the methodology reported by Elkjaer *et al.* (2010b) Crohn's disease (CD) patients received 3 hours of face-to-face disease and website psychoeducation, and then engaged in web-based monitoring (and if needed, modified their IFX medication as recommended by the website). When compared to the treatment-as-usual control group, patients utilising the web-based monitoring program were less likely to report adverse events (e.g. allergic reaction, infection) and tended to seek, and attain, their IFX infusions at the most appropriate times.

Further, there were no differences between the control group and the experimental group in terms of hospitalisations, across the groups, use of corticosteroids or frequency of surgical interventions. Consent with Elkjaer *et al.* (2010b) findings, Pedersen and colleagues concluded that the use of web-based monitoring program was both safe and practical.

Cross and colleagues (Cross *et al.* 2006, 2012; Cross and Finkelstein 2007) have conducted a number of studies evaluating the benefits of a telemanagement service for patients with IBD. In these studies, patients access a computer and complete a symptom diary and questions about possible medication side effects over the past week. Current weight is also provided via a digital scale connected to the computer. A customised action plan is then provided to the patient via the computer along with a psychoeducation program about IBD. The results indicated that individuals utilising the telemanagement service reported significant improvement in disease-specific QoL (Cross *et al.* 2012; Cross and Finkelstein 2007) and knowledge (Cross and Finkelstein 2007) compared to baseline and a positive attitude toward its ongoing use (Cross *et al.* 2006; Cross and Finkelstein 2007).

Although only based on a limited number of studies, the research, and two recent systematic reviews of this literature (Huang *et al.* 2014; Knowles and Mikocka-Walus 2014), suggest that eHealth technology can be used not only to enhance patient IBD-specific knowledge, but more importantly, encourage and empower patients to monitor and take ownership of their IBD treatment in a safe and reliable way. Further, this technology may also assist in both increasing medical treatment adherence rates and adapting medication interventions quickly and at the most critical times, therefore, leading to improved quality of life and continued best-care approaches.

Evidence for the efficacy of eHealth psychological distress management in IBD cohorts

Research to date demonstrates that online psychotherapies can be equally informative and efficacious (Barak *et al.* 2008), and provide significant cost savings (Kaltenthaler *et al.* 2006) comparing to face-to-face treatments. Several studies involving Irritable Bowel Syndrome (IBS) patients have demonstrated the efficacy of eHealth intervention programs in reducing IBS symptoms and improving quality of life (Hunt *et al.* 2009; Ljotsson *et al.* 2010, 2011a, 2011b, 2011c).

Patients with IBD have been found to be at an increased risk of anxiety and mood disorders (Fuller-Thomson and Sulman 2006; Kurina *et al.* 2001; Walker *et al.* 2008) and associated illness-related issues, including reduced self-esteem, body image concerns and sexual problems (Casati *et al.* 2000; Joachim and Milne 1987; Maunder *et al.* 1999). Given this, efficacious treatments for IBD-specific psychological distress is needed (Knowles *et al.* 2013). One recent recommendation is the utilisation of Internet-delivered programs to identify and reduce mental-health distress in IBD cohorts (McCombie *et al.* 2013). To date, there are multiple research groups evaluating the efficacy of eHealth technology in reducing distress in IBD cohorts, including some open-trial studies (e.g. www.IBDclinic. org.au). Over the coming years, it is hoped that these studies will provide a strong empirical foundation from which health professionals can recommend, and patients can seek and attain, high quality IBD-specific psychological healthcare.

Conclusions

eHealth technology is becoming an increasingly important component in facilitating patient education and ongoing disease management. Research to date suggests that patients with IBD are regularly utilising the Internet to attain information about IBD and attain advice by communicating with other individuals with IBD via online discussion forums/groups and IBD organisations. Initial studies involving IBD cohorts suggest that the utilisation of Internet-based disease management programs may not only enhance adherence, but also provide a mechanism to identify and begin treatment at more optimal times. It is clear that eHealth technology will become an increasingly important component of integrated healthcare in IBD management. However, much more research is needed to be undertaken to identify how and where this technology can be used to enhance patient care.

Current limitations and future considerations

- Increasing healthcare demands and limited resources will be a primary driving factor in the development of eHealth Technology for IBD management
- eHealth interventions can be expensive to develop and difficult to individualise
- Most Internet information is not peer reviewed and may contribute to misinformation and patient concerns/distress
- Optimal health care is likely to be based on the combination of traditional healthcare practices (e.g. one-on-one assessments) and eHealth technology
- While mobile applications are plentiful and can provide information and a mechanism to monitor symptoms, they have yet to be validated or evaluated for their effectiveness and usability
- eHealth interventions specifically developed for patients with IBD are yet to show to be efficacious in reducing mental-health concerns

Practical recommendations

- eHealth technology should be integrated into a holistic treatment approach to promote optimal patient care
- The Internet is readily seen as a key source of easy-to-access information by patients; however, this information may not always be valid or reliable. Given this, clinicians should help patients by directing them to sites that they see as reliable and authoritative in the area

Learning points

- eHealth technology is used by the majority of patients as a way to attain information about IBD and to facilitate support
- Several IBD-specific studies have shown that eHealth technology can be utilised to enhance patient disease management in a safe and reliable way
- While eHealth has been shown to reduce psychological distress and enhance QoL in other gastroenterological conditions, such as irritable bowel syndrome, its efficacy in IBD cohorts is unknown
- eHealth technology should be considered as an important component of optimal care and integrated into models of healthcare for patients with IBD

References

Barak, A, Hen, L, Boniel-Nissim, M and Shapira, N (2008). A comprehensive review and a meta-analysis of the effectiveness of internet-based psychotherapeutic interventions. *J Technol Hum Serv*, vol. 26, no. 2-4, pp. 109–60.

Bernard, A, Langille, M, Hughes, S, Rose, C, Leddin, D and Veldhuyzen van Zanten, S (2007). A systematic review of patient inflammatory bowel disease information resources on the World Wide Web. *Am J Gastroenterol*, vol. 102, no. 9, pp. 2070–7.

Casati, J, Toner, BB, de Rooy, EC, Drossman, DA and Maunder, RG (2000). Concerns of patients with inflammatory bowel disease: a review of emerging themes. *Dig Dis Sci*, vol. 45, no. 1, pp. 26–31.

Castro, HK, Cross, RK and Finkelstein, J (2006). Using a home automated telemanagement (HAT) system: experiences and perceptions of patients with inflammatory bowel disease. *AMIA Annu Symp Proc*, p. 872.

Cima, RR, Anderson, KJ, Larson, DW, Dozois, EJ, Hassan, I, Sandborn, WJ, Loftus, EV and Pemberton, JH (2007). Internet use by patients in an inflammatory bowel disease specialty clinic. *Inflamm Bowel Dis*, vol. 13, no. 10, pp. 1266–70.

Cross, RK, Arora, M and Finkelstein, J (2006). Acceptance of telemanagement is high in patients with inflammatory bowel disease. *J Clin Gastroenterol*, vol. 40, no. 3, pp. 200–8.

Cross, RK, Cheevers, N, Rustgi, A, Langenberg, P and Finkelstein, J (2012). Randomized, controlled trial of home telemanagement in patients with ulcerative colitis (UC HAT). *Inflamm Bowel Dis*, vol. 18, no. 6, pp. 1018–25.

Cross, RK and Finkelstein, J (2007). Feasibility and acceptance of a home telemanagement system in patients with inflammatory bowel disease: a 6-month pilot study. *Dig Dis Sci*, vol. 52, no. 2, pp. 357–64.

de Jongh, T, Gurol-Urganci, I, Vodopivec-Jamsek, V, Car, J and Atun, R (2012). Mobile phone messaging for facilitating self-management of long-term illnesses. *Cochrane Database Syst Rev*, vol. 12, p. CD007459.

Donker, T, Petrie, K, Proudfoot, J, Clarke, J, Birch, MR and Christensen, H (2013). Smartphones for smarter delivery of mental health programs: a systematic review. *J Med Internet Res*, vol. 15, no. 11, p. e247.

Elkjaer, M (2012). E-health: web-guided therapy and disease self-management in ulcerative colitis. Impact on disease outcome, quality of life and compliance. *Dan Med J*, vol. 59, no. 7, p. B4478.

Elkjaer, M, Burisch, J, Avnstrom, S, Lynge, E and Munkholm, P (2010a). Development of a Web-based concept for patients with ulcerative colitis and 5-aminosalicylic acid treatment. *Eur J Gastroenterol Hepatol*, vol. 22, no. 6, pp. 695–704.

Elkjaer, M, Shuhaibar, M, Burisch, J, Bailey, Y, Scherfig, H, Laugesen, B, Avnstrom, S, Langholz, E, O'Morain, C, Lynge, E and Munkholm, P (2010b). E-health empowers patients with ulcerative colitis: a randomised controlled trial of the web-guided 'constant-care' approach. *Gut*, vol. 59, no. 12, pp. 1652–61.

Eysenbach, G (2001). What is e-health? *J Med Internet Res*, vol. 3, no. 2, p. E20.

Fortinsky, KJ, Fournier, MR and Benchimol, EI (2012). Internet and electronic resources for inflammatory bowel disease: a primer for providers and patients. *Inflamm Bowel Dis*, vol. 18, no. 6, pp. 1156–63.

Fuller-Thomson, E and Sulman, J (2006). Depression and inflammatory bowel disease: findings from two nationally representative Canadian surveys. *Inflamm Bowel Dis*, vol. 12, no. 8, pp. 697–707.

Huang, VW, Reich, KM and Fedorak, RN (2014). Distance management of inflammatory bowel disease: Systematic review and meta-analysis. *World J Gastroenterol*, vol. 20, no. 3, pp. 829–42.

Hunt, MG, Moshier, S and Milonova, M (2009). Brief cognitive-behavioral internet therapy for irritable bowel syndrome. *Behav Res Ther*, vol. 47, no. 9, pp. 797–802.

Joachim, G and Milne, B (1987). Inflammatory bowel disease: effects on lifestyle. *J Adv Nurs*, vol. 12, no. 4, pp. 483–7.

Kaltenthaler, E, Brazier, J, De Nigris, E, Tumur, I, Ferriter, M, Beverley, C, Parry, G, Rooney, G and Sutcliffe, P (2006). Computerised cognitive behaviour therapy for depression and anxiety update: a systematic review and economic evaluation. *Health Technol Assess*, vol. 10, no. 33, pp. iii, xi–xiv, 1–168.

Knowles, SR and Mikocka-Walus, A (2014). Utilization and efficacy of internet-based eHealth technology in gastroenterology: a systematic review. *Scand J Gastroenterol*, pp. 1–16.

Knowles, SR, Monshat, K and Castle, DJ (2013). The efficacy and methodological challenges of psychotherapy for adults with inflammatory bowel disease: a review. *Inflamm Bowel Dis*, vol. 19, no. 12, pp. 2704–15.

Kurina, LM, Goldacre, MJ, Yeates, D and Gill, LE (2001). Depression and anxiety in people with inflammatory bowel disease. *J Epidemiol Community Health*, vol. 55, no. 10, pp. 716–20.

Langille, M., et al. (2010). Systematic review of the quality of patient information on the internet regarding inflammatory bowel disease treatments. *Clin Gastroenterol Hepatol*, vol. 8, no. 4, pp. 322–8.

Ljotsson, B, Andersson, G, Andersson, E, Hedman, E, Lindfors, P, Andreewitch, S, Ruck, C and Lindefors, N (2011a). Acceptability, effectiveness, and cost-effectiveness of internet-based exposure treatment for irritable bowel syndrome in a clinical sample: a randomized controlled trial. *BMC Gastroenterol*, vol. 11, p. 110.

Ljotsson, B, Falk, L, Vesterlund, AW, Hedman, E, Lindfors, P, Ruck, C, Hursti, T, Andreewitch, S, Jansson, L, Lindefors, N and Andersson, G (2010). Internet-delivered exposure and mindfulness based therapy for irritable bowel syndrome – a randomized controlled trial. *Behav Res Ther*, vol. 48, no. 6, pp. 531–9.

Ljotsson, B, Hedman, E, Andersson, E, Hesser, H, Lindfors, P, Hursti, T, Rydh, S, Ruck, C, Lindefors, N and Andersson, G (2011b). Internet-delivered exposure-based treatment vs. stress management for irritable bowel syndrome: a randomized trial. *Am J Gastroenterol*, vol. 106, no. 8, pp. 1481–91.

Future directions in IBD: eHealth 215

Ljotsson, B, Hedman, E, Lindfors, P, Hursti, T, Lindefors, N, Andersson, G and Ruck, C (2011c). Long-term follow-up of internet-delivered exposure and mindfulness based treatment for irritable bowel syndrome. *Behav Res Ther*, vol. 49, no. 1, pp. 58–61.

Malik, S and Coulson, NS (2011). The therapeutic potential of the internet: exploring self-help processes in an internet forum for young people with inflammatory bowel disease. *Gastroenterol Nurs*, vol. 34, no. 6, pp. 439–48.

Maunder, R, Toner, B, de Rooy, E and Moskovitz, D (1999). Influence of sex and disease on illness-related concerns in inflammatory bowel disease. *Can J Gastroenterol*, vol. 13, no. 9, pp. 728–32.

McCombie, AM, Mulder, RT and Gearry, RB (2013). Psychotherapy for inflammatory bowel disease: a review and update. *J Crohns Colitis*, vol. 7, no. 12, pp. 935–49.

Molnar, T, Farkas, K, Szepes, Z, Nagy, F and Wittmann, T (2010). Ask the doctor about inflammatory bowel disease on the Internet: experience after more than 1000 questions. *Inflamm Bowel Dis*, vol. 16, no. 12, pp. 2010–1.

Panes, J, de Lacy, AM, Sans, M, Soriano, A and Pique, JM (2002). [Frequent Internet use among Catalan patients with inflammatory bowel disease]. *Gastroenterol Hepatol*, vol. 25, no. 5, pp. 306–9. [In Spanish].

Pedersen, N, Elkjaer, M, Duricova, D, Burisch, J, Dobrzanski, C, Andersen, NN, Jess, T, Bendtsen, F, Langholz, E, Leotta, S, Knudsen, T, Thorsgaard, N and Munkholm, P (2012). eHealth: individualisation of infliximab treatment and disease course via a self-managed web-based solution in Crohn's disease. *Aliment Pharmacol Ther*, vol. 36, no. 9, pp. 840–9.

Vodopivec-Jamsek, V, de Jongh, T, Gurol-Urganci, I, Atun, R and Car, J (2012). Mobile phone messaging for preventive health care. *Cochrane Database Syst Rev*, vol. 12, p. CD007457.

Walker, JR, Ediger, JP, Graff, LA, Greenfeld, JM, Clara, I, Lix, L, Rawsthorne, P, Miller, N, Rogala, L, McPhail, CM and Bernstein, CN (2008). The Manitoba IBD cohort study: a population-based study of the prevalence of lifetime and 12-month anxiety and mood disorders. *Am J Gastroenterol*, vol. 103, no. 8, pp. 1989–97.

Chapter 24

Future directions in IBD
The biopsychosocial care, the integrated care

Antonina A. Mikocka-Walus

Introduction

The present book was written with the goal of demonstrating that inflammatory bowel disease (IBD) is a biopsychosocial condition rather than just a purely physiological gastrointestinal (GI) disorder. Although historically, the link between psychological and gastrointestinal functioning has been well recognized, with the term 'nervous diarrhea' appearing in medical texts in the mid-1800s. The first decades of the twentieth century promoted the psychodynamic understanding of IBD (perhaps because of the influential works by Freud at the time but also likely due to poor understanding of the differences between organic and functional GI disorders). The second half of the twentieth century and the discovery of novel anti-inflammatory therapies shifted the understanding of IBD towards mostly physiological processes.

While the biopsychosocial medicine as a term was coined in the 1970s (Engel 1977) and has been endorsed by the increasing number of health opinion leaders and practitioners to this day, the understanding of IBD remained for many years biomedical. Only the last 20 years of research into the role of stress and depression in disease progression, and more recently, aetiology, have shaken this view of IBD. IBD is nowadays considered a result of an exaggerated immune response to normal microbes in the intestine, activated by environmental factors in those with a genetic susceptibility. Albeit, recent research in animal models has shown that colitis can be triggered by stress and healed by antidepressants (Ghia *et al.* 2008, 2009). Although more studies are needed to better understand the relevance of these findings in humans, there is now little doubt that co-morbid psychiatric disorders shorten remission times (Rampton 2009) and that stress is, in fact, associated with increased inflammation and IBD symptoms (Maunder and Levenstein 2008), with a recent prospective study confirming higher stress levels in the periods preceding symptomatic disease flare (Bernstein *et al.* 2010).

The present book demonstrates that biopsychosocial influences are present and apparent in practically any aspect of disease course and management, through drug and surgical treatment, complementary medicine use, diet and nutrition, as well as associated procedures. They are also in the process of transition from

Future directions in IBD   217

child/adolescent care to adult services, in addressing sexuality, pregnancy and fertility issues, in experience of comorbid functional symptoms, fatigue and colorectal cancer, and finally, in diagnosis and treatment of psychiatric co-morbidities, such as anxiety and depression, using various traditional and novel psychotherapies (including online therapies) and antidepressants. Those who contributed to the present book represent a variety of disciplines; however, in their report of a particular area of their interest and expertise, a clear picture of psychosocial and cultural influences on the whole experience of IBD as an illness and its treatment transpires. The picture of IBD presented here hopefully demonstrates the need for the interdisciplinary approach to its understanding and management; only through combining different perspectives and specialties can IBD be addressed adequately in clinical practice and research.

The present final chapter of the book is concerned with bringing the perspectives presented in the above chapters together to paint a uniform picture of the new model of care for IBD. The next sections will introduce the concept of the integrated model of care, highlighting the roles of health professionals involved as part of the model as well as recommending changes to current IBD curricula and relevant further research on models of care in IBD.

The integrated model of care

The biopsychosocial approach we used in this book lends itself well to applications in health settings, particularly those practicing the integrated model of care (IMoC). The World Health Organization defines the IMoC as 'bringing together inputs, delivery, management and organization of services related to diagnosis, treatment, care, rehabilitation and health promotion' (Grone and Garcia-Barbero 2001) and recommends it as current best practice in chronic illness management. The model enables personalised and flexible patient-centred care, abandoning supply driven care provision (Lloyd and Wait 2005). It has been applied in a variety of settings to manage different chronic conditions (Bolibar *et al.* 2009; de Stampa *et al.* 2010; Renders *et al.* 2010; Vedel *et al.* 2009), resulting in improvements in patient outcomes and reduced health-care costs (Phan *et al.* 2012; Sack *et al.* 2012).

The integrated model of care in IBD

Within IBD care, only a few IBD centres around the world have applied a variant of the IMoC (Mikocka-Walus, A *et al.* 2012). From their reports, the IMoC is thought to best work in specialist-led clinics rather than in primary care (Mikocka-Walus *et al.* 2013), given reports from general practitioners of not feeling adequately prepared to manage IBD (Tan *et al.* 2012). However, gastroenterology clinics around the world, in the majority of cases, still work within a reactive model of acute care and the service delivery needs to be redesigned to provide more optimal care for IBD patients. Recommendations for such changes

218   Antonina A. Mikocka-Walus

in the delivery have recently been provided and include: care that involves patients in service development; mechanisms for active and regular follow-up of patients; patient education; comprehensive assessment of biopsychosocial functioning; a significant role of IBD nurses; good transition arrangements between child and adult services; and access to a variety of health professionals knowledgeable about IBD, with a significant role of mental health providers (Mikocka-Walus, A *et al.* 2012).

Design of the integrated model of care in IBD

The integrated models of care are conceptualised to provide access to various specialists at one site, to prevent delays in diagnosis and treatment but also to avoid mutually exclusive recommendations from different specialists. As part of each clinic, various specialists should have the opportunity to discuss diagnosis and treatment with colleagues before providing patients with recommendations for treatment. Thus, the prescribed treatment should result from the combined expertise of several disciplines, such as gastroenterology, nursing and mental health, but often also surgery, dietetics, radiology and others. In reality, patients rarely meet with all these specialists in person. They are usually introduced to a small basic team comprising their gastroenterologist and an IBD nurse (in some alternative models, a mental health professional is also included). Other specialists meet as a group with the basic team in regular intervals (fortnightly or monthly) and the patients learn about their recommendations from the providers better known to them (gastroenterologists and nurses) and with whom they have established a relationship.

The patient-centred aspect of the integrated model of care (or the so called 'balanced power care') (Mikocka-Walus *et al.* 2013) relates to the care provision in which patient's opinions and preferences but also their socio-demographic characteristics, culture and values are taken into account. Thus, meetings at the clinic are built around a conversation and exchange of views with equal partners – patients and health professionals – arriving at a mutually acceptable treatment strategy.

How effective are integrated models of care in IBD?

Research on efficacy and costs of the integrated model of care in IBD has only recently commenced (Mikocka-Walus, AA *et al.* 2012; Phan *et al.* 2012; Sack *et al.* 2012). The Adelaide-based group has provided the first analysis in this respect. A drop in the use of opiates ($p = 0.037$) and hospitalisation rates (from 48 per cent to 30 per cent) in IBD patients has been noted as a result of introducing the changed model of care. The group further demonstrated that savings offset additional expenses incurred while establishing the integrated model clinic, for example the mean total cost of inpatient care was lower for people using the new IBD service than in IBD controls [US\$12,857 (SD = US\$15,236) vs. US\$30,467

Future directions in IBD 219

(SD = US$53,760), p = 0.005] (Sack *et al.* 2012). These savings have resulted from less frequent visits to the clinic, fewer hospital admissions and fewer referrals for unneeded examinations, as well as reduced medication use with optimised treatment regimens (Phan *et al.* 2012). Despite these promising results, further research is strongly recommended to promote the model and to document any resulting problems in the hope of continuing the improvement in the quality of care in IBD clinics. Given that the model has only been tested in one clinic in Australia, future studies should evaluate its usefulness in other countries and cultural contexts.

Biopsychosocial awareness

The omnipresence of biopsychosocial influences in management of IBD means that IBD clinicians of all specialties should be made aware of their existence and relevance to treatment. While mental health providers (psychologists, sociologists, psychiatrists and general practitioners) usually have a good grasp of the biopsychosocial paradigm, other clinicians (for example, gastroenterologists and surgeons) rarely do, which results from a biomedical focus of the current medical curricula worldwide. Current curricula include some modules on communication with patients (anecdotally not very well attended as students prefer to learn about 'real medicine') and many courses now refer to the biopsychosocial medicine, yet these early signs of change do not always translate into changed practice in gastroenterology. A major shift in the approach to teaching in medicine and its philosophy by medical educators, but also senior clinicians, who supervise students, particularly when providing information about complex conditions such as IBD, is urgently needed. Continuous professional development (CPD) can also add to the basic training by providing recent evidence-based knowledge on the topic. The present book may become a good introductory resource on the biopsychosocial approach to IBD. It can be used in both standard curricula and CPD in relevant disciplines, supporting life-long learning about the most optimal approach to IBD management.

Conclusions

The integrated model of care is receiving increasing interest from researchers and policy makers around the world. It is recommended as the current best practice to manage chronic illness. However, very few gastroenterology centres have applied the model to manage IBD. Those that have attempted it report better patient outcomes and reduced costs in comparison with the acute biomedical approach. However, there is limited published research exploring the effectiveness and costs of the model in IBD. Studies are needed to evaluate existing models and propose improvements. Given the encouraging observations from Australian studies on applying the elements of the model, in terms of improved patient outcomes and reduced healthcare use, further research is warranted.

Given the significant biopsychosocial influences in the overall experience of IBD, the integrated biopsychosocial model of care may be the answer to current frequently suboptimal care of IBD worldwide.

Current limitations and future considerations

- Clinicians are rarely aware of the importance of biopsychosocial issues in the experience and treatment of IBD and this may translate into suboptimal care
- More focus on the biopsychosocial issues in IBD but also other GI conditions is needed in medical programs
- There is strong evidence of the efficacy of the integrated model of care coming from studies on other chronic conditions, although very few studies are available specifically on IBD
- Research on the integrated model of care has only recently started and although the results are encouraging, further studies are needed to demonstrate its efficacy in IBD populations in different countries

Practical recommendations

- Biomedical approach to IBD care may lead to suboptimal care and poorer IBD outcomes
- The omnipresence of biopsychosocial influences in management of IBD means that IBD clinicians of all specialties should be made aware of their existence and relevance to treatment
- Standard medical curricula and CPD courses on IBD should reflect changes in understanding of IBD resulting from recent biopsychosocial research

Learning points

- There is increasing evidence of the role of stress and psychiatric co-morbidity in IBD course and possibly its aetiology
- Current models of IBD care rely on its understanding as a biomedical disorder which is in disagreement with contemporary research in the area
- Biopsychosocial influences are present and impact on all aspects of IBD experience and treatment
- The biopsychosocial integrated approach to understanding and treatment of IBD is likely to benefit patients and the healthcare system and should be promoted in medical schools around the world

References

Bernstein, CN, Singh, S, Graff, LA, Walker, JR, Miller, N and Cheang, M (2010). A prospective population-based study of triggers of symptomatic flares in IBD. *Am J Gastroenterol*, vol. 105, no. 9, pp. 1994–2002.

Bolibar, I, Plaza, V, Llauger, M, Amado, E, Anton, PA, Espinosa, A, Dominguez, L, Fraga, M, Freixas, M, de la Fuente, JA, Liguerre, I, Medrano, C, Peiro, M, Pou, M, Sanchis, J, Solanes, I, Valero, C and Valverde, P (2009). Assessment of a primary and tertiary care integrated management model for chronic obstructive pulmonary disease. *BMC Public Health*, vol. 9, p. 68.

de Stampa, M, Vedel, I, Mauriat, C, Bagaragaza, E, Routelous, C, Bergman, H, Lapointe, L, Cassou, B, Ankri, J and Henrard, JC (2010). Diagnostic study, design and implementation of an integrated model of care in France: a bottom-up process with continuous leadership. *Int J Integr Care*, vol. 10, p. e034.

Engel, GL (1977). The need for a new medical model: a challenge for biomedicine. *Science*, vol. 196, no. 4286, pp. 129–36.

Ghia, JE, Blennerhassett, P and Collins, SM (2008). Impaired parasympathetic function increases susceptibility to inflammatory bowel disease in a mouse model of depression. *J Clin Invest*, vol. 118, no. 6, pp. 2209–18.

Ghia, JE, Blennerhassett, P, Deng, Y, Verdu, EF, Khan, WI and Collins, SM (2009). Reactivation of inflammatory bowel disease in a mouse model of depression. *Gastroenterology*, vol. 136, no. 7, pp. 2280–8.e1–4.

Grone, O and Garcia-Barbero, M (2001). Integrated care: a position paper of the WHO European Office for Integrated Health Care Services. *Int J Integr Care*, vol. 1, p. e21.

Lloyd, J, Wait, S (2005). Integrated care: a guide for policy makers. Alliance for Health and the Future. Available online from www.ilcuk.org.uk/files/pdf_pdf_7.pdf (accessed 14 December 2010).

Maunder, RG and Levenstein, S (2008). The role of stress in the development and clinical course of inflammatory bowel disease: epidemiological evidence. *Curr Mol Med*, vol. 8, no. 4, pp. 247–52.

Mikocka-Walus, A, Andrews, JM, Bernstein, CN, Graff, LA, Walker, JR, Spinelli, A, Danese, S, van der Woude, CJ, Goodhand, J, Rampton, D and Moser, G (2012). Integrated models of care in managing inflammatory bowel disease: a discussion. *Inflamm Bowel Dis*, vol. 18, no. 8, pp. 1582–7.

Mikocka-Walus, AA, Andrews, JM, von Kanel, R and Moser, G (2013). What are the implications of changing treatment delivery models for patients with inflammatory bowel disease: a discussion paper. *Eur J Gastroenterol Hepatol*, vol. 25, no. 4, pp. 393–8.

Mikocka-Walus, AA, Turnbull, D, Holtmann, G and Andrews, JM (2012). An integrated model of care for inflammatory bowel disease sufferers in Australia: development and the effects of its implementation. *Inflamm Bowel Dis*, vol. 18, no. 8, pp. 1573–81.

Phan, VA, van Langenberg, DR, Grafton, R and Andrews, JM (2012). A dedicated inflammatory bowel disease service quantitatively and qualitatively improves outcomes in less than 18 months: a prospective cohort study in a large metropolitan centre. *Frontline Gastroenterol*, vol. 3, pp. 137–42.

Rampton, D (2009). Does stress influence inflammatory bowel disease? The clinical data. *Dig Dis*, vol. 27 (Suppl 1), pp. 76–9.

Renders, CM, Halberstadt, J, Frenkel, CS, Rosenmoller, P, Seidell, JC and Hirasing, RA (2010). Tackling the problem of overweight and obesity: the Dutch approach. *Obes Facts*, vol. 3, no. 4, pp. 267–72.

Sack, C, Phan, VA, Grafton, R, Van Langenberg, DR, Holtmann, G and Andrews, JM (2012). A chronic care model significantly decreases costs and healthcare utilisation in patients with inflammatory bowel disease. *J Crohns Colitis*, vol. 6, no. 3, pp. 302–10.

Tan, M, Holloway, RH, Lange, K and Andrews, JM (2012). General practitioners' knowledge of and attitudes to inflammatory bowel disease. *Intern Med J*, vol. 42, no. 7, pp. 801–7.

Vedel, I, De Stampa, M, Bergman, H, Ankri, J, Cassou, B, Mauriat, C, Blanchard, F, Bagaragaza, E and Lapointe, L (2009). A novel model of integrated care for the elderly: COPA, Coordination of Professional Care for the Elderly. *Aging Clin Exp Res*, vol. 21, no. 6, pp. 414–23.

Index

abdominal pain 23–4
acceptance of diagnosis 113–14
acetylcholine 13
acupuncture 199, 200, 202
adalimumab 77, 113
adherence to treatment 50, 113–15, 127, 142
adherent invasive *E. coli* 32–3
adolescent patients 47–52
aetiology of IBD 2
alternative medicine 144–5, 199–204
anorexia 120
anti-tumour necrosis factor (anti-TNF) therapy 48, 76, 95, 109, 112
antibiotics 34
antidepressants 191–6
antioxidants 121
anxiety 166; disease activity 1, 10–11, 12; IBD-IBS 87–8; individualised therapy 61; nutritional status 124, 127; onset of IBD 12; post-surgery 105; questionnaires 157; sexual function 66
apps 209–10
5-ASA 95, 112, 210
autoimmune disease 2
autonomic nervous system 13, 14, 21, 87

balanced power care 218
barrier contraceptives 69
best outcome, definition 57
biologics 59, 67, 77, 95
biomedical model xviii
biopsychosocial model xviii
blood tests 41, 43
body image 65–6, 165
body weight 119–20
brain-gut axis 13, 20–7, 33
brain imaging 24–6

calcitonin gene-related peptide 23
calprotectin 85–7
cancer 93–8
candidate microorganism strategy 32–3
capsule endoscopy 42
childhood IBD 3, 47–52, 120
chronic care model 4
cyclosporine 112, 113
clinical nurse specialists 166–8
clinician–patient relationship 60, 141–2
cognitive behavioural therapy (CBT) 61, 89, 136, 173, 174–5, 184–6, 187–8
cognitive function 24
colonoscopy 41–2, 43
colorectal cancer 93–4, 95
complementary and alternative medicine 144–5, 199–204
congenital malformations 76
constant-care website 210–11
contraception 67–9, 70
coping questionnaires 157–8
coping strategies 114, 136, 142, 144
cortical thickness 25
corticosteroid therapy 48, 67, 76, 77, 109, 112, 113, 120, 132
corticotrophin-releasing factor 13, 14
counselling: preconceptional 77–9; psychological 174
cultural aspects of IBD 140–6; coping strategies 142, 144; doctor–patient relationship 141–2; elderly patients 59; epidemiology 140–1; ethnic differences in phenotype 141; patient concerns 143–4; patient knowledge and understanding 142–3; perception of disease 143; treatment preferences 144–5
cytokines 23, 24

224 Index

demyelinating disease 25
dendritic cells 31
depression 33, 166; adherence to treatment 114; adolescents with IBD 48, 49; antidepressants for 193–5; disease activity 1, 10–11, 12; fatigue and 132; IBD-IBS 87–8; individualised therapy 61; nutritional status 121, 124, 127; onset of IBD 12; post-surgery 105; questionnaires 157; sexual function 66
diagnosis of IBD 40–5
diagnostic imaging 42, 43–4
diet and nutrition 89, 118–28; body weight 119–20; enteral nutrition 35, 120–1; fat malabsorption 124; fatigue 133; fluid intake 121; FODMAP diet 89, 121, 123–4, 125–6, 133; food avoidance 121; gut microbiota 35; lactose intolerance 122; low residue diet 122; malnutrition 118, 119; nutritional therapy 120–1; psychological comorbidity 121, 124, 127; vitamins and minerals 121–2, 133
discharge summary 51
disease activity questionnaires 156
distress 10–13, 49, 96–7
doctor–patient relationship 60, 141–2
drug interactions 56–7
drug therapy *see* medical treatment
dysbiosis 31, 32, 33
dyspareunia 67

education: in biopsychosocial awareness 219; of patients 167–8, 173
eHealth 207–13
elderly IBD patients 56–62
emotional function 24, 65–6
emotional motor system 21
endoscopy 41–2, 43
enteral nutrition 35, 120–1
enteric nervous system 23, 85, 86
enteric neuroplasticity 23
enterochromaffin cells 23
environmental factors 2
epidemiology of IBD 2–3, 140–1
erectile dysfunction 67, 75
Escherichia coli 32–3
Escherichia coli Nissle 122
ethnicity 141, 142
exclusive enteral nutrition 35

Facebook 209
faecal calprotectin 85–7
faecal incontinence 164–5

faecal microbiota transplantation 34–5
faecal tests 41, 43
Faecalibacterium prausznitzii 31, 32
family planning 5, 67, 111
fat malabsorption 124
fatigue 130–7; assessment 131; biopsychosocial approach 133, 135–6; causes 132–3, 134; complementary and alternative medicine use 202; definition 131; diet and nutrition 133; impact of 130–1, 165; inflammation and 132; multidimensional nature 131; prevalence 131; psychological comorbidity 132–3; sleep disturbance 132; solution focused therapy 185–6
fear 103–4, 111
fertility 74–80, 111
financial issues 57, 59, 60
fluid intake 121
FODMAP diet 89, 121, 123–4, 125–6, 133
folate deficiency 121
food avoidance 121
formulation 151, 153
fructose malabsorption 89
functional core microbiome 30
functional magnetic resonance imaging (fMRI) 25

genetic factors: IBD 2, 31; IBD-IBS 85
global description strategy 31, 32
glucocorticoids 14
grey matter 25
grief, stages of 113
growth delay 48, 120
gut associated lymphoid tissue (GALT) 21–2
gut microbiota 2, 13, 30–6

handover letters 51
heat shock proteins 14
herbal medicine 202
holistic approach 6
homeopathy 199
hospitalization 103–4
host-bacterial mutualism 31
host immunity 31
5HT 23
hypnotherapy 89, 173, 175, 186–8
hypolactasia 89
hypothalamic-autonomic nervous system (HANS) axis 13–14
hypothalamic-pituitary-adrenal (HPA) axis 13–14

Index 225

I-Thou relationship 114–15
illness perception questionnaires 157
immigrants 140–1
immune regulation 31
incidence of IBD 2–3, 47
individualised therapy 61, 88, 167
industrialisation 141
inflammation 2; brain-gut axis 22–6; fatigue 132; IBD-IBS 85–7; neuro-immune model 1; psychological status and 1; symptoms and 5
infliximab 77, 113
insula 22
insurance issues 59
integrated model of care 217–19
interleukins (IL-1/IL-6) 23, 132, 194
internalizing disorders 49
Internet 207–13
interoception 22
intrauterine devices 69
iron deficiency 121, 133
irritable bowel syndrome (IBS): in IBD 5, 33, 84–90; overlapping with IBD 123; post-infectious 85

K-Dub rap 115
Kubler-Ross stages of grief 113

lactose intolerance 122
laparoscopic sterilisation 69
libido 66
low residue diet 122
lymphoma 95

malnutrition 118, 119
MAP 32
mast cells 13, 14
medical treatment 3–4, 109–16; adverse effects 111–13; cancer prevention 94–5; cancer risk 95; eHealth 210–11; elderly patients 56–7, 58; fertility issues 75; I-Thou relationship 114–15; IBD-IBS 89; intermittent 4; paediatric patients 48; pregnancy outcomes 75–7; psychological wellbeing and 109–13; sexual function 67
medium chain triglyceride supplements 124
metagenomics 30
methotrexate 67, 75, 76, 112
microbial factors 2, 13, 30–6
microbiome 21–2, 30
migrants 140–1
minerals 121–2, 133

mobile applications 209–10
mood disorders 10–11; *see also* anxiety; depression
Mycobacterium avium subsp. *paratuberculosis* (MAP) 32
MyHealth passport 51

nerve growth factor 13
neurokinin-1 receptor (NK-1R) 26
neurotransmitters 13, 24
nitric oxide 14
non-adherence *see* adherence to treatment
non-melanoma skin cancer 95
NSAIDs 95
nurse specialist 166–8
nutrition *see* diet and nutrition

onset of IBD xix, xx, 12
opiates 5–6
oral contraceptive pill 68–9, 70
ownership of disease 115

paediatric patients 3, 47–52, 120
pain: brain-gut axis 23–4; impact of 165
parasympathetic nervous system 21
partner relationships 66
patient support groups 167
perceived stress 10, 11, 12
perception of disease 143; questionnaires 157
perianal disease 41, 165
pharmacotherapy *see* medical treatment
phylogenetic core 30
physical examination 40–1, 43
poly-pharmacy 56–7
positron emission tomography (PET) 25–6
post-infectious IBS 85
prebiotics 34
preconceptional care 77–9
pregnancy 5, 74–80, 111
prevalence of IBD 3
primary sclerosing cholangitis 42, 94
probiotics 31, 34, 122
progesterone only contraceptives 69
proinflammatory cytokines 23, 24
Project Management study 185
pseudo-acceptance 113
psychodynamic therapy 173, 174, 175
psychoeducation 173
psychological assessment 150–61
psychological comorbidity: diet and nutrition 121, 124, 127; disease course 5–6; evidence of 4–5; fatigue 132–3; IBD-IDS 87–8

psychological distress 10–13, 49, 96–7
psychological treatment 89, 166, 172–80, 183; adaptive design 179; online 211–12; randomized controlled trials 176, 179; standardization 176; *see also specific treatments*
psychological wellbeing: questionnaires 156; standard medical care 109–13
psychosocial functioning 164–8; adolescents with IBD 48–9; cancer and IBD 96–7; elderly 57–61
pubertal delay 48

quality of life: adolescents with IBD 49; complementary and alternative medicine use 201–2; medical treatment 109; post-surgery 104–5; questionnaires 158; stress and distress 12–13

relationship function 66
religious issues 59
restorative proctocolectomy 67
retrograde ejaculation 67, 75

segmented filamentous bacteria 31
selenium 121
self-efficacy 184
self-management 167–8, 185–6
self-report questionnaires 155, 156–9
serotonin 23
SERT 23
sexual function 65–7, 69–70, 75, 105
short chain fatty acids 35
sickness behaviour 23, 24, 130
skin cancer 95
sleep 132
smoking 2, 95
smooth muscle 22–3
social media 209
social normality 110
social support 58–9, 60
solution focused therapy 61, 185–6
specialist nurses 166–8
steatorrhoea 124
steroids *see* corticosteroid therapy
stigma 43, 59, 111, 143, 164
stoma issues 105, 165
stool samples 41, 43

stress xix–xx, 10–16, 33, 124, 166; disease activity 1, 11–13; IBD-IBS 87; nutritional status 124; onset of IBD 12; quality of life 12–13; questionnaires 157
stress management techniques 173, 174, 184, 185
structured psychological assessments 159
structured transition programmes 50
substance P 14, 23
sulphasalazine 75
support groups 167
surgical treatment 3, 102–7; attitudes to 102; decision-making process 102–3; expectations and fears 103–4; fertility 75; psychological symptoms after 105; quality of life after 104–5; sexual function 67, 75, 105
sympathetic nervous system 14, 21, 33

tacrolimus 113
telemanagement 211
thalidomide 76
thiopurine 48, 76, 95, 112
topical treatment 111
total parenteral nutrition 120
transfer of care 49, 51–2
transition of care 49–52
treatment approaches 3–4; clinical nurse specialist role 167; cultural influences 144–5; gut microbiota manipulation 34–5; IBD-IBS 88–9; paediatrics 48; *see also* medical treatment; psychological treatment; surgical treatment
tumour necrosis factor-α 13, 14, 23, 132, 194
Twitter 209

vagus nerve 13, 14, 21, 22, 23
vasoactive intestinal proteins 14
venous thromboembolism 68–9
visceral hyperalgesia 23–4
vitamins 121–2, 133

weight loss 119–20
work settings 59, 60

YouTube 209

CPSIA information can be obtained
at www.ICGtesting.com
Printed in the USA
JSHW021510221219
3113JS00001BA/75